"Connie writes in such a way th..... you're actually attending a James Ray event. Her insight into what was really going on behind the scenes at James Ray International and with James Ray is uncanny and dead on."

Amy Hall
Former employee of James Ray International

"This book is a gift to the world. I loved every page—happy, sad, frustrating, exultant, tragic, and everything in-between. As a reader, I was right beside her at every event, every conversation, every new insight, and every puzzlement. Thank you, Connie, for taking me along!"

Arlene Bartle Harris
Regional Advisor Emeritus of San Diego
Society of Children's Book Writers and Illustrators

"Connie is going to take you into the world of James Ray. I have attended many of these same events and she accurately described them and highlighted both the good and the bad. I loved reading it and I think it is a must read for anybody wanting to understand why people followed James into that sweat lodge."

Erwin Bosma
San Diego, CA

"Powerful! Fascinating! I couldn't put it down. You'll love every word! Ms Joy draws you into her amazing journey of Spirituality with James Ray and holds you captive!"

Katie Gallagher Goese
Artist in La Jolla, CA

"A powerfully honest account of personal and spiritual growth, and of overcoming and learning from adversity."

Emily Johnston
San Marcos, CA

"Connie has captured the essence of how intelligent, successful people can find themselves in the clutches of a true charlatan. I attended many of these events, some of them with her, and find her description to be accurate to what I experienced. She has poignantly and honestly written about her own Journey and her lessons along the way. This is a must-read for all who are lifelong learners and who venture to find a true teacher to guide them."

Nancy Ogilvie
New York, NY

"James, who came from very humble beginnings, had all it takes to finally live the life of his dreams. When money became his #1 goal, his Universe came tumbling down around him in a matter of months. It is a tragedy innocent people had to die to stop his ego trip. Connie Joy does an outstanding job telling the story from the inside. I couldn't put this book down and would recommend it to anyone who wants to know how James Ray got to this point."

Fatima Bosma
2008 Spiritual Warrior Graduate

"Connie Joy is brilliant, courageous, and at times, even funny. In this beautifully written book, she shares the painful beauty of her honesty not only with the reader, but with herself, of her spiritual journey before, during and after James Ray. I laughed out loud and ached with empathy. A great, riveting read. She holds herself and James Ray accountable on every level. A must read for anyone who questions what is truly meaningful and important."

Arlene Pollard
Licensed Clinical Social Worker, San Diego, CA

"*Tragedy in Sedona* is unquestionably thought-provoking! Kudos to Connie Joy for having the courage to speak out. Join her on the emotional rollercoaster that gave rise to this book. You will not be disappointed!"

Gale Jensen Krause
San Diego, CA

Tragedy in Sedona

MY LIFE IN
JAMES ARTHUR RAY'S
INNER CIRCLE

CONNIE JOY

Transformation Media Books

Transformation Media Books

Published by Transformation Media Books, USA
www.TransformationMediaBooks.com

An imprint of Pen & Publish, Inc.
Bloomington, Indiana
(812) 837-9226
info@PenandPublish.com
www.PenandPublish.com

Cover photos of James Arthur Ray and Sedona sweat
lodge courtesy of the Yavapai County Sheriff's Office
Cover photo of Connie Joy with James Ray
courtesy of Meredith Ann Murray
Cover photos of Egypt and Peru courtesy of Richard Joy
Cover design and text layout by Jane Hagaman

ISBN: 978-0-9845751-6-9
Library of Congress Control Number: 2010933445

This book is printed on acid free paper.

Printed in the USA

*This book is dedicated to
my husband Richard and my daughter Erica.*

My greatest blessing is that you are in my life.

Table of Contents

Acknowledgments

I would like to express my love and deepest gratitude to the following people:

First to Vera Lopez of Spirits of the Earth®; without your encouragement that snowy December morning in Sedona this memoir might not have been completed. You heard and understood my concern to keep my spiritual journey from getting lost in the very public story that was unfolding. You are a selfless point of light on this planet. Thank you for also guiding me to the publisher who would best understand and honor my story and message.

To Ginny Weissman and Paul Burt of Transformation Media Books; thank you for your professionalism and integrity in nurturing this memoir through to completion. Your patience in taking on a "non writer" and expertly guiding me through the publishing process is deeply appreciated.

To my editor, Robert Yehling of Word Journeys, Inc.; you helped me hone my words while keeping the integrity of my journey. Your editorial brilliance and valuable input improved this book tremendously. It was such an amazing coincidence you have been to many of the same places I have, and even climbed Huana Picchu the "wrong way" too by going up the steep stone steps! It was a blessing to have someone with your background in life and writing to help me shape this memoir.

To my publicist, Sara Sgarlat of Sgarlat Publicity; thank you for using your considerable skills in getting the word out.

To those who reviewed pertinent chapters for accuracy; I thank Richard Joy, Erwin Bosma, and Stephen Ray for their time and integrity.

To those people who took the time to read and give feedback on the manuscript; Amy Hall, Arlene Bartle Harris, Erwin Bosma, Katie Gallagher Goese, Nancy Ogilvie, Fatima Bosma, Arlene Pollard, Gale Jensen Krause and Emily Johnston.

To my dearest husband Richard; I thank God everyday for the gift of spending my life and spiritual journey with you. You give me unconditional love and support, and are my soul mate, best friend and business partner. Thank you for the countless hours you spent proofing my writing.

To my daughter Erica; thank you for your infectious smile and cheerful disposition. I appreciated your patience while this book was being completed.

To my parents Mary and Albert Petak; I thank you for setting me on the path of a lifelong learner.

To the San Diego Warriors group; our monthly dinners and deep conversations are something I treasure and look forward to. I am deeply honored to call you my friends.

To all those who are on "the journey" with me; your help, encouragement and support guides my way.

In memory of Colleen Conaway, James Shore, Kirby Brown, and Liz Neuman; your light continues to shine bright in our lives. We will never forget you.

Publisher's Note

I agreed to publish this book only when the author assured me this would not be a muck-racking "tell-all" tome written to frighten the reader about the spiritual self-help movement. Transformation Media Books focuses on publishing authors who are dedicated to improving the lives of their readers in the Mind, Body, Spirit genre.

Personally, I have experienced and benefited from many of the books, workshops and seminars that the media and general public have considered "brainwashing" or "cults." While I never attended a James Arthur Ray event, I did meet him once at the start of his career and found him to be as charismatic and engaging as described in this book.

This is the story of one woman who followed a spiritual path and heard a message that did improve her life but she did not, as the saying goes, "mix up the message with the messenger." As this book is released, James Arthur Ray goes to trial on three counts of manslaughter and is facing numerous civil suits. The courts will decide his fate.

To the best of the author's ability, this is an accurate account of her experience and that of other participants at James Ray International events. References and photos are available at:

www.tragedyinsedona.com.

Many individuals' names in this book have been changed to protect their privacy.

This book is in memory of Colleen Conaway, Kirby Brown, Liz Neuman and James Shore who paid the ultimate price in a quest to improve their lives. They will not be forgotten.

Ginny Weissman, Publisher
Transformation Media Books

Foreword

By Carole Lieberman, M.D.

If the Law of Attraction is true, then James Arthur Ray must have been thinking some mighty powerful self-sabotaging thoughts to have 'attracted' the debacle he's in now.

In his book, *Harmonic Wealth: The Secret of Attracting the Life You Want,* published a year before the sweat lodge incident in Sedona, James unwittingly revealed the clues that explain why and how he unconsciously attracted this tragedy. As with all unconscious manifestations, the seeds began in his childhood.

"I was the kid with the big Coke bottle glasses and buckteeth who everyone made fun of . . . . To make matters worse, I failed at every sport. I just curled up inside myself to avoid the pain. Since I knew I'd never get the girls being a nerd . . . I became a workoutaholic . . . . Becoming a competitive bodybuilder seemed like the answer to all of my problems. But getting attention from girls for the first time in my life didn't squelch my feelings of being a loser, an imposter. If anything, it made me more nervous . . . . My body had become big and strong, and yet in my mind, I was still that weakling who sat alone in the cafeteria, terrified of his own shadow. So I got a new motorcycle, believing that having monster horsepower at my command and all the physical freedom that comes with that would finally do the trick and morph me into a bona fide stud. The last thing I remember about my first ride was a set of headlights coming straight on. Then I woke up in the emergency room. That sense of power was gone, replaced by searing pain . . . . I felt cursed, doomed to remain small and insignificant." And what better antidote to such a curse than becoming a world famous guru? Since the motorcycle didn't do it for James, he undoubtedly hoped that having lots of devotees and lavish toys would.

"The hardest part of my childhood was reconciling how Dad poured his heart into his work, how he helped so many people, and yet couldn't even afford to pay for haircuts for me and my brother. Mom would sit on the front porch to give us buzz cuts while the neighbor kids would stand nearby and laugh . . . . How could a loving God keep me from the Cub Scouts on account of not being able to afford a uniform?"

From the time he was a little boy, sitting in the front pew of his father's Midwest church, listening to sermons about how hard it would be for a rich man to be close to God, James began searching for ways to rationalize how he could possess money, status symbols, fame, eternal youth, sex appeal, and meaningless relationships, while still being spiritual. It did not seem to dawn on him that the concept of being a 'billionaire spiritual guru' was an oxymoron.

Becoming a guru was simply a cover-up for James to feel less insecure and inadequate, a false self that he hung on his shoulders like a shroud. It was a psychological defense that precariously hid his 'inner nerd'. And as his flock and his bank account grew, he fell into the trap of believing his own PR.

James' debut in the film, *The Secret*, thrust him into the spotlight—with the appearances on *Oprah* and *Larry King Live* that he'd been trying to attract for years. He thought his newfound paradise would never end. But, as the buzz wore off, and his popularity and income began to wane, his arrogance, desperation and obsession with death soared. The psychological defenses he had constructed—his hopes of being the first 'billionaire spiritual guru', so that he would have the last laugh on his childhood tormenters—were failing fast. No longer protected from the demons that haunted him, his repressed painful memories washed over him, and drove him to the edge of the cliff he had boasted of in the past. It is no wonder that he attracted the self-sabotaging 'death' that occurred at the Spiritual Warrior retreat in Sedona.

Call it a messiah complex, imposter syndrome, wounded narcissism, sociopathy, too many experimental drugs, sadism or a death wish for himself—no one should be recklessly damaged or die in the pursuit of spiritual awakening.

In regard to an earlier time when his life had imploded, James wrote, "My first big lesson was that everything appearing in my world was of my own creation . . . . I had no choice but to go deep and look at my life and ask, 'How have I created all this pain for myself? How have I gotten so hideously off track?' . . . . I wasn't living as a spiritual person. I had only thought I was . . . . Maybe the lesson is that when you begin to think you're 'the bomb,' the universe loves you enough to drop the bomb. Thump."

If his earlier bomb dropped with a "thump," the 2009 Sedona sweat lodge tragedy dropped a bomb that went nuclear, decimating his credibility and the James Ray Empire. Unfortunately, the bomb also landed on some of his most devoted followers and, literally, decimated them in the process.

James needs to go back and read his own writings. Some of his spiritual lessons are quite insightful. But, somewhere between shopping for a Porsche and a house in Beverly Hills, taking countless supplements and steroids to try to look like a perpetually young stud, and clinging desperately to the fame and fortune that his appearance in "The Secret" brought him . . . he lost his way.

Ironically, James wrote, "One day, I saw a mother duck and her ducklings crossing the highway. The path was dangerous, but the mother waddled with great purpose. Her babies followed without hesitation, marching in perfect step . . . . It provided me with a valuable insight. Being a teacher and an author is a big responsibility. It's a precarious dance I do: provoking, encouraging, stimulating my students without disempowering them . . . . I'm always wary of those spiritual leaders who encourage their students to follow them in blind faith like ducklings, without questioning the path ahead or checking in with their own inner guidance system—spiritual leaders who are unaware that they may be leading their students right into oncoming traffic. I don't want you to follow. I want you to explore."

Really? The sweat lodge participants tell quite a different story. Indeed, James' use of neuro-linguistic programming, hypnosis, crying on cue and other persuasive sales techniques was more insidious than a mother duck's intentions. His 'playing God' and commanding his followers to die, in a game purportedly designed to teach some esoteric lesson, desensitized them to the real danger of his acting like God in the sweat lodge, where he commanded them to be "bigger" than what their inner voice was telling them, and to stay inside. So when he reassured them, "You may feel like you're gonna die, but you're not," they believed him. Before they marched into the sweat lodge, James had painstakingly promoted a growing trust in him by showing his followers that they could accomplish bigger feats than they had ever imagined: breaking blocks of wood and concrete with their bare hands, bending rebar and arrows held to their throat, joining him in his death-defying dance . . . until it was too late.

Tragedy in Sedona is a behind the scenes look at the rise and fall of the James Ray Empire, through the eyes of an ultimately disenchanted follower. Connie Joy takes you on her personal and authentic journey—from being a devoted member of James' inner circle and Dream Team to realizing that the Emperor has no clothes and trying to warn others. Connie's instincts for self-preservation stopped her in her tracks before it was too late. Others, who followed James into his ill-conceived sweat lodge, were not as fortunate. Three were cooked alive, and the rest were traumatized physically and emotionally, leaving visible and invisible scars that will remain with them forever.

James' megalomaniacal behavior has left a trail strewn with victims—not only those in the Sedona sweat lodge, but those whom he previously disappointed, deluded, and drove into bankruptcy or misery. Yet it would be far more unfortunate if the self-serving actions of this one troubled man, haunted by his childhood demons and driven to increasingly desperate attempts to rid himself of his 'inner nerd,' were to discourage others from pursuing their quest to find answers to life's mysteries and fulfill their most cherished dreams. One shouldn't throw the baby out with the fancy bottled bath water . . . or the aromatherapy candles. One should follow one's own path, study the wisdom that's been handed down through the ages, and even some carefully chosen New Age or modern gurus. But when one's inner voice is shouting a warning to get out of the heat . . . or away from the guru's persuasive psychopathological manipulation . . . it's time to run!

In *Harmonic Wealth,* James wrote, "The Darth Vader move, as I call it—the transition from a man of light to a monster of darkness—can happen at any level. Regardless of how high you grow and evolve, you can still fall . . . . You need to guard against this as if your very life depends on it . . . . The allure of increasing wealth and fame is always a seductive reality, slithering around your ankles, ready to strike in the blink of an eye. It's even seductive for me, and I know what to watch out for, my anti-venom always at the ready because it gets really comfortable receiving adulation and gifts, the accoutrements of success." His own words lead us to the inescapable and ultimate question: where was his "anti-venom" when he needed it most—in Sedona?

Carole Lieberman, M.D., M.P.H. is a Beverly Hills forensic psychiatrist, who examined two of James Ray's followers who were in the sweat lodge that fateful day of tragedy in Sedona. Her background encompasses additional experiences that give her deep insights into self-styled gurus like James Arthur Ray. These include having: spent weeks in the Peruvian Amazon convening with shamans and experiencing their ayahuasca ceremonies, hiked to the vortexes of Sedona with guides of the spiritual and llama variety, been in the 'inner' orbit of other gurus, written *Bad Boys: Why We Love Them, How To Live with Them and When to Leave Them*, and—like James—been on *Oprah* and *Larry King Live.*

Introduction

When I first started writing this book, its title was going to be, *My Spiritual Journey to Egypt and Peru as a Member of James Arthur Ray's Inner Circle.* I even hoped the charismatic and highly intelligent James Ray would write the introduction. A lot has changed in the last year.

To be more precise, it changed in an instant.

On October 8, 2009, while vacationing in Maui, my husband Richard and I started receiving phone calls and texts from friends who were in Sedona and participating in the now infamous sweat lodge run by James Arthur Ray. Other mutual friends relayed messages from those who were too ill to call us directly. We heard an acceleration of tragic news: many of our friends were injured, some severe enough to be treated at a hospital; one dear friend was on a ventilator; one was in critical condition (and eventually died); and two were dead. After experiencing a James Ray sweat lodge two years earlier, I knew his version of this ancient ritual was an accident waiting to happen. At most, I was expecting someone to suffer some degree of brain damage. Even I did not foresee James going so far as to literally bake his clients to death!

Our minds immediately filled with should haves, would haves, and could haves. Should we have been there? We had planned to serve as volunteers at the seminar, but we backed out for several reasons. I felt the sweat lodge run "James Ray style" was dangerous and, sooner or later, something really bad was going to happen. We were growing more and more disillusioned by his rapidly growing aggressive behavior. Had we been at Spiritual Warrior 2009 in Sedona, we would have been among the people most likely to stand up to James, as we had in the past.

Earlier in 2009 in Peru, James called us "the trouble makers in the World Wealth Society." It's a designation we are not ashamed to hold, especially considering what happened just two months later at Spiritual Warrior 2009. The World Wealth Society (WWS) consisted of the people to whom James referred to as his "inner circle." We were among the original-founding members. Could we have been even more vocal about our concerns? How could we have communicated more clearly to those whom we had previously warned? At what point do you have to let people follow their own path?

After the tragic events took place in Sedona, I stopped writing my book. Who would be interested in what I had seen and learned, especially when it concerned what I had been taught by James?

During Christmas 2009, we visited my parents in Prescott, a town close to Sedona. We also decided to visit our friend, Vera, the tour organizer of our trip to Peru with James. She convinced me the message of my journey still needed to be told, maybe now more than ever, so people could better understand the events that led up to that tragic day, how it could have happened, and why the people who suffered and died in that lodge were there in the first place.

From January of 2007 until the end of 2009, Richard and I attended twenty-seven seminars and events presented by James Arthur Ray. The media dubbed him "The Rock Star of Personal Transformation," a term he liked to use, even at the end of his emails. He promised to instruct us in a mix of spirituality and quantum physics that would transform our lives. We would have to agree there has been a transformation in our lives; we now have a regular meditation, supplementation, diet, and exercise program. We have traveled to Egypt and Peru with him, and explored the ancient spiritual teachings from those areas. Through James, we met our current financial advisor, our anti-aging doctor, and many of our dearest friends. This all came at a very high cost, somewhere around $200,000.

We did not set out to spend this much money on our spiritual growth. Before we met James and started to follow his teaching to "live (and spend) from the outcome" (translation: don't let your current situations dictate how you live now), we would have been considered financially conservative. To James, our current state is a result of how we thought in the past. He spoke of basing current decisions on how we want to be in the future. For many things, this approach works well. Financially, this worked very well for James, though not necessarily for his students. Was that a flaw in his teaching, or by his design? I will let you, the reader, decide.

All of this would have continued if not for a very sad, disastrous day on October 8, 2009. We felt certain after the problems with the 2007, and especially the 2008, sweat lodges James would tone down the heat and number of rounds he administered to a more reasonable level. After the injuries at his previous events, why didn't he get the message he was literally playing with fire?

A lot of questions to be sure. Many I hope to answer in this book. I will show you the James we knew before his appearance on *Oprah* and *Larry King Live*, the "old" James, and what happened after those appearances that led up to this disaster. Since the Spiritual Warrior seminar in September 2007, I voiced my concerns about the safety of the participants in James' extreme sweat lodge experience. I sent out an email on October 10, 2007, rating that activity 0 out of 10 because of its danger. This email appears later in the book. Our vocal opposition to his practice of pushing people too hard, and our attempts to find less dangerous options for all of us, is partially why we locked horns with James in the lobby of a Peruvian hotel, where a heated argument took place just weeks before the Sedona tragedy.

At the same time, we are very appreciative for all we have learned from James. Therein lies the dilemma we and his other students face: separating James the man from the often-deep quality and wisdom of his teachings. We need to be able to separate the message from the messenger.

It is my primary intention to show those who attended his seminars were not mindless cult followers. We are like-minded people, many very successful in our careers and businesses, who knew the way we treat each other and our environment can and must improve. We are people who constantly endeavor to hold ourselves to a higher level of integrity in our daily actions. Because of our association with James, we learned and made tremendous strides in our lives.

When you finish reading this account of my experience, I hope you are better able to understand how intelligent and caring people could follow James Ray into a grossly overheated tent and stay there while he slowly cooked them to death. Why is it important for you to know this? So something similar doesn't happen to you or someone you love. Our instructor was a human being with his own agenda and issues. At what point did his prime directive switch from helping his students improve themselves—and the world around them—to focusing squarely on himself, his ego, and his personal financial wealth?

Our extended family of James Ray seminar participants and WWS members are struggling to find closure, which will not come for most until long after the forthcoming trials are completed, and the legal system metes out its determination. We are working together to find and validate the value of the lessons we learned and the changes we made in our lives, while identifying and finding a way to accept our teacher's shortcomings. What do they say about converting and manifesting skills and talents? Those who can, do; those who can't, teach.

As with any issue, especially one as emotionally charged as this, two main camps have formed. First, there is the group who want to see James thrown in jail for a very long time. The other side of the spectrum consists of chronically co-dependent people. It doesn't matter what James does; they will continue to hold him on a pedestal. As Buddha taught, the true way is the middle path. To find peace in your soul the answer will lie somewhere in the middle of these two extremes. That's where many of us fall now.

Most of all, I do not want James' actions to cast a permanent shadow on the desire of many people to learn and grow. There are many great teachers out there, but at some point, we have to become our own gurus, take what we have learned, and apply it to how we live. The unfortunate reality is that with spiritual teaching, like any other product being sold, we have to be careful consumers—even if our teachers are of a religious or spiritual nature. I am not a big fan of regulation, but unless some steps are taken to provide full disclosure of event contents and the presenter's qualifications, this type of tragedy can happen again.

Connie Joy
July, 2010

CHAPTER 1

The Sphinx

Giza Plateau, Egypt · October 4, 2008

I have always sent you all the help you ever needed,
before you even knew what to ask for.

—The Sphinx

The alarm jolts us awake. Exhausted, our heads fall back into our pillows. It's 3:30 a.m. in Cairo, Egypt, another early start of a day. This was common fare for a trip with James Ray.

We're staying in a beautiful modern hotel overlooking the Nile. It's partly a waste, considering how little time we have spent in our room since returning to Cairo. A few minutes later, the phone rings with our secondary wakeup call. This is not our earliest morning call. That would have been the first day, when we awoke at 2:00 a.m., packed our bags and placed them outside our door by 2:15 a.m., then arrived in the lobby by 2:30 a.m. That day, we were headed off to the airport for the first of three separate flights around Egypt in a single day.

Today, there were no flights scheduled, just a pre-dawn bus ride to the Giza Plateau. This was the last day of a busy weeklong trip with the World Wealth Society (WWS). If I had any idea what was waiting for me in the dark stillness of that timeless place, I would've been more excited.

It was time to meet the Sphinx and the Great Pyramid.

James often said that you could *know about* something by learning about it, but to truly *know* it, you must experience it. Today, we are going to get to *know* the Sphinx and the Great Pyramid. It is James' M. O. to make the end of an event or trip the "grand finale." This past week in Egypt has truly been a trip of a lifetime for my husband, Richard, and me, so I'm equally apprehensive and excited to see what our day on the Giza plateau will yield. My mild apprehension stems from the fact that each day thus far, a growth opportunity sprung up that forced me to take a hard look at my core beliefs, particularly untrue belief patterns that do not serve me. While ultimately rewarding, this is often a painful experience. What would I learn today—and what would be the "cost" of that lesson?

As our bus moves along the mostly deserted Cairo streets, my trepidation quickly yields to awe as the top of one pyramid becomes visible over the surrounding apartment buildings in the predawn light. There they are! They're real! There would be no disappointment here today. Our bus is the first to pull up to the guarded gate at the base of the plateau. After much "discussion" in Arabic, the guards, brandishing automatic rifles, pull open the gates and step aside to let the two buses pass. A jeep with heavily armed military men falls into line behind us as we drive by the Great Pyramid.

The magnificence of the pyramid exceeds anything I have ever imagined. The entire Giza plateau sits silent and empty, as if frozen in time—the time of millennia past, yet also seemingly devoid of time. It seems completely out of sync with our understanding of time. Our large buses appear as mere toys next to the huge solid unmovable expanse of history beside us. From the moment we passed through the gates, everyone in the bus fell silent. Any spoken words would only violate the private experience each of us was having. Especially words spoken in English, a language three millennia removed from this sacred giant.

It was just a few minutes before dawn. In just a few hours, the entire area would swarm with tourists, buses, camels, horses and locals hawking anything they can sell. But for now, the entire plateau is ours and ours alone.

We drive slowly on the road past the Great Pyramid, and then proceed further along until we pull to a stop alongside the Sphinx. Its appearance doesn't disappoint. The Sphinx wears a deep rose color in the predawn light, a perfect color for the first activity on our final day in Egypt: a meditation between the paws of the Sphinx at sunrise!

The Sphinx faces east, greeting the rising sun. It is a symbol of eternal rebirth for both the new day and, possibly, the birth of our new selves. With each "spiritual" experience perceived as either "good" or "bad," we change. Each time, an aspect of our old selves "dies" so a new self can come forward. Like the experience of a paradigm shift where we see or feel something we never perceived before, we alter our conscious perception to the point that we can never see the old way again. Whether or not you believe Leonardo da Vinci purposely left a V-shaped space to the right of Jesus in his painting of the "Last Supper" to illustrate the sacred feminine, you cannot avoid seeing it every time you view the image once pointed out. This also goes for the feminine appearance of the first person to his right, which some believe to be Mary Magdalene. Nothing changed in the painting, but your perception of it changes forever. There is no turning back to the way you viewed the painting before.

The acknowledgment of rebirth represents just one facet of the Sphinx. In nature, rebirth happens effortlessly at the triumphant rising of the sun every morning. The Sphinx is also thought to be an earth-based keeper of the Akashic Records, the detailed record of everything that has happened in the past and will ever happen in the future.

Such encounters with the deepest aspects of the spiritual life have been daily occurrences all week. Earlier, we followed the ancient path of the initiate. It began with a visit to the feminine (emotional) energies of Philae Island and the Temple of Isis, followed by an acknowledgment of the masculine (logical) energies at Abu Simbel on the Egypt/Sudan border. In these visits, we were reminded of the need for emotion and intellect to work harmoniously within each of us. Our history is dotted with leaders who ranged too far to one side or the other. No one wants to be led by someone who is very smart but without compassion, nor do we want to follow a person who makes decisions purely on emotional grounds without logical thought being applied. This is the same whether we are male or female. We need both to be complete and effective.

During the week, we traveled up the Nile, which in Egyptian cosmology represents a spinal column. We stopped at the temples built on locations thought to represent the energies of the seven chakras in the human body. James gave us an assignment: to review and fine-tune our goals and intentions for our lives. We formed and wrote down short, intermediate, and long-term goals, evaluated them for the "negative" consequences that accompany any goal, adjusted where necessary, and recommitted to them. Now we were ready to compare the activities or achievements to which we were going to commit our energies, and strive to attune the plan for our lives to the Akashic records already held by the Sphinx. That was just one possible experience we could have during our meditation between its paws.

As the sun rose in the east, we became aware we are always capable of a rebirth, a fresh start, and the dropping away of some more of our limiting beliefs that have kept us from attaining our goals. That was then (our old selves), and this is now (who we are at this very moment). The sunrise heralds a new day, a new beginning, as it does every day. It signifies the "Now," each moment of the new day in which everything and anything is possible if you're willing to commit to doing what it takes to bring your goals into form. In our plane of existence, this movement progresses from thoughts to feelings, then accelerates into the action that produces results.

But we're not there yet. We wait for the guards to unlock the gate that blocks the path to the Sphinx. A large fence surrounds it and prevents visitors from getting near the monument. We're allowed in as members of a trip full of special features and privileges.

After facing east to offer a brief salutation to the rising sun, we move between the Sphinx's paws to find our places to sit for meditation. James offers a quick discussion that touches upon the reasons why this ground is so hallowed. The granite altar between the Sphinx's paws was likely used by Moses, and if you believe Jesus spent time in Egypt, he surely sat in silent contemplation where we were now sitting. Next, James pointed out the large granite slab standing against the chest of the Sphinx, drawing our attention to the rectangular squares that many believe represent the Akashic Records. Whether they are stored physically in the Sphinx or in a room below, or delivered via infusion of thought directly from the Sphinx to you, is a matter of speculation and debate. Anyway you look at it, we are sitting on a very special place on our planet and my butt is firmly planted on the ground with my back resting on the inside of the Sphinx's left paw. As the sun ascends higher over the horizon, directly between the Sphinx's paws, I feel its heat bathe the left side of my face. As I look up to my right, the rose-colored face of the Sphinx lightens.

James instructs us to close our eyes and then resumes his talk. I truly don't remember much of what he says; his voice is melting away behind the chant of gratitude I have begun. My legs start to vibrate, and small energy tremors move through my body and exit from the tips of my fingers. I just let it flow; for how long, I have no idea. I'm at peace. I feel gently stroked and rocked in the arms of this mighty statue. Everything was perfect, as it should be.

In an instant, I'm jerked to attention: time to go over the life plan I had developed for myself over the last week. I did not know how much time would be available for me to finish. With nervous excitement, I started to review some of my "easier" goals. Within my mind, I ask if a desired goal will happen in the next six months. If I perceive a "No" answer, then I ask if it will manifest within the next year. If still not, then I would ask about the next two years. Throughout this deeply inner exercise, I "feel" or get the impression of a yes or no answer.

After moving quickly through the goals in which I was less personally vested, I tentatively move to my two "big goals." For most of my adult life, I've struggled with a weight that has hovered somewhere in the 350 lbs. range. I say "somewhere," because I stopped weighing myself a long time before. Why subject myself to the heartbreak every morning of having a scale confirm what I already knew? I was a failure. How can I be successful at anything if I am constantly failing at such a basic discipline as keeping my weight in line? Anything that would appear as success in my life did not seem real to me; how could it be real? I lived in fear "they," the people around me, would figure out I was an incompetent individual.

Did that make sense, given the many successes I had already created in my life? No, but this fat-equals-failure dynamic constantly accompanied me like an unwelcome shadow. I would lose weight and then put it all back on—and then some. In my life, I have lost more than 100 lbs. three different times, only to gain it all back. I just didn't want to think about the possibility of going through the physical, mental and emotional rollercoaster for a fourth time. The only thing worse than being severely overweight is to make the Herculean effort to lose so much, then have the effort be for naught when the weight returned.

That being said, as I sit at the base of the Sphinx, my current weight is severely impacting my health and limiting my abilities to undertake the activities I desire. I am blessed with a husband who loves me independent of my weight, but he became rightfully alarmed at the results of recent blood tests and physicals. Richard is Mr. Fit, a two-time marathon runner and disciplined exerciser. Even though he loves me unconditionally, he could not understand why I failed to keep the weight off. My excess weight made it difficult for us to share the activities we loved to do together, like hiking and snorkeling. He told me often he feared losing me, his best friend, to a heart attack or stroke.

So once again I went to battle and worked hard to understand why I used the excess weight for protection. I lost a lot of weight, which I could tell by the bagginess of my clothing, and was starting to feel hopeful that this lifetime enemy could be beaten back one more time. When I stepped on the scale, the number 308 stared up at me. What should have felt like a proud, successful moment instead sank my heart and brought tears to my eyes. Even if I lost another hundred pounds, I would still be obese. I had such a long way to go. Even with all the personal work, the spiritual journey over the last few years, and gaining a strong understanding of how I used food for protection from a dangerous world, did I have the audacity to think I could finally succeed?

I tried to quiet my racing mind of these negative thoughts. I ask, "Will I lose enough weight in this coming year so that my health will improve?"

The answer races to me, a clear "Yes!" Stunned, I ask again. Did I misunderstand the answer? Or had I not asked the question clearly? I asked the question from different angles three more times; on each occasion, the answer is the same—"Yes." I didn't know whether to be terrified or exhilarated! Deep, profound relief poured from my heart. Tears rolled down my cheeks. All I could think of was, "Please let this be true, please!"

I received a clear thought from somewhere in the universe, not from within me: "Trust the process and good results will come about over the next year."

That left one main goal to confirm. I worked to quiet my mind again. Since our honeymoon trip almost 27 years ago, Richard and I felt the peaceful spiritual energy of the Hawaiian Islands. We instinctively *know* we belong there. In 1994, we made the bold move of buying a one-bedroom condo overlooking the channel between Maui and the island of Molokai. It became our sanctuary. To be able to afford it, we've rented it as a vacation home except for a two or three week period each year when we spend truly heavenly time there. Knowing we have "our place" on the island makes it more tolerable to leave and return to the mainland. It has always been our dream and intention to retire there. We know it will happen, but the big question remains, when? I wanted to find out from the Sphinx.

After several deep, calming and focusing breaths, I ask, "Will we move permanently to Maui before the end of this year?" Quickly, the answer comes back, "No." No big deal; I did not expect to be able to move so quickly anyway. Next I ask, "Will we move permanently to Maui next year?" Again, the answer is "No." It seems the answer forms way too quickly, more like a "no way, not even close" response.

A feeling of fear and dread develops in my solar plexus. OK, now this is getting serious. I started to ask the question again; this time prepared to ask about the following year. I cannot even release the question before I am interrupted with the thought that there is more I must do first on the mainland. When I inquire as to the nature of what I'm supposed to do, many images flash quickly through my mind. I see people who I need to help through our real estate business. I envision us taking an ownership and operating role in our real estate office. I perceive I am responsible for sharing a message; and, most shockingly, I learn I am supposed to write a book!

A book? *No way!* I really mean NO WAY! Richard is in his 70's; it's time for us to slow down, not assume more responsibilities. As for the idea of me writing a book? Ridiculous! I am NOT a writer. My favorite subjects in school were always science, math and history. My early work and degree came as a Medical Laboratory Technician. I ran electron microscopes, worked for Union Carbide as a Microbiologist, and served IBM as a Chemical Engineer. I also earned a BS degree in Computer Science in the school of Mathematics. I have been blessed with a quick and intelligent mind, but not when it comes to English and writing. Truth be told, I found both subjects to be painful. I always thought of myself as a "creative" speller, the person for whom spell check was invented. I'm just not a liberal arts kind of a person. I know that 95% of people say they want to write a book, but count me among the 5% who happily lived her life with absolutely no interest. This was *not* my plan for how I wanted my life to go in the next few years at all, not even a little bit. No, no, no!

Help me out here, Sphinx!

James' voice returns to my consciousness. He's wrapping up the meditation by talking about gratitude for the messages and experiences we have received. He reminds us to remain in silence for a while after the meditation to allow the messages to sink in, to be absorbed and assimilated by our physical, emotional, mental and spiritual bodies, in our hearts and souls. People start to hug each other, bliss-filled tears running down their faces.

However, I am majorly pissed off. The ageless lion boy and I are not done. Not by a long shot!

James has begun hugging people; many still sit, kneel or stand in the area between the paws. Richard looks over at me. I nod, but I don't remember much more than that. Instinctively, without any thought or plan of what I am going to do, I work my way around the mass of people and approach the plate of granite against the chest of the Sphinx. The armed guards who followed us in their jeep and opened the gate to let us approach the Sphinx continue to keep a watchful eye on us. What I do not know is what I can get away with as far as approaching the granite slab, nor if I can actually touch it once I arrive.

I stepped on the platform in front of the Sphinx, my forehead just a few inches away and my hands held up at shoulder level, also inches from the slab. I become aware of someone stepping up to join me; when I turn my head slightly to the left, I see Whitney, a member of our group. Turning back to the stone, I listen for a moment to hear if any of the guards are ordering me down. I hear nothing but the shuffling of the group members behind me.

Whitney, myself, and several other people in the group are "sensitive" to energy. We can sometimes sense its flow in places and objects and can direct that flow inward if we choose. It's easier for me to actually touch the object but it is not necessary, depending on the strength of the flow. Everyone can sense energy to some extent. You know the feeling you get when you step into a room where there has just been an argument? Or when two people are having a fight and you don't know about it but you can feel that something is wrong? You're feeling the negative energy generated. To feel the "good vibe," positive energy, you just need to walk outdoors in nature, or stand near a group of supportive, loving people. The energy that surrounds us constantly affects us.

I was upset from what I'd just "learned" in my meditation. I hoped by picking up on the energy coming from the Sphinx, I can settle down quickly to get back into communication with whatever is passing these messages to me.

Standing very close to the granite slab, I closed my eyes and said my usual request when I do not know what to ask for—and leave it to the higher power to tell me what I must know. I really need the guidance now, because I am having trouble settling down.

"Talk to me," I say. "Tell me what I need to know most right now."

The next thing I know, I'm pulled toward the slab with my forehead, bridge of my nose, and hands firmly pressed against it. It feels cool in the already high heat of the desert morning. For a split second, I wonder if the guards are going to let me get away with actually touching it and then . . . I'm *gone,* focused completely on my "conversation." Nothing else matters. The group could have boarded the buses and left me there; I wouldn't know. It's just the lion boy and me, and I'm not giving up on him seeing it from my perspective without a fight.

You may be asking yourself to whom is this woman speaking? I am not picky when it comes to the originating sources of important messages. Call it my guardian angel, my spirit guide, a member of the council of elders, a friend or relative who has passed or a higher power. It all comes from God, and I have grown to learn that it really does not matter who the messenger is.

This time though the "voice" is unique. It is compassionate and patient, but firm. It feels like I'm not getting away with anything, no matter how hard I whine and complain. The images return; one by one, I try to argue them away with debates of reason. Why in the world would we invest a hefty amount of money into a real estate office when we are heading into a very tough time in the real estate business? Large companies and offices were folding, yet I was shown that we were going to not just invest, but also be the managing partner. That made no sense at all. As for the book? That was just plain lame; I didn't have the time. Why can't we move to Maui and work from there? Why do we have to do these things first before we leave California?

The guiding presence meets each of my arguments with either the sense of utter silence, compassionately waiting for me to wear myself out, or by giving a reasonable answer. All were equally annoying responses. At one point, I realize I am whining to God, and chuckle at the absurdity of threatening not to cooperate in my attempt to negotiate with the Almighty. But like a small child being told they can't have something, I'm pitching a fit that ranges from arguing facts to sobbing that this was not fair.

Eventually, I see the bottom line, the root of these images and directives: I had agreed to do all of these things in this lifetime before I got here, before I was born, and that they were just helping me stick to my plan. They also knew me very well, and I have to begrudgingly admit they are right. God being "right"—now there's a wild thought! If I went to Maui now, I would confine myself to my home and garden and never work on any of these other projects. They were doing me a favor by holding me to my plan.

Crap! I am plainly not going to win this argument. "OK," I reluctantly say. Not the way you say "OK" when everything is perfectly agreeable, but the resigned OK of realizing all further resistance is futile. Through one last sob, with pangs of perceived unfairness still echoing in my head, I demand, "If you expect me to get all of these things done, then you better at least send me some help!"

What comes back is the message meant for anyone who is facing a challenge in their lives: "I have always sent you all the help you ever needed before you even knew what to ask for."

With that, I knew I was out of arguments. Whatever I felt about the whole task now becomes a moot point. It is really going to be more than OK. It is going to be perfect.

The next message I received was the sensation of being told to go, turn around, and get on with my life. As suddenly as I had been pulled into the slab, I am now gently propelled away. I noticed for the first time others on both sides of me, taking turns standing with their heads and hands against the slab.

Turning around and stepping down, I search the group of 60+ people for Richard. We are supposed to be in silence for a while after the meditation, so I quietly scan the group for his face. I find him and walk next to him. Not being able to tell him what I just experienced is torture, but I followed the rules. I did not want him to miss out on the chance to stand at the slab as I did and see if he experiences something similar. I kept gesturing at him to walk up to the slab.

He wasn't moving. I made a final, desperate attempt. I whispered to him to place his head against the slab. "I already have," he whispered back. Not thinking I've heard him correctly, I asked him to repeat what he just said. How is that possible? I wonder. I surely would have known if he had been up there with me, unless he was there for just a second.

I asked him again if he had stayed there for a while. "Yes."

Later that morning, I'm still confused. How could he have been up on the platform with the Sphinx? I asked him how long he thought I was up there, thinking it had to be four, maybe five minutes. He replied, "You were up there with your head against the slab for a good 25-30 minutes!" How did I manage to stand still for so long?

Losing track of time is a sign of being in an altered state, a state of consciousness different from your "normal". When you sleep every night, you are in an altered state of consciousness. Engrossed in a book without noticing hours have slipped by; when you are doing something fun "time flies." When you are working on something that impassions and inspires you—in-spirit—time seems to move at a more rapid pace.

When Richard told me my "couple of minutes" of seeking answers from the Sphinx was really close to half an hour, I took that as confirmation of a spiritual experience.

It was still very early in the morning. The day had already been incredible. It was mind-boggling to know our grand finale experience was yet to come that afternoon: three hours alone inside the Great Pyramid! We were free to explore all three levels inside the pyramid, two of which were usually off-limits to the general public. Each of us would receive our own personal meditation time while lying inside the red granite sarcophagus in the King's Chamber. I was already pretty wiped out from the events of the morning, certain I would be processing my experience for days and weeks to come. What more could possibly be waiting for me in the Great Pyramid, the grand finale of this amazing trip?

CHAPTER 2

A Lifetime Learner Meets James Arthur Ray

Harmonic Wealth Weekend February 2007

Intellectual growth should commence at birth and cease only at death.

—Albert Einstein

How did I come to meet James Arthur Ray? What drew me to his teachings? What had set me on this path of learning? Nothing is by accident or coincidence; I was exactly where I was supposed to be.

I was raised Roman Catholic by a family that considered themselves very religious. We never missed Sunday Mass, even in the worst blizzards. My father is a member of the Knights of Columbus, and both parents trained and served as Eucharistic ministers for the distribution of Communion. I attended Catholic schools through the university level. I always had an intense desire to learn about and know God, but the more I was forced to follow the rigid Catholic way, and the limitations on thought, I was increasingly repelled.

I saw an ad for hypnosis sessions when I was 19 promising to teach self-hypnosis. By practicing regularly, they said, I would be able to thrive with much less sleep. I was working full time and attending university with a heavy course load, so sleep was in short supply. Self-hypnosis looked very appealing. During one of the sessions, I experienced my first major paradigm shift. When the hypnotist took me back in time through my childhood, I slipped back into a previous life as a man. I learned I was eternal and what I was experiencing now was just one of my many lives. If the Catholic Church was wrong about something as fundamental as reincarnation, then they could be wrong about everything else I was taught to believe as well. This paradigm shift set me on my path as a lifelong spiritual aspirant and learner. To find the truth, I would have to search for it myself.

Just before I married Richard, I met a man while attending a health retreat for women who became a long time friend. Robert, a psychic, was a friend of the resort owner, and as a favor, he would come in after dinner and demonstrate his psychic abilities to the guests. Each person in the room would place something they carried with them often on a tray. Robert was not in the room. Being a skeptic of psychics, I thought I would trick him. Most people were offering keys, pens, or pieces of jewelry. I placed a very small pinkie ring on the tray. There were several small girls playing in the room, and I thought he would mistakenly assume the ring belonged to one of them.

One by one, Robert picked up the articles from the tray and did a mini-reading on what he felt about the person, a practice known as psychometry. He said one woman was there to recover from the recent suicide of her son. Not only was it true, but she had told no one there about it! He relayed a message from her son that his suicide was due to a chemical imbalance in his brain and that she was not to feel responsible. He was happy and safe now. What an amazing gift of peace! None of us had any idea of the loss she'd suffered.

There were happy readings, too. One woman learned she was pregnant and was going to have a boy, which later proved correct on both counts. Finally Robert picked up my tiny ring. He said at first look one might think it was a child's ring because it was so small. "I don't know how this can fit on a woman's finger but it belongs to a woman who is about to get married." I was busted! He described Richard to a "T" and he told me we were going to have a long and happy marriage. I now knew there was validity to psychic phenomenon.

In 1988 I had a near-death experience during an ectopic pregnancy rupture. I learned we have multiple exit points built into our lives and it is our choice if we want to take an earlier one. It was during this experience I "met" my future daughter, Erica, and at which time I first consciously remembered the state of total and complete unconditional love.

Later I talked to Robert on the phone, before he knew about my hospitalization. I was getting ready to tell him when he stopped in mid-sentence and asked me, "How was it to meet your future daughter?" I was surprised; psychically he already knew what happened!

I picked up one side effect of the near-death experience: the ability to feel what other people were feeling. Being an empath was a mixed "blessing," to be sure. I could share in someone's joy, I could tell when they were really in pain and trying to hide it, but at times it was a real curse because I did not yet have the ability to turn it off. I had no idea that most people were in so much pain! I couldn't even watch the news, because I picked up the grieving family's pain at the loss of a loved one—even on TV. When I say I could feel their emotions, I mean I could feel the physical sensations attached to their emotions.

Over time, I learned how to minimize this connection. I improved at cutting the link totally when it became overwhelming, such as during severe grief, but sometimes the emotions and feelings were so strong they could not be blocked. In 2003, the Cedar Fire incinerated much of our neighborhood, including many houses on our road. Numerous people lost not just their homes, but all of their possessions as well, including memorabilia such as photos and videos. No one was killed in my area, but many lost their beloved pets. As one of the surviving homes in the middle of this sea of destruction, we were surrounded by a growing vortex of grief as people sifted through their homes to find nothing salvageable. Many felt like we lost our tight knit community as well; so many families were displaced and would rent homes in other areas for years to come as they struggled through the rebuilding process.

At the same time, one of Richard's sons had a daughter born with a serious heart defect and was struggling to stay alive in a hospital in Oregon, and our daughter Erica's beloved horse became seriously ill and landed in an equine hospital. Grief was all around, all hitting me at one time. I folded myself into the fetal position and asked for it to all stop; it was too much. I couldn't function anymore. I couldn't breathe.

Suddenly the physical feelings stopped. I still knew about the pain, and could feel my own emotions and physical sensations. However the huge wave of other people's physical sensations stopped. After that I intuitively picked up on other people's emotions if I chose, but not their physical sensations.

The gift from this experience was I became a kinder, gentler Connie. I wasn't as tough on others, now that I understood that everyone was just working through their pain the best they could. People can't get away with telling me they are "fine," because intuitively, I know when they are not. My decision is whether I call them on it, or not.

Robert had been encouraging me to meet Sylvia Browne for as long as I had known him. I told him I did not need to go seek out another psychic when I already knew him. He insisted her information for me would be "different." Robert also started to tell Richard and me that both of us would meet and spend a lot of time with a famous man who appeared on TV and would have a profound effect on our lives. He always had a concerned look on his face when he talked about this man. I asked him if the effect on our lives would be good for us, to which he always replied, "Yes," but he sensed trouble. He was concerned about the man's intentions.

I had known Robert long enough not to argue with him when he told me something. Like the time he told us we would be moving. I said, "Yep, our new house is almost ready!" We were a few weeks away from moving into our newly built home in San Jose.

"I'm sorry that you will not be able to continue working on your Master's degree. How do you feel about that?"

"Why?" I asked.

"Because you're moving away from the area. You're moving to San Diego."

"You're correct about the move but very wrong about San Diego," I protested.

We never moved into the San Jose house. Shortly after the conversation with Robert, Richard accepted a job offer in San Diego.

I learned whenever Robert showed concern while telling you something about your future, don't take it lightly. At the time, I had no idea who the famous man on TV was and why we should be leery.

A couple of years later, I saw Gary Zukav discussing his book *The Seat of The Soul* on *Oprah!* I was immediately drawn to the material. I had been thinking about many of the same things but had no idea where to turn for more information. I bought his book and related with much of what he said. Especially in the chapter that discussed reincarnation, I found validation for what I had experienced. It was real and now I was determined to learn more about it.

A little while later, I "accidentally" switched the TV channel and watched the last few minutes of a *Montel Williams* show in which Sylvia Browne made her weekly guest appearance. I was busy making dinner, but when I heard her name, I remembered that this was the woman Robert wanted me to meet. She was discussing her book, *Past Lives, Future Healing,* which was all about reincarnation and the effect of our past lives on our current one. I stopped at a bookstore the next day. Again much of my experience was validated, including my near-death experience, and I wanted to know more. I returned to the store the next day and bought every book Sylvia had written.

I joined one of Sylvia Browne's groups, became a small group coordinator for Southern California, and led a study group in my home. During a phone session, Sylvia told me I was supposed to be doing past life regressions. She verified it when we met in person during a book signing. During my phone reading, I thought she meant I needed to have another hypnotic regression done on me. She told me three times to learn how to do them, that I had a natural gift for it, before I realized what she meant. I was to take *someone else* through the process. I went up to San Jose to be trained and certified in performing past life regressions.

I belonged to several spiritual book groups. In 2006, at the end of one of these meetings, I saw *The Secret.* It engrossed me. I suspected our positive and negative thoughts were far more powerful than we acknowledged, and we were the creators of what surrounded us. I wanted to know more. Immediately, I bought the DVD and shared it with other people. One person heard one of movie's contributors was conducting a short lecture in San Diego. A group of us, including Richard and I, attended.

Soon after James Ray started his talk, he asked us to introduce ourselves to each other. No one was approaching him, so I did. When I shook his hand and introduced myself, he commented on my name badge, The Joys of Real Estate, and how that was a great company name. I was impressed he would notice, considering all the people moving around the room. He seemed open and friendly, charismatic and approachable. He talked about practical applications of ancient wisdom and spiritual practices in today's world. He meshed quantum physics with spirituality. He said that quantum physicists were today's mystics, that our forward-thinking scientists were proving that the teachings of ancient mystics were true. In college, I loved physics, but was always too busy getting the formulas correct to spend time contemplating what it all meant; time folding back on itself, parallel universes, alternate realities, and now the proof that more than one atom can occupy the same place at the same time.

Richard has a PhD in Engineering from Stanford and I have a BS in Computer Science from Santa Clara University's school of Mathematics. We were drawn to the blending of science and spirituality. It appealed to us and we wanted to know more. Richard told me to hurry to the back of the room and sign us up for James' next seminar. That was uncharacteristic of him; usually, he needed time to think about it. I was usually quicker to make snap decisions and act on my gut feelings.

Two red flags popped up that I brushed off. I noticed the extremely hard-sell techniques James used to get participants to sign up for one of his future events. Early in this lecture, he asked, "If I can show you a way guaranteed to get you everything you want in life, would you do it?" The crowd responded loudly and affirmatively. He repeated the question again, this time asking us to raise our hand if we would do what he said. A little while later, he challenged us to fill out the credit card information at the bottom of the event enrollment form "just so you will be ready in case you decide to take the next step." It was James' way of showing us what to do to get what we wanted in life.

He introduced his next event, an entry-level seminar, Harmonic Wealth Weekend (HWW). I thought the price was very inflated. He went on to tell us all the things he would throw in for "free," one at a time, if we signed up right now. After that he dramatically reduced the price—if we signed up right now! And then the grand finale: if we sign up today, we receive two tickets for the price of one!

In retrospect, this was very clever. James motivated us to bring someone to the seminar. Once there, he deployed these same high-pressure sales techniques to get both parties to sign up for much pricier seminar packages.

The second red flag launched us from our seats to the back of the room. He announced a HWW seminar coming up in San Diego, but it had been sold out for many months. Too bad, he said, because it would be a long time before another was offered locally, and we'd have to pay for travel and other expenses to attend in another city. BUT, he added, we were in luck! Amazingly, his staff made room for 20 more people to get into the San Diego seminar. To be fair, they'd release those spots on a first-come, first-served basis at the back table now! Everyone else would have to be waitlisted. Richard and I had already decided we wanted to attend, so I scurried to the registration table. When I arrived, Megan, James Ray International's (JRI) Chief of Operations, was handing out slips of paper with the number 1 to 20 written on them. There were easily more than 50 people crowded around the back table. *Miraculously,* they agreed to accommodate everyone, so no one would be left out. How nice of them!

I was somewhat amused. I knew what James was up to. It was the slickest and pushiest sales pitch/manipulation I had ever seen. I was interested in the material, and I was one of the "lucky" ones who got a piece of paper with a number on it, so I didn't care much at the time. I had seen similar sales pitches for other seminars. I should have considered he wasn't trying to sell me some real estate sales training, or new gadget; he was supposed to be a spiritual teacher. How did his approach fit into taking the high road in business and life?

After the talk, we walked up front to get our picture taken with James. He seemed pretty open and friendly, and we already looked forward to his next seminar.

Harmonic Wealth Weekend started a month later in February. From the first moment, we experienced quite a spectacle. When the doors opened, we were met with a wave of very loud upbeat music. People raced past us, aiming for the tables in the front by the stage. The volunteers known as the Dream Team, danced in unison on the stage. When we got to our seats, we were encouraged to stand and dance as well.

The energy level in the room was very high, and the speaker about to introduce James was trying to whip the crowd into a loud cheer. There was plenty to see for the visual people, and the music rocked for the auditory people. As soon as the music stopped we were asked to hug three people. Even the "touchy feely" people received something. He engaged each type of person from the very start; smart. Nothing was left to chance.

At the beginning, we were given our mantra: You must constantly study, understand and immerse yourself in that which brings you power (strengthens you) and avoid everything that weakens us, and EVERYTHING counts. During the ensuing seminar, James demonstrated a technique of Applied Kinesiology (AK) discussed in length in David Hawkins book, Power vs. Force. It utilizes the apparent increase or decrease of your body's muscle strength to gauge if something in close proximity to your body is "good" or "bad" for you. If it is good, or the answer to a question is true, you will stay strong. If the opposite is the case, your body will show weakness.

The process involves two people who have removed their watches or any electromechanical devices. The first person asks the questions and applies pressure on the other person's outstretched arm to gauge whether the arm remains *strong* in response to the question or goes *weak*. If the person can keep their arm in the air, even when pressure is applied to their wrist, then the answer to the question is true. If they cannot hold their arm up under the same pressure, the answer to the question is false. If they are holding an object close to them and remain strong, it is good for them. If they go weak, then it is not. Before beginning the test, questions are asked with obvious "yes" and "no" answers, to give a feeling for what a strong yes/true reaction feels like, likewise for no/false reactions.

James used this principle to demonstrate that artificial sweeteners are bad for your body. He put several into an unmarked white envelope and asked different people to test it. Everyone's bodies went weak when they were tested while holding the envelope to their solar plexus. He passed around another unmarked white envelope; this time, everyone tested strong. The second envelope contained natural sugar in the raw. He went on to test different music CD's and different emotions. The results were amazing. Our bodies instinctively knew what was good and true, proving that a bad environment and/or negative feelings affect our physical health in a detrimental way.

One of James' most effective ways of getting a point across was to act it out. He told us to offset the negative effect of one cup of coffee or one glass of soda, we needed 32 times the volume in water! Richard, a lifetime lover of Pepsi, never drank another after that day. James demonstrated how we set ourselves up for a difficult day from the moment we awaken. We first get out of bed, likely with too little sleep, the body still working out the toxins from the prior day. We head into the kitchen to our first cup of battery acid . . . oops . . . coffee. While drinking we turn on the news and listen to what is wrong with the world, what disastrous things happened since we last watched the evening news the night before. As we shower, we anticipate a difficult employee/client/boss who we'll have to deal with. While on the subject of difficult people, it reminds us of another difficult or obnoxious person we don't like. So, just how much bad stuff and negative feeling do we stuff into our bodies during the first few minutes of each day? "You have just made yourself weaker without ever realizing what you are doing," he said.

James also told us not to watch the evening news, and to never fall asleep with the TV on. What we hear and think about before falling asleep become auto-suggestions for our brains to mull over all night. Also while falling asleep; the unconscious mind still hears what is being said and what commercials are pitching, even though our conscious minds are not alert to filter the messages. The unconscious mind considers everything truth; without the conscious mind to evaluate the input, it all goes straight in as fact. James desfined two types of people: peasants, who fear and resist change; and warriors, who embrace change as an opportunity to learn and grow.

He told us the difference between intention and attention. Intention is what you intend to achieve in your life. Attention equals love. We give our attention to what we really care about; unfortunately, some are in love with their misery. If you want to know what people really care about, look at their checkbooks and calendars. Everything else is empty words.

James taught us what he called the Harmonic Wealth Wheel. I have seen other presenters use a similar circle to determine how balanced our lives are; a great tool. Each spoke of the wheel represented one area, or pillar, of our lives: Financial, Relational, Intellectual, Physical, & Spiritual. According to James, these areas need to be in harmony with each other for us to feel that we have harmonious, happy lives. Complete harmony will never happen. It is a constant dance. If one spoke is seriously out of whack, it will affect the others. People often mistake money for wealth, but you can have a lot of money but not an abundant life. James used the timely example of Brittany Spears as someone who had many gifts in her life, but not happiness. Now you can replace her example with Tiger Woods. The man definitely has a strong financial pillar. Money is not a problem for him. From all reports, he is very smart. His physical pillar is strong in both body and environment. His beautiful house and surroundings, as well as the best playing conditions possible, have allowed him to continue to improve and excel. With all that going for him, is he currently living a happy and fulfilling life? I don't think so; his relational pillar is a very public mess. Shortly after his infidelities had become public and his marriage was in serious trouble, he was named Athlete of the Decade. I could not help but think it must feel like a sad, hollow achievement, because he had no one with whom to share the joy.

Could his fame and athletic skills alone be enough to give him a happy life? No. We need all spokes of our wheel to function well. If one pillar is in serious trouble, it will negatively affect the others. Do you think Tiger's family troubles affected his career? Judging from the way he faded down the stretch in the last several major golf tournaments, it's a safe assumption. He is still famous, but is he proud of what people think of when they hear his name? While his family life was in shambles, could any amount of money make life fulfilling for him? Money is important, but it alone cannot bring happiness. James taught us that money is a magnifier; it will magnify who you really are. If you have an off-kilter pillar, then the lack or abundance of money will throw gas on the fire in that particular area.

A wealthy life contains more than money. This was one of the more common misconceptions when people heard us talk about wealth or the Harmonic Wealth Weekend, or later the World Wealth Society. To them, it always meant trying to acquire more money. While it is true many people were working on that particular pillar, there were others working to improve different areas.

To have a more wealthy and abundant life, I needed to fortify my physical pillar. I needed to improve my health. Money was not my main focus. In fact, it was behind my intention to create a stronger relationship between my God and me, and to improve the time I spent with my daughter before she headed off to college. I also wanted to improve an already good relationship with my husband. So after the physical, relational and spiritual pillars, I then turned my attention to the financial one. Even in the weekend seminar, the money pillar was discussed last.

I like the idea behind the Harmonic Wealth Wheel. However, I split Physical into two distinct pillars—Physical Body and Environment. You could be in great physical condition, but living or working in a mess. Or, you could be living in a palace but not caring for your body; consequently, your health is at risk. For these reasons, I don't think you can lump them together. This concept was similar to one taught to us by our real estate coach/mentor, Brian Buffini. Instead of calling one area the Physical pillar, Brian called it the Personal circle, containing both your physical and emotional state. He taught us this was one of five overlapping circles (aspects) of your life. There, the similarities ended. Brian would stage an event such as Mastermind, where he would bring in great guest speakers to talk to us about different aspects of our lives. His seminars drew 5,000 to 6,000 people, a number about which James could only dream.

Whether Brian was speaking in a packed convention center or to a couple hundred people in a Turning Point workshop, he always spent time discussing our financial pillar/circle, specifically about budgeting and living within our means, saving and investing. People hear about the big commission checks a real estate agent makes, but what they don't realize is it is expensive to market and sell a home. We incur high overhead costs such as licensing and fees. It is easy for an agent to get caught up in purchasing all of the latest gadgets and gimmicks that promise to make selling a home easier and quicker, only to learn these expensive items often do little to actually sell the home. Our clients want us to buy and use them because they believe them to be effective, but experienced agents know that it takes just a few good tools, a lot of hard work, and a competitively priced home to sell it successfully. Sadly we have seen agents get recognized at a national event for being one of a company's top agents in gross commissions, often taking in millions of dollars, only to find out a few months later they are bankrupt. Controlling overhead expenses in both business and personal life is essential, and Brian knows and preaches it to us every chance he gets.

James bragged about his car, multiple homes, traveling first class, Armani Suits and the like. Brian confided he lived for many years without furniture in some of his new home's rooms. It was not yet in his budget. Saving for his kid's college or making a new investment took priority. Wisely investing in his business took priority. Avoiding too much debt and saving were the verses of Brian's gospel. James saw credit cards and credit as unlimited tools; leverage was a good investment strategy. Brian saw them as a tool to tightly control, and to cut up if you could not manage them. James saw no problem with us paying for his expensive seminars by credit card, even though we might have no way of paying for it when the bill came due. He always told the story in HWW of how he once charged about $10,000 to his company credit card when he worked for AT&T for a class he wanted to attend, knowing it was not the policy for his company to reimburse him for that type of an expense. He managed to miraculously increase his value to the company by bringing in more revenue; as a reward, they paid for his class. Interestingly, James's favorite examples of how it was OK to overspend and take a big financial risk were for a class or seminar. He justified it because you would improve yourself, making you more valuable. That, in turn, would result in making more money and paying off the seminar fee investment many times over.

James always pushed the idea that if the class, or any item for that matter, was going to make you more successful or skilled, then you needed to live/spend now. He called it "living from the outcome" (being successful in your future). James taught us to live and spend now with abundance, as the person you were going to be (rich and successful) and you would attract that vibration into your life. If we act as though we are not abundant, or react to the scarcity in our lives, we will continue to attract that vibration into our lives instead. I know teaching to spend from the outcome was prompting many to over-use their credit cards and purchase very expensive seminar packages they could not afford, for which they might be paying years later.

Brian would teach the vital importance of living within our means, and that we needed to do so even if it meant canceling a seminar or our calls with one of his coaches until we could afford to put it back into our budgets. Even though Brian knew how valuable his seminars were to increase our businesses and growing our client skills, he always insisted that staying within our budgets was more important—even if it meant not attending an event for a while. He considered it preferable to stay out of debt for most everything, even his classes. James was the direct opposite. I never heard him advise someone to lower their credit card debt before signing up for more of his seminars. Instead, he openly encouraged charging—"and you should think of that charge on your credit card as investing in yourself for your future."

Who was right? Well, James claims to be broke now, while Brian enjoys a comfortable debt-free life with a lot of passive income from his investments. Brian cared about his client's financial health and longevity far more than he cared about making money from them, while James seemed to be more concerned with persuading people to pay for more of his seminars. They both believe they delivered an excellent product to their clientele. One didn't want us to go broke doing it. James was throwing out mixed messages, especially about money. On one hand, he would talk about acquiring or manifesting the things you wanted in your life, and then, "It's not about the $2 million house, but about the person you need to become to create that house." I was especially confused about this living/spending from the outcome concept.

We moved to a different subject. If we want to change our lives and results, we *must* change our mindset. One of the main ways was by examining and dispelling limiting beliefs. These are the self-imposed beliefs that hold us back— "I am not smart enough, strong enough, quick enough, pretty enough, I don't deserve it, and I am not good enough to be successful and achieve what I want in life." These beliefs were formed while we were very young, usually before the age of 6, and imposed or passed along by parents, siblings, teachers, family, and friends. We're aware of some of these; others lie outside conscious awareness. For the rest of the day, we zeroed in on the one limiting belief that contributes most to holding us back in life. We were given 8x11 inch pieces of wood, ¾ of an inch thick. On one side of the board, we wrote the limiting belief that we wanted to vanquish; on the other, what it would be like when we shattered the belief. This was tough work, requiring a hard look at yourself and what was going on in your life. I was able to write with my green Sharpie, "I AM INSUFFICIENT, I AM NOT GOOD ENOUGH, I AM LACKING!" Most people held their boards close so no one else could read them.

On the other side of my board, I wrote what I was breaking through to: "I am Good Enough! I CAN DO ANYTHING!" After instruction from James on how to break our boards with the flat section of the bottom of our hand, we walked to the back of the room and made a big circle. James was in the middle, pumping people up by demonstrating the technique —without ever actually hitting a board. Emotions were running all over the place. Some attendees were stoked and couldn't wait to get going, while others slowly worked their way to the back of the group, clearly less than thrilled at the "opportunity" before them. I vacillated between each camp. James said our physical size had nothing to do with whether or not we broke our boards. It was all in our heads. We are energy, and the board is energy that only appeared solid. Mind over matter! Are we ready to give up our limiting belief? If not then we would unconsciously pull up just before hitting the board and not break through. We had to want it to be gone!

James then asked who thought they might not even try to break through their board. Several sheepish hands went up. James looked around, pulled the owner of one of those hands forward, a woman, from the back, and told her she was going to break her board in front of the whole group! Loud music started playing and the group started cheering. After several attempts, she finally broke through her board. After a larger cheer, we lined up into about 10 lines to take our turn at breaking our own boards. For my turn, the popular 1980s song "Eye of the Tiger" was playing, which helped focus me. This was either going to be easy or hard; I was hoping for easy. I followed directions to the T, oriented my board in the holder's hands so I could clearly read the I AM NOT GOOD ENOUGH printed on its center, pulled my hand back and slammed the board with all I had. It made a big thump, but the board was still solid. "Oh no, not again!" I exclaimed. I feared this could become a very public failure. Everyone was turning their attention to the woman struggling with her board. Me. I hated the attention, bad enough to fail, but now I had an audience. The crowd was rooting me on, wanting me to succeed. I was not used to that. My lifelong struggle with my weight was obvious to anyone who saw me; I didn't need to draw attention to other ways I could fail. I was definitely not a secure person, nor confident in who I was and what I was capable of attaining.

A woman Dream Teamer ran over and talked to me, her face just a few inches from mine. She had to get that close so I could hear her; the volume level of the music and crowd noise was deafening. I kept my eyes on my board. She told me I had to *want* to break through my limiting beliefs. "Well of course I do; that's not the problem," I said. She kept insisting otherwise. We reviewed my form; I worked on calming down, centering and focusing, and pulled my hand back. I hit the board with less force than the first time. What's up with that? I wanted to break that board and get out of there as quickly as possible. What was going on? Thoughts were now running through my head; had anyone ever *not* broken their board? Was I going to be the first? Was I going to be the only one tonight not to break the board? I didn't want that notoriety. More people came over to my side of the room and screamed encouragement to me. Meanwhile, my hand was throbbing. *Great, a bigger audience, just what I did not want!*

The Dream Teamer took the board and looked on the backside "What part of 'I AM good enough' and 'I CAN do anything' do you not believe?" she asked. She pulled my attention away from the board and told me to look at her. She repeated the question. I didn't believe it yet. I had just dug deeply to find out my major limiting belief was I was not good enough, and I didn't have enough time to get through to the other side. Together we said, "I am good enough" several times until I could raise an emotional charge and truly believe it was possible. I was really sick of feeling inadequate, and I wanted that to end. I again squared up my body to the board, shaking, trying to hold back tears. I had forgotten half of what I was supposed to do, but I pulled my hand back and held it there for a moment. *I've had enough of feel-*

ing like I am inadequate; I am good enough, and I am good enough to break this damn board. I pulled my hand forward and aimed for a point behind the board, on its other side, just above the chest of the man holding my board in front of him. The sound was different this time. I didn't feel the board. *I must have missed it.* Then disbelief, as I watched the board break into two, with wood splinters flying all around us!

The man holding my board grabbed me in a big hug, while still holding one piece of it in each hand. I think he was more relieved than me! I thanked him for his patience, and then was directed to the other side of the room, where the other successful board break-ers were waiting. The first person I saw was Richard and his big beam-ing smile! We hugged and then moved further to the back, where it was a bit quieter, and hugged some more. He kept saying, "You did it." *Yes I did.* I faced down my biggest enemy—fear.

I then accomplished a second thing I had never done before: cry-ing on Richard's shoulder. I don't cry easily, especially in public. I prefer to hold that card close to my chest and suck in the tears. This time, I was not sure exactly what I was experiencing, but I could feel the weight release from carrying the belief for as long as I can remem-ber. It was almost two a.m., what a long and draining, but liberating day!

The next morning, we worked on adding three new beliefs to our systems. For me, they were:

1) When I commit to something, there is always a way

2) There is no failure, only feedback, and a real master knows this as it happens

3) The past does not equal my future; anything is possible.

So now we were on to our BHAG—Big Hairy Audacious Goals.

Several other lecturers had taught me this approach to goal-set-ting as well. If we set our goals to a level we can achieve by ourselves they are not large enough. We tell the universe we don't need its help, and we are left on our own. First step is to become very clear about EXACTLY what we want and write it down. When the intention is clear, then the way to achieve will appear; don't worry now about the "how." Our goal had to be measurable, with exact amounts and dates. There would always be a gestation period we cannot bypass, but we can accelerate it with our actions. We ended up with clear, measurable goals written on a small card to carry in a clear plastic pouch. James' session on goal setting was one of the best I had ever experienced. Despite James' numerous annoying commercials in which he pitched his very expensive packages of future seminars, we were learning some really good stuff. We gained a lot from the seminar and were interested in learning more so we signed up for a couple more events in one of his packages.

At every event he told us he was a kahuna and had studied extensively in Hawaii, and a shaman with two different groups and had studied in Peru and the Amazon. We decided to study with him because we wanted to be exposed to a wide diversity of spiritual teachings, and then choose the path that felt the most "right" for us. As another long day neared its end, we moved to our final pillar: Financial. James was telling us money is just green energy that starts as a thought, and our current income is the result of our past consciousness and our consistent and programmed thinking. Many of us have been taught it is selfish and sinful to desire money, so we unconsciously push it away. We forget you can do a lot of good for yourself and others with money. "Love people and use money," so the saying goes; it is the love of money that is the root of evil. James talked about the importance of not walking around with just a few bills in your wallet. Doing so promoted a feeling of lack and scarcity. He recommended carrying several $100 bills, with Benjamin Franklin looking back each time you opened your wallet, reminding you of your abundance.

I was among those people guilty of carrying very little cash in my wallet. Almost all of my purchases were by credit card, since it was easier and often more convenient. It also made business expenses much easier and more efficient to track for accounting purposes. But more than once, I paid for something with a few wrinkly dollar bills and a lot of change. I didn't feel abundant at all, so I understood what he was saying.

Later I found his approach useful in another way. If I saw something that was going to be purely an impulse buy, then I made myself pay for it in cash. Seeing the bills pass from my hand to the clerk's made a greater impact on me than swiping my credit card. I had to deal with the total amount on the spot, tax and all, and not wait for the credit card statement. Also, it removed the feeling that I needed to splurge on something to feel abundant. I could now look at the item and know I was more than capable of buying it with just the cash in my wallet. That knowledge made me feel more powerful and abundant than buying the item. Since making that change, I've rarely decided to buy a splurge or impulse item.

The last participation exercise was the "money game." Some thought James told us to reach for our wallets and "take out the amount of cash that you are willing to invest in your education." Others would argue he had told us to "take out *all* the money in our wallets." Either way he then told everyone to hold the money over their heads. "Now go and exchange money!" That turned out to be the only direction volunteers could repeat when participants asked for further guidance: "Go and exchange money."

There was a broad range of behaviors at this seminar, which I later learned to be the case at all of James' seminars. This time I had a problem: I was not in the habit of carrying cash, so I had to borrow a five dollar bill from Richard to start playing the game, or so I thought at the time. Pink Floyd's "Money" was blaring in the background, and people were looking at each other, bewildered. We started to ask each other what we were supposed to do. Every once in a while, James would yell from the stage, "exchange money." We started exchanging exact amounts with each other. I would give someone my five; they would give me five ones. We did that for a few minutes. Bored, some people decided to move around the room, exchanging the cash in their hand for whatever amount another person carried. It didn't matter how much it was. That felt pretty daring to me, even though I had started out with only $5. Eventually, most of the people exchanged their cash with others without stopping to look at what they received. At one point, I held a giant wad of bills; minutes later, I held a few coins. Once, I handed off several bills and ended up with nothing. The other person sheepishly said "sorry," but I knew that they had received nothing from another person. At my next exchange, I handed off air and said "sorry," to which the other person said that it was quite all right.

Suddenly James yelled, "Stop and return to your seats." To my amazement, there were several people who never moved from their seats at any time during the game. Did they sit out of fear of losing their money? The point of the game James said was to recognize how you approached money in your life. Some people never stopped conducting even exchanges, winding up exactly with their starting amount. Some started with little and ended up with a lot, while others were not so "lucky" since it appeared they supplied the others' windfalls. I started out with Richard's five-dollar bill and ended up with a couple of Canadian dollars. I still have them floating around my office somewhere.

What would you have done? From my experience, the fun and the excitement lay in the rapid exchanges. You were "up" or "down" quickly, then moved on to the next person. Some hedged their bets in one of two ways. One was to stop and remove a bill or two from their hands and put it into their pockets, then exchange what was left in their hands. The other was to split the money and make an exchange with each hand, therefore cutting in half your chances of ending up with nothing. Needless to say, the people pocketing bills at each exchange had a lot of money. Many felt they were cheating by not exchanging everything they received. There was no cheating since there really were no rules. The point was to see how each of us reacted during and after the game. There was always one person who ended up with very little or nothing; this time, it was a college student who stood up and said he used all of his money in the exchange and did not have enough for gas to get back to school. "What did you learn from the exercise?" James asked.

"I should not have taken out all of the money that I had, because now, I have nothing and I am stuck."

"Really, do you really have nothing?" James asked in a leading way. James went on to say the amount of our resources does not matter, but how resourceful we are. In the end, the student found out that all he had to do was ask the group for some money. Within a few seconds, he had more than he started with.

In other seminars, James would prod the "stuck" person to think of something of value they could do for another person in the room, a service or action for which the latter would be willing to pay. To my knowledge no one ever had to walk home. Sometimes we make things harder than they need to be. After this exercise, we took a break. I noticed something unusual as I was walking to the back of the room. Many people left their cash sitting on the table in plain view—after they had left the room! When I returned to my seat, I looked down to find my wallet sitting on my workbook. It seems that the money game did something to lessen our fear of losing our money, since we were clearly not protecting it like we did before the game. Did we feel if we lost it, we could obtain more?

James shared his proudest announcement during the seminar: in a few days, he would be a guest on *Oprah!* Though we didn't yet know it at the time, this marked the turning point—*his* turning point. (People who had studied with James for awhile referred to his pre-*Oprah!* demeanor as the "old James.") After the seminar, he pulled his chair around to face the left side of the stage. People lined up to get their photo taken with him and talk for a minute or two. He kept the interactions short because of the long line, but he was warm and friendly. I'm glad we got to see that side of him.

CHAPTER 3

Homeless in San Diego

Creating Absolute Wealth • May 2007

Reflect upon your present blessings, of which every man has plenty;
not on your past misfortunes of which all men have some.
—Charles Dickens

We entered a room with loud upbeat music, people dancing on the stage, and participants ready to dance and clap along. Since we had already been "broken in" at the previous event we knew life was a participation sport and this no longer felt unusual. The first day involved lectures and exercises in the room, and for the next day we were told we were going to be going "off site" a lot.

Creating Absolute Wealth, took place in our hometown of San Diego so we drove back and forth from home to the hotel to keep the high cost of the seminar down. The staffers at James Ray International (JRI) frowned on people not staying at the event hotel; later I learned why.

After Harmonic Wealth Weekend, we did consider the hotel option. Each day started around 8 a.m. and ran until 1 to 2 a.m. the following morning. By the time we got home, cleaned up, and did our "homework," we had few precious hours of sleep. James taught us to affirm to ourselves, "I will sleep soundly and deeply and wake up refreshed and ready to rock!" James also said frequently, "Sleep is over-rated." Frankly, I was feeling less than refreshed on day two, and this seminar was going to last for three days instead of just two. I would need all the sleep I could get.

James breaks much later than usual for lunch and dinner. It was not uncommon to stop for lunch at 2 or 3 pm, and dinner at 7, 8 or 9 pm. For that reason, he encouraged us to bring healthy snacks to keep our energy up. On day two, it seemed like lunch was going to be very late. We were hungry when he announced we were going on an excursion away from the hotel.

During the previous quick break, the Dream Teamers made two piles of what looked like donated clothing. Women's clothes were in the front by the stage, and men's garments were in the back of the room. James told us to walk to one of the piles and select clothes to wear on the outing. He told us that after we had our clothes, leave the room and change. When we returned, he added, we were to wear only our own underwear, shoes and socks, name badge and the clothes from the piles. We were to remove all makeup and jewelry. No money, ID, cell phones, watches, or anything else was permitted. Eyeglasses were allowed.

James had selected special outfits for some of the participants to "up their game." He pulled a dress from a box on stage and, while holding it up, called the name of one of the guys! He threw the dress over to him and pulled out two more dresses. One of the men, Dr. John as we called him, is a chiropractor in downtown San Diego. Walking around the city looking homeless was not something that would push Dr. John out of his comfort zone far. James spent a lot of time in both Harmonic Wealth Weekend, and in this seminar, on the importance of being outside your comfort zone in order to grow. The premise was if you are comfortable, you are not doing anything new; therefore you are not growing. The strappy little number Dr. John was just tossed would definitely stretch his comfort zone!

The rest of us had only 15 minutes to select our clothes, change and be back in the room. Ready, set, GO! People ran to the clothing piles and started digging through them. Some of the women were putting together outfits, while the rest of us—especially me at over 300 lbs.—were just trying to find anything that might fit. I took what I could find to the ladies room to see if I fit into any of it. I was wondering if they would notice if I was wearing some of my own clothes. Something did fit— a pair of stretch pants with bright, wide horizontal stripes. The only top I could find that was not too revealing when stretched was a bright red Christmas sweat shirt with a Christmas tree imprint and little gold ornaments hanging from it. It was now late spring in San Diego. Lovely!

Back in the meeting room, the JRI staff and Dream Teamers rubbed makeup "dirt" on the participant's faces and hands, and smeared some kind of grease in their hair. I received the full make over. Even more lovely! I could not remove my wedding band, so they used tape to cover it up. One of the Dream Teamers noticed my nice "fake nail" French manicure, picked up an old ripped up bathrobe, and told me to wrap it around my hands to hide them. Each of us was given a small piece of paper with a phone number to call in case of emergency. JRI Staffers used scissors or knife blades to cut holes in any clothes that looked too "good."

James stood up front and gave instructions: We would be taken by bus to downtown San Diego, where we would be "homeless" for the afternoon. We were not allowed to speak or make eye contact with anyone from the seminar after we got off the buses. If we were hungry, it was up to us to figure out how to get something to eat. Our mission: to learn how to not just survive, but thrive as a homeless person. James again said that success was not determined by the resources you had, but by your resourcefulness. It was now time to get very resourceful!

I looked really bad, but so did everyone else. Richard wore a pair of girl's jeans that apparently crept into the men's clothing by accident. He couldn't figure out why they fit so strangely until we pointed it out. He wore a plaid flannel shirt with several buttons missing. He tried to find a hat to protect his head from sunburn. He located the cut-off arm of a sweater that when rolled up would pull over the top of his head so the wrist opening pointed straight up. You would have crossed to the other side of the street if you saw him approaching. The two of us made quite a couple!

We didn't have to worry about being the strangest looking people in town; the guys in the dresses locked up that honor. One large man's dress didn't close in the back so he wore a small pink and blue ruffled jacket. He was trying to talk one woman out of her long sweater but there was no way she was going to give it up. Finder's keepers! Dr. John, however, was actually looking good in his slinky little number!

We piled onto the buses. During the ride to downtown San Diego, we had to find "buddies" to check in with when we returned to the bus to make sure everyone was accounted for. My bus deposited us in front of Horton Plaza, a large downtown open-air shopping mall and, for many years, a gathering spot for San Diego's homeless community.

We were told to return to the bus stop by 4 p.m. sharp. No watch to tell time? Better get in the habit of asking strangers for the time, the Dream Teamers said.

We each scattered in our own direction. I kept on the move. I was unaccustomed to having nowhere specific to go and nothing to do. I had no idea how people were going to react to me, especially the police. I was walking around in a Christmas sweatshirt in May with hanging gold ornaments on it:" Merry Christmas," the bold letters proclaimed across my chest. I can't tell you how many people walked by me and said, "Merry Christmas!"

"Merry Christmas to you, too!" I responded. What else could I say?

One man said to his wife as they passed me, "Now, there's someone who is all ready for the holidays!" But something else was moving through my mind. If a cop saw me, would I be taken straight in for a psych evaluation? The law of attraction was working fast. As I came around the next corner, I almost walked head first into two cops on bicycles. They stopped, one on each side of me, and the younger one said, "You're new here." To which I just smiled and nodded. He asked me where I was going to be spending the night and I told him I had a good spot with a couple of other people down by the convention center. He kept eyeing me up and down, and I kept wondering, *just what is it they do to you in a psych ward these days?* He looked at his watch and said it was too late for tonight, but if I went to the Salvation Army building and told them I needed a place to stay, they would set me up with something for tomorrow. "You do know where the Salvation Army building is, right?" he asked. I nodded and smiled.

"They're closed now, but if you go to the back gate and tell them you need new clothes, they will let you grab some," the bike cop said.

"I have clothes."

"Yes, I can see that, but they can give you some different clothes. You are going there for dinner, right?"

Again, I just nodded and smiled. He looked at me for what seemed like a long time, but it was probably no more than 10 seconds. I almost laughed out loud: if I had to find someone to vouch for my sanity, who would that be? Richard, the guy walking around with a sweater sleeve on his head?

The officer looked at his partner, who stood behind me, then nodded at her. They exchanged some form of non-verbal communication. He then turned to mount his bike. "Remember to get into line early for dinner, the place fills up fast, and stay close to other people tonight."

I had no idea the police actually looked out for the homeless on their patrol. The young cop seemed genuinely concerned for me; he also noticed I was a true neophyte to the street scene. I breathed a sigh of relief. No psych ward, at least not now!

No matter how bizarre I looked, I was certainly not the worst. There were people on the streets who were clearly mentally ill. One woman pushing a baby carriage yelled at light poles. When she walked away from her carriage, I peeked in. To my relief, it was empty. I don't know how I would have approached a cop looking as I did and say, "Hey, there is a crazy lady over there with a baby, you better check her out!"

Then there were the people from the other end of the homeless spectrum. They did not look bad, but if you watched them long enough, you saw they were not going anywhere. After talking with a few, I found out they either just became homeless or they were "temporarily" homeless while waiting to get their next job.

In downtown San Diego there is an unofficial mayor of the homeless. An older African American gentleman walked past me, pushing a bike with numerous plastic bags hanging from it. "You're new, right?" I just nodded and smiled. He asked, "Got a place to stay?" Again, I just nodded and smiled. "Are you hungry?"

This time, I spoke: "Yes."

"It will be time soon to start lining up for dinner at the Salvation Army."

"I hear they fill up fast."

"Damn right they do so you better get your butt in line early," he ordered gruffly as he started walking away. Over his shoulder he yelled back to me, "See you there!"

I was still on the move; I figured I might as well make up for the weekend's lack of exercise walking. Unfortunately, I had increasing chronic pain in my knee and hip. It hurt less if I didn't lift my leg up all the way when I stepped, and since I didn't care what I looked like, I just started to drag my leg along as I walked. Unbeknownst to me, Richard was coming up fast behind me; later, he told me my limp really made my look "complete." He had spent some time in a bar watching a game. Eventually, he asked some of the guys there if they would buy him a beer, and they said no, but they would get him something else if he wanted. He saw them eyeing his "hat" and couldn't resist saying to them, "Do you like my hat, it's new!"

They agreed it was one cool hat. To his amazement, no one bothered him or tried to push him out of the bar. As long as he did not bother customers, the employees were OK to let him be. That is also what I experienced. Even the security patrol in the upscale Horton Plaza shopping mall simply walked past as I sat with my leg up on one of the park benches. They saw this every day; no big deal.

While walking through the mall, I passed a cell phone kiosk and was immediately approached by a young salesman. "I have no money to pay for a cell phone," I said.

"No problem: the phone is free."

"For how long?"

"Long enough; you just have to buy a plan."

"I don't have a credit card to buy a plan," I said as I continued to walk out of the mall.

"No problem; instant credit!"

"But I have bad credit." I really thought that would drive him off.

Instead, without missing a beat, he said, "No one is turned down on this plan; it doesn't matter how bad your credit is."

I admired his persistence, but it was time for us to part ways. I had to firmly tell him no several times before he finally left me alone. Amazing: no credit, no money for food, no place to stay . . . but I could get a cell phone!

I headed down 5th St. towards the Convention Center, when I passed a man and a woman with convention visitor ID badges hanging around their necks. The man smiled and said "Merry Christmas!"

"Merry Christmas to you to . . . and welcome to San Diego!"

When they had taken a few more steps, and the man thought I was out of hearing range, he said to the woman, "God, San Diego has a really big homeless problem, doesn't it!"

That made me laugh. Our class must be the Chamber of Commerce and the San Diego Convention and Visitors Bureau's worst nightmare!

I saw Dr. John waiting at a street corner. Two guys were eyeing him up and down. As I crossed the road on the other side, one approached him and said something. I thought, *Poor John, I hope he can keep his sense of humor about this!*

I decided to walk into a couple of real estate offices to see how they would react. I did not expect anyone would recognize me, and I was curious as to how they would greet the likes of me.

I remembered a story told to me by the owner of the previous real estate company for which we worked: It concerned Skippy, a man who came into our exclusive Fairbanks Ranch office looking like an older version of the Gorton's fisherman. On a rainy day, he wore oversized bright yellow plastic pants, jacket, and rain hat. He passed one agent who was leaving; the agent took one look at him and kept walking. Skippy (his real name) walked up to the main desk and asked if someone could show him a couple of houses he was interested in seeing. Figuring he had nothing else to do, the owner stepped up to the desk and introduced himself. To his surprise, Skippy had a clear idea of exactly what he was looking for—pricey homes. Never one to miss out on an adventure, the owner took Skippy to see the homes. He bought one. Over the next 20 years, Skippy bought over $20 million in real estate from the owner. Think the real estate agent who rushed by him has kicked himself a few times over his rash judgment?

I walked first to an office in a prominent street corner location. As I entered, two people immediately looked up. One was in the process of rising, but after seeing me, she sat back down and ignored me. The other woman looked away as well. I stood there for a few minutes at the front desk but it was clear no one would give me the time of day, never mind answer a question about local real estate. After waiting for a few minutes, I moved on. I did have fun eating a couple of candies out of their candy dish while I was waiting.

My next stop was at a smaller office of a large franchise—the same company for which we had previously worked. It was possible I would run into someone I knew; the idea of that was both disconcerting and fun. I picked up a free copy of *Dream Homes* magazine, which features only very high-end homes, most in the $2 million-plus range. I viewed the home flyers posted on their front window. I knew many of these neighborhoods, and was catching up on the current inventory, when a young male agent came out and cheerfully greeted me. I asked him the time; didn't want to miss my bus. I only had about an hour left. He asked me which homes had caught my eye in the window and I pointed to a couple of them. He told me the good points with each of the properties, then in mid-sentence stopped and said, "Shouldn't you be heading over to get in line at the Salvation Army?"

"No worries; a friend is saving me a place." I also told him I was not in the market to buy a home right now but could I have his card for later. He gladly obliged, and told me to call him when I was ready. He continued talking about the homes in the window and started to describe a home on a golf course in a gated community.

"Do you mean the one on Obsidian Drive?" I asked.

Surprised, he said, "Yes, but I don't see it." His eyes scanned the flyers posted in the widow.

I spotted it first. "There it is!"

He followed my arm up to the flyer but stopped short. "Wait a minute; look at those nails! You're not homeless, what's up?" Looking around, he said, "Am I on camera? I know you; you look familiar!"

My cover was blown. Looking directly at me now, he asked, "Who are you?"

I said I was a real estate agent and my husband and I used to work for his company. He kept asking who I was, and finally I told him he would have known us as The Joys of Real Estate. Immediately, his eyes flew wide with recognition. He ran back into the office to see if anyone else was still there so he could show him or her what I looked like; fortunately for me, they had all left. He kept saying they aren't going to believe this! Again he asked, "What's up, why are you dressed like this?"

"Well, you know, the real estate market has been tough lately," I said with a solemn face.

He laughed. "No really; what are you doing?"

I told him I couldn't say right now but I would tell him later. I had to start heading back towards the bus stop. "Well I am late to get in line at the Salvation Army so I am off."

"Yeah . . . sure you are!" he said.

I later sent him a note with a couple of free dessert cards in it. I told him I knew he was going to be very successful in life. In the card, I also included one of our business cards. I looked at the photo of Richard and me. Would he be able to recognize the woman who stood at his office window from the glamour photo on our business card?

On the walk back to the bus stop, I mulled over the reactions I received from some of the people I approached to ask the time. One bus boy was clearing a table at an outside restaurant when I asked him for the time. I thought he would just have to twist his wrist and look. Instead, he put the heavy tray down against a chair and, while balancing it with one hand. He reached under his apron to get his watch. He looked up, smiled, and told me the time. I had no intention of inconveniencing him, but clearly he did not mind. A little while later, I asked a young, well-dressed woman walking her little dog, also dressed in an accessorized little outfit, but she pushed by me, annoyed. Clearly some people care more about an animal than they do about people.

I asked for change to make a phone call once and was turned down. I did not ask for money again. The truth is I have never been comfortable asking anyone for money. My reluctance has to do with my sense of self-reliance. It was definitely outside my comfort zone to "beg."

I sat down at the bus stop and started reading the copy of *Dream Homes*, studying the styles of ads the other agents were using. Having spare time for this was a luxury in my "normal" life. One man, sitting by me on the bench, couldn't resist asking me if I saw anything I liked.

"No, not yet."

"Well, keep looking, you should be able to find something tolerable in there," he said.

A young man came by and offered me a large cookie that came with his meal, but because of one of its ingredients, he could not eat it. Later, both on the bus ride back and inside the meeting room, many people came up and said that the funniest thing they saw all day was me sitting in my "rags," smeared face and greasy hair, carefully reading every page in a *Dream Homes* magazine while eating a giant cookie!

When we arrived at the hotel, we were allowed to change back into our real clothes, but there was not enough time to do more than wash our faces. The messed-up hair and lack of makeup would have to stay for a while. People shared a wide range of experiences. It shocked me to find out several of the young women were so upset about what they looked like they locked themselves into a bathroom stall in the shopping mall and stayed there the entire time. They only spoke to people from inside the booth to ask what time it was. Their identity was completely wrapped up in how they looked.

Another man's story touched me deeply. He spent a good deal of the time sitting alone on a bench in a small park, crying. The homeless exercise gave him time to think about his family's current lifestyle. He felt his life was a lie because he could not afford it; he was quickly going broke. He resisted making changes because he felt it was his responsibility as the man, husband, and father to provide well for his family. Anything other than that was a failure. His family had no idea of how bad their financial situation was. He feared if he didn't do something quickly to severely curtail their spending, he was going to end up homeless and alone. This was a tiny taste of what he would receive if he didn't make the necessary changes quickly. He knew he had to go home and face the situation head on. He dreaded it.

The purpose of this exercise was to show we could be without what we consider critical resources—money, friends and family—and still survive by being resourceful. Many people turned asking for money into a game. They managed to gather quite a bit of cash and at the end they left it with some real homeless people. We needed to know we would be OK even if we lost everything. I knew the liberation of that truth: I had already been broke once in my life.

My experience happened after I was divorced from my first husband. I was left with an apartment I could not afford on my salary, but I couldn't leave it because my parents had cosigned the lease. I had to stick it out. Paying rent became the priority; consequently, I had to live on what was left. It wasn't much. For food, I would make a big bowl of potato salad and have it for breakfast and lunch for an entire week. For dinner, I would hit "happy hour" with my friends. Back then, free hot hors d'oeuvres were served in a restaurant's bar for a couple of hours before they started serving dinner. Someone would buy me a drink and I would nurse it through the entire happy hour. Even though it was the middle of winter in upstate New York, I had the middle upstairs unit in the apartment complex so I could turn off my heat without worrying about the pipes freezing. The surrounding apartments acted as insulation. I was rarely home, because I worked two jobs. After my ex-husband left, I found out he had skipped paying many of the bills, like the electric bill; they were seriously past due. On top of that, I had to pay his part of the lawyer's fees just to have the divorce go through.

One night, I returned home to change my clothes after making the long commute from my day job. It was cold and windy with deep snow piled up all around. After I opened my front door, I reached in and flipped the light switch at the base of the stairs. Nothing. I flipped the switch several times . . . *Great, the power company has turned off the electricity!* I walked up my stairwell, saying, "Damn, damn, damn," or words to that effect. When I reached the top step, I sat down and cried. I was tired, frustrated, alone, overworked, and sitting in the dark in my cold apartment.

That's when I *knew* what it felt like to hit rock bottom. After crying, I carried on. I found my oil hurricane lamp and lit it. I went to the freezer, took out the two small bags of frozen vegetables, and put them outside in the snow on my balcony to keep them frozen. Then

I changed my clothes and went to work. Thankfully, in the 1970's I had a wind-up alarm clock and very little in the way of electronic gadgets that relied on electricity, plus no food to cook, so I dealt with the inconvenience of having no lights.

I lived this way for over a week. One night, a friend came over to pick me up on our way out to find a good Happy Hour. Before we left, she had to use the bathroom. She knew the power was off, but out of habit, when she went into the dark bathroom, she flipped the switch. The light came on. When I saw the light, I flipped the switch in the living room. The lights came on in there as well. They turned the power back on! Or did they?

I went to the stairwell that led up from the front door to my apartment. When I flipped the switch, the stairwell light did not come on. I tried it several times, but no light. Finally I figured it out; the light bulb in the stair well was blown. The power had been on the whole time!

Was this a gift? Yes, it was. I survived and eventually dug myself out of the financial hole and thrived. With the fear I would not be able to survive if I lost everything now gone, I was able to concentrate on growing instead of hoarding. It can be a real gift to hit rock bottom once in your life and come out the other end stronger and wiser. Knowing I could survive gave me the courage to take risks that eventually got me to where I am today. Many in the seminar never experienced life on the financial edge before, so being "homeless" was scary for them.

I already knew I could survive most anything and eventually thrive. I knew how to be resourceful. What did I gain from this exercise? *True wealth begins with gratitude for what you do have.* Even if you were grateful for being homeless on the streets of San Diego and not Bangladesh.

In just the few hours I was on the streets, I began to "forget" this was just an exercise. I started to feel homeless. I didn't have to worry about maintaining my homes, cars, bills, clothing, and calendars, because in the "homeless" world they didn't exist. It felt amazingly liberating. I decided I wanted to simplify my life and start getting rid of the "stuff" that I didn't really need.

The exercise was a lot like life. I am here for a short while to play a part, to learn and grow, but the part I am playing does not constitute the real me. I am much more, as is everyone else. I need to live every minute to the fullest, because unlike the exercise, we don't know exactly when the bus is coming to take us home.

We still had a second outing that day: a scavenger hunt in the affluent community of La Jolla. Given only enough time to change back into our own cloths, but not time to clean up, we were off again. On the bus we were given a list of items to find. The winner who found the most received dinner with James at the black tie dinner dance, which would culminate the seminar the following evening. James was on our bus. When I looked over the list of items, I saw there was also a list of questions worth a lot of points as well. One question: "What was James' mother's maiden name?" How would we find that out unless we asked James or his brother directly? When we left the bus, I simply asked James his mother's maiden name. He told me and kept walking. Later, James commented on how many people did not come up and ask him for the answer. They felt either they couldn't approach James, or it was a trick question. Just how hard do we have to make things for ourselves?

Richard and I could not get jazzed about this activity. We knew the lesson was to use what resources we had, other than money, to get what we need, but in reality this activity was way too easy for us to win. We had our cell phones back, and I had two friends who lived a couple of miles from where they had dropped us off. One call from us, and they likely would have shown up with bags of the stuff that we needed. Also, since we knew the area well, even if we decided to find the items on our own, we knew where to look. We did not feel this would be fair to the other participants who were running around like crazy people looking for this stuff.

We weren't excited about the competition for another reason. If Richard or I won, then one of us would sit with James while the other would be alone at the dinner dance. What fun was that?

After we returned from the scavenger hunt, a buffet dinner awaited us. We talked about our lessons learned during the long day with the others at our table. During the dinner, each table had to write a song or jingle, to be judged in a contest. Some of these were very clever or really funny. There were a lot of very talented people in the room! Many of the songs and skits poked fun at James and especially at the way he used his hard-sell techniques during the seminar to sell other events. James seemed to take it all in good humor.

On day three, a scheduled field trip to work at a women and children's shelter was canceled, so we made toiletry kits for them instead. The lesson: part of being wealthy and abundant is to give of your time and resources to others. The purpose is to give out of gratitude for what you have, and not because it is something you should do.

We also had a trust exercise. We were blindfolded and silently led around the hotel grounds by another person. I found out I still had trust issues, especially with men, and was relieved it was Richard leading me around. I would not have been comfortable with someone else as my partner. Of course, James mixed things up a bit. He moved through the group and grabbed someone's arm or hand and ran them around the area quickly. He also liked to swing them around in circles, pushing their comfort level as much as he felt they needed. After he was done, he would return each person to his or her original partner. The blindfolded person would wonder what on earth had gotten into their partner. When the blindfold came off the other person quickly explained it was James, not them, who spun them around so wildly.

This was the second event we attended with Edward and his wife, Faith. They had both been in our extended study/support group, known as a Warrior Group, after Harmonic Wealth Weekend (HWW). We were quickly becoming good friends. Back in HWW, I had heard Edward's loud booming voice over the crowd and immediately concluded I had known him before. He was way too familiar to me. I likely knew him in a previous life. To verify this, I did a past life regression on myself and simply asked my unconscious mind, "Did I known Edward in a previous life?"

The answer: "Yes."

"Show me."

I was taken directly to a time and place where we were brother and sister. He was around 9 and I was about 8. We had other brothers and sisters, but they were much older. I got the impression our father remarried and we were his children with his second wife. Edward was a prankster, always getting into trouble. Even when he knew he would get severely paddled, he would go ahead with the offending act. On the rare occasion I would get into trouble, they would punish him, too, because they thought he was likely to blame in some way. I could see us running through fields of high grass, free to play and explore as much as we wanted to. We were close, and we would continue to look out for each other throughout that lifetime. Going back further in time, I saw many lives with him. Richard and I have had many past lives together and Edward was also there in many of them. Richard and Edward have either been related to each other, close friends, or fellow warriors. All three of us fought in battles together, and as Scotsmen, we resisted English occupation. Our past life experiences were tightly interconnected; we knew each other well before meeting each other in this life.

We all experience instantly liking or disliking someone. Some of us experience love at first sight. They are all our unconscious mind's recognition of someone from a past life. Often we meet up again and again to help and support each other. Other times we run into each other again just to see if we have finally figured out to stay away from each other. Nothing is an accident, and life is a miraculously woven tapestry more complex than we could ever understand while in human form.

We closed with the black-tie dinner dance to celebrate our abundance. It was a far stretch from what we looked like on the streets of San Diego to men in tuxedoes and women in gowns. To me, it was all about gratitude. I had attended many black tie events over my lifetime, but that evening I was especially grateful for the wine, good food, and great people around me. I was appreciative for the opportunity to participate in the seminar. James had put together a learning experience unlike anything I had ever encountered. I was starting to see just how brilliant he was at orchestrating classes in which one would have numerous opportunities to learn and grow from whatever level one was. I was also grateful we would be heading to Practical Mysticism and the forest around Lake Tahoe in just a few weeks. I was eager to learn more! What new challenges and "opportunities" would await us at the five-day event?

CHAPTER 4

Most Empowering Week of My Life

Practical Mysticism • July 2007

The unexamined life is not worth living.

—Socrates

The most empowering event I have ever attended almost didn't happen for me. Just two weeks prior to Practical Mysticism, after already being sick for several weeks, I was diagnosed with post pneumonia asthma. I was prescribed two different types of inhalers, which kept me breathing, but I quickly noticed when I used them, I felt the jitters, like I had ingested too much caffeine. I wondered how I was going sit in lectures for hours at a time. Only after I arrived did I learn I had an additional problem.

Practical Mysticism was held in an absolutely beautiful location on the shores of Lake Tahoe in California. Ponderosa pines, sugar pines and other ancient, giant fir trees surrounded the property; Lake Tahoe is one of the few places in the Sierra where one can see the same pine trees the Nisean and Miwok Indians saw 400 years ago. We stopped to take in the beautiful crystal-clear high mountain lake. The problem for me was the word "high." The altitude at the lake's surface is 6,225 feet above sea level. I live at sea level. Post pneumonia asthma and climbing more than a mile in altitude don't mix very well. It would be a struggle not to be using the inhalers constantly.

We arrived on Sunday afternoon. After registration and dinner, we convened the first of many evening fire circles. It was kind of fun to be around a large roaring campfire, with a clear sky showing off a dazzling array of stars. The first evening went pleasantly enough. We each took a turn telling the group what brought us to this seminar. For a James Ray event, it ended early and I enjoyed a reasonable night's sleep.

The first full day began with a yoga class led by James. He advised us to develop our own yoga practice and to do it daily. This week he said we would have class every morning because we would be releasing a lot of issues. The emotional work stresses your mind and body by, among other things, releasing toxins into your system. Yoga kept us loose and allowed for the energy to move freely through all parts of our body; practicing daily would get this new habit off to a good start. Afterward we moved to the meeting room and immediately sat for a 40-minute long guided meditation from one of James' CDs. I used my inhalers before yoga, and I wasn't able to relax or stretch my muscles, and could still feel the hyper effects during the meditation. I kept the inhalers in my pocket but only to use as a last resort.

James lectured on the different types of meditation. He first discussed Guided Visualization, focusing our train of thought by following guided images or instructions given by the group facilitator during the session (or on a CD). This type of meditation is easier for Western minds, since it offers the mind something "to do" while it is settling into the process of "being." He then moved into Zen meditation, the most disciplined of the many Buddhist meditation techniques, where you sit still and pay attention to where your mind goes, without judgment or attempting to suppress your thoughts. After that is Transcendental Meditation (TM), the famous technique that set off an international meditation frenzy in 1967, when Maharishi Maresh Yogi taught it to the Beatles in India. In TM, you turn off your thoughts completely. James said that in Zen it takes around 20 years to get to Transcendence. I don't agree with him on that. I believe the time each individual needs to reach this state varies, from a couple of months to a lifetime. Finally there is Mobile Transcendence, "pray without ceasing" as described by the Apostle Paul. When we experience "heaven on earth" we turn our entire life into a walking prayer, exemplified by the rishis and gurus of India, or the wandering monks of Japan, but something that is entirely possible to achieve while living an ordinary life in, say, Southern California.

James spent some time discussing the special window of time in which we sit; from 2000-2012 there is a rapid escalation of consciousness in the universe. *"For something new to live, something old must die,"* he said. *"*We are all here for a special reason." He also told us the world around us is a biofeedback mechanism and shows us who we are by the results we receive. "Everything around you is your responsibility," he said.

Then a man asked this question: "Exactly how is everything my responsibility?"

"Everything is your responsibility and nothing is your fault," James said. "Fault means there is something wrong with you. *When you take responsibility for your actions and results then you are standing in your power.*"

Before we were dismissed for lunch, we were told James had given some directions to the cooks regarding what they would serve us in the buffet. However there were other guests in the resort and items were being served that were not the healthiest choices. As we found out over the week, the rabbit food and lean proteins were aimed at us, and a lot of other good-looking items were not. James reminded us about how coffee, sodas, and sugars affect our systems; he directed us to choose wisely. As far as I could see, everyone in the seminar gave it their best shot, although many experienced severe coffee withdrawal while sitting just a few feet away from the dining room coffee pots!

I am not a coffee drinker, but I had my own challenge. Our room was on the hill above the meeting room, so at breaks I hurried up the path in order to get to my room with as much time as possible to check emails and make a few phone calls. After lunch, I moved way too quickly. The inhalers I used before morning yoga had worn off. I was wheezing and gasping; I had to sit down. I removed the inhaler from my jacket pocket, but really didn't want to use it. James did not say much of what to expect as far as scheduling goes; for all I knew, we might be having another meditation right after lunch. The inhaler would ruin the experience for me.

As I sat on the steps, hanging on to the railing with one hand and the inhaler with the other, James and his assistant came walking out of the building. I was embarrassed; I'm sure he thought I was way out of shape, which I was, but the asthma made it worse. He didn't stop or ask me if I was OK. You would think a person sitting gasping for air, holding an inhaler, might cause some concern. Not with James. He probably thought I deserved to be gasping because I was so fat. This triggered a week of beating myself up over my weight.

When we got back into the meeting room, we started to work on our life maps. We were directed to use photos cut from magazines to put together the "story" of our lives on a large piece of poster board. After working all afternoon, we broke up into groups and told each other our stories, using the images on the boards. It was really funny to see the difference between the men's and most of the women's boards. The men would have, at most, a handful of photos glued to their boards in a very haphazard way. The women used so many photos some of their stories ran over onto the back of their boards. In addition to the pictures, they also decorated their boards with different color markers, sparkles, stickers, you name it and it was on there! One woman loved her life map so much she was going to frame it when she got home.

We looked at our boards to find repeating patterns in our lives, particularly those wrapped around significant emotional events. Some people already recognized repeating patterns while telling their stories. Others needed some quiet time to either see the patterns or admit to them. One woman in our group realized she would sabotage her relationships within a year. She felt if it went longer, then the pain of its potential loss would be too great. She would leave before she had too much time invested in the relationship.

I could see my pattern but did not want to acknowledge it, especially not with the group. My life had been a series of weight gains, then weight losses, followed again by weight gains. Looking at my life map for the first time, it was finally clear what triggered each of the weight gains. I am sure I already knew at some level, but now, it was visible in my map and obvious to me.

Was I ready to talk about it yet? Not with my small group that afternoon.

When I was around 10 years old I was sexually molested by my swimming instructor/coach. Even now, it is still hard to type out the words.

I grew up in a small town in upstate New York. A major attraction of the local YMCA was its large indoor pool. Just to the right of the reception desk was a large staircase that led to the second floor, where rooms were rented out to men. We called one of those men "Coach." I loved my time in the pool because swimming was one of the few things I felt I could do well. At first, I was awkward, but over the course of one winter it all came together and I became fast. I felt like I could swim forever. It was a thrill to be made captain of our team! Even though there were no other teams to swim against in the area due to lack of pools, we raced against each other. My job was to decide who would be in what race and how the relay teams were going to be comprised and ordered. I was always the anchor of one of the "older kids" relay teams, because if we were behind I would just put my head down and go. I even impressed myself with the distance I could make up if we were behind. There were two other co-captains, one for the "younger kid's teams" and another for the "older kid's teams." The three of us became the cheerleaders, organizers and scorekeepers for the group.

After practice, Coach met with us upstairs in his room to plan the next week's races. Every once in a while, one of the other kids missed practice and wasn't there for the meeting. On one occasion, both of the other captains were out sick and it was just Coach and me. He exposed himself and kept on with our meeting as if nothing out of the ordinary just happened. I left when the meeting was over, confused as to what *did* happen.

Then came the next meeting, and I was the only one there, even though both of the other kids had been at practice. I later found out from them Coach had told them not to attend any more meetings, because I would "fill them in on what they needed to know." I found myself alone with a man who was getting more daring each time we met. It was even spilling over into our practices. He would come over to talk to a group in the water that was hanging onto the side of the pool. He would orient himself so when we looked up to talk with him, we would be looking straight up the baggy loose trunk leg of his bathing suit. While talking to us, he would hide his arm behind his clipboard and rub his genitals. From our angle in the pool, there was no way we could miss it. If we looked down, he said to look at him; it wasn't polite not to be looking at someone when they were talking to you.

I was in an impossible position. Parents didn't often talk with their children back then about what to do when someone does something to make you uncomfortable. Coach was an elder, a teacher, and someone to be respected. His behavior escalated from indecent exposure to full-blown molestation. When I protested, he told me as the captain of the team, it was my job to work closely with the coach. If I wasn't willing to do what I was supposed to do, then he would have to get another captain. He said he wasn't asking that much from me, considering all he had done to make me a great swimmer. He said I had great potential, everyone saw that, and with his help I could really go far. I just had to do my part and be a good captain.

I kept trying to figure out how to get out of the situation. Finally he grabbed me by both arms and was pulling me towards him. I didn't care anymore about his threats. I kicked him hard and twisted my body until he finally let go. I ran out of his room and down the stairs, grabbing my stuff on the way out the front door. I waited outside for my ride even though it was very cold. I knew Coach would be furious and I would have to deal with that when I saw him again, but I was not walking up those stairs again no matter what he said.

At the next practice, Coach acted like nothing had happened. At the end, he simply said to me, "I'll see you upstairs."

I shook my head.

"Yes!" he said forcefully.

"No." I said.

He glared at me. For a moment, I thought he was going to slap me in front of the other kids, but eventually he turned and walked away. I was scared and relieved—scared because I didn't know what he was going to do next, and relieved because I would never have anything to do with going upstairs with him again. At the next practice, Coach surprised me when he announced we had a new captain. He told them I had decided I did not want to be the captain anymore.

Over the next few weeks, Coach and the new captain entered me in fewer and fewer races. In one of my last relay races, my team was far behind when I dove into the pool as the anchor leg. The guy swimming against me was close to half way done already; it was going to be one of those races where I put my head down, swam as hard and far as I could between breaths, and gave it my all.

Everyone else was cheering at the other end of the pool when I hit the water. I knew I was moving well, and when I touched the wall at the end I was completely out of breath. I beat the other swimmer by an inch. We popped our heads up at the same time and looked at each other to see who had touched first. He made some comment that he almost won, and then we both looked around because it was quiet. Everyone was gone. They had moved to the other end of the pool before we finished the race.

Surprised, he looked at me, then he yelled to the kids from both teams to be a little more supportive of their teammates. "What was that all about?"

It was Coach's way of telling me my spectacular finishes were no longer of interest to him.

I was no longer selected to be on any relay teams afterward. When the other kids asked him about it, he replied it was time for some of the other swimmers to get their chance to race and I didn't need any more practice. He also told them it was time for them to work harder and stop expecting me to save their butts every time they were behind. Over the rest of the swimming season, I would sometimes see the girl who was our new captain head up the stairs with him after practice, so relieved that it wasn't me.

A couple of weeks before the end of the season, my father could not leave work to pick me up. He sent a cab to get me—my first cab ride! Excited, I told a couple of my friends, who were waiting with me just inside the front door. I did not see Coach standing at the foot of the stairs behind me. He walked over, startling me, and said my Dad didn't need to send a taxi; he could give me a ride.

"No." I emphatically shook my head.

He kept trying to persuade me to accept his offer. I kept refusing. I looked around to see if there was another adult who I could stand by, but there was no one at the front desk.

Finally, the cab arrived. I ran past him and didn't stop until I jumped in the cab. I still remember him standing at the front door, watching the cab pull away. To this day it still makes me sick to think what could have happened had I gotten into his car.

I didn't return to swimming the next year. I was happy to be away from him and sad not to be swimming. I had finally found something at which I was good; and, it was gone. After that ordeal, whenever a man said I looked nice, or gave me a compliment of any type, it sent shivers down my spine and turned my stomach. I figured out if I didn't look nice, especially after putting on weight since I wasn't swimming anymore, they would stop complimenting me. I felt downright invisible; that suited me just fine.

I also learned when I was around six, a car pulled up to our front yard. A man opened the passenger side door and asked me to "go for a ride" with him.

I hesitated. Luckily, my great-grandmother saw what was happening and ran from her usual seat on the front porch. She yelled something at him in Polish, and he drove off.

Shortly thereafter, the local newspaper apparently ran a story about a man offering rides and sexually molesting young girls. I didn't understand. I just knew that a bad man had come to our house and great-grandma scared him off. After that, I was limited to playing only in the back yard.

Between that experience which I had forgotten, and what happened with coach, the world did not feel like a safe place to this 10-year-old girl.

I hit my later teen years and thinned down, partly because of my ongoing ballet practice. I did not love it, and it did not love me. I was very self-conscious of the fact I was tall and always stood out in any group. I was not comfortable with attention. It was also through ballet that I developed my unhealthy habit of eating far too little. I was now thinner, and had a boyfriend. The latter gave me a sense of protection, since I was rarely alone. Everything was fine for now.

Years later, I was leaving a shopping mall late at night, after the stores were closed and most cars had left the parking lot. My car was parked at the far end of the mostly deserted lot. I heard a car start up close to the mall and then head towards me. I was walking along the main lane out of the parking lot, not think anything of it, until the van stopped abruptly alongside me and the door slid open—fast! A man stepped one foot out, grabbed me and started to pull me into the van. I kicked and screamed. My sweater ripped, and he failed to grasp anywhere else as I fell to the ground and kept on kicking. The driver yelled to the guy that he was taking too long. Headlights popped into my peripheral vision; coming towards us was another car. The men in the white van gave up and took off.

I shook so hard I was barely able to get up, pick up my keys, and run to my car. One of my shoes was missing; I didn't bother to look for it. I limped along as quickly as possible and threw myself into my car. As I was getting in, I heard a man's voice calling to me, asking if I was OK, could he help me. I never even looked his way. I was out of there.

Again the world proved it was a dangerous place and it wasn't safe to look pretty. Without ever consciously thinking about it, I started doing what I knew would divert that type of attention away from me—gaining weight. After putting on weight, the compliments and unwanted attention stopped again.

After my divorce, I was broke. I didn't feel much like eating so the weight dropped away quickly. A few years after I married Richard, I received some unwanted attention at work. Again, unconsciously, I brought my weight back up until the attention and comments stopped.

We moved to a new city and I had a new job, which meant my weight could go back down since I was now away from the perceived "threat" at my previous job. I got pregnant and after two ectopic ruptures, I finally was able to carry a baby all the way to term, worrying and nervously eating all the way through it. After I had my daughter, I let my weight fall again. This time it plummeted to the point that friends were telling me I was skin and bones. Even Richard hugged me and said, "You have lost enough weight, stop it now."

But I stayed trim, worked out with a trainer and thought I was in the best shape of my life, until . . . I was heading to my station wagon after working a local Oktoberfest craft show. It was very late; rowdy groups of young men moved through the streets. I walked down several side streets to get to my car while pulling a handcart that carried a box of supplies and my cash box. I just started down the last road and sensed I was being followed by a group of men on the sidewalk on the opposite side. They crossed the road behind me and were slowly catching up. I walked out to the center of the street and moved quickly towards my car when two came onto the street and gained on me. I figured (and hoped) they wanted the cash box, so I left the handcart on the center of the road and ran for my car.

I looked back: they had run past the handcart and were still coming towards me! Just as I was ready to scream, a police car made a slow left turn onto the road well in front of me. It was a long road, and the police car was far away, but I saw him—and so did my pursuers. They yelled to each other to get out of there. Then a few men ran across the road in front of me. *Oh my God!* A couple of men stood between me and my car. I was actually running towards some of them without knowing it!

The police car sped up and pursued them down the road. I glanced around—only the street and me now. I ran to where I left my handcart, grabbed it and sprinted to my car. I threw the whole cart into the back in one piece. I could hear the money in the change box flying everywhere. I shook so hard I could barely open my door. Once inside, I started the car, locked all the doors and split. I did not wait to see if the police would come back for a statement. I just wanted to go home.

The damage was done. Again it reinforced it was not safe to be pretty or to look sexy, so I returned to what I knew would keep me safe. Being overweight hurt, but not as bad as the fear. If that wasn't enough, the cycle had to repeat one more time. After again beating the weight back down, I was holding an open house and Richard was out putting up the directional signs. An insurance broker came in and asked if he could tell me about his homeowner's policies. I politely listened to him, but I noticed he kept moving closer and closer to me. Finally, he reached out and put his hand on the back of my arm while he was talking. I pulled away and moved to one side of the dining room table. When he moved, I moved, so that the table was always between us.

Richard came back to pick up something before heading back out to finish putting out the rest of the signs. He looked at me and could tell something wasn't right. "Do you think I have enough signs up?"

"I think you have plenty of signs up." He knew both the code and the look in my eyes; *don't leave!*

Richard stood by me. The man took off without leaving a brochure or business card.

I didn't look like my "thin" photo on my business card much longer.

Looking at my life map, it was clear gaining weight was a direct reaction to feeling threatened. Fat was my protection. Attention was dangerous; fat stopped it. If I could not break the connection, I would be locked in this cycle forever. There had been a lot of discussion in the seminar about how you needed to see your patterns to stop the destructive cycles. Own them; don't try to hide from them.

I clearly saw the cycle. Would I be willing to claim and own it?

That night around the fire circle, one by one we talked about what we had learned from our life maps. I was trying to listen to each person; at the same time, my mind was racing. I never talked about what had happened to me with anyone. Even Richard knew very little. Could I verbally own the source of my lifelong weight issues? Thank goodness it was dark, with just the campfire to illuminate the faces sitting around it.

My turn. I took a deep breath and just said it. I didn't go into any details, and I think I only brought up that I had been sexually abused as a child. I didn't mention any of the later incidents. I didn't need to. Just saying aloud what Coach did to me was a huge step.

As we headed back to our rooms, many women came up and told me the same thing happened to them. I was shocked at first. How could this be a shared experience among so many people? The next day, James said if you were not abused in some manner when you were a child you were in the minority. How sad is that realization? Later, a friend admitted to the group his father had sexually abused him. Now that people were freely talking, I could see how common the problem was. It was a relief to not carry around my "secret" anymore, and also to know it wasn't just me. People can say it wasn't your fault all they want, but deep down, you think there must have been something you were doing that caused these things to happen. I felt somehow it was my fault. All the fear and shame is way too much for an adult to carry, let alone a trusting child.

The real work of healing had begun for me. I think most people in our seminar would say that they got amazing insights from just some magazine pictures glued to a poster board.

CHAPTER 5

If I Can Do That, I Can Do Anything!

Practical Mysticism • July 2007

Strength does not come from physical capacity.
It comes from an indomitable will.

—Mohandas Gandhi

James was using every possible moment to write his new book. On the second day, he showed up just as the meditation CD was winding down. Some women were still putting the finishing touches on their life maps.

That afternoon, he talked about the relationship between courage and fear. Courage is not the absence of fear, but taking action even while feeling fear. Fear is a natural feeling, an instinct, so we should not be surprised when we feel it. When an important life event choice comes, he continued, you have two choices: step into your power and face it head on; or step back into fear and lose the lesson and the opportunity. He talked about how it's more powerful to know than to believe.

All his talk about experiencing fear and displaying courage caused me to wonder what he had planned for us.

The second day drew toward an uneventful close. We headed off to the nightly fire circle, this time paired up with the person we worked with most of the day on different assignments. We expected we would have to share our progress with the entire group. We came in with our partners and took our seats.

There was always drumming at the nightly fire circle. We were told to bring a drum to the event—or in the case of Edward, the loudest, most annoying rattle on the face of the Earth! Several people danced around the fire to the beat of the drums.

When everyone was seated again, James stood up. He had something in his hand, which was hard to see in the dark. Soon, it became apparent he was moving around the fire with a five-foot piece of rebar, the metal rod that strengthens concrete. He waved it around. Every once in a while, he held it like a spear; he even touched one end to someone's throat. Then he danced around the fire, stopped and repeated this process several more times. What was he doing?

The drums stopped. James explained we were going to bend a piece of rebar with our partners. Those who paid attention to the release waivers we signed at registration already knew this: bending rebar, participating in Holotropic Breathwork™, and walking on fire were all listed. We all thought that bending rebar would be no big deal. I mean, how hard could he make *that*? Either you did it or you didn't.

However all of us were concerned about walking on fire. Several times during the week, Edward, Richard and I had a conversation where we said these exact words to each other: "James is a businessman. He wouldn't have us do anything that was really dangerous and let us get hurt, because it would be bad for business." We must have said that to each other about 20 times over the next couple of years. We said it as a statement of fact. Later on, we would say it as a question.

The smiles left the faces around the fire; we knew whatever James had in store was going to be serious. He explained we were not going to put our hands on the bar, but our *throats*! Did I hear him right? Now I knew what that discussion about fear was all about! What did he say, *it was normal to feel fear*? Well then I was feeling very normal.

I couldn't believe he meant it until he asked for a pair of volunteers. Two jumped up and one of them was Stephen Ray (no relation to James). I sat there, my mouth hanging open, as James placed a folded up dollar bill on each exposed tip of the rebar and then placed the ends in the lower v section of each of their throats. Their hands could not touch the rebar. Instead, they held their hands just under their chins to guard their faces in case the end of the bar flew up. The folded up bills helped protect the participants from the sharp edges of the metal pole cutting into their skin.

The road to success was simple: Keep heading towards each other until the rebar gave way and the partners ended up hugging with a piece of bent over rebar between them. Do I really have to say it? DON'T TRY THIS AT HOME!

Within a few seconds, the first pair bent their rebar. Everyone else lined up to wait his or her turn. This is one of those times where you could see a wide array of reactions. Some wanted to go quickly, either because they were excited, or they couldn't wait to finish. Many admitted later to being afraid if they waited too long, they would chicken out. Others were undecided about bending rebar at all, and were hugging the back of the line, waiting to see if anyone managed to push a metal rod through their throats before they got up there. Richard and I are of the mindset once we decide we are going to do something, it is best just to get it done and over with as quickly as possible. Waiting prolongs the agony of being fearful.

We moved up in line, and were among the first 15 pairs to go. I watched to see if anyone bit it big-time before us, but with each passing successful couple, it looked more and more like we could do this. The thought crossed my mind that whoever created this "activity," it must have involved men and alcohol! Women wouldn't have come up with something like this.

Some people bent their rebar on the first try; others did not. It became evident it was far more preferable to bend it on the first go around. If you didn't succeed, then your throat was already sore before you tried again. It hurt, and people were gagging, but it was best to keep going and get it over with.

Before I knew it, it was our turn. I was trembling. James stood on my side as a coach, and one of the Dream Teamers assisted Richard. "You ready to do this?" James asked.

"No."

James immediately lowered my end of the rebar and looked me squarely in the eyes. The group cheered us on loudly; some were singing a chant we learned the night before. It was very hard to hear James. He got to within a couple of inches of my face and said, "Well, you better get ready, or else you won't be doing this."

I nodded and said I was ready, but how can you really be ready to do something like this? Since Richard and I paid all that money and invested so much time to be standing here, it looked like we were going to do it—so let's get it done! I kept hearing Edward's words in my head: "James is a businessman. He wouldn't have us do anything that was really dangerous and let us get hurt because it would be bad for business."

We were nearing the step where one partner makes eye contact with the other. James was explaining the bar was just energy, that we are energy, we are more than the bar, with our will we can do anything . . . and the bar doesn't stand a chance of resisting the power of our will. As I made eye contact with Richard, I still felt very wimpy.

Then I saw his eyes. Richard swears he was fine with the whole thing, but what I saw when I looked down that long metal bar was his eyes bugging out.

Over the roar of the crowd, I heard some people calling our names. "GO!" James yelled into my ear.

I lunged forward. One of the more difficult things was gaining traction with the loose dirt sliding under our feet. I was looking down the bar at Richard. For a second, I thought I would have to pull up because I was gagging and it was starting to hurt too much, but before I did, I gave it one more hard push. The center of the bar bent beyond my field of vision.

Next thing I knew, I was hugging Richard and the crowd was cheering. When we let go of each other, I saw the bent piece of rebar—we really did it! I hugged James, then Richard again. We left with our souvenir bent metal bar and found a place to sit on the logs around the fire. I touched the spot on my throat where the end of the rebar had rested. It was tender but not painful. It seemed like an eternity while we were doing it, but those who watched us said we were done in a couple of seconds. Did it hurt while we were doing it? Hell yes! Was it unbearable? Heck no.

Talk about a bonding experience! How many people can you say that you bent rebar with? As we watched the other pairs, I could not help but think I was very lucky to experience this with Richard. How could I ever go home and try to explain this to my significant other? Such a unique sharing also tied you with your partner for eternity; a moment of fear, followed by surrender, and finally victory over your fear. I was very grateful Richard was my partner at these events.

Last to go was a pair of James Ray International employees, the marketing director and event coordinator. I didn't think of this at first, but they were under some added pressure. They were not only doing this for the first time, but also performing in front of their boss. Apparently, the pressure affected them; they must have tried five or six times before succeeding.

Every group of participants bent their rebar. According to James, this was the first time everyone in the group had been successful.

What did I learn from this exercise? That it was a lot like life. You attempt to accomplish something hard. It may even appear to be impossible, and along the way its gets really difficult and you think you can't do it. That point usually comes just before you break through and become successful. Unfortunately, many people give up precisely at that point, when one more hard push would break the resistance and lead to achieving their goal.

I also learned it is far easier on both partners in a dual effort if I just stick it out and get it done the first time, and not start and stop several times. Indecision on one person's part hurts both. Lastly, it often takes someone else to help me achieve something difficult, and *both people* have to be willing to give full effort. Choose partners carefully. Several times, we saw one person pull up on the rebar while the other held ground and kept pushing. All the partner could do was encourage their teammate, because it wasn't going to happen unless both people gave it their all.

At breakfast the next morning, we all wore small red marks on our throats. We called them "James Ray hickies." These spots served as a reminder that we really did bend rebar; it wasn't a dream. We had our yoga session followed by a guided meditation from one of James' CDs.

The day consisted mostly of lectures. James talked about how important it is to choose your friends wisely. If you grow, then your peer group must change. I thought it was an interesting concept: if you want to see who you really are, then take a look at your friends. At the very least, your values must be similar. I gave some thought as to how my friends had changed over the years. Some were far away and I stayed close to them, while others lived nearby, but we had grown distant. Being closer physically may make it easier, but if you are changing and they are not, or vice versa, your common ground slowly slips away.

James spoke about annually evaluating your goals and where you stand. He said most people take more time to plan a vacation than their life. I agree with him. For years I followed a New Years Day ritual of taking out my goals/resolutions I had written on the previous January 1st and grading myself on how I did the past year. I did not beat myself up for what I had not accomplished, but used it to determine what was slipping through the cracks of time. It was an opportunity to reevaluate and reprioritize my action items. Since then I do it quarterly, because a year is too long to let something I deemed important go unaddressed.

He also talked about first impressions. He said you only have 30 seconds to make a first impression, and people have a tendency to hang on the first impression, even if it is wrong. While reviewing my notes, I find his next statement interesting, and prophetic: **"Juries make their decisions within the first five to seven minutes of the trial and spend the rest of the trial convincing themselves they are right."**

Richard and I often comment that homebuyers decide within the first two minutes of walking in the front door if they are standing in their next home. They spend the rest of the time walking through the house to validate their decision. We constantly work with our home-selling clients to make their homes as welcoming as possible, especially what prospective buyers see when they first walk through the door.

That evening, we reported back to the meeting room with our life maps, blankets and pillows. We were told not to eat much for dinner. When we arrived all of the chairs were gone, and the lights were very low. We sat down on the floor in front of the stage. James told us a story about how, when he was in Peru with his shaman teacher don Javier Ruis (the man's name has been changed for his privacy), he climbed a steep mountain to get to the shaman's graveyard. He talked about how we carry our life's story around with us and it is constantly sapping our energy and holding us back. Maintaining our story keeps us dwelling on the past rather than living in the now. I knew what he was getting at; I had already grown tired of looking at my life map. I wanted to let the past and the destructive cycles go. Start fresh.

James continued. When he reached the top of the mountain, don Javier Ruis told him he was still carrying too much of his life's story around. The shaman rolled back the large stone to a grave and told James to get in. James reluctantly did. Don Javier Ruis rolled the stone back into place, entombing James. He was to stay there until he was ready to release his old life, let it die, and be reborn.

He never finished the story, even though we prodded him many times over the next couple of years to tell us what happened next.

James delivered this story very dramatically. It was a very effective story for what we were about to do. James told us to leave our pillows and blankets behind, and take only our life maps. We were going to be "climbing a mountain!" In this case, following a trail through the dark woods to our own "burial ground." No flashlights were allowed, and no talking from now until 9 a.m. the following morning; more than 12 hours of silence. After "climbing a mountain," we would return to the room for a session of Holotropic Breathwork™. After 9 a.m., we were to discuss our experiences within the small group of six participants—our "warrior group." For Richard and me, these six people would remain the warrior group with which we would continue to work, just as we did after Harmonic Wealth Weekend and Creating Absolute Wealth. Edward and Faith were in our group as they were in the previous two events.

I knew I would have a few challenges: first, my asthma; second, poor night vision. I am practically blind in the dark.

We lined up single-file and headed straight up the hill above the meeting center. Walking in a line meant I had to keep pace with the person in front of me. We were only a few minutes into the hike and I was already wheezing and gasping for air. I had my inhaler but did not want to use it. I knew Holotropic Breathwork™ waited when we returned to the meeting room, and I had no idea how the inhaler's jittery side effects would impair my ability to participate in the session. So I literally sucked it up and kept going.

Other than struggling over the hills, I was moving along OK. The person in front of me wore a white sweatshirt I could barely make out. If I stayed really close, I could at least see which direction we were heading. The major pain in the butt was the life map; carrying this big square of poster paper through the woods was difficult. It kept getting hit and tangled in the tree branches, throwing me off balance. Some people were being very careful just before and during the hike not to "mess up" their maps. I was over any love or attachment to my story.

At one point, the line backed up and we stopped for a minute. I used that opportunity to fold my life map until it was small enough to fit into the back of my jeans waistband. Once it was tucked in, I had free use of my hands for balance and to protect me from tree limbs.

During this pause, the two people in front of me switched places. Now I was following someone who wore a dark shirt. Even up close I couldn't make them out much at all. We were walking through the darkest part of the woods; eventually, I could see absolutely nothing. We tried to warn the people behind us of large steps up or down by tapping our feet several times on them, but the more we did that, the further we risked falling behind the person ahead. Big gaps formed throughout the line; you just had to stumble along the best you could.

Later I found out Richard had a good idea of where we were and knew the terrain. His morning run included parts of the trail. Every once in a while he would tug one of my arms from behind, signaling I was to head in that direction. At one point he broke silence and told me to stop and veer hard right to keep me from heading towards an area with a sharp drop-off.

We came to a dirt road that led up a very steep hill. The trail opened up, allowing everyone to proceed up the hill at his or her own pace. We could see a large campfire burning in the distance. The steep hill was really taking its toll on my breathing, and I had to stop a few times on my way up just to catch my breath. Despite how slow I felt I was walking, we still reached the top ahead of about a quarter of the group.

As we stood facing the fire, one thought coursed through my mind: *I would love to throw this life map into the fire!* The only thing stopping me was I did not know if I needed it for some other activity.

James talked about how we waste too much energy carrying our life stories around with us. We tend to our stories, finding proof of their correctness by looking for things that are wrong with the world around us now. He compared our life story to a minimized computer program. It was off screen and residing on the lower status bar, but still very much active, and taking precious resources from our system. Every once in a while, it maximizes to a full screen to see if we are ready to deal with it yet; most of the time we decide to stuff it back down again. Out of sight and out of mind, but not completely. Our unconscious mind always "sees" it. After many years of stuffing it back down, we start to put layers of other stuff over it. It is still very much there, even if we don't "see" it anymore on a conscious level. At some point, our systems will slow down so much we need to maximize our life stories back into full view and deal with them to free up space and keep our systems running.

I knew where he was going. I took out my folded life map and had it ready to discard the second he gave the word. I was ready to be rid of it. I didn't want to carry it any more. I didn't even want it near me.

I wasn't alone. Some people were already leaning forward with their maps. When James gave the word, Richard and I were among the first to walk up to the fire and throw our maps in. This act has a sacred Eastern corollary, the Hindu fire ceremony, where people seeking purification throw their unwanted karmic seeds, compressed stories of life actions among other things, into a fire superheated with ghee butter.

The fire flared up and grew to bonfire size, fueled by the sheer number of maps. Sometimes, maps wouldn't burn completely, so participants would return to the fire and move unburned sections of maps into the flames.

To my surprise, many people held back, still looking at their maps, unable to let them go. One by one, they released their maps over the next few minutes, except for one lady who would not part with her stories. Everyone watched quietly as their life maps burned, bidding adieu to what they held.

After we were satisfied that our maps had been completely consumed by the fire, we followed the group back down the hill to the meeting room. The lights were turned way down and lit candles were grouped throughout the room. We were directed to lie on our pillows and blankets in lines on the floor, feet to feet with the adjacent line, but leaving walkways open by our heads. I was about to be introduced to Holotropic Breathwork™. James told us he was trained by Dr. Stanislav Grof, whose book, *The Holotropic Mind,* was required reading for this seminar. James said, "Altered states can be achieved via psychoactive drugs, breathing, love, and meditation. They all expand your consciousness." He added all four take us beyond the thinking that we are just a "meat suit" living only within what we can experience with our five senses. He described altered states as putting "stretch marks" on our minds. Later, James would tell us not to do this type of Holotropic Breathwork™ without him, because it could be dangerous. "If you use it too much," he said, "You could start to lose your solid connection to this reality." I remember writing in my notes, "Don't even think about it!" James said he had the special training to bring us back, no matter how far "out there" we got.

Looking back on this now, was he just trying to get us to buy more of his events so we could have this experience? Or did we really need to have him with us because it was so dangerous to do alone? Grof's book actually described the process. Why would Dr. Grof describe something that was so dangerous to do unsupervised?

Dr. Grof, a psychiatrist and researcher in the US and Europe, wrote about his studies with "non-ordinary" states of consciousness, which began with the assistance of LSD until LSD became illegal in 1965. He then developed the process he called Holotropic Breathwork™, in which a similar altered state could be achieved just by the way you breathed. Grof was convinced that altered states of consciousness are the gateways by which we experience spiritual realms beyond the bounds of normal waking consciousness.

This fascinated me. I never tried any hallucinogenic drugs or substances, mostly because I was a big chicken. My first degree in Medical Laboratory Technology left me with a profound respect for the human body and its sensitive and complicated chemical and hormonal workings. It concerned me to ingest a chemical substance that could really mess with that process. In Holotropic Breathwork™, the altered state was "induced" by your own breathing pattern—and I was definitely curious and nervous about experiencing this altered state.

James said each time you do Holotropic Breathwork™, you can have a completely different experience. "You could be in the depths of hell or the euphoria of heaven." Personally I was hoping for the heaven experience.

I tucked my inhaler into my jacket pocket as I was lying down on my blanket. I looked up and saw the woman who laid feet to feet with me place her inhaler by her pillow. We nodded at each other, acknowledging each other's extra challenge. To do this, you had to be able to breathe vigorously.

The session started loudly, with a lot of drumming and loud music that sounded tribal. The music was supposed to keep your conscious mind busy so it would not interfere with the process. We started the pattern of quickly inhaling through our noses and exhaling hard through our mouths. We continued to breathe this way for the two-plus hours of the session. After a few of these extremely tiring breath cycles, I thought, *no way I can keep it up for two hours.* My skin started to feel tingly. Little by little, I could not feel parts of my body anymore. The entire process was not alarming, because if something happened you did not like, you slowed your breath down and it stopped. I liked having the feeling of control over the experience, unlike what I imagined I would have from a drug-induced altered state. During this session, I floated at the top of the room and looked down at everyone below me. I was able to float further and further up while watching the earth move farther and farther away.

Finally, I stopped "expanding" when I could see other planets around me. It was peaceful, freeing, and heavenly. While there, an entity appeared and handed me a book, a journal. They told me to start writing and keep good notes because I was going to need them someday. "They" would send me messages while I journaled.

A gentle pull tugged me back to earth and eventually into my body. The music had stopped; I was now lying on my side, in the fetal position, feeling fine except I was freezing cold. I slowly sat up and looked around. On the floor were white pieces of paper with a large black circle drawn on each of them, and color markers nearby. It was time to draw our Mandalas. James said before we started to forget what we experienced, we were to draw what we could remember. "The mind thinks in pictures, so draw pictures and avoid words."

I started to draw what I remembered. Several people were still breathing hard; Richard was one of them. Apparently, this husband of mine who originally was not sure of his interest in Holotropic Breath-work™ didn't want to stop now that it was over. Eventually, James came over, held his hand on Richard's chest and talked to him until eventually Richard's breathing slowed to normal. Watching this was difficult because my first reaction was to try to help my husband. I had to trust James to do what was best for him. Other than his eyes being bugged out and shaky, Richard seemed none the worse for wear. Some did not come back so easily; a few still needed more of James' attention after the rest of us were finished drawing our Mandalas.

Day Four began without yoga; we remained in silence. We sat with our Warrior Group for breakfast and waited for 9 a.m. when we could talk about our experiences the night before. I pulled out my journal, in which I had been sporadically writing the last few years. I have been blessed with the ability to retain information for long periods—a great memory—so I haven't needed to be as thorough in taking notes as others. After my experience the previous night I started to journal more regularly.

After nine, we pulled out our Mandalas and shared our experiences with our group. Most of us had amazing experiences and insights to share. Faith said she experienced nothing during the Holotropic Breathwork™, even thought she had been looking forward to it. I remembered reading somewhere even if you had no immediate reaction or memory of a session, that you may still experience such after-effects as "seeing" energy flowing or people's auras, so we told her to just be patient and pay attention. Still she was very disappointed.

The day continued with another of James' guided meditations from his CD set. After that he lectured for the rest of the morning. One particular series of comments are very revealing, in hindsight. He told us if we don't pay attention, then we would pay with pain. "A warrior's path is never crowded, and if you follow that path, it won't be easy but it will be fulfilling. You have to be careful that what you are doing is coming from 'heart', not ego." Then he stressed, "Anytime you start to think that you are 'the bomb,' the universe will drop a bomb on you."

According to James, when we are tapping into higher levels of consciousness, we are edged out of our comfort zones to keep growing. If we start to think we are the "Second Coming" then Ego is talking, not the Divine. James warned us not to fall into that trap. He gave us examples on how the universe had blown him up in the past when he started to think too highly of himself. He said again, "If you start to think that you are the bomb, then the universe will show you what a bomb really looks like." James reiterated these same words over and over again throughout the next couple of years.

At one point, James discussed the craziness of some disclaimers and releases used by others. "Why would you ever sign something like that anyway?" he asked. I found it odd, since he made us sign them when we arrived at his events. If we refused, we had to leave—with no refund. Some participants were giving James a bit of a hard time because we were being made to sign a release form that day to participate in another activity. On our tables were releases from a separate group that ran a Sierra Ropes Course; the list of possible results from participating included serious injury and death.

James laughed it off. We still had no idea what we were signing up for. Earlier in the day, he said, "some people would be flying this afternoon," which set off speculation we would be skydiving, hang-gliding, or something like that. I could not imagine taking this many people through a sky dive in the allotted time, which brought me back to square one: I had no idea what was in store for us.

After signing our releases, we broke into groups of about thirty people and hiked to a nearby challenge course. My group's first stop was at "The Wall." Before us was an approximately 15-ft. high by 10-ft. wide shear wooden wall. Our first task: to get every member of our group over the wall in a limited amount of time.

There were many rules. You could have no more than three people at the top of the wall at any time. The maximum time any person could stay at the top was long enough to help no more than three people over. If you had already scaled the wall, you could spot from below, but could not touch or otherwise help a person with their climb. Strategy was really important! We were dealing with people of all different sizes and ages, and the order of their climbs was critical.

My team's strategy didn't matter to me. I was terrified and embarrassed. How could my team be expected to get my 300-pound-plus body over that wall? I tried to negotiate with the person running the challenge to not include me, but *everyone* had to make it over in the allotted time or the entire group failed. If someone wanted to scream "No Fair!" while pointing at me, they didn't show it. But everyone knew what they were up against and they were already deep into their strategy session. I told them even though it would be a "challenge" to get me up there, once on top I was very strong and could pull another large person over easily, so send a couple of big men and women up after me. I wasn't the only heavy person, so we decided to send some of the strongest men up just before me to help pull me over. Then it would be up to me working with two of them to pull some of the other big people up behind us. We also had to make allowances for some of the smaller or older ladies who could scale the wall, but would be of little help pulling anyone over. We had to maximize our strengths and minimize our weaknesses and liabilities.

It was now my turn, and my heart pounded in my chest. I stepped up on the thighs of two of the men and worked my way up to their shoulders. The man under my right foot was Edward. Once standing on top of them, I was still a good foot away from reaching anyone's downward extended hands from above. It was up to me to figure out how to make up the difference. I could get no traction from the smooth wall. The men grabbed my feet and pushed me up while, at the same time, I sprung off their shoulders as hard as I could. God, I was scared! But it worked! I was able to work myself to a hanging position off of the top edge of the wall. Attempts to work myself *over* the edge kept failing, because they were trying to pull me straight up and over. There is no delicate way to say this, but ladies with larger chests cannot be easily pulled straight over an edge.

While I was hanging from the top, we tried to come up with another way to get my legs high enough so that someone could grab one and pull me over sideways. Let's make it fast: I couldn't hang much longer! I seriously contemplated letting go and falling back to the ground, even though it was a long way down and getting injured was a distinct possibility. I was at the end of my strength. The only thing that stopped me was my fear of hurting someone else from my team if I fell. What I couldn't see was that a couple of the women, including Faith, were climbing up the wall below me. They were standing on the men's shoulders, and pushing each other up, hoping they could reach my feet and give me the extra push that I needed to get my leg high enough for someone on top to grab. "Go!" Someone yelled.

I was pushed up a couple of inches from below. It was just enough for me to throw my left leg up. Richard grabbed it from above. With everyone's help, I was able to work my way sideways over the top edge of the wall.

As my group cheered wildly I had to look around to believe I was really up there! Have I mentioned I am not a big fan of heights? I looked down at my teammates and thought about how close I had come to letting go and falling. It sent shivers down my spine. There was limited time for celebration. I had to work to pull up the next two big people from our group. We succeeded in getting everyone over the top in the allotted time. Big hugs and high fives all around!

One of the James Ray International staffers came over and said watching me go over the wall was one of the most amazing things she had ever seen, and she congratulated me. I still could not believe it! I was overcome by the love and unconditional support my team gave me. If only it could be that way in the "real" world, where we love and support each other totally rather than always being in competition with each other. I felt like I was seeing and feeling a "snapshot" of our true human potential. Would our race ever be able to actually achieve it someday?

Our next stop was the Trust Fall. Climbing onto a platform planted four feet up the side of a tree; we took turns falling backwards into the arms of our teammates. This wigged me out, too, because I didn't want my team to have to catch me after their huge effort to get me over the wall. Perhaps this was just my "story" to get out of something that involved the word "trust." Trust still did not come easily to me.

Finally, we reached the last person in our group. "You're next," Richard said.

"I'm not going," I said, and then laid out my reasons.

He called me on it. "That has nothing to do with it; it has to do with trust."

Richard then turned and called the biggest men to gather beneath the platform, because I was going to fall. Yikes, Yikes, Yikes! But he was right. I climbed up the platform. The woman in charge of the station was wonderful, and she talked me through the whole thing. It took a lot for me to let go and fall backwards—now I'm glad to have had the opportunity.

Did I mention I was part of a great team? Later that night, we spent hours around the fire circle as each person spoke about their day's experiences. Most of us felt compelled to thank our wonderful and supportive team. I was not the only one feeling the love!

The final day of the seminar arrived. We started off with yoga, then to the meeting room for our morning mediation. Immediately after meditating, James started to talk to us. These are my notes from what he said:

Why are we here? We are here to remember and unite with the God capabilities and power that we have forgotten. To do that, we must first grow and it requires change. We can't grow spiritually and remain the same. We must change. Everything we think that we know must change. Every relationship must change—including the one with ourselves. Have we not done things that by appearances would mean death and realize that death was just an illusion? When is now the time for us to have the life that is our destiny no matter what the external appearances? When we are away from here, we will not have a lot of people to talk to. We can have superficial conversations with others, but for the next several years there won't be many people to talk to outside these events and during our calls, but that is changing quickly. We are part of that change and that is why we are here.

According to legend, when we leave this life we will see our higher council and they will ask us two questions: First, did we love enough? And second, did we learn and grow enough?

Don Javier Ruis would ask [James], "How do you know the path is the right path? It's the right path when you don't feel prepared to take it." When we feel prepared, then doing that won't help us grow. We have to be open to the being more. The good news for us is that we have found our path in this special time in history, welcome home! The bad news is that we have found the path and we can't make any more excuses for not growing. Ancient traditions say that to be attracted to this work we must have already spent at least three lives dedicated to growth. We are now ready and that is our call.

We prepared for the "grand finale"—the fire walk. After the rebar bending exercise, we all felt trepidation. James usually increases the difficultly of the activities as the seminar progresses, yet we couldn't imagine something harder to take on than bending rebar with our throats. Every day, whenever the subject came up, several of us would remind each other, "James wouldn't have us do anything that was really dangerous. He's a business man and getting a client hurt would be bad for business."

We walked to the site where two large wooden fires were assembled, but not yet lit. We were each given a piece of paper to imbed with our intentions and our DNA just by holding it; we would later tuck the paper between the fire logs. James talked more about letting our old way of living die. For something new to be born, something old must first die. Death and rebirth were natural cycles.

While James talked, I thought about how happy I would be to release all of the issues surrounding my weight. They had been with me for so long, hurt so much, and sapped energy from my spirit. If it was possible to let that all die and be reborn, then I was all for it! My eyes welled with tears. I took the paper and blotted the tear rolling down my cheek. It was time to let the sadness burn away in the fire.

After our pieces of paper were all tucked between the logs, the fires were lit. Soon the flames from the two giant bonfires reached toward the sky. While James chanted, Faith looked over at me, wonder in her eyes, "Can you see the swirls of energy moving around the group?" I could make out something, but judging from the expression on her face nowhere as vibrant as her vision. I teased her for complaining she didn't get anything from her Holotropic Breathwork™ session. Even standing around the outside of the circle, you could feel the intense heat. I thought the same thing as everyone else: *We are going to walk through those?*

We returned to the meeting room and waited for the firewood to break down into glowing red-hot coals. James explained the Fire Walk, and why we were doing it. We would start by entering a medicine wheel, a sacred circle and living altar. Each direction on the wheel has significance. The west equals engagement; this is how you show up in the world now. The north is the direction of silence or night. East relates to your vision and clarity for the future. South signifies transformation. When we walk fire, we go from the west to the east—from how we show up now towards our new commitments and vision.

Then James delivered the directives. He would guide the ceremony—and our minds—by using languages with high vibrational quality, such as Hebrew, Latin, and native Hawaiian. We needed to control and focus our minds. We were to hold our hands out to our sides and ask our spiritual guardians to give us a sign when we were ready to walk through the fire. We were to walk with purpose, and never run. At the end of fire and hot coals, we were to wipe our feet on the provided pieces of sod and then step into water buckets. Then, in James' words, "celebrate your ass off!"

We practiced the movements several times, until they were ingrained in our minds, then we headed back to the fires. Edward, Faith, Richard and I said to each other one more time, "James wouldn't have us do anything that was really dangerous. He's a business man and getting a client hurt would be bad for business." We nervously laughed as we said it. Once in the fire ring, James called on four of the archangels for protection, he chanted in several different languages, and we lined up to go. The fires were spread out over two strips of burning coals; one by one, people started walking through. We never saw James walk fire. In fact, we never saw James do any of the activities like bending rebar or breaking a board with his hands.

The four of us ended up towards the back of one of the lines. We had plenty of time to observe the firewalkers as we slowly moved by them on our way to the start of the fire path. We had been teasing Faith that she was a Digital In Denial (DID). During the week, James had discussed different personality types. Since Edward, Richard and I all had science/engineering backgrounds, it was no surprise that a short test deemed us to be Digital in our behavior. We want the facts. After we have gathered all of the data, we will make a logical decision and act on it. Faith's test suggested she was a Digital, too—which she totally rejected. In her opinion, she was nothing like us.

The three of us stood in line, settling our minds and preparing ourselves. Faith kept counting exactly how many steps it took for each walker to cross through the fire. Excitedly, she updated us on any corrections to her calculations. The three of us laughed. From that day on, we referred to her as a DID.

Of the four of us, I went last; Richard right ahead of me. Just before I started, James ordered the man tending the fire to stir up the coals on my side. As he turned over the coals, they glowed bright red with renewed heat; the flames came up. I had already rolled up the hems on my jeans a bit, and now I reached down and rolled each one up a bit higher until they were just below my knees. When the fire master was done, he gave me a nod: it was OK to go when I was ready. I held out my hands at my sides like I had been instructed, and asked my spirit guide to tell me when I was ready to go.

After a few seconds, I felt a slight nudge at my back. I took my first step onto the coals. It felt a bit like walking on popcorn. I truly never felt any heat on my feet. Before I knew it, I was wiping off my feet on the sod and standing in the two buckets of water. I then found Richard in the crowd on the other side and "celebrated my ass off!" Compared to bending the rebar, this was a cinch! Many of us wanted to do it again, but we were cautioned to be respectful of the ceremony and settle for one pass. We had made it; we were done for now.

After everything I had done during the week, one question remained: could I finally let myself believe I could accomplish anything that I set my mind to do? Time would tell, but I was determined to do something: to give our teenage daughter the opportunity to experience this empowering week as her present for graduating high school the following year.

The meeting room was in celebration mode—and moneymaking mode. Participants could get their photo taken with James onstage and say a few words with him. It was also our last chance to sign up for expensive seminar packages at a discount offered only during his events. The prices were rising regularly. In just a few months, Spiritual Warrior had climbed from about $5,000 to $7,695 a person—and there was no discount offered. It was always sold out, so all you could do was pay and be placed on the waiting list. Concerned James' growing popularity would drive the prices even higher, we both signed up for the Spiritual Warrior event—and were told there was a large wait list ahead of us. At this time, the other events were listed on his registration form as follows:

> Harmonic Wealth Weekend, regular $1,297 today only $1,097 (we had originally signed up for two of us for $895 less than a year earlier)
>
> Quantum Leap, regularly $3,495 today only $2,995
>
> Creating Absolute Wealth, regularly $3,495 today only $2,995
>
> Modern Magick, regular price $5,695 today only $4,795

James was clearly riding the wave of popularity from his appearances on *Larry King Live* and *Oprah!* Not only were prices swelling, but the number of participants at most of the events. Instead of breaking up the longer events into multiple separate sessions, he grew them to the maximum amount the resort or room could hold. In order to pack in even more, he eliminated the round tables that made it easier to write notes and work on. From now on, we would be sitting in rows of chairs. The ability to interact with James dropped dramatically as the number of participants increased. He was delegating the work of personally interacting with and answering many of the participant's questions to his Dream Team volunteers.

But it was the one-on-one interaction with James that people were willing to pay these huge event prices for. If he was going to continue to pull away and delegate much of that interaction to his staff and volunteers then is the experience still worth the big bucks he was charging? The personal interaction with him was going down while his prices were going up.

I told James we were on the wait list for Spiritual Warrior. He asked us if we were signed up for Quantum Leap, the event just after Spiritual Warrior. Yes, we were. When we left, he said he would see us next at Spiritual Warrior. I didn't catch it until we had left the stage. Spiritual Warrior was before Quantum Leap. We were enrolled in Quantum Leap but behind a sizable wait list for Spiritual Warrior. He must have misspoke.

After getting home, we called the office to see how far down the Spiritual Warrior wait list we stood. There was a delay, and then the woman said she had to check on something. After quite a wait, she told us we weren't on the wait list—we had two confirmed spots! I was confused, but glad we would not have to wait another full year. We were going to complete all of James' events in just over one year!

CHAPTER 6

I Am NOT My Hair!

Spiritual Warrior • September 2007

*Enlightenment may be our birthright, but spiritual transformation
James Ray style was downright expensive!*

—Connie Joy

It was a long ride from San Diego to Sedona, AZ. We drove down
the dirt Forest Service Road 89B for about two miles before the main
gate of Angel Valley, the facility for the week's seminar—Spiritual Warrior 2007. Richard and I were already tired from the hectic pace of
taking care of our clients before we left, then undertaking the 7+
hour drive was exhausting.

It's not good to start off a James Ray event while tired, since he
likes to schedule participants from early in the morning until very
late at night. Once, while on stage, he said the Spiritual Warrior event
was the one in which you got the least amount of sleep. I took this
warning seriously since no one got much sleep at any of his events, a
fact he barely acknowledges. So to have him actually comment on the
lack of down time meant this was going to be extreme.

Extreme is a good word to describe James and his events. He
often spoke of being a Scorpio and how Scorpios like to do everything in extremes. I am one as well and understand the mind-set. We
can't imagine doing anything halfway. If you are going to bother to
do something, do it well, do it totally, commit fully, and get results as
fast as possible.

There were, however, several main differences between James and
me. A couple are easier to see than others, beginning with James'

challenges in the area of finance and relationships. But there is another critical difference, one that would become clear before the end of 2009.

Why would I say this self-proclaimed millionaire has an issue with money? For starters, he often talked about his own finances. He regularly told us stories about how he lost it all several times and got it all back each time. It was also clear from his steep and steadily climbing prices he charged for his events. Prices rose even more when he received the notoriety of appearing in *The Secret,* and on *Oprah* and *Larry King Live.* Then in his blog on April 19, 2007, entitled "It Is A Sin To Be Poor," he wrote:

> Quite frankly, I've never had a money goal for the entirety of my life until just recently . . . and yet I've become a multi-millionaire. Why? My entire focus has been to learn, grow, love and give more value to myself and others.
>
> . . . and money has come as a byproduct of this focus.
>
> "Why do you have one now?" you may ask. Only because I believe that in our society, like Warren Buffett states, "Money is just a convenient way of keeping score." I use the money my company generates as a feedback mechanism to how much value we're providing to the world.

Making more money had become one of his official, on-the-record goals. I agree there is nothing wrong with accruing money as a by-product of the value you give to others. The key word here is *by-product.* A Spiritual Leader's moral compass must always be checked. Is your motivation really coming from the heart? At what point is your activity financially benefiting you more than it is helping others? When is enough money more than enough?

At his Spiritual Warrior event, James stated he wanted to be the first billionaire in the Spiritual Teaching arena. His statement floored both Richard and me: *That is his goal?* Again, how much money is enough? James often told us about a study of people who were worth over $30 million, and how the vast majority reported feeling financially insecure. That leads to a rather simple question most people who get by just fine on less than $30 million might ask: *What does it take to feel financially secure?* Will $50 million do it? The answer is no amount of money will make you feel secure if you are an insecure person. No amount of money will guarantee your happiness if you don't feel happy and wealthy.

From our beginnings with James, he discussed all pillars of your life need to be working well together for true wealth and abundance. So why is he now proclaiming one of his new goals to be a billionaire? Why is he shooting off into the wild blue financial extreme? What changed inside him to make it necessary to have a billion dollars to be successful financially?

Only he can answer that. I know he would argue it means he is giving a billion dollars worth of value to the world. My retort is, as a Spiritual Teacher, he should deliver a billion dollars worth of value to the world—and the money will take care of itself. When someone complained about how expensive his seminars were, James liked to ask "compared to what?" If he teaches you how to live a wealthy life, how can you compare that to a dollar amount? What was peace of mind worth?

Well, attaining peace of mind through James' services cost a lot! For some of his packages it was comparable to the price of a new car or a year's worth of house payments. Joining the WWS costs the same as a new BMW M3! Enlightenment may be our birthright, but spiritual transformation James Ray style was downright expensive!

When it came to relationships, James' challenges were revealed by his own words and actions. He would often say he never remarried because people were not meant to be together "forever." While I will agree people can grow apart, they can also grow together, whether they are married or not. Whenever he talked about this, I felt he had plain old commitment issues and he was trying to make his situation sound noble. He considered having children as the parents' vain attempt at immortality; hardly the type of statement you'd expect from a spiritual warrior. Both statements did not ring true to me. You have the right to choose whatever lifestyle you want, and I know first-hand it is better to be alone than in a relationship where everyone is miserable. I personally have flourished in the 27-year marriage with my husband, and one of the most wonderful experiences in my life was the addition of my daughter, Erica. I think commitment, compromise, and vulnerability bother James.

His actions spoke louder than his words when it came to relationships. Richard and I are both real estate brokers. We could not survive long if we did't enjoy being around people, and we can usually get along with just about anyone. We invite complete strangers into our car and spend the day with them as they sift through the stressful procedure of making one of the biggest financial decisions of their lives. If they are selling their home, they likely have an emotional attachment to it. Mix in a divorce, the loss of their job and/or dream home, and possible loss of easy access to their children, and they can get overwhelmed emotionally.

That's where we come in. At one moment, we have to literally blend into the background during an emotional confrontation between soon-to-be separated spouses. Simultaneously, we have to be present and hold space as the trusted advisors on which they can count to have their backs, no matter what happens during the transaction. In the end, 95% of them become a part of our ever-growing family.

Even without a divorce, buying or selling a home can be stressful. We sold one couple's country home so they could move closer to downtown San Diego. We found out later the husband did not agree with the choice of location his wife had picked out, but went along with it since she wanted it so much. Just three months later, we received a call: the couple couldn't stand it and wanted to sell the home and move again. Later, during a conversation on the costs involved, they ramped up to a lively discussion as to whose fault it was they were in this situation in the first place. The wife yelled she was sorry; she made a mistake, but couldn't live with the mistake anymore. To which the husband replied he made a big mistake 35 years ago [when they got married] and he still had to live with it, so she could put up with her mistake a little longer. I flashed the universal sign for "call me;" and Richard and I made a hasty retreat out the front door. We see clients at their best in situations both good and bad. We also see them at their worst. We love and support them always the best that we can.

The reason I mention this is, even though we get along with most people, I originally held the distinct feeling James did not like us. Being older can have its advantages. One of them is we know who we are, and we also know you cannot and should not try to please everyone. We were not enamored by James' persona or fame. We were not among his groupies, so his lack of friendliness did not cause us to lose sleep at night. It did make us wonder what we did to apparently piss him off. We interacted well with several people who were more famous. I like solving puzzles so I continued to try and figure it out.

It did not take long for me to see what was going on. Since we have known him, James has not mixed easily or naturally with most people. Even those who "Dream Teamed" as volunteers rarely had direct contact with him. Those who knew James for a long time said he hadn't always been that way. The James who emerged after his appearance in *The Secret* was quickly growing distant. You could see many members of his staff were afraid of approaching him. The exception was Megan, his Chief of Operations, and her husband, Josh, who interacted with him better than most. What we were seeing and feeling was not he didn't like us, but he didn't like being around people.

The other part of James' relationship issue was clearly his love life. I don't envy anyone who does not have a life partner with whom to share his or her life. If you choose to go it alone, that is your option. I have found one of my biggest strengths is having Richard as my partner in life, parenthood, and our business. I often make excuses for those who may not be making the wisest choices while they are alone and searching for someone to share their life and dreams. It can be a very lonely path. It was pointed out to me that James would scan the audience during an event to decide the person with whom he was going to have dinner that night.

I would be the first to acknowledge that temptation was constantly thrown in his face. On stage he appeared confident and in control of the room. He presented material designed to facilitate spiritual transformation. He was a media star featured in a best-selling book! He sat on Oprah's couch, and rarely missed an opportunity to mention he was a multi-millionaire. These qualities attract single women, especially those 35 and older who have suffered through less than outstanding relationships. During breaks, it was not uncommon for me to have to work for sink space in the ladies room because women were sprucing themselves up. Some were pulling down their blouses to show their cleavage, prepping for the moment they would stand in line to ask James a question. These women would shamelessly flirt when they got their shot to talk with him. For the most part, especially early on, James seemed to ignore their advances—to his credit. Over time, that was no longer the case.

One of the assignments for a Dream Team volunteer was to serve as James' point person. Essentially, the job entailed getting James whatever he requested; in some locations, it might mean escorting him to and from his room, or even to and from the airport. One woman who held the job complained to another volunteer that James would keep calling her up on breaks and point out a woman in the audience. It became her job to go and ask the "lucky" woman if she would join him for dinner.

During one seminar, I noticed a woman sobbing in the back of the room. Nothing James had covered could have elicited such an intense emotional reaction. I feared she had received terrible news. She was alone, and it seemed odd none of the Dream Team members were trying to console her. I started to head her way when I saw Edward, who had volunteered to work the event. I motioned to him as to whether or not she needed help. He waved me off with an odd look on his face.

At the break, I asked Edward what was wrong with her. He told me she believed she had a dinner date with James that evening, only to learn he had cancelled in favor of dining with someone else. I gave Edward the "you've got to be kidding look."

"Exactly," he replied.

As mentioned, I often made the excuse that James was lonely and traveling most of the time so it was hard for him to meet women. But there's an all-important flip side: he wanted the role of Spiritual Teacher. He *chose* the role and as such had a unique influence over his audience. With the role comes an even greater responsibility for one's actions. If you are going to call yourself a master, you had best hold yourself accountable to a higher standard of behavior. What made this increasingly more difficult to overlook was his lack of discretion. Maybe he thought he was keeping it under wraps, but a woman sobbing in the back of a ballroom during a seminar is hard not to notice.

Another point person's experience demonstrated how James distanced himself. She was given the assignment to ride to the airport with the hotel manager to pick up James. She was told under no circumstances was she to talk to James unless he specifically asked her a question. She sat in sad silence for the entire ride back as James engaged in a lively conversation with the hotel manager. This volunteer had not only taken his seminars, but now was donating her time and paying money to help him. She was not worth acknowledging—yet a stranger was OK to talk to. Which leads to my point: James is a human being with his own unique set of issues that are decidedly unmasterful—as the world would later learn.

Richard and I were in Sedona to work on our issues.

We pulled into the parking lot outside the large registration tent. Inside, we were greeted by a big hug from Sam, a Dream Team member from Scotland. We saw a few other members of the team we knew: Mike, a dentist; Joan, a lovely young woman; and Liz Neuman, whom I would befriend at this event—the same Liz Neuman who died in the Spiritual Warrior sweat lodge in 2009.

Even though we were standing in a desert, the sky turned dark with ominous black rainclouds. It was going to rain at any second. Volunteers told us to leave our luggage, carry what bags we could, and head for our accommodations. I learned quickly why the "accommodations" were giving people fits. Richard and I were not happy to find out I was assigned a cabin with two other women, and he was assigned to join two other men. Apparently all the couples were broken up and assigned roommates. I learned later to be grateful for the cabins and the assigned bathrooms in a separate building which we shared with our cabin mates.

When the rain came, it pounded the area with water. The cabin dwellers and the few really lucky women assigned to share a house stayed relatively dry. Some people were assigned to tents and tepees. The tent people had a particularly long walk to their communal bathrooms, and the rainstorm soaked their tents, beds, bags, and them. The tepees were not much better. The poles met in a large hole at the top that allowed smoke to escape from fires built inside. It was great for heat, but not for rain. Neither group ever fully dried out the entire week. (Note the cost of this event: close to $10,000 *plus* a $1,363 fee to the center *per person.*) I know everyone gets exactly what they need, even though it may not be what we want. So even though I was not happy about being away from Richard, I was grateful not to need the wet tent experience. I had already suffered through that many times in my life.

I grabbed as much of my gear as possible, including my computer laptop bag, and walked briskly to find my cabin. Big raindrops started to fall just as l located the building. The sky broke open, and the wind whipped into a frenzy when I cleared the door. I don't think I've ever seen that much water pour down so hard and so fast in my life!

Within a few minutes, a soaked man showed up with our bags in the back of his pick-up. Enduring, he still flashed us a big smile as he arrived at our door. He handed me my bag; water literally dripped out from the zipper. Everything inside was soaked. My funk level rose. I masked my disappointment to the delivery man. I was tired and just about everything I owned was wet.

Part of why I enjoyed taking these seminars with Richard was at the end of the day we could discuss what we had learned and what we could apply to both our individual lives and our life as a couple. Now he was bunked separately, and knowing him, didn't mind his stuff was wet. As it turned out, his bags arrived before it started to really pour, so his stuff was fine . . . which elevated my funk even higher! Anything that even remotely looked like camping made him . . . well, a happy camper. So in a way I should have been very grateful I was not with him, and especially grateful I was not with him in one of the tents. His cheerfulness would have really ticked me off!

I met my roommates—Sally, a lovely lady from San Francisco, and Elaine, a young woman from New York. While waiting for the rain to taper enough to head for the dining hall, I tried to turn on my computer. It started to boot when suddenly, the blue screen of death flashed, followed by the black screen of despair. My computer was dead, just like that. No warning! *I'm going to be away for almost a week from work, and I have no internet access and no email.*

Did I mention my funk rising?

Finally the rain started to relent. We made a dash in the direction pointed out by the guy who delivered our bags and managed to find the dining hall. Following the directions on the sign taped to the door, we removed our hiking shoes and stepped inside. We sat at one of the tables and acquainted ourselves with the other people as they slowly filtered in.

After a few minutes, James, his assistant, and Megan showed up. He informed us the food would be ultra healthy and all vegan, at which point I pointed out the stack of what looked like chocolate pudding cups at the end of the buffet table. "Well, at least we still have chocolate." James frowned. I'm still not sure if it was because there was chocolate, or because I had spoken to him directly. He can be difficult to read. He told Megan to escort everyone out of the building until he was "ready." She asked us to leave even though we were only a few feet away from him. Why didn't *he* ask us to go? He is strange in that sense. It appears his motto is, "Never do yourself what you can get someone else to do for you."

Heading outside was not pleasant. Our muddy hiking boots were stacked by the door; there was no easy place at which to sit down and put them back on. Many of us stuffed our feet in them the best we could. It started raining again, so we huddled against the wall to try and stay under the eaves for protection. As the water ran off the roof, it splattered in puddles on the ground, and then splashed up on our legs.

My funk level continued to rise.

Eventually, the king summoned his serfs. We sat at the tables and awaited further directions. I immediately noticed the chocolate pudding was gone, replaced by apple slices. I thought about the chocolate . . . so close, yet so far away. James reiterated we would be eating a healthy vegan diet. The absence of protein, he said, would cause us to be less grounded, satisfying one of his stated purposes for the week—to become less grounded and move into a higher, more aware state of consciousness through yoga, meditation, and other activities.

James discussed an "opportunity." I already knew about this particular surprise. A week earlier, Richard and I, along with our friends Edward and Faith attended the grand opening reception for James Ray International's new office in Carlsbad, CA. James was there and I mentioned to him his haircut was unusually short. He told us he did it in preparation for Spiritual Warrior. The warriors of some traditions, he explained, buzzed their heads before going to war to remove all distractions and show their forthcoming actions were serious and demanded their full attention. He usually buzzed his head at the event along with the other participants, but the buzz job was always so choppy, he said, he decided to let his hair stylist do it instead.

Faith immediately picked up on his statement. "You don't mean the women buzz their heads too?"

"Yes, the women too."

"You mean that Connie will have to buzz her head?"

Looking seriously at me, he said, "Only if she intends to play full-on."

Faith kept saying he was kidding; he assured her he was not. She then asked me if I was going to do it. I responded truthfully: "I don't know." I never thought about doing anything like it before. Richard was quick to say he did not want me to cut my hair and together, over the next week, we came up with a good list of reasons why it was not a good idea. They included but were not limited to: it would be bad for business; I would not look like my photos on any of our stationery or advertising (as if looked anything like my photo for the past several years, but it was still a reasonable objection); I would look like I was sick; I would look like I had cancer; I don't look good in short hair; Richard likes my hair longer and he did not want me to cut it; my head is bumpy and would not look OK in short hair; it would take years to grow back. On and on it went. Let's just say my list of reasons was satisfactorily long.

During the Carlsbad reception, I changed the subject by asking James about the photos around the office, taken in beautiful places throughout the world. Some were from Egypt; others were from Peru. I asked him if he had taken the photos himself. He said he did not. He brought up he had recently tried to organize a trip to Egypt but he could not get enough people interested to go. I told him Richard and I would definitely go if he put another trip together. Photos of Egypt and Peru adorned both of our vision boards; they always did. It was on our short list of what we wanted to do in this lifetime. James told us he was planning on starting a group of "movers and shakers" who would be going to places like those in the photos. I again told him we would go, to which he responded, "Maybe." Now I know he was contemplating the formation of the World Wealth Society (WWS), and his doubt likely had to do with whether or not we would be able to come up with enough money to join the group.

Back at Sedona, the moment of reckoning had arrived in Angel Valley. Mike, the dentist and "keeper of the shears," set up shop under an awning just outside the dinner hall. Men and women were invited to walk outside to get their hair buzzed off. After the event was over, on October 10, 2007, I described this in an email I wrote to friends and coworkers. (Throughout the rest of this chapter, I will include sections from that email that contained my thoughts and opinions on the different activities in which we participated during the week.) About this "opportunity," I wrote:

> On the first night, we were given the "opportunity" to buzz our heads. If you were hesitant about buzzing your hair you were to consider whether or not you believed that your identity had anything to do with your hair. We did a lot of writing that week where you filled in pages of—I am _____, and I am not _____. If you could not get to, I am not my hair, then you needed to lose that attachment or illusion, because we are really not our hair, or our bodies for that matter either. If you had any doubt then there was one way to get over your hair attachment and that is to do without it. To my surprise more women buzzed their hair then men did!! Men believe that they are their hair more that women . . . go figure?!? This went across gender lines,

race, age, and religious backgrounds. I learned that I am not
my hair.

Immediately, a woman jumped up and walked outside. I later
learned she and her husband, Albert, a psychiatrist, were return visitors to this event. She enjoyed the advantage of previous experience
to consider whether she was going to shear her locks. In a few minutes, she returned minus her hair. James led the group applause; he
congratulated her for "playing full-on."

Several others walked outside, including my husband. I expected
the men to go easily. After all, it would just be a closer cut than usual,
and hardly noticed when they returned home. In a couple of weeks,
they would be back to where they started, none the worse for wear. On
the other hand, women were buying into as many as several years of
waiting for their hair to grow back. In the end, more women than
men buzzed their heads.

Those of us who decided to keep our hair (for now) grabbed our
dinner from the buffet. As I ate, I was torn inside over my next step.
As a Scorpio, I never wanted to consider myself as doing anything less
than playing full-on. However, Richard, usually very agreeable to most
anything I choose to do, was adamant about me not cutting my hair.
Nor was I in a hurry to see my hair lying on the ground. I still weighed
well over 300 lbs. In my book that left me with exactly two appealing
attributes: my great hair, and my blue eyes. If I lost the hair, that eliminated half of my physically attractive qualities. Giving up my hair
meant giving up a lot . . . almost everything! I felt this was not going
to help my terrible self-image of my body at all.

I didn't want to buzz my head. At the same time, I didn't want to
miss out on the possible lessons learned from doing it. What I had yet
to realize was my lesson had already been in full swing for a week. I
had to decide if I thought I was my hair. Did I know the real me had
nothing to do with my physical body? I knew about the concept, but
did I *know* it down deep in my soul? There was no question I had my
doubts about believing I was not my hair. How this "opportunity" was
going to resolve itself for me was still in question.

Soon a woman walked back inside. The way she approached her
hair-cutting offered me an acceptable compromise. She just cut her
ponytail off. Her hair was short, but not buzzed. Not so bad. It would
certainly grow out quicker and not look so extreme in the meantime.
Even though Richard was still not happy with the compromise, I went

for it! One of the participants, a hairdresser, used her good scissors to clean up some of the spiky chopped hunks of hair stuck out from people's heads. After Mike cut off my ponytail, she walked over to me and offered to see what she could do with the remaining hair. The spot formerly occupied by my ponytail was really short, but the front hair remained long after I removed the hair tie. She worked until it seemed "presentable;" people commented it looked pretty good.

James strolled outside to watch the activity. After a few minutes, he stopped the hairdresser and told her she was turning my hair into a "fashion do." "That is not the intent," he said. He grabbed for her scissors, but she pulled them away in time. I bolted out of the chair, afraid he was going to use the scissors to cut off my longer pieces of hair. In hindsight, I realized he probably was only going to take the scissors away, but I was not willing to risk it. Deep down, I still held an attachment to what hair I had left—and the amputated ponytail did nothing to crack my belief that in some way I was my hair.

Later that night, I ran into the hairdresser again. I gratefully accepted her offer to finish "fixing" my hair. She was very good; when she finished, my hair didn't look half bad. At worst, I reasoned, people who knew me would just think I had gotten very adventurous and stylish with my hair.

I slept soundly that night, unusual for me in a new place. It usually took a few nights for me to reach the point of exhaustion where I could fall asleep.

Morning dawned quickly. It was chilly; most of my clothes were still wet. Even the "dry" ones remained damp. We were three women sharing the same small bathroom, and we had to act quickly at the same time every morning. Luckily, none of us considered wearing makeup, but Elaine New York, as she would later be known, spent some extra time grooming her long, dark hair. Obviously, she never considered buzzing her head. She certainly thought she was her hair and she was OK with that. My other roommate, Sally, never buzzed her head either; her hair was short to medium short in length. Between the two of us, we needed to move extra fast to make up for Elaine's coiffeur time.

We headed off to breakfast. After only two meals, I realized the food and I were not going to get along. Contrary to what you may think, overweight people do not eat everything with which they come in contact. In fact, we can be downright picky. For me, it has to taste good or I would rather skip it—and this "gourmet" vegan food didn't taste good. After awhile I figured out a particular spice they were using interacted poorly with my digestive system. If I could get to the buffet early enough to score a banana, then I'd consider that a good meal; well, good enough.

It turned out I wasn't alone in my "less than desirable" food rating. Even Richard, the least picky eater I know left food on his plate and hunted for alternatives. One morning, he proudly brought me what looked like a cold hardboiled egg. I was thrilled to have it—until I cracked it open and found it partly raw. Cold and partly raw . . . icky! There was usually some type of sliced fruit, but the mystery seasoning covered it too, so I took some pieces over to the sink and tried to wash them off. In the mornings, they would often serve peanut butter and toast. Problem was, if you didn't get there really early, it was all gone. After a while people would rate the quality of the food by the number of barely touched plates pushed to the middle of the table when they entered the dining hall. To be fair, one person found the food to be just fine. Al, a young college student, would snarf up his plate of food and often returned for seconds. We watched in awe as he ate heartily every meal. Then again, he was a young male college student, so I don't know if culinary refinement even registered with him.

After a fast breakfast, we hustled off to class. It was Sunday, our first official day. It kicked off with a lecture from James. Beforehand, he said Mike, the keeper of the shears, would be standing by all week. If we decided the time had come to release our hair and whatever it meant to us, Mike would be outside the door at our service. James' lecture moved into the topic of remorse, one of the worst feelings with which to live. Regret and remorse . . . things we should have done, should not have done, and things we could have done better. Many times in life we are given an opportunity and we waste it. Well, not really. Someone seizes every opportunity; it does not go to waste. If you don't take it, someone else will.

During the week James said we would receive many opportunities to challenge our belief systems and dig for black bags—those dark things we try to suppress but remain with us. James again gave the example they are just like a minimized program on a computer. A black bag may be reduced to a small icon on the bottom bar of our screen, but it is not gone.

Black bags include limiting beliefs we hold about ourselves, such as: I am not good enough; I am not smart enough; I am not fast enough; I don't deserve good things; I am selfish; and good things

just don't happen for me. Those are the more common self-sabo-
teurs. Likely, they were implanted by our parents, other family members, or teachers when we were still very young. Regardless, we are
left to deal with them. These beliefs hold us back from being all we
can and want to be. A traumatic event may cause a black bag to be
formed or enhanced.

Working on releasing them is like peeling an onion. We peel away
a layer, and there is still another deeper layer below it. We have to
keep peeling one layer at a time until we arrive at the core issue.

While James talked, I thought about my hair and opportunities
lost. *Regret.* I was attached to my hair. I did believe it was one of my
only two good features. If I lost that, then what would I have left? Who
would I be after it was gone? I would hit rock bottom physically. Then
I would experience another layer of regret, this time over not having
taken the opportunity to prove to myself I could let it go. I would survive; I was more than that! I was more than my appearance.

I picked up my notebook and quickly wrote a note to Richard. In
it, I stated I would not live with regret. I would not miss this opportunity. I respected his opinion, but this was about me and something
I had to do.

James then took a short break before delivering our main assignment for the week. Richard hurried out to find the nearest bathroom
before I had a chance to hand him the note. I picked up my pen and
wrote one more thing at the bottom: "I love you and I hope you won't
be mad, but I have to do this for myself." It struck me as I put the
note on his seat that I was usually not so forceful about insisting on
doing things for myself. This was new for me.

Concerned it would not be long before James started the class up
again, I hurried to find Mike and his shears. As soon as we made eye
contact, he asked, "Are you ready"? I nodded, and he led me behind
the building, where he had already set up a chair. A couple of quick
swipes across my scalp with the electric hair clippers and it was too late
to turn back. My hair dropped in hunks on my lap and onto the
ground. Mike found it somewhat troublesome to move the clippers
evenly through my hair because it was so fine. He made numerous
passes in an attempt to even it out.

After he finished, I saw myself for the first time in a mirror. I
chuckled; it was a good thing he makes a successful living as a dentist—because he really stank as a barber!

People stood around us, patiently waiting for their turn with the shear master. When we were about three-quarters of the way through my shearing, I spotted Richard coming quickly around the corner of the building. He had apparently just found my note, and figured out where we were. The look of shock on his face worried me. He later said it was more the initial shock of seeing me with most of my hair gone while big sections were still sticking out from my scalp in all directions. Not a good look for anyone, I'm sure. True to his nature, he quickly got over it. When I finally stood up, he kissed me and said, "It doesn't look bad at all." That amazed me. It would definitely take longer for me to get over the change than Richard. When I returned to the room, I noticed some of the women who buzzed their heads the night before now wore long beautiful earrings. With their hair gone, the earrings really stood out. *Note to self: as soon as I get home, I am going to go shopping for some big, long earrings.*

Looking back, I believe this experience was one of the most empowering I have ever undertaken. With what I considered to be one of my last good physical characteristics now gone, I needed to develop a completely different way of seeing myself. I was still there. After people got over the surprise, they still treated me the same as they did when I had my hair. The hair made no real difference in my life. I was not my hair. My husband and daughter did not love me any less. My friends did not love me any less. My co-workers did not treat me any differently, even though everyone was trying to figure out why I did it! What they really wanted to know was if they would ever have the nerve. They were all smiling at me, but at the same time, busily saying to themselves they *were* their hair. Many of them even told me they couldn't do that! But here is the amazing thing my decision and action did for me: If I could do without my hair, then I am not my hair. Then by extension, I was not my clothing, my makeup, and my nails (the fake nails came off right after I got back home). I was not my car, my job title, my home, my furniture, or the meals I cooked. A stain on my jacket, a run in my stockings, chipped nail polish, scuffed shoes, or a bad hair day was not me; therefore, it didn't really matter. I was not my friends, my wrinkles, or even my intellect. I AM more than that!

As my hair grew out, I was OK with coloring or not coloring it. I was OK with whatever length it was; I was in no hurry for it to grow out. In the interest of full disclosure, there was one period about four weeks into my hair's re-growth where the length was too long to stick straight out and too short to lay down next to my head. It literally shot in every possible direction, no matter what I did with it. Some women looked very stylish during this phase, but I looked like I had just crawled out of bed. Luckily, my hair was growing very fast, so this phase didn't last long. I didn't really mind . . . I was not my hair; it didn't matter what it was doing. The end result of this seized opportunity: I was truly set free! An entire set of limiting beliefs were shattered forever with the simple act of letting my hair go the way of Mike's erratic shears.

After the break, James led us into a one-hour group meditation using the Holosync Meditation CD from Centerpointe. He had recommended we use this technology to help train us to meditate better, so we were all expected to own a copy of this disc. He helped us find our way to the vendor by sending an email with the internet link to purchase it. I'm sure he received a cut. He did email promotion often for different products.

I like the Centerpointe meditation product and use it often. I have found whenever you meditate with a group, your experience intensifies. It is said the group adjusts to the frequency of the member with the most organized theta brain wave patterns. The entire group combines and amplifies each person's experience. This was the case when the group meditated to the Holosync CD. Even though I had used the CD for many weeks, I heard many more tones and experienced a deeper level of mediation when with the group. This was by far my favorite part of each day during the seminar.

In my email on October 10, 2007, I described this activity:

> Other activities included daily group yoga, and several hour-long group meditations a day. I give those a 10/10.

After the meditation, James told us our main assignment for the week: to write about every person who made an impact on our life. He wanted us to start with everyone with whom we ever had sexual contact. After we wrote about them, we were to move on to our parents, then siblings, children, other family members, teachers, friends, people who hurt us and people who helped us.

We started by writing everything we remembered: when we first met each person; what they looked like; where we were; what they said; how they acted; how we acted and what we said. Then came the most important questions to answer: What emotions did you feel around them? What physical sensations did we feel during our interactions with them?

When we came across a strong emotion such as anger or love, we would write on the side, "Anger is_____. Anger is not_____. For example, we might be experiencing love. We would then write, "Love is compassionate, love is not manipulative. Love is patient, love is not possessive." We kept going until we ran out of things to write on the subject.

Whenever we'd approach James or one of the volunteers for help, the answer was always the same: "Keep writing." I stuck with it, and the most amazing things popped up. I realized my conscious mind had been busily minimizing these things on my computer screen's lower activity bar. Things I unconsciously thought were too hurtful to deal with were coming up and reintroducing themselves to me.

One of the purposes of this exercise was to find the good in every interaction, regardless of how painful it was. For example, I had already done quite a bit of work with being sexually molested by my swim coach, and was able to quickly come to the good result from this horrible experience: I got away from him. Even when faced with someone who was many times bigger, many times stronger, and in a position of authority, I figured my way out of it. I outsmarted him. *Keep trying and don't give up.* I was a survivor. Even when the situation looked impossible and I felt like I was all alone, it would work out and I would survive! How many people go through their entire lives never knowing they can prevail no matter the circumstances in which they find themselves? By the time I was 10 years old, I did not only know about surviving; I knew I could survive anything if I kept my wits about me and didn't give up.

This writing exercise was to keep digging through the crap until you find the "pearl." It reminds me of the story about two young boys who, on Christmas Day, were led into a room. In the middle sat a huge pile of horse manure. One boy smelled the pile and retreated in revulsion. The other boy immediately jumped in and started digging around in it. The first boy asked, "What on earth are you doing?"

"With all this horse poop, there must be a pony in here somewhere!"

Our job is to dig through all of the crap until we find the pony. No matter how deep and how long we have to dig to find it.

Once we started writing, we would continue to write, most likely all night long. James told us not to move onto the next person or subject until we were finished with the person on which we were focusing. We were told the Dream Teamers would remain in the classroom, and at least one of them would be available all night long at the dining hall if we got stuck and needed help. We were welcome to write in the classroom, in our cabins, outside, or later in the dining hall. The expectation was clear: to stay up all or at least most of the night working on this assignment. We would continue writing on this for the rest of the week.

James said we would practice yoga in the morning. As with the Practical Mysticism seminar, it was important to stretch and relax the body to move and release the toxins that we were accumulating and dislodging while undertaking this intense emotional work. We were ordered to turn off our cell phones for the entire week. We had invested all of this time and money to be at the seminar, James said, and we were going to give it our 100% attention. We were put on our honor not to use our cell phones. Yikes! Richard and I had arranged to have one of our real estate team members cover for us while we were gone, but we still intended to check in every once in a while to make sure everything was OK. We had a teenage daughter staying with a neighbor, and intended see how she was doing as well.

With those instructions, we were dismissed.

As soon as we walked away from the classroom, Richard and I discussed the cell phone "situation." As it was, Verizon's ubiquitous pitchman, Mr. "Can you hear me now," had never been to Angel Valley, because he would have known our phones had absolutely no coverage here. Our last known connection came just before the main road. So, like two high school kids sneaking off school grounds, we covertly made our way to our car, jumped in and quickly headed out the gate and up the dirt road. Once at the top, we changed our voice mail to direct all calls to our covering team member, and then called her to let her know she was on her own. We also called our daughter, who was having so much fun with our neighbor she didn't care that we were going to be unavailable. We gave everyone the Angel Valley main number in case of emergency.

For the first time ever, The Joys of Real Estate signed off for five straight days!

It was scary, yet liberating not to be "on call" every second of the day. Would our world survive? We were about to find out!

Before heading back, we kidded about parking somewhere to make out. This would be our last "alone time" for the next five days, and we were feeling pretty naughty for leaving the facility and making our calls. That turned out to be the extent of our daring; we hurried back before we were missed.

With a quick kiss goodbye, we went our separate ways. For a good part of the week, we only saw each other at class or at some of the activities. We often did not even see each other or sit together at dinner. This brought up some interesting feelings for me. It was like we were dating again: together, and at the same time apart. We had been married almost 25 years, and had spent many years mostly apart due to Richard working in other countries. When that was not the case we were very much together. For the past several years, we had worked side-by-side.

This current living arrangement seemed very strange. I would often see Richard walking at a distance with his roommates, or arriving for dinner as I was leaving. A quick "Hi" to each other, and that was it. It didn't feel right. He didn't seem troubled by it at all. *Well, fine. See if I say Hi first to you next time!* I told you it felt like we were in high school, and apparently that feeling ran deep. "FINE" does stand for something else: Flipped out, Insecure, Neurotic, & Emotional. That summed me up nicely.

I wrote until about 3:30 a.m. when I decided it would be better to take a shower and free up some bathroom time for my other two roommates in the morning. In the shower, I discovered another big benefit of no hair. I could take a shower, dry my head with a hand towel, and go straight to bed for a couple of hours of sleep before breakfast. Had I still had my hair to take care of, it would have cut my sleep time in half.

On Monday morning, the lecture started early, right after yoga. It began with one guy receiving praise for staying up all night and writing by the dining hall. He was held up as the example of playing full-on. For those of us who had decided to go to bed, well, it was our loss of opportunity. James told us to continue writing, and then he started talking about what it meant to live an honorable life. He used the example of the Samurai of Japan and showed scenes from the movie *The Last Samurai*, starring Tom Cruise, to demonstrate his points. In summary, he said, it is better to die with honor than to live without it.

We were asked to examine where in our lives we had not lived with honor and been true to our word in every way. Was our word law? Did we keep our word to everyone but ourselves? Did we make resolutions, promises to ourselves that were quickly forgotten? What is it like to live in such a way that your word was truly your bond? Always! What would it be like to live in a world where everyone else's word was their bond, always?

In the meantime . . . keep writing.

CHAPTER 7

Be Careful About Volunteering

Spiritual Warrior • September 2007

*Change is the essence of life. Be willing to
surrender what you are for what you could become.*

—Unknown

That evening, James and his assistants told us to eat lightly because we were going to do a session of Holotropic Breathwork™. Yeah! My first and only other experience with Holotropic Breathwork™ had been a few months earlier at Practical Mysticism in Lake Tahoe; the process still fascinated me. I was looking forward to doing it again.

This is what I said about it in my email:

> We did one session of Holotropic Breathwork™, where you breathe very rhythmically and deeply which puts you into an "altered state" of awareness. Very much like lucid dreaming, where you are aware of what images come to you and can ask questions of your images for clarification. This process goes on for 2 hours and is physically exhausting. However, it is well worth the work in my opinion. This was my second experience with it and both were great . . . I would give this experience a 10/10 and would gladly do it again given the opportunity. Whatever your spiritual beliefs are this can help you to experience a direct connection between yourself and the universe, whatever your belief of God is.

This experience was even more amazing than my first. It was also very different. Because of the white color of the large tent in which we practiced yoga, the space did not seem as dark and ominous to me as it did in the large conference room in Tahoe. On the down side, they could not seem to make the music as loud as it was inside a solid building. For me, the overload and distraction that very loud tribal music presented to my conscious, ever-thinking mind made it easier and quicker to move into an altered state. Despite that, it still worked out very well for me.

I knew what I wanted from the session: to "meet" and communicate directly with my unconscious mind. If I could get a clearer, more direct flow of communication started, then I hoped to improve at seeing and interpreting the messages it fed me in the form of symbols, especially when I was dreaming.

I set my intention to meet my unconscious mind and started the pattern of heavy, hard breathing. Very quickly, a numb sensation moved up and down my arms and legs. It felt like they had fallen asleep. Even though my eyes would remain closed for the entire session, I could soon "see" around the room. Looking up, I saw a small black man wearing a long white mask that came to points well above his head, and around his chest area. Only two eyeholes were visible on the mask itself; I could not see his eyes. He seemed to be looking at me as I lay on the floor. He danced around a bit, and then resumed his observation of me. My first thought was this African native image appeared due to the tribal drumming and occasional yells being made by the music. I watched him dance around for a while, and then felt myself lift up and move freely from my body. I was able to travel to the top of the tent, then beyond it. In deep meditation and during Holotropic Breathwork™ sessions, it is common for me to move my consciousness through the levels of our atmosphere, then past the moon until I float between the planets—and that was happening again.

I was startled when I looked around and again I saw my tribal friend continuing to stare down at me—from deepest space. Down "there" on Earth it seemed natural to see him with tribal music and drumming, but he seemed out of place among the planets. It did not dawn on me that *I* was the one out of place among the planets.

Still . . . what was he doing here?

My next action made a huge impact on my future dreaming experiences. I turned, looked directly at him, and asked him who he was and what he wanted from me. Immediately, he responded he was my unconscious mind and he was present because I asked to meet him. That was all it took! I could simply ask for what I wanted to see, and it would show up!! And if I saw something that I did not understand, I only needed to ask what it was and it would tell me. How easy is that?

How often in your dreams are you chased by some unknown force, held down by something you can't see, or repeatedly visited by some person or thing and you can't figure out why? What are they, your unconscious mind, trying to tell you? To get the answer, you just have to stop running or struggling, and ask the being who they are and what they want. Since learning this, I have never suffered through a bad dream. When something scary shows up, I face it down and demand to know who or what it is. It tells me, it's not scary any more, and I don't have to experience the dream or another like it again; I got the message.

Excited I could summon up my unconscious mind, I asked to see my conscious mind. It manifested as a wiry, jerky dude, and my higher conscious mind appeared as a white glowing being, neither male nor female. We were so happy to be together that the four of us moved around in a joyous circle. I asked my unconscious mind what it needed from us; it asked that my conscious mind stop being in control all of the time and trying to block the communication funneling down directly from my higher conscious mind. It wanted me to pay more attention to the messages coming from my higher conscious mind in the form of gut feelings and intuition, and to clear my conscious mind out of the way during meditations so the messages could flow freely. My conscious mind agreed. With that, all three of "them" merged back into me.

Realizing all I had to do was ask to see or experience someone or something, I thought, *whom would I most want to meet*? The answer came out of me before my conscious mind had a chance to point out the audacity of my request. I wanted to meet and be close to God! With that thought, a large sweeping hook of blue white energy came about me and pulled me to God. I am in no way skillful enough with words to describe this experience, other than to say it bathed me in total and complete unconditional love.

I felt this same unconditional love once before, during a near death experience in 1988. An ectopic pregnancy burst my fallopian tube, and I nearly bled to death. Anyone who has experienced this knows the pain is excruciating. All I could think of as I drifted in and out of consciousness was, "I don't want to die!"

Then there was a delay. I had to wait on the operating table while they tried to find an anesthesiologist. I remember hearing one of the doctors yelling for them to find anyone. Next, someone bent over and, while gently stroking my cheek, told me, "Everything is going to be OK."

A sudden "pop" followed—then nothing. I felt no pain, no pressure, no restriction in my chest, no struggle to breathe . . . no breathing at all. Peace.

I saw myself lying on the table. The operation had started; blood flew everywhere. From my experience as a Medical Laboratory Technologist, I knew the condition of the woman below looked very bad. It did not concern me at all that the woman was me! It was OK. I had somewhere to go.

There was no effort involved with soaring up and out of the room. I found the tunnel, or it found me, and I knew where to go and how to get there. At the end of my pleasant trip, I was met by a woman I knew and was very happy to see. I was home! Quickly, we were joined by a male figure, a member of my council of elders. He was there for an important, "official" reason. I could tell there was a gathering to my right, behind the woman. Before I could go to them, I needed to make a decision. I was joined by a female entity I would later know as my daughter Erica. We already knew each other and were overjoyed to see each other again! I was again reminded by the male figure I had to make a decision, quickly. As in, *now!!*

I was at one of my exit points, one of five opportunities we are given to leave our current life "early," if we so choose. If I felt I had accomplished enough in my life, or felt it complete, I could stay. I instantly understood if I made the decision to stay, I could join the group forming over to the side for, essentially, my "welcome home" party. However, my staying would hugely complicate Erica's plans for her next life. I was preordained to be her mom, and if I stayed, she would have to find another mother. Her circumstances would not be as good as what we had laid out together before I came down into my current life. I would really mess up her plans if I stayed, but it was totally OK either way. I was surrounded by true and complete unconditional love. Whatever I decided to do, it would be perfect. I was loved. I loved them. Something around us loved us all.

Quickly, I looked at Erica and asked if she was going to be a boy or a girl. She smiled and responded, "A girl, of course." No actual words passed between us, but this flow of non-verbal conversation and knowledge entered our minds as complete thoughts. My next thought was life was hard, but I felt I had made an agreement to Erica and I was going to keep it. Within a split second, I was slammed back into my body—very rudely I might add. It felt like someone dropped a layer of lead over me. One second I was light and free, and the next I was heavily weighted down and in intense pain. I went from thinking I didn't want to die to thinking, *Crap, I am alive!*

Even after a second ectopic rupture later that same year left me without any fallopian tubes and essentially sterile, I knew Erica was coming, and she would be a girl. We elected to try In Vitro Fertilization, which was pretty new and not very reliable in the late 1980s—a real leap of faith. Within a couple of years of my first ectopic rupture, we welcomed Erica into this world. I'd painted her nursery pink months ahead of her arrival, much to her Dad's concern: "What if this is a boy?"

"He'll have to learn to like pink!" I replied.

I recognized the unconditional love of the Holotropic Breathwork™ session as this same feeling of complete peace and love. I allowed myself to immerse in it. I then asked if I could be with Mother God. Another light hook surrounded me and pulled me towards her. Again, I experienced more unconditional love and peace. I told her I often sensed her in the beauty of nature. She then told me, "my spot was her place." I had no idea what that meant, and I didn't care. This was overwhelmingly wonderful. I left her and was aware the music had stopped and my body was no longer breathing quickly. I sensed it had stopped breathing hard quite a while ago. Coming back into my body was smooth and easy. I rolled over and started to draw the images of my spiritual journey on my Mandala.

Often during the week, we were told to maintain silence to keep our attention inward and not allow ourselves to be distracted by idle chit-chat. It is usual with James to be in silence after Holotropic Breathwork™; this was no exception. We remained in silence through the rest of the night, and again the next day through breakfast, yoga, and then up until we met for class again on Tuesday. I welcomed the silence as a way to help me hold the joy within myself, as vividly as possible, for as long as possible. Before lying down to get some sleep, I scanned the brochures we had been given when we checked in. One showed a map of the vortexes and angel spots on the property. I studied the map for locations near our cabin, and also close to the classroom. I had already stumbled on several of them, and I really felt the energy coming from one of the vortexes just outside the classroom's front door. Richard was drawn to it as well. Whenever we got a chance, we would go and sit on the benches there while waiting for class to start. A second spot had different markings, which I took to mean it was an angel spot. These locations were believed to be good places to make contact with specific angels. Rose quartz stones surrounded the location that attracted me the most; for some reason, that quickly became my special place. Sitting there brought me peace. When not sitting with Richard in the vortex, I would always spend time outside of the classroom alone there. I was curious which angel was associated with the spot. Clearly, it brought me something I must have needed, since it was the one part of the property that constantly drew me.

Meanwhile, my roommate, Sally, was not feeling well the night before, but now it was official; she was very sick. We were supposed to maintain silence, so we signaled back and forth to figure out what we could do to help her. It came down to finding a garbage can for her to heave in, plus being present for her. Elaine of New York was MIA for most of that night. She had likely found a warmer spot to write. The cabin was cold and damp; many of our clothes were still wet. So much for my previous impression that the desert is always hot and dry. Sally had chills, a fever, and was wearing everything she brought to try to stay warm. After a while, she drifted off to a fitful sleep and I used my small flashlight to read the map that showed the angel and vortexes locations. Again, I was curious as to which angel was associated with "my spot." I worked my way through the list and locations until I finally found my special spot on the map, then I cross-referenced it with the list of Angels. I was shocked: my spot was not an angel's spot. My spot was Mother God's place!! During Holotropic Breathwork™, she had told me my spot was her place. I now understood what she meant.

In the pitch black night, I put on my jacket and shoes and made my way down the dirt roads and paths to *Our* place. Some people call her Mother God, Mother Mary, Mother Azna, Divine Mother, Pachamama, or Isis. A name is just a title we humans put to things. I often just call her Mom. Sitting there under the stars on the small bench, I cried happy tears, and I was very grateful for everyone and everything in my life. I thanked her and sat in peace, reminded that everything was perfectly as it should be and I was loved unconditionally.

Back at the cabin, Sally seemed to have grown sicker. When I returned an hour before dawn, she was still sleeping, but shaking with chills. I ran up to the bathrooms to take a quick shower; when I returned, she was sitting on her bed. She looked terrible. I know I was supposed to be in silence but I had to ask her if she was OK. She told me no, and we then discussed whether or not she should go to yoga. I did not want to leave her in the room alone. Elaine came and went quickly; she'd spent the night writing with a couple of other people, and rushed herself off to yoga. After a bit of discussion, using the fewest words possible, I encouraged Sally to join me for yoga. If nothing else, she could lay on her mat in *sivasana*, the corpse pose, so named because of the degree of stillness and relaxation you can attain.

We made our way to the yoga tent very slowly. Sally could barely stand up, and I was starting to contemplate if I would be able to carry her if necessary. No matter what, I did not want her to be alone. When I could finally see the tent, I noticed two of the Dream Team members, Sam and Joan, were talking outside. Sam came running when I called for help. After he reached her I hurried over to the tent for yoga. I received a quick lecture about breaking silence from a James Ray International employee at the tent door, and then joined the yoga class. When Sally returned to the meeting room later that day, she told me Sam took great care of her, which I figured he would because he is such a kind soul.

When the lecture started, James released us from silence and we broke up into small groups to share our experiences from the Holotropic Breathwork™ session. He said numerous people had been seen using their cell phones, and he was passing around a box for everyone to deposit their phones. They would be returned at the end of the seminar. Even though Richard and I had long since turned off and put away our phones in our suitcases, I sympathized for the parents now being forced to give up contact with their children, especially those with small children. I know since James did not have any children, he was not sensitive to this situation. At the same time, I do understand cell phones at retreats are distracting. Since our writing work was not pleasant, any of us could easily be tempted to use our phones as a convenient mechanism to keep from facing something we did not want to see about ourselves. I was surprised to see how many cell phones emerged from peoples' bags and pockets. Apparently, Richard and I, and others who put away their phones on day one, were in the minority.

James talked more about integrity and the life of a Samurai. He told us to keep writing between sessions. After lunch, we learned we would be participating in something referred to as the Samurai game. This was based upon a game played out during some corporate retreats, but our version would take place James Ray style. In other words, it would be the extreme or "X game" version. We were divided into two teams and told to choose a leader, our Daimyo. Each Daimyo chose a priest and several other people to play parts such as our team's Ninja. James would be "God" (who else?), and team members had to completely obey their Daimyo. Only the priest could talk to "God." Anyone who made eye contact with the other team's Ninja was dead. Later that day we would engage in combat with the other team by pairing off. It was up to the Daimyos to approve the pairs. Later over dinner we could strategize within our teams. Any disobedience of "God," the rules or your Daimyo meant immediate death.

Have you ever been told to be careful what you volunteer for? We have later warned friends to be careful about volunteering at Spiritual Warrior because of what was about to happen next. The group pointed out one person to be their Daimyo; it was up to them to volunteer to accept the position. They selected people for the other positions. The Daimyos and their priests then approached "God." "God" would bellow the question, "Do you accept the title of Daimyo for your team?" He did this to the other team's Daimyo first.

"Yes," the Daimyo replied.

"DIE!" "God" yelled while pointing to the floor. The Daimyo dropped to the ground immediately, without question.

We were all pretty shocked by the exchange. James then said, loudly, "No one but the priest can talk directly to 'God!'"

He then turned to our Daimyo, Albert who had attended Spiritual Warrior before, and asked him the same question. To our amazement Albert did exactly the same thing as the other Daimyo. Likewise, he was ordered by "God" to instantly die.

With both Daimyos now "dead," the teams met to choose new leaders. Needless to say, the next round of volunteers was not so quick to accept the position. We told them for gosh sakes, when "God" asks you if you accept the position of Daimyo tell your answer to the priest and have them tell it to "God" for you. No one but the priests can talk to "God!"

We repeated the previous steps. This time, both Daimyos told their priests to answer for them, and both teams managed to move past step one with their Daimyos remaining alive. We were then ordered by

"God" to go into silence until we were released by him to talk again. In the meantime, we kept writing in our journals until we later went to dinner and plotted our strategy. Those who were "dead" had to stay on the meeting room floor without moving, even during dinner time. If they moved, then another person from their team would be ordered to "die" as well. If you spoke for any reason, you were ordered back to the lecture room—where you were to "die" immediately.

Anyone who "died" early was dealing with a harsh aftermath. Lying flat on a floor without moving for hours is very painful. I later found out Albert suffered back spasms from lying on the floor after a few hours. I felt this level of punishment was unnecessary and just plain mean, but it was not my show or my rules. Within a couple of days, I found out, as bad as this was, it was not the worst thing on the agenda. At least this "game" didn't *really* put your life in danger.

The corporate version of this game contained major differences from the James Ray version. In it, the "dead" person sat in silence in a corner or another room. Any further movement would not "kill" a fellow teammate. I have been told there was also no "God" in the corporate version, either. It was up to the Daimyos to declare someone dead. We were playing James' more extreme version now.

At dinner, we quickly figured out we needed to communicate by writing on paper napkins and passing them around. The first question from our new Daimyo: whom should we target to "kill" first? I immediately wrote, "Angel Valley's cook," and passed the napkin around. Those who agreed either put a strike mark on the napkin or wrote "Yes" on it and passed it on. It was unanimous that the cook was the first to go! Unfortunately, the cook was not on the other team. Heck, I would've gotten rid of him first even if he were on our team! Either way, the cook was safe from being targeted.

We continued to suggest pairings. After dinner, we returned to the classroom. The room was now rearranged in two circles of chairs, one circle on each side. In the center of the room, two "dead" Daimyos lay on the floor parallel to the front of the room. A few additional people had joined them; we were not told about their infractions. Members of the Dream Team and the JRI staff were now dressed as angels of death, in black. James wore a white-robed "God" outfit. We reached our respective circle of chairs and sat down.

Our next exercise: to write our own eulogies. Shortly, many of us would enter battle. Many would die. If we were to die right now, what would be said about our lives? What did we stand for? What did we accomplish? This is a great exercise. If I like what the eulogy said, then great: I'm living my life with purpose and meaning. If not much can be said about me, then I need to decide if I am really living or just taking up space. During this exercise areas that need improvement might come up. Wouldn't it be nice to get a second chance to work on those areas that returned less than desirable results?

After we finished our eulogies, we returned to our main writing. I felt like I was at a dead end. I thought I had written everything possible, but the usual response from the support team was to keep writing, so I did. It felt more like just babbling now; I wasn't discovering anything more about my "black bags" or myself than I already knew. That morning, I overheard a support team member tell one person to write one more paragraph on each of the main people in their lives. So I tried that. When I got to Erica, I started to write about my concern over her unhealthy weight. That really scares me, and throughout her life I have been unable to successfully assist her with it. We took her to different counselors and diet centers, but nothing seemed to help. She used to be a very picky eater until she was about six. It took everything we had to get her to eat anything. Now, we had the opposite problem. I considered it partly my fault. I was her mother, and she watched my weight yo-yo up and down. On paper I admitted I was a terrible example for her. I drove towards something: at what exact point did her eating swing from very little to too much—and what did I do to cause that? Why did I let it go so far before we started to take more direct action? At first, I wrote, we were relieved to see her eat. It certainly made lunch and dinner time more enjoyable for everyone at the table. But then I could see it was going too far the other way, and I didn't react until her bad habits were well instilled. Why? I love her and only wanted the best for her. Why did I think this was going to be OK?

Then it hit me, literally squeezing the air out of my lungs. I let her gain weight for exactly the same reason—to protect her from experiencing childhood sexual abuse as I had! Being fat in this world is painful for a child, but sexual abuse is far worse. I let Erica put on the weight! Never in my conscious mind would I have made that choice, but unconsciously I was protecting my child in the only way I knew. I did not consciously know I was using food and fat for my own protection when Erica was a child. I never thought or made the connection I was setting her up as well. At that moment, I felt it was my fault entirely; I was the world's worst mother. I sobbed.

When I could see again through the tears, I started another round of writing with a series of sentences to complete: Love is_____. Love is not _____. Being a good Mother is_____. Being a good Mother is not_____. Trying my best is_____ . Trying my best is not _____. Eventually, I realized I did the best I knew at that time to keep her safe. I would have to forgive myself and move on, so . . . Forgiveness is _____. Forgiveness is not _____.

The pony in this pile is Erica who has grown to become a wonderful young woman. Since she chose me to be her mother in this life, then everything must be perfectly as it should be. She is more intelligent than I am, and will figure out her own food issues and correct them. *Please God, let that be quicker than the length of time it took me to do it!* There are far worst addictions in this life. Eventually, we will both get past this one.

God was I a mess! I had been crying on Richard's arm while he was trying to write and simultaneously console me by patting me on the back. I don't think he had ever seen me cry like that. At one point or another, most of the people attending the seminar experienced one or more of those personal realizations, so my sobbing looked pretty "normal.". When someone found one of their "black bags," we just passed the tissue box to them and kept writing.

We were about to take a break. James released us from silence. After the battle, he said, we would be going on a Vision Quest and needed to come back with just the few supplies allowed. There would be no food, water, or flashlights. We would be in the desert alone for two nights. We could and should journal, he said. Additional instructions were given on how to wrap chewing tobacco into small cloth pouches and tie them together on a long string. We were to move to a new location in our medicine wheel, a circle of rocks we would make as soon as we got to our assigned spot, and infuse each pouch with specific intentions and commitments we wanted to make. Once inside the wheel, you could not leave it for any reason until one of the Dream Team members came and released you from it.

We were to collect a stone and, with its permission, infuse it with the things we wanted to remove from our lives. To gain permission, we would pick up the stone and ask it if it was willing to be part of our quest. If the stone agreed, we would sense it; if not, we needed to carefully put it back where we found it and try another stone. That sounded easy enough.

Now, in case you were wondering, he really meant we could not leave the circle for *any* reason. On this one, the men had a definite advantage over the women! We carried a small amount of toilet paper and plastic bags with us. Nothing was to be left in the desert after we left. Even the rocks we used to outline our medicine wheel had to be returned to where we found them.

The vision quest represented a place where we go when we die. While there, we were to review our lives and plan what we would do differently should we get another chance at life. We would be led to our assigned places by the angels of death, and later welcomed to rejoin life by the Dream Teamers. While James continued talking, a man noticed a pair of eagles flying in a circle above our small lecture building. As we all looked out of the windows to see them, James commented this was a very good omen for us. Later, when I researched the animal totem energies represented by the eagle, I learned the eagle teaches us to soar to great heights, if we will find the courage to do so.

I returned to my cabin to gather up the few allowable supplies. On the way back to the yoga tent, I stopped to look for my stone. On the dirt road, I found a spot with a lot of small rocks from which to choose. One grabbed my attention. I picked it up, and asked aloud if it was willing to join me on my quest. I had expected little to no reply, so was very surprised to receive a definite feeling: "No!" Ok then! I gently put the stone back where I found it, and chose another. I repeated the process. To my shock, again I got a "No" response from the darned stone! I kept this up through a good fifteen stones. Admittedly, I was no longer placing them gently back down after the first few negative responses. I was pretty much tossing them back down in frustration.

Now I was feeling really silly, standing on a desert dirt road, talking to stones and asking for their permission to take them with me. I really needed rest! The frustrating thing was that I was clearly getting "No" for an answer, so I could not guess that it said "OK" if I received no answer at all. Just when I was reaching the point of seriously considering just taking one, I picked up a plain looking gray stone and asked the question yet again: "Are you willing to come with me on my quest?"

I got the impression of a definite "Yes" answer!

"Really, are you sure? You know that I am going to put my negative things into you."

Again I got the impression: "Yes!"

I put my little gray stone carefully into my jeans pocket and hurried off to the yoga tent.

Inside the tent, both teams grouped together at opposite sides. A "graveyard" had been set up at the back of the tent that the "dead" people were moved to. One by one, people came forward to challenge a person from the other side. After both Daimyos consented to the pairing, they moved to the middle and awaited "God" to tell them what their challenge would be. Meanwhile, a person from each team created "bombs" from aluminum foil mashed into balls. If they could throw bombs across the tent and hit the Daimyo of the other team, then the game was over and they won. You can also win the game if the other side runs out of warriors for the challenges. The loser of each of the challenges dies instantly and is carried to the graveyard. Challenges included: Who can stand on one foot the longest? Who can balance a book on their heads the longest? Or chant Om the longest? No one knew what the challenge would be until after you chose your counterpart in battle and moved to the center of the tent.

One pair at a time proceeded with the challenge. Very early into the battle, our Daimyo was unexpectedly hit by a "bomb" while distracted. "God" immediately ordered him to die; our team had to swear allegiance to the other Daimyo. Then for some infraction, which I never understood, we were all ordered to die. At that point, the angels of death came to line us up into groups and lead us out to the desert. Once we were dead, we returned to silence.

I had been assigned spot number two in my group, according to the #2 written on my hand by one of the angels. Each angel headed out in the night in different directions, followed by their line of "dead" people. We hiked for a while until we stopped and the angel pointed to the person with #1 on her hand and signaled for her to stay. Our angel then proceeded. After a while she stopped again and she signaled to me to stay. I watched the group head off. It only took a few steps in the darkness for them to leave my sight.

I fumbled around for rocks to make my medicine wheel circle. It took awhile and I could occasionally hear movement in the distance, which I took to be the sounds of other people foraging for their rocks. When my circle was complete, I entered it and placed the last rock behind me, figuratively sealing me in. I was exhausted and would have loved to sleep, but my back was nearly in spasm. I tried different yoga stretches to see if I could release the tension.

The day before we left for Sedona, I moved a large laser printer by myself and managed to throw out my lower back. For some reason, either Richard or I, or both of us, always managed to hurt ourselves or get sick just before attending one of these events. We kiddingly say we must be advanced souls, since the universe is always increasing our degree of difficulty for the seminar activities.

I heard rumors that something like a vision quest might be one of the activities. I looked forward to the time alone in nature to meditate and journal. My back was so messed up I could not sit on the ground at all. It had been torture to sit in a chair since we first arrived. Now the least painful position was standing. When I became too exhausted to stand, I laid on my side for a few minutes before I had to stand up again.

When the sun came up the following morning, I occasionally caught glimpses of the woman in position #1 through the trees. I could barely make out some movement and the color of her top. I could not see or hear anything from the man in position #3. It still was reassuring to know someone was out there. Later that day though I stopped seeing #1. Just before sunset, I felt she was no longer there. Previously, she sat to the left of me in class. Early in the seminar, we gathered in our small groups to discuss something, and she had been sitting on the floor. When we rose to return to our chairs she tried to raise herself up backwards directly onto her seat, her hand slipped and she fell and landed on the floor. She was no more than a foot away from me when it happened; it did not seem like a big deal, because she did not fall far. After she sprung back up and into her seat, she held her arm strangely. After a few minutes, she walked to the back of the room. I saw her talking with Sam while they examined her arm. Later that day, she returned with a cast on it. I wondered if the pain meds had worn off and if she decided to bail and return to the main buildings. Hopefully, she was OK.

There are some things you can't escape, even in the wilderness. While standing and trying to journal at the same time, I heard a very familiar truck sound in the distance. As it approached, I knew I'd heard that sound before. I did not know where I was in relation to a road, since we did not see one when we hiked into our places. After a few seconds, I spotted the rooftop of a brown UPS truck moving behind a section of trees about a half-mile away from me. It was reassuring to know civilization was not far away.

After awhile, Joan, our angel of death, arrived with a note pad and paper. Without making any eye contact, she marked down I was present and accounted for. She continued in the direction she'd followed with the rest of the group after leaving me behind. That was the only time during the quest I saw anyone from the support team.

Among the activities was to spot the creatures who visited us. I *was* constantly visited by mosquitoes; in the desert! These mean dudes bit me non-stop right through my jeans, day and night. The only thing I could do was cover up in my sleeping bag. During the heat of the day it was particularly uncomfortable; the last thing I wanted to wrap around me was a sleeping bag. But it was still better than being constantly bitten. My vision of angelic meditation and journaling in peace-filled nature was not working out the way I hoped. That night, again unable to lie down because of my back, I watched the full moon march slowly across the night sky. I kept hearing something large moving around on the hill above me, but I could not spot anything.

It was a long night, and I could not wait for daylight to signal the approaching end of my solitude. I took out my little gray stone, and holding it, imagined everything I perceived to be negative in my life flowing into it. When I was done, I put the stone into a backpack pocket, never to hold near me again.

Sometime after sunrise, Joan appeared and signaled it was OK for me to exit my wheel. After I got my big hug from her, she went off to release the next person. I placed my stones where I thought I originally found them. By the time I was finished, she had returned with a line of people behind her. I fell in behind the last person, and we hiked back to the main facility.

The entire time I was in the desert I was extremely thirsty. Once back, I filled my water bottle with fresh water but could do no more than make myself sip it. Apparently, my thirst reflex had stopped working correctly. I was exhausted from lack of sleep, my back was just shy of full spasm, and I was dehydrated. The good news was I was no longer hungry, but I was definitely not feeling well.

This is what I wrote to my friends about the Vision Quest:

Our week in Sedona (Sept 22-29). Its purpose was to be a spiritual quest facilitated by breaking down our barriers facilitated by putting us in extremely difficult physical and mental conditions. The physical challenges were the lack of sleep (for me at least, Richard has once again proven that he can sleep on a rock and did so instead of staying up and doing his written assignments).

Very controlled & limited diet—no protein—vegan at its worst to break your attachment to food as pleasure (here they succeeded completely with both of us; I actually welcomed the days without their food), and days without water in the desert . . . It is when you symbolically die and are in the "after life," contemplating your past life's ups and downs. At the end you come back to this life and get a second chance to improve it.

Activities included a Vision Quest (survival camping with the only equipment being a sleeping bag, compass, toilet paper, plastic bags, note book, pen, and the clothes on your back. No food or water.). This included Hiking at night to my assigned "spot" where I was to spend the next couple of days and nights alone. Building a "medicine wheel" in the dark. A Medicine Wheel is made up of a circle of rocks about 8 ft in diameter with larger rocks at the north, south, east & west poles. Yes, I did feel some wiggly things when I was picking up my rocks in the dark! Once you enter the wheel you or any part of you cannot leave it, don't matter what comes your way or for any reason. Indian tradition believes that larger animals respect your circle and not pass into it . . . I am glad that I did not have to test this theory. However, smaller animals, reptiles and insects found great pleasure in joining me in the circle! Once there you were to spend time at each compass point writing in our notebook as to what inspirations you received, and to have time to meet and converse with your animal totem guides. Mine turned out to be a dragonet fly, which means that I am about to reap the rewards of 2 years of hard transformational work. A lizard, which symbolizes strength in psychic and intuitive abilities, and that I should listen to my own intuition over anyone else's. When a lizard shows up it also means that we are about to break from the past and explore new areas and information. A spider, which reminds me to maintain my balance between my past and future, and use my creative abilities to their maximum. (This is the second time that I have been told to make sure that I use my creative abilities to their fullest or have to answer to the "elders" after I pass over as to why I wasted the ability). In case you are wondering where all of this came from it can be looked up in the book, Animal Speak by Ted Andrews. It lists many of the animal totems and what Native American Indians say about their purpose in our totems.

While I was typing the above paragraph, a very large red dragon fly (same description applies to both insects, the dragon fly and the dragonet fly, from a mystical point of view) banged into the screen on my window before sitting on a nearby leaf. It continued to watch me. You know that it is a visit from an animal in your totem when they approach you much closer than usual, do not seem frightened by you, and spend a considerable amount of time being with you. During the vision quest, my dragonet fly spent an entire day with me and then came back to me just before I was greeted by my guide to leave the circle. She sat on my hat, stayed there while I showed the other hikers, and rode on the hat on my head until we left the wilderness area.

Overall, I gave the vision quest a 9 out of 10. I did not mind the lack of food, but the lack of water concerned me as far as the health ramifications of dehydration. I would not want to go any longer without water. It also did not help that I had thrown out my back the day we left for Arizona. I know that it was "perfect," for what I needed to learn, but it made enjoying nature difficult. It was great, however, to spend that much uninterrupted time in nature alone. I also learned that there are mosquitoes in the desert, a lot of them, and they bite you all day and night.

CHAPTER 8

Meet James' Sweat Lodge

Spiritual Warrior • September 2007

At the time I gave it 0 out of 10.

—Connie Joy

I joined the group for breakfast in the dining hall. All I could find that I would eat was a piece of bread. The peanut butter was already gone. I really didn't care about the food anymore; what I really needed was water and sleep. Neither was going to happen since it was time to return to class. Once there, we were released from silence. We celebrated our return to the living and shared our vision quest experience with our small groups. After that, we were warned not to eat much of anything for lunch (again, no problem there) because that afternoon, we were going to have our final activity—a sweat lodge. Yeah! I had not been warm much since arriving in Sedona except for when I wrapped up in my sleeping bag to save myself from the mosquitoes. I love saunas and steam rooms. I sit in a 170-degree sauna for 20 minutes almost every day at my exercise club. I hoped the heat in the sweat lodge would help my back relax.

Our instructions from James were simple: drink water between now and then; avoid food; wear a bathing suit and/or old pair of shorts that we will not mind getting very dirty; and bring the tobacco pouches we made during the vision quest, along with our stone we infused with what we wanted to be rid of in our lives. When we entered the lodge, two rows would surround the inner pit; an outside row and, when that filled with people, an inside row. Super-heated rocks would be placed inside the pit. We were instructed that it would be dark and crowded, so don't try to get up during a round and watch out not to fall into the pit with the hot rocks. We were also told that we could only move clockwise inside the lodge, both when entering and leaving. James said it would be very hot in the lodge and we may be tempted to leave, but we were more than just our physical bodies. Resist the urge to leave. We were in there to detoxify through sweating. We might not think we could make it to the end, but we had to face our fears and overcome them.

I do not remember any discussion from James or his staff about leaving before the sweat lodge was over, and I am certain there was no discussion about returning for those who left early. I do remember being told by James that when the ceremony was over we were to exit moving only clockwise around the lodge. We were to keep writing in our notebooks until it was time for the sweat and then bring them with us.

When we arrived at the lodge, a raging fire burned next to it. A Native American Indian (so we were told) watched another man tend the fire. We made a circle around the fire and placed our stones into the flames so it could be purified of what we had put inside them and returned to Mother Earth. Next, we took our notebooks, and our writings we had worked on all week, and added them to the fire, releasing their contents from our lives.

We formed a line behind James. As the Native American drummed and chanted, we headed into the lodge.

We circled around clockwise. James stopped at the right side of the door, then told us to sit as close as possible to each other and to the tent wall, but not to put any weight on the tent itself. After the outside row filled up, the inside row formed with people packed tightly next to each other, their backs just in front of our knees, which we pulled up against us. No one could move. I knew I was going to have serious issues with my back. I kept shifting my legs around while trying not to bump anyone in front of me; it was pure agony. I started to hope this was going to be over quickly.

Several people who were there told me later, from start to finish, our group spent a total of three hours in the sweat lodge.

After everyone was in and seated, James called for the first batch of super-heated stones, which we called grandfathers. When asked by the men outside of the tent how many he wanted, I believe he asked for eight to ten stones. One at a time, they used a pitchfork to pass a stone to Joan, seated on the left side of the door. She took the stone in her pitchfork and placed it in the pit. Each time, we said, "Hail Grandfather," to acknowledge the stone had joined us. This continued until all of the requested stones glowed in the pit. Then Joan took a five-gallon white painter's bucket filled with water and poured it all onto the stones. As soon as she backed up to her spot and sat down the people outside dropped a cover over the doorway.

Round One began.

The lodge was pitch black. Scalding hot steam moved along my body and scorched my mouth and throat as I inhaled. This was far hotter than any sauna or steam room I'd ever entered. This was nuts! James led us in a chant. Frankly I was not interested in chanting since I wanted to minimize the amount of steam I inhaled. Later, other participants told me, according to their watches, each round lasted around 20 minutes.

About halfway through the first round, I started to grow dizzy. In the darkness, I had nothing I could focus on which worsened my dizziness. The week of limited sleep, little food, and insufficient water had caught up to me. The good news was it took my mind completely off my back.

When the first round was finally over and they opened the tent flap, I tried to focus on anything to stop the dizziness, but it was not working. I grew more nauseous by the second. Concerned I would get sick on the people packed tightly around me, I covered my mouth and got up and worked my way through the bodies to the door. Richard said something to me about it only being round one. It didn't matter: I was out of there!

Once outside, a Dream Team member, Liz Neuman, sprayed water on me with a hose and directed me to the water. As I drank, I started to feel better immediately. The nauseous feeling still came and went but I was not so dizzy. Liz suggested I try to throw up so I would feel better. I walked by a large woodpile and waited to see if I could vomit. I leaned over and waited. After a few minutes, I threw up a little bit of water. I did not have much in my stomach; other than the one piece of bread from that morning. I had not eaten in three days. I forced myself to drink more water.

The second round was well under way when Liz came over to check on me. She said something that surprised me—when I felt better, I could go back in. The thought of going back in never crossed my mind. Why would I want to? I told her something was wrong; it was way too hot in there. I explained I spend a lot of time, just about every day, in a very hot sauna, but that this was far hotter—and not safe. I told her she needed to let James know it was too hot. She replied James wanted it this hot to really challenge people, and that it was still safe. She reminded me that he conducted sweat lodges every year and no one got hurt.

Maybe it was just me. In my tired state, maybe I was more susceptible to the heat than usual. Maybe I was just getting sick.

After a couple of more rounds, the tent flap opened. A group of people rushed out. What I saw alarmed me. They were disoriented, throwing up, and after they were sprayed with water, a couple of people were shaking on the ground. It wasn't just me; *it was way too hot in there*! After a minute or two, more people staggered out in the same or worse condition. Because the two outside helpers were busy with the people who came out first, Liz asked me to hose down the second group of people. I used my thumb to create a better spray. Within a few minutes, my thumb was becoming numb from the cold temperature of the water coming out of the hose.

This too was wrong. You don't spray cold water on a burn or a heat stroke victim, because their blood veins and capillaries are super-dilated in an attempt to remove as much heat as possible from the body. Hitting them with cold water will cause their vascular system to quickly constrict, often enough to send someone into shock. I questioned Liz about the wisdom of hosing people down. She replied that they do the same thing every year; it was OK.

Well it was not OK with me. I put the hose down and grabbed towels for the people who were already wet and shaking. James saw me from his seated position by the open door and called for me by name to come back in. *No way! This is crazy!* I shook my head and continued to help the people now lying on the ground.

One of the women who emerged from the lodge said she had just undergone a cornea transplant and her eye was starting to weep. Did I think it was OK for her to stay out? I assured her her eyesight was more important than participating. Later I found out one of Richard's roommates had a pacemaker—and he was still in there!

I became really concerned for Richard. He is the type of person who will try to stick it out, no matter how he feels. I heard from inside the lodge right after I left that someone was down. It turned out to be him. He said he was OK; it was just his back giving him problems and he needed to lie down. I knew there was more to his need to lie down than a sore back.

I would have to go inside to check on him.

I re-entered. Richard was lying down on the far right of the lodge. He looked up. I asked him if he was OK. He nodded. While I moved clockwise around the stone pit in the center, they announced the door flap was going down. I didn't have enough time to circle my way to him. I had to take the first open spot, directly across from the entrance. Ladies on both sides of me were lying down, and told me to do the same because it would feel less hot than sitting up. It would also be easier on my back. I lay between them with my head pointing towards the outside wall. One of them told me to press my face as low as possible toward the bottom edge of the lodge. Outside air was seeping through; it helped me breathe more easily. I made it through the round fine.

When the flap opened again, quite a few people left. Sam was busy dragging out several who could not make it on their own. I looked over to Richard; there was nowhere for me to sit by him so I decided to stay put for now. Between each round, James continued to add many rocks. I had not been in a traditional sweat lodge, but experienced sweat lodge participants told me a sweat usually consists of four stones per round, with four rounds total. James was calling for eight to ten grandfathers per round. By now we were to at least round five with no sign of stopping. I noticed location in the lodge made a big difference in the heat and how much air you had to breathe. Next to the door, it was considerably cooler, and plenty of fresh air flowed through when the flap opened. That's where James sat. On the far side of the lodge where I sat it was much hotter, with little to no cool air.

Just before the flap came down again, Sam returned to his spot directly in front of me on the inner circle. James called for a volunteer to switch places with him, because he knew it was hotter on the inside circle, next to the pit that held the grandfathers. No one volunteered; no surprise. Then I forgot my own advice about not volunteering. Because I felt OK during the previous round, I offered to switch places with him.

As soon as I sat up, I knew I had made a mistake. My head started spinning again, but it was too late to renege on my offer, so I crawled on my hands and knees to the center ring and Sam lay down in my place. The bucket of water was poured over the rocks, and it splattered steaming hot water all over my legs. It took everything in me to make it through the round.

Finally over, I had to get out of there. I wobbled to my feet and grabbed the wooden sticks that held up the lodge to steady myself. I remember someone saying something about not touching the sticks because they could not support our weight. I would fall down if I didn't use them—and I was walking right at the edge of the open pit! Just as I reached the three-quarter point around the lodge, someone grabbed my leg and shorts. It was two different people; both trying to follow me out. Neither could stand without assistance, and I could not walk with someone holding onto my left leg. I grabbed an arm and tried to drag them behind me. Someone behind partially picked them up and between the two of us we got the people outside.

Once out, the spray from the water hose hit our group, but that was about all I could make out. I was dizzy, disoriented, and looking for a place to sit. People were lying in front of the door, and I did not want to step on any of them. I made a sharp right and headed for an open spot on the ground. I watched as more people came out behind us. Liquid ran from their noses; they were disoriented as well. One woman emerged, only to fall headfirst into the dirt just outside the lodge door. She scraped her face badly, and was bleeding in several spots.

James observed all of this from his spot by the door. I could not understand why he continued with the next round. When Liz walked past me, I again told her it was too hot and she needed to tell James. She pointed to James, while he was looking right at us, and said he knew what was happening and that it was OK. James called more people who were sitting outside the lodge to come back in. He asked one man in particular several times by name to return. The man just shook his head.

Another round came and went. Each time, he added numerous hot rocks to the pit and doused them with a full five-gallon bucket of water. Inside the lodge, people encouraged each other to stick it out. I had not heard my husband Richard's voice for quite a while; if he did not come out at the end of the next round, I'd have to return to check on him. The round ended, the flap opened, people came crawling out . . . but no Richard.

I took my towel, soaked it with cold water, threw it over my shoulders and headed back in. This time I would lie down next to him regardless of whether there was room. I found a vacant spot, and laid between him and a woman I did not know well. I gave them the ends of my soaked towel and told them to hold it against their faces. Richard told me to put my face down close to the bottom edge, where you could get some air. I hunkered down with him until this thing was over.

James called for ten more grandfathers. The guy on the other side of Richard was so out of it he was babbling to himself and making no sense at all. When each stone was brought in, and people greeted it with "Hail, Grandfather!" he was yelling, "F— you Grandfather!"

My sentiments exactly, there was nothing spiritual or sacred about this sweat; it was a matter of pure endurance and nothing else.

Again I was dizzy. The woman encouraged me to breathe slower and deeper, but nothing helped. We passed through another couple of rounds and then James decided to wrap it up—and not a minute too soon. He told us later he planned on at least another round, but became inspired during his last chant and it seemed like the best place to end it.

Finally, it was over. The flap was opened. We were instructed to remove our tobacco bags hung above our heads and take them out with us. People were so disoriented and confused that they hesitated to leave. A blond-headed woman I did not know walked into the lodge and loudly told us to get out. That snapped everyone into forward movement. Unfortunately, not everyone could move. Sam carried out a small Asian lady, Henrietta. She was conscious; she could still talk but had lost all ability to move on her own. Richard told me when he saw her she appeared to be convulsing violently. According to Sam, the Dream Teamer who took care of her, "While I have no medical qualifications, I would say she was suffering from hyperthermia."

James was first out of the lodge, followed by Megan and then his personal assistant. The rest of us followed. He was hosed off and then sat down on a chair. His assistant brought water and a towel, and he placed the towel over his shoulders. He did not seem concerned that many people were still on the ground and not doing very well. We all looked like hell. After a few minutes, he got up, stepped into his golf cart and took off, leaving the volunteers to deal with the aftermath. Henrietta was still in serious physical distress.

I returned to my cabin, showered, changed and walked to the dining hall, only to find out Henrietta had still not fully recovered. Sam worked for over an hour to cool her down in tepid water and get her back to a normal state.

When I saw Richard again, I told him this sweat lodge was dangerous. They were playing with a potentially life threatening condition—heat stroke—and you don't raise people's body temperature like that and not expect to have serious problems. It was a miracle no one suffered brain damage.

I knew about heat stroke; I dealt with it while working the emergency room as a Medical Laboratory Technologist. One particular example haunts me to this day. A man brought in his wife fairly often because she was constantly hurting herself by walking into things, burning her hand on a stove, or falling victim to any number of strange accidents. He was constantly reminding her of things like where her ID was so I knew she had some form of brain damage, but I did not know the full extent. One day, while I was drawing blood from her, she told me I was good; she didn't feel the needle at all. "Are you new here?" she asked. I told her I had taken her blood many times before. She insisted she had never seen me. I looked at her husband as he worked to calm her down. He explained to her she did know me and to stop fussing about it. She settled down after a few minutes and I sent her off to the bathroom for a urine sample.

While she was away, her husband told me her mother died a couple of years earlier. In the days between her death and the funeral, a terrible heat wave struck and his wife did not drink enough water. On the day of the funeral, she suffered severe heat stroke, and her high body temperature caused permanent brain damage. She was left with only very short-term memory. She didn't even remember her mother was dead.

At that moment, she walked around the corner; she'd heard the end of our discussion. She reacted with shock and sadness at the "news" of her mother's death. Heat stroke destroyed her life.

I thought of her and the still struggling Henrietta, and how I watched so many people suffering from obvious heat stroke with very little concern on the faces of the JRI Staffers.

As for James, he and his golf cart undoubtedly rode to a cool, comfortable place.

This is what I said about the sweat lodge in my email:

> The final activity was a Sweat Lodge. Again a Native American Indian tradition usually done before a vision quest, but we did it the same day we came back from the quest. The group enters a low hut and we sit facing the middle pit where the heated rocks are put. You are packed in very tight and it is difficult to move (again having a back in spasm made the sitting position almost

impossible). After the glowing hot rocks are put in the pit the opening to the lodge is covered and it is pitch black inside. Water is thrown on the rocks to make steam. Like a steam room (which I love to be in), but way more intense. Tradition calls for usually 4 rocks to be added at a time, and for four times total (one addressing each major compass point). Our guide used 10 rocks at a time and did the process 8 times! Way over the top!! Between not eating and little chance to rehydrate after the vision quest, this was not fun. It lasted about 3 hours straight and most people crawled out of the hut at the end. I did not find any spiritual connection here and just had a terrible time. **I would give this a 0/10 and I would not ever do a sweat lodge of this intensity again. I believe that it is dangerous** from a health point of view to be so dehydrated. I would consider doing the "easier" traditional sweat lodge of 4 rocks at a time for 4 times total.

Part of what I find interesting today is that I gave the sweat lodge experience a zero out of ten points. I usually give events and activities one or two points just for happening. I saw no purpose then, or any time since. I was so against James' sweat lodge I discouraged people from going to Spiritual Warrior. Eventually when someone told me they were going to attend, I broke the rule about not telling someone what we do at an event. I warned them it was too dangerous. I fully expected someone would suffer permanent brain damage from overheating.

I never anticipated James would literally bake people to death.

After dinner we met as a group one final time in the lecture room. We celebrated our completion of this grueling week, and many said their goodbyes. Some people needed to head to Phoenix for early morning flights. If breakfast was the same thing I had seen all week, I would skip it, so this would be the last time I would see many of the participants and get a chance to say goodbye.

When Liz and I hugged, she asked me if I was feeling better. "Yes, but I am worried about what happened."

I told her it was way too hot for way too long, and that I really needed to talk to someone who works for James about it. I asked for the senior JRI person; she told me it was Megan. "You need to know first that the sweat lodge is Megan's favorite activity," she said.

I was shocked. "You're kidding!"

Liz shook her head. I saw Megan only about 10 feet away from me, so I walked over to her. She gave me a hug and I asked her, "Is the sweat lodge really your favorite activity?"

With a big smile and nod, she said an emphatic, "Yes, I love it!"

"You don't think that it was too hot?"

"No, not at all." Megan replied shaking her head no.

With Megan's enthusiasm for the lodge, I knew she would never talk to James about reducing the intensity. Megan spun around to give her next hug to another attendee, and I sought out my backpack.

The next morning, I was awake and packing early. I placed everything on the cabin's deck, ready to be loaded in our car. All week, Richard and I had discussed taking most of the day to hike to the different vortex and angel spots, since we did not get a chance to see many of them during the event. I had my map out and our course plotted. Richard showed up shortly thereafter, but he came with the car. He backed up the car to the porch and started literally throwing everything into the back. I thought he wanted to get all of the gear in the car first before we walked around, but it turned out that he was anxious to leave as quickly as possible. He wanted "normal" food—eggs, pancakes, things like that. I thought, with the event over, and James not dictating our menu options, that the dining hall would return to serving some protein with breakfast. Besides, I really wanted to see what we had been too busy to check out during the week.

At that moment, two people walked down the road from the dining hall. They stopped to say goodbye. I asked if there was anything good for breakfast, and they shook their heads; it was the same stuff we ate all week. Hearing that, Richard told me to get into the car. He was out of here!

Off we went. He wanted to stop at the first restaurant or diner. Just before the intersection in Cottonwood, he spotted at a Denny's. I have never seen him pull a sharper U turn. When the waitress came over to our table, we never looked at the menu. He ordered several eggs and a big stack of pancakes. I ordered steak and eggs, protein with protein.

While waiting for the food, we talked about our experience. Richard said even though he stuck it out to the end, he gained nothing spiritually from the sweat lodge and would never do it again. He enjoyed the vision quest, and I became an even bigger fan of

Holotropic Breathwork™. Neither of us could figure out a reason to make the "dead" people in the Samurai game lay still on the cold hard floor for so long. That seemed just plain mean.

My parents live in the area, so we were accustomed to taking short cuts on back roads to move around the area quickly. This time, both of us were completely wiped out, so we stuck with the highways the entire way home. For the first time in his life, Mr. Speedy remained in the slow lane all the way back to San Diego. The protein from our breakfast restored some of our energy, but it still took several weeks to feel well and grounded again.

I learned many things that week, and I experienced some significant spiritual breakthroughs. I also learned I would not automatically do everything that James asked me to do. From that point on, I no longer held unconditional trust in his judgment of how far I should be pushed. Some of my trust in James had eroded forever.

CHAPTER 9

World Wealth Society Is Born

Quantum Leap • November 2007

Anyone who doesn't take truth seriously in small matters
cannot be trusted in large ones either.

—Albert Einstein

Our daughter Erica was using James' phrases against us. "So what did you do to attract that into your life?" popped up often. Be careful what you teach your teenagers! She liked the Harmonic Wealth Weekend she had just attended, and was also excited about future events.

Later she asked me if she could attend Spiritual Warrior. "No, it's too expensive," I said.

She asked if she could go if she paid with her own money. "No," I repeated. "You'll have to attend all of the other events first, because it's the hardest."

I was stalling. There was no way I was going to let her attend that seminar unless I accompanied her. I had to be sure she would not stay in the sweat lodge too long—and I wasn't planning on attending anytime soon. She did tell us something we found later to be true. Bodyguards now followed James everywhere and were stationed at both ends of the stage to prevent anyone from approaching him. I talked to Richard, wondering what it was all about. James had grown more distant and less approachable over the year. We couldn't imagine the addition of bodyguards would improve the situation. Were they really necessary? Soon enough, we saw for ourselves.

Richard and I drove to Las Vegas to attend Quantum Leap for

the first time. Many of the "old timers" said this was one of their favorite events, so I was excited, but not about returning to Las Vegas. Even before I understood I was sensitive to the energy places carry, the Las Vegas strip gave me the creeps. I picked up feelings of desperation, hopelessness and greed, imprinted by untold numbers of gamblers who had come there to make their fortune.

James owned a couple of homes there, so having a seminar in town was convenient for him, but I still had to wonder if there wasn't a better place to conduct an uplifting spiritual event.

To my delight it did not feel so bad this time. The bad vibes were still there, but not as overwhelming. Either I was getting better at shielding myself from them or the newer "family friendly" attitude was diluting the negative energy. Our hotel in Henderson was away from the strip, but I could still feel the negative undercurrent. Every morning I would leave the elevator and pass through the casino to get to the conference room. There were times when the same people sitting at the machines had been there since the night before. To avoid getting sucked into their sadness I would cheerfully say, "Good morning Mr. Desperation, sorry I can't stay. I'm off to an exciting meeting!"

James' movie theme for this event was *The Matrix*. He had written a treatise on the film, saying, " . . . this movie is laden with messages regarding the advancement of consciousness and the birthing of the great Initiate." In the treatise he again asks, *"Are you ready to die to the old self?"* His premise was, like the movie, we live in a world that is not showing us the truth or the total picture of who we are and what we are capable of. Once we decide to explore that and learn the "truth," there is no going back to our "old" limited way of thinking. During the event we had to choose which path we wanted to follow: continue on our current path, living the illusion of a limited existence; or find out the "truth" and all the challenges that come with that knowledge.

Part of the seminar was dedicated to some of the principles of Huna, an ancient Hawaiian spiritual tradition. James said he was a kahuna, and had studied in Hawaii. From my reading on the subject over the years, I know there are basically three types of kahunas: expert canoe makers; expert navigators; and expert healers. In all cases, they develop and earn their expert status by long study and apprenticeship under a more experienced kahuna. I was familiar with both Huna practices James discussed in this seminar. The first, *Ho'o-ponopono* (loose translation: to make right twice), is an ancient Hawaiian practice of reconciliation and forgiveness, a loving and effective tradition. In it, extended family members meet to "make right" broken family relationships. When there is a disturbance in a family or group they gather together, often with the assistance of a kahuna, and they talk it out until the problem is resolved. Hard feelings are not allowed to fester since in Huna teachings they will lead to disease if not handled and eliminated.

James was teaching a form of *Ho'oponopono* that uses a guided meditation to forgive those who have wronged us and ask forgiveness of anything we may have done that was not in everyone's highest good. At that point we cut the Aka cords, the treads of energy that connect us with them, and pull our energy from those cords back into ourselves. Believing those established connecting cords drain you of your life energy, we can stop the outward flow of this energy and keep it for ourselves. What James taught us was a private form of *Ho'oponopono* to do by ourselves while in meditation. I was familiar with it as more of a group activity.

The other Huna practice is *Hakalau*. Pick a spot on the wall to look at, preferably above eye level. As you stare at the spot let your mind relax and focus all your attention on the spot. Within a matter of moments, your vision begins to spread out, and you see more in your peripheral vision than in the central part. Remain in this state for as long as possible and notice how it feels. You may begin to feel an ecstatic state; it is said that it is impossible to feel anger while in it. When you get angry, your vision collapses to "tunnel vision," your focus to a single narrow viewpoint. You may no longer be capable of seeing the other person's point of view. If you practice *Hakalau*, your anger dissolves almost instantly, enabling you to tackle problems or disagreements much more calmly.

I have used this technique for years when I feel fearful or angry, and it does send away my "negative" emotions quickly. It is a great tool for anyone to use.

James' version is slightly different. We begin by looking up at a black round spot above the stage and allow our peripheral vision to expand. We lower our gaze, trying to maintain extended peripheral vision even as we move around during the day. Eventually, you will notice your peripheral vision is growing wider over time. Those who excel at this technique can eventually extend their peripheral vision to see and sense behind them, like having "eyes in the back of your head." It's quite an effective tool if you are a warrior and your enemy is trying to sneak up behind you.

Huna was not on my mind when I asked James a question during the "open frame" section of the seminar when participants are allowed to ask him something on any subject. I was still confused about his concept of living and spending from the outcome. If I don't have the money now to spend on things like I would in my more abundant future, how is it reasonable to spend money now like I would then? I had asked different versions of this question many times at different events, and apparently I was not alone in my confusion.

James asked me to give him an example of something useful to my work for which I was reluctant to spend money. I told him my current color printer was giving me fits, and I wanted to replace it, but our company's financial person said to keep using the printer until more money came into the business. (I'm not talking about a simple printer here. This is a fairly expensive business laser printer for our color flyers and booklets; the toner cartridges alone run more than a thousand dollars a month).

"Will the new printer mean we can make higher quality prints?" he asked.

"Yes."

"Can it bring you more business?"

No question about it. "Yes."

James said this example showed why we should buy the item now as a tool to generate more business/income, thus aiding us toward our goal of providing the absolute best quality service and products for our clients. I finally understand James' reasoning, even though I still held some reservations about his budget-be-damned approach.

James told me to go back and tell my financial person why it was important to buy the new printer now. "I don't have to do that, because the financial person is Richard and he's sitting right next to me," I said

With that, James started to bounce all over the stage, partly in jest, saying he couldn't believe after all the seminars Richard had attended, he would still be fighting me over a printer. He called for his secret weapon! One of his staff people ran behind the stage, only to emerge with the biggest water-soaking cannon I have ever seen. James pumped it up and told me to give the microphone to Richard. The rest of us tried to get as far as from Richard as possible. Richard held up the mic, hoping James would not soak him and risk soaking the mic as well. He soaked Richard! This was all done in good fun, so

Richard did not mind it. They were both laughing. Considering how James had been biting off heads lately when someone asked a question, I think we got off pretty easy.

The example I shared with James resulted in me being known as the "printer lady." I was merely trying to pin down how this process should work. I just couldn't wrap my head around how you should be out there "spending money you didn't have, on things you don't need, to impress people you don't know." That's how Brian Buffini, our real estate mentor, would have put it.

So James wanted us to spend on items that were going to improve our futures or help us attain our goals. For example, you might buy a new suit for a job interview, a far different experience than buying expensive clothing just because we liked it. Of course he always counted spending on his seminars as a good example of preparing for a better future. Buying his expensive seminars now, even if it meant maxing out our credit cards, meant we were giving ourselves the necessary tools to succeed. I think James partly believed it but I can't help thinking spending without restraint to attend his seminars was very self-serving.

The big challenge activity for this event turned out to be breaking an arrow. The metal tip of an archery arrow was placed against your throat, in the same place where the end of the rebar had been placed during Practical Mysticism, and the other end was held high above your head by a Dream Teamer. We had to push into the arrow until it shattered. Another "DO NOT TRY THIS AT HOME!" activity. When it was my turn, I felt a moment of fear, but it proved anticlimactic, especially compared to bending the rebar. James used to insist we take the events in a particular order, something that is very familiar to people who have practiced Eastern disciplines and martial arts, but we didn't. Normally, the arrow break would have come before rebar bending. It was designed as a warm-up.

James' policy changed when his popularity soared. He now allowed people to take the seminars in any order they could schedule, which resulted in getting them to events quicker, while the going was hot (more money to James quicker). Consequently, the arrow break offered little challenge to those of us who had already taken Practical Mysticism. However, as nonchalant as some of us were about the arrow break, it still carried risk. One man was injured by the shattering wooden part of the arrow. It pierced his eyelid. I was grateful it wasn't his eye.

But there was a flip side: some people were taking Spiritual Warrior, the one with the sweat lodge, as their first event. I found it hard to believe these people ever took another seminar with him again after being indoctrinated through Spiritual Warrior!

Money was firmly on James' mind. In Las Vegas he announced the formation of the World Wealth Society (WWS) which he described as a group of like-minded people who would come together and be actively involved in projects to significantly improve and impact the planet. He talked about a couple of things that really interested us. First, there would be a WWS philanthropic project to support a more conscious and spiritual long-term approach to solving a world problem. Second, we would travel as a group to see ancient historical locations from a spiritual perspective. Due to his personal inside connections at many of these locations, James added, we would get to experience these sites in a way unavailable to the general public. How do we have these experiences? You get them through James by signing up for a membership in the WWS. He said not everyone was going to be able to join the WWS because the membership fee necessary to support the project and events would be steep.

Richard and I looked at each other. We had to be willing to play and pay at a very high level to be part of this group. To keep the membership exclusive, he was limiting the group to no more than 60 people. Interested parties needed to get to the back table and sign up quickly. Members would attend all future events without paying event fees, with the exception of Spiritual Warrior. We could also send our family members to the events free. At that time James included parents, brothers and sisters in this group.

At the break, we went straight to the back table to check it out. We definitely were interested in the travel portion, as we told James during his Grand Opening Celebration. We were already sending our daughter Erica to some of the events, and if her remaining events were included as part of our membership, so much the better. We also wanted to extend the opportunity for more family members to attend the seminars, such as Richard's three sons from a previous marriage and their families. We weren't sure if any of our brothers or Richard's sister would be interested, but it would be nice to offer anyway. We talked seriously about the importance of gratitude and giving back. We worked very hard for what we had, but we also felt very blessed. We had reached the point in our lives where we needed to give a bit extra to a cause in which we both believed. The WWS sounded like the vehicle where we might be able to accomplish all of these things at the same time.

I was concerned when I heard James say it would be pricey. All of his events were very pricey, with costs often comparable to or higher than week-long stays at the world's most exclusive resorts, but you would never hear him admit that. Since he came right out and said membership would be expensive, I thought the number could be truly scary.

It was! An individual membership was $60,000, and a couple/team membership was $75,000! I know we were thinking about giving until it hurts, but this would be very painful!

At the back table, we were told for this first year only, the money we had already paid for his events, other than Spiritual Warrior, would be credited to our membership fee since these events were now included in the overall package. This helped quite a bit on the total price, since we had already made a hefty "investment" in his seminars over the previous year. We felt giving to the WWS project would be hard, but worth it—especially since we could also send our family members to the events. We hurried to make our decision and sign up because we did not want to miss the chance of getting in before it had reached its maximum membership number of 60 people.

Later at the seminar we were announced as two of the six inaugural members of the WWS.

Over time we discovered several promises would not be honored. First, we were not able to enroll our siblings, just our children. After awhile, James even attempted to put a cap on their ages to further pare back the seminar "comp list." Another lie: The maximum membership number. Later, he would claim he said his *goal* was to have 60 members in the first year, but we and others clearly heard him say otherwise: there would be a *maximum* of 60 members. If there were no limit on the membership number, we would not have been in any hurry to enroll.

This reminded me of the time back in his intro event when he claimed to have only 20 spots left open for the next Harmonic Wealth Weekend in San Diego. That night, many times that number of people enrolled. At the time I was amused by his "hurry or the opportunity will be gone" sales tactic to rush us into a purchase, but this time the lie did not entertain me.

It was just over a year later when I learned the biggest misrepresentation he made about the WWS. I was stunned.

At the end of the seminar we could still get a photo with James but his assistants hustled people through the line. Due to the larger number of participants, I thought. James was reaching his peak of popularity, and riding high with the announcement of his new pet project, the WWS.

In January and August 2008, Richard and I volunteered to Dream Team James' Harmonic Wealth Weekends. During the year we would also Dream Team Practical Mysticism. In addition to wanting to be of service, we thought it would be interesting to see the events from behind the scenes. We also figured we would get more time interacting with James, only to find out that wasn't true.

One of my biggest surprises as a volunteer involved the board break exercise. I knew many women had the issue of "I'm not good enough", written on their boards. What I did not know was most men had it on their boards as well. Overall close to 95% of both the men and the women fought this same issue.

How is it our society manages to impart this message on almost all of its children? And why are we, as adults, unable to collectively shake this limiting belief off? The only difference I saw was men didn't want you to see what they had written on their boards; women didn't mind so much. It was part of the macho image to appear confident, while in reality, men felt as incompetent and vulnerable as the women. As I watched them go through the exercise to evaluate where they stood on their different life pillars, the men were developing a body image view as distorted as the women already possessed. Great looking, healthy and fit guys rated themselves low physically. Apparently, the commercial message of buying more to become more socially acceptable was working on the men, too.

Volunteering was hard work, but it was also rewarding, especially coaching people through the activities like the board break exercise. I loved watching the tiny older ladies come up and smash their boards to pieces with one whack. I also felt compassion for the big guys who would take a swing at their board and nothing would happen. It became clear to me there was no coincidence or luck involved. If you were not ready to break through the limiting belief you had written on your board, the board was not going to break no matter how strong you were or how many times you took a smack at it. The mind has much more unconscious control over the body than I ever thought possible.

One of the participants was undergoing chemotherapy for cancer. She was afraid to hit her board, because she was concerned her bones were brittle. I could tell she was going to have trouble before she even handed her board to the volunteer holder. Her body language spelled defeat. I asked her if she really was concerned about her bones; if so, she should not do this exercise. She nodded both "yes" and "no" to my question.

I asked her what really frightened her. After several minutes, she told me she had reached the point with her cancer when she had to fight for her life with everything she had. She couldn't afford to lose a single battle now, even the battle to break her board. She was afraid any additional failure would break her spirit; without that, she would have nothing left to fight with. She was afraid to even try, because her body had failed her so many times before and was failing her now. She felt it would just fail her again with the board. She sobbed; she was tired of fighting with her body; she was tired of fighting with everything.

We let her try a couple of times, because she wanted to, but she barely tapped the board each time. I could see she was pulling up at the last second, emotionally red-lining with the exercise. For those who could not break a board with their hands, we set up a place where they could attempt to break their boards with their feet by stomping on it. For some, it was less intimidating than using their hands. We would just say they liked the freedom to do things a bit differently than others, and that, as in life, it really doesn't matter how you get something done, it just matters that you do it, however creatively you choose. I told her this as I led her over to the other station.

"I cannot fail to break my board," she repeated.

"Then go ahead and put your foot down on the cancer and say, 'I'm not going to take it anymore!'"

With that, she straightened up, picked up her foot and smashed it through her board with great intention. Her friends were ecstatic; big hugs all around. Some people do stay in our memories forever.

It was fascinating to watch the money game as well. We could see the people who never moved out of their seats nervously looking around. Meanwhile, those who very quickly moved to freely exchanging money along the outside perimeter of the room looked like they didn't have a care in the world. Each time we watched, several people would come up to us and demand to know what they were supposed to be doing, and each time we would repeat the instruction they had been given. James was still saying from the stage, "exchange money." We needed to allow them to figure out what those words meant to them.

On the less positive side, we observed the volunteers were being taken advantage of. The hours we worked were ridiculous—from 5 a.m. until 2 or 3 the following *morning*. Even though you paid your own way, including travel, hotel and food expenses, took off from work and arranged for childcare, James and his staff were still very demanding and often didn't seem very appreciative. God help you if you took a phone call at any time during your volunteer weekend, because they felt they completely owned you every second you were there. Some of the staffers would micromanage the volunteers. I think it was because they were afraid of James. If something did not go exactly according to schedule they freaked. What a schedule it was. Events timed to the minute, every detail laid out, planned and practiced. Even a task as simple as turning down the lights required many practice runs, and a couple of people to join you for backup. I don't know why. Maybe because you might pass out at the light switch from lack of sleep. All the volunteers had syntaxes that scheduled out every action and part of the seminar in detail.

Another thing bugged me. Volunteers were not given enough time to go and get something to eat, because when the participants left the room, we usually had a task to finish before they got back. We could eat in whatever minutes or seconds remained. We had to scarf our food down during those quick breaks. It was a big deal because someone from our group had to take everyone's orders, collect the money, go and get it, and bring it back fast. Honestly, it was the biggest pain in the butt job there. With all of the money James made off of these seminars, and the expenses the volunteers had to cover just to be there, would it have killed him to provide the volunteers with some sandwiches during those quick meal breaks? I have run several charitable events and rule number one is you always take good care of your volunteers. James stunk at caring for his volunteers.

There was a single dinner during the event for which James would pay, and he would eat with us. Food was served in the seminar room and we would pull the tables together to make a big square. In every event at which we volunteered, James would sit at one of those tables and put someone from his staff or his brother on either side of him so he did not have to sit next to one of the volunteers. We all thought this strange. We had the feeling he did not want to be there with us at all. This was his sole opportunity to personally talk with volunteers who had paid considerable money for their own transportation, hotel and meals to be there—not to mention either lopping off a week of paid vacation time from work or losing a week's wages entirely—but he always seemed to keep his distance. He was an amazing charismatic force on stage, but when dealing one-on-one, he looked awkward and pained at best. What I discovered was the charismatic "Rock Star of Personal Transformation," as the media dubbed him, was either painfully shy or he simply did not like to be around people. It's odd someone who makes a living from teaching spiritual development would be so unsociable with volunteers.

Something else mystified me. It happened after we became members of his "inner circle," the World Wealth Society (WWS). Many of the other members approached either Richard or me with a concern they wanted us to take up with James. When I asked why they didn't ask themselves, they usually suggested we had a closer relationship with James than they did. I found this amazing, since James was often very distant from us. Apparently they felt he was even more distant with them.

Over the year, we discovered what several of the volunteers and attendees already knew. Not only did the volunteers pay for their own hotel rooms, but James' company was getting a kickback on each hotel room at the events. Not only were we working for free, but James was making money off what we were paying for our rooms!

James' staff did not stop taking liberal chunks of our time even after the seminars were over. Participants were broken up into Warrior Groups, and instructed to have weekly conference calls to do exercises handed out to them in a worksheet or packet. We were expected to keep track of as many as four or five of these groups at a time, listen in to some of their conference calls, and make sure they were still meeting. Each person had our contact information in case they had a question or problem. After the seminars, we were their only live support. These group meetings would go on for months. If you volunteered for several of the events, it was not uncommon to deal with overlapping groups. At one point, I was the soul support for eight Warrior Groups. Did I mention I have a full-time job and a family? In addition to the group calls, we had to attend a couple of calls each session between the volunteers and a staff person. All of this took up considerable hunks of time.

Why did we do it? Simple, we wanted to help others. We could see the attendees benefitting tremendously from both the event and their Warrior Support Groups. That is why we tolerated the treatment. The process wore out volunteers, but more people were waiting in the wings to take their places. After we were finished with supporting the Warrior Groups, a staff person decided if we had done a good enough job and give us some of James' "Manna" money which could be used as a credit towards a seminar. To get "paid" you had to buy more seminars. The amount of the Manna money was trivial compared to the cost of the events.

Please don't get me wrong. I loved the volunteers with whom I worked, and the people who I supported during and after the events. We volunteered because we wanted the best for all of them, even though we knew we were being used by a man making a lot of money from the events, *and from our hotel rooms!* Of the entire group, only James was in it to make money. We sought only a little respect and appreciation for our hard work. It didn't seem like the man was walking his talk. He wasn't showing gratitude, and he certainly wasn't coming from an attitude of abundance—both cornerstones of his teachings.

We watched James go through his material over and over again. The benefit was we were really getting to know it! But we also noticed James was orchestrating some of his emotions. For example, there was one part in his story about what it was like growing up as a nerd where he always cried. After seeing it a few times, we all noticed he cried at exactly the same spot, on cue each time. What any reasonable participant would see in a single viewing as real emotion now looked like an act; the realization was unsettling. Even now people still talk about James' ability to cry on cue.

It sparked a memory within me. At our first Harmonic Wealth Weekend, James mentioned to us he had taken lessons but decided not to pursue acting.

Maybe he did pursue it after all.

CHAPTER 10

Magick Isn't What It Used to Be

Modern Magick & World Wealth Congress • April 2008

Do or do not, there is no try.

—Yoda

I always love being in Hawaii. Maui is our favorite, but I am grateful to spend time on any of these magical islands. From the very first time we stepped foot on the islands in 1982, we knew we were home. There is a healing energy unlike any we have experienced elsewhere. This feeling of well-being could arise from being surrounded by the lush greens of the tropics. Maybe it's because I am a water sign. Between the Pacific Ocean, translucent waterfalls, and natural rain forests, I am always near water. As mentioned earlier, I am also drawn to the study of Huna, the mystical ancient Hawaiian practice of healing and spiritual development, and hope to investigate it more thoroughly someday.

We returned to Hawaii for the Modern Magick & World Wealth Congress, followed by a few days of plain fun with Edward and Faith in Maui. This was a fun seminar. The content changes every year, so there are no graduates who would be qualified to Dream Team it. It started later in the day than James' other events, giving you most of the morning to workout or chill out. The seminar was manned by just the James Ray International (JRI) employees, giving us volunteers the

chance to spend time with each other and play. This was also one of
the times I saw Liz Neuman when we were not working. Seeing her
there in Kona, so full of life and happy, will always be my fondest
memory of her. Most of our other friends were there as well. Stephen
Ray was there too. It really felt more like a family reunion than a seminar.

Some things about this Modern Magick were very different from
the previous event, but not in what I would consider an improved
way. After James' appearances on *Oprah!* and *Larry King Live,* he was
determined to mold himself into a more mainstream seminar leader
who could appeal to a wider audience. During previous years, Modern Magick was centered on mysticism. The seminar size was much
smaller and far more intimate. James' "insider group" was called the
Messengers of the Light (MOTL). A few months back, James
announced the formation of the World Wealth Society (WWS) and he
intended to replace the MOTL with it. The WWS was already turning
into more of a business networking group, with very high membership fees, and would appear to be much more mainstream than the
MOTL. James hoped it would attract more members and more
money for him.

The MOTL would follow ancient mystical ceremonies and practices, often while wearing ceremonial robes. Their main meeting
every year was at Modern Magick. While part of the title included the
word "Magick," there was nothing Satanic about the group. I have
never seen or heard of anything remotely Satanic around James and
the people who studied with him. Many of the ceremonies would
involve evoking archangels like Michael, Raphael, Gabriel, or Auriel
(or Uriel) for protection and guidance. The people in the MOTL
who I knew were members of many different traditional faiths who
studied and participated in some of the ancient rituals and ceremonies as well. I was not a member of the MOTL, but I know many
who were. They are some of the kindest people I have ever met.

The entire subject matter intrigued me, beginning with the word
"Magick." The "k" is used at the end of the word to differentiate it
from illusionary magic, which is more sleight of hand. Shake off the
Hollywood image. This is ceremonial Magick which involves ancient
spiritual rituals. One of the main areas involves the study of the Kabbalah, the mystical aspect of Judaism. Since Christianity sprang from
Judaism, it should not be surprising that many aspects of Christian
mysticism are similar to and/or have roots in Jewish mysticism. I am

a Gnostic Christian who enjoys studying ancient traditions and finding the deep similarities between many of the teachings and belief systems. The main themes for these ceremonies and rituals are love, light and healing.

But James suddenly had a problem with the MOTL. He wanted to appear more mainstream and felt the need to distance himself from the very group he'd created. He telephoned the group to disband it, and told them, among other reasons, "What would Oprah say if she saw us in our robes?" James was becoming all about appearances. One MOTL member told me he forbade any of them from using the name Messengers of the Light anymore; that's how badly he wanted them to go away.

I have a more cynical view of why he disbanded the MOTL and formed the WWS. He was concerned about his image, but he also saw the opportunity to bring in more money if his insider group followed a more business networking orientation. He would keep the study of Kabbalah and some of the ancient mystical teachings, but would nix the robes and much of the rituals and ceremonies. He orientated the yearly Modern Magick event so it would appeal to a wider audience, bring in a bigger crowd, and rake in more money. I believe James treated the members of the MOTL badly in the end. I don't blame some of them for ignoring his "command" to disband and abandon their group and name. Really, who did he think he was to proclaim the right to approve or disapprove their spiritual practices?

As James hoped, a larger audience turned out at Modern Magick. So large, in fact, some of the core activities, like Holotropic Breathwork™ sessions, were replaced by Trance Dancing, which could handle larger groups at one time. Talk about knocking it down a spiritual notch or two! In Trance Dancing, we put on a blindfold and moved and dance freely while listening to loud music. Part of the idea was to become attuned to surrounding vibrations, one of which was sound. I had become a fan of Holotropic Breathwork™. Trance Dancing did not impress me, at all. People started running around and often crashed into other people. I found I had to keep my arms around my face for protection, and I am tall. I could only imagine how hard the shorter people were getting hammered! I wound up with a swollen lip from someone's flaying arm, and never felt any type of trance-induced happy state. I would rate the experience a 1 out of 10. There was no question many of us greatly preferred a session of Holotropic Breathwork™, and we let the staffers know it.

On the final day, James spent some time talking about giving it our all, because we often only receive one chance in life; we have to seize the opportunity. Sounds like a build-up to the grand finale, doesn't it? After we returned from a break, we walked into the room to see a large pile of concrete slabs stacked on a wooden pallet. Next to it was a smaller stack of wooden boards, like the ones we broke in the Harmonic Wealth Weekend seminar. The pieces of concrete were 1½ inches thick, 5½ inches wide and about 12 inches long—and they were heavy! James told us to walk to the back of the room and decide between breaking either a wooden board, one or two together, or a concrete slab. We would be breaking them with our hands!

Since we were sitting in the front of the room, we were among the last to get to the back. By the time I arrived, all of the concrete slabs were gone. For the previous two weeks, I read a quote from a Greek general taped to the bottom of my computer screen: "It is more glorious to fail at a difficult task than to succeed at a trivial one." Looking at the pile of wooden boards that remained, I felt like I had just gotten the "trivial task." In reality that wasn't true, because I chose two boards, and there is nothing trivial about attempting to break through two wooden boards at one time. It's just that it felt like I would be taking one step up from Harmonic Wealth Weekend, but not making it all the way to the landing of the stairway where those attempting to break the concrete slabs would be operating. It felt like a repeat of a previous challenge instead of a new one. When we returned to our seats, everyone was checking out the weight of their slabs. I tossed the two boards under the seat in front of me. I was ticked off about the whole thing. When I looked up, I saw James looking right at me. I was sitting in the reserved WWS priority seats, so I know he had a clear view of my hissy fit. I could not read any reaction in him, though. James wore one of the best poker faces I have ever seen.

James said there were not enough slabs for everyone, so some would have to break boards instead. Several of us booed, which he acknowledged by saying he knew some of us might not be too happy about it. But for some holding concrete, he added, "I know you don't have it in you to break them." He said we would each have only ONE chance to break the slabs. This was different than breaking the boards, where we were given all the chances we needed. He added there were people who don't have the determination to go after it 100%—what it would take to break through the concrete. The slightest hesitation and we would fail, just like we do in life. Some of us don't give anything 100% so we fail over and over again.

This was different. James usually told us we could surmount the challenge, we were more than whatever lay before us. That it was all in our heads and we could do it. I never heard him say before that some of us couldn't succeed before we started.

We were given very little instruction as to how to hit the concrete with the side of our hand before James called up a guy from the audience to demonstrate. He enthusiastically ran up on stage with his slab and suspended it on top of two cinderblocks. After a few practice swings while loud music filled the room, he brought his hand down hard and smashed through the concrete. A big cheer rose from the audience. Everyone jumped up and proceeded to one of the stations set up at the back of the room. I walked to the sad little station in back, set up for breaking boards. Others were whacking away at theirs, but I was still in a funk. I just held back and watched for a while.

After a few minutes, I noticed the two guys manning the concrete station were taking unbroken slabs from unsuccessful attempts and asking people holding wooden boards if they wanted to break the slabs instead. I immediately moved in line behind a small group of people waiting for more slabs to become available. A couple of women ahead of me asked one of the guys, Scott, if he thought these "used" slabs held negative energy from the person who just missed, and therefore were not "good" anymore. I had Dream Teamed with Scott, who was getting impatient with the two women who could not make up their minds. I stepped in and told them it had nothing to do with the slab, the energy and power to break through was inside of *them*. They still were unsure. Scott looked at me, I put my hands up, and he passed me the slab over their heads.

I saw Edward, Faith and Richard near the front of the line. I signaled to Richard that I had a slab. He was surprised I managed to get one. Richard and Edward broke their slabs, but Faith did not succeed. The frequency of successful attempts was dropping off quickly. Now mostly the people who received "used" slabs took their turns. It seemed like even less of them were succeeding. Talk among the group now was maybe these re-used slabs were thicker or harder than the others, that is why the original person failed, and why the second person was failing too. Trying . . . I caught the word and it immediately transported my mind to another quote I keep on my computer screen. "Do or do not, there is no try." One of my favorites, from the

Star Wars Magick man himself, Yoda. I thought maybe the problem is they were trying and not doing. I started saying over and over to myself, "Do or do not, there is no try."

A woman set up for her attempt. She looked strong, very determined, like someone who could do it. Our side of the room had grown quiet, as person after person failed. We were not used to this. As a group, we were accustomed to succeeding; this was really messing with everyone's heads. The woman swung down her hand, hard. *Something's wrong.* From my angle, it looked like she either broke or severely dislocated the bones in her hand and/or wrist. If the room had been completely quiet, we would have heard the bones snap. She pulled back her arm and cradled it against her chest, then was directed towards the back table for help.

Several people exited the line in front of me; suddenly, I'd progressed from the very back of a long line to almost the front. A couple of other people tried it; a man succeeded, a woman failed. I reminded myself I would have only one try. Ooops, no try, do or do not, do or do not! My friend, Stephen Ray, now manned the station. He would later say to me that he could feel the energy on our side of the room dropping quickly because of the lack of success people, especially the women, were having with the slabs. Another woman missed, and then it was my turn. As I walked over to the spot where the two cinderblocks were lined up for me to put my block on, I noticed the growing pile of unbroken "used" slabs next to Stephen. A thought occurred to me: James was not concerned about running out of slabs because he knew that there would be more than enough "used" ones to go around.

I set my slab down and Stephen came over to watch. I asked him if he had any words of advice. He was into martial arts, so I figured he had experience with this. He shook his head and just told me to focus. A man behind me said, "Come on Connie, we need a win, you can do it!" *Focus,* I thought. I pictured the end point of my swing to strike below the slab, just above the floor, but not on the slab itself. *Do or do not, Do or do not.* I recited it over and over. Stephen said something to me, but I did not hear him. I took my practice swings . . . *do* . . . *do* . . . *do* . . .

I pulled my hand down with every bit of energy I had. I heard a sharp crunch. I didn't even feel the side of my hand contact the slab, but I was looking down at two pieces of concrete lying on the ground where my slab had just been suspended. *What was this . . . why . . . I did it!* The group around me cheered, and Stephen grabbed me in a big hug before I even had a chance to pick up my two pieces. Richard ran behind him and hugged the two of us. I think the two guys were more excited I had broken through the concrete slab than me, and I was pretty excited!

I picked up my two pieces of concrete and walked toward the back tables, where it appeared most of the people headed when they were done. Richard grabbed me and yelled, "Do you get it now? You can do anything you set your mind to do!" I really didn't know the answer to his question. I still had not absorbed what I had done. After a lifetime of feeling you are not good enough, is it possible to fully realize, at a single moment, you are powerful? Or does it require a succession of moments, where you break through boards or concrete or life challenges, before you finally break through the barrier around your heart?

At the back table, they were frantically handing out Ziploc bags with ice in them. One was handed to me, so I took it and headed through the crowded center aisle to my seat. About half way up the aisle, I looked up and saw James on stage, peering at me. He was trying to see what was in my hands. When we made eye contact, he gestured by tilting and moving his head up my way, asking how I did. I just smiled and held up the two pieces of concrete above my head. He returned my smile and nodded his acknowledgment.

After I got to my seat, I gave away the ice bag. I didn't need it. The ring finger on my right hand felt a bit strange, so I grabbed it with my left hand and gave it a good tug straight out. It felt much better. Richard and Edward were still icing their hands and complaining. I teased them about being wimps. For weeks thereafter, it would still hurt Richard to shake someone's hand.

Not all was lighthearted. It was clear from looking around the room many people were hurt. The final count ranged from 8 to 12 people with broken bones, plus one woman taken away by ambulance, and countless others with bruised hands and/or bones. Even the man who demonstrated how to break concrete was not immune. Edward told me he, too, had broken a bone. I asked Edward whatever happened to: "James is a business man. He wouldn't have us do anything that was really dangerous and let us get hurt because it would be bad for business?"

Edward shook his head. "I don't know."

Stephen also told me later why he didn't have words of advice when I asked him: because James' instructions on how to hit the concrete were different from what he knew to work best. He felt there was nothing he could tell me quickly that would have made a difference. The next day I saw Scott, the man who handed me my slab, and *his* arm was in a cast! Many people broke their hands or arms, but James said nothing about it during the remainder of the seminar.

At this point, trust in James started to erode among his general clientele.

Richard and I were grateful neither of us was seriously hurt. We took our pieces of concrete with us to Maui, and left half of each slab there in our storage cabinet and brought the other halves back to San Diego. It is our intention to reunite the pieces in our garden once we reach our goal and move to Maui permanently. Until then, a piece of us is always there.

A luau culminated the event. We could still approach James pretty easily, but there was usually a long line. When Richard and I got to within a couple of people of him after waiting for awhile, he saw us, pulled us out of line, and said we were WWS and didn't need to stand in line to see him. We were not very comfortable about "cutting" the line, so from then on; we still waited in the "regular" line when we wanted to have a photo taken with him.

A new event followed Modern Magick: the World Wealth Congress. It was a two-day seminar with guest speakers James described as the "best of the best" in each of the pillars of our lives. Later it would be called the WW Extravaganza when it followed Quantum Leap. Eventually it would become a stand-alone event called the WW Summit. The Congress would become a WWS members-only event, meeting once a year. Are you confused yet? Like a long rural road that changes its name several times as it winds through different towns, we were attending the same event. It just had different names.

Between Modern Magick and the World Wealth Congress, we had a day off. The majority of the WWS had decided to do some type of volunteer work for a local group. We ended up working for Habitat for Humanity in Kona, painting a church and adjacent buildings on the property. The congregation could not afford to get the work done, and they felt too old to do it for themselves. For some reason, several of the new WWS members decided they did not want to participate. Instead they explored the island. For those of us who did work, it was a lot of fun, a great bonding experience for our members, and something that benefitted the local community. It was a great idea by some of our members to organize it!

The World Wealth Congress was free that year to anyone who attended Modern Magick. We enjoyed some fantastic speakers. One of them became, and still is, our family doctor. He conveniently lives and practices in San Diego. Another speaker now handles some of our investment portfolio. This James Ray event, independent of its name changes, became one of our favorites. It was here James announced our first WWS excursion. To my great delight we were going to Egypt! I remembered being a bit surprised we were going to be paying for the trip ourselves after what we had just paid in membership fees, but I shrugged it off, thinking it would leave more money for the WWS humanitarian project, whatever it turned out to be.

Our "souvenir" of Modern Magick turned out to be a case containing copies of James's new book. It seemed very important to him to be on the *New York Times* bestseller list, so he pushed each of us to buy a case or two. As a joke from Edward and Faith, they gave me a gift beautifully wrapped in Christmas paper that year . . . his book! We all still had a few copies left over, and were trying to figure out creative ways to get rid of them.

CHAPTER 11

Guiding Others Through Their Empowering Week

Practical Mysticism • July 2008

I've learned that people will forget what you said, people will forget what you did, but people will never forget how you made them feel.

—Maya Angelou

Edward's car was totally packed; every possible space filled. Richard and I joined him as part of the Practical Mysticism Dream Team, and our daughter, Erica, was riding with us to attend for the first time. The event was five and a half days long and the volunteers had to arrive a couple of days ahead of time to set up the meeting room and activities. At least this time I didn't feel sick at altitude, although the asthma that resulted from the pneumonia never completely went away. At sea level it was rarely an issue, but at altitude, I did not know if I would be symptom-free. On top of the altitude, a terrible forest fire gripped the Lake Tahoe area and smoke almost obscured the entire lake. My improved asthma situation was compromised by my allergies, kicked up from the smoke. I was not alone. Many people suffered from watery eyes and congestion. On the drive from San Diego to Tahoe, we wondered if they would even let us build a fire this year with the extreme dryness and the fact they were currently battling a fire with all available resources.

When we arrived, we received our job assignments for the week. Apparently, the number of participants had doubled from the previous year, when we attended. To handle the increased volume, staff members divided the participants and volunteers into two equal groups—red and blue. Richard and I were put on different teams. Already, I had been around James' events long enough to know nothing is by accident. He thought we were together too much, and tried to separate us whenever possible. I don't think James understood we liked being together, though we were quite capable of being on our own. When Richard worked internationally he was gone for months at a time and we survived, but James didn't know that. I wondered if he viewed us as living contradictions to his notion that people were not meant to be together for too long. Maybe by splitting us up, he thought he was challenging us. He likely thought we relied on each other too much. Since he had only been married once, briefly, he might not understand how we could be best friends *and* married.

The question about fires was answered pretty quickly. On the night before the event started, we had a staff/Dream Team fire walk. We were testing the wood. The specific wood used in a fire walk was known for burning both long and evenly. If we managed to get through the walk with the skin on the bottoms of our feet still intact, then the participants should be fine. Customarily James led this walk to create special time with his volunteers before the event started, but mixing with the troops was no longer a priority for him. One of his staff members led us and did a great job. We were becoming used to seeing less and less of James.

While waiting for the fire to burn down, Richard and Edward leaned on the rakes we had just used to prepare the area for the event. It was dark, and the air cool and crisp. The only noise came from the cracking logs. I sat behind them on one of the large logs that ringed the fire circle, twisting some twine that had worked its way loose on the supply box. The guys were laughing about something, enjoying the fire and the beautiful sky.

Suddenly, my ears popped like I had just changed altitude. I looked over at the guys. I saw them still standing in front of a fire, but they leaned on swords, not rakes. The battle was just hours away; these two men, friends over many lifetimes, were now appearing to me as they existed in another incarnation. Sylvia Browne and others call this phenomenon a "bleed through" in time. It's more than just a surfacing memory; you actually feel the sensations of *being there*. I also perceived myself not twisting twine, but making a scraping motion, like sharpening a blade. Much heavier clothing hung on my body; the air was very cold. There was an odd, unfamiliar, pungent smell in the air.

A "bleed through" lasts only a few seconds. If one is not paying attention and aware of what is happening, it would be easy to dismiss it as a quick daydream, which it is not. They happen to everyone; we just don't pay enough attention or recognize what we are sensing. It is easier to spot it while it is happening, rather than catching it in hindsight. I knew from doing a past life regression that Edward, Richard and I have been in many battles together, so when I suddenly saw the flash of them leaning on swords, I made the connection it was a past life and not just the current fire reflecting strangely on their rakes.

What triggers a "bleed through"? From my experience, it is either a strong emotion in common with the past life experience, a very similar physical situation, or both working together. In this case, they were in front of a large fire, it was night, they leaned on the rakes like they once leaned on swords, and they stood on the same side of each other. I was almost exactly the same distance and position behind them, doing something with my hands, enjoying their shared laughter. Then and now, it felt good to me.

This was a short "bleed through." I experienced a longer one in 2003, during the Cedar Fire in San Diego. Californians are concerned about earthquakes, but fire is what terrifies me. I was so concerned I wondered if it was a premonition, so I asked Sylvia Browne if my home was ever going to burn down. She reassured me I was not experiencing a premonition, but a past life memory of my home being burnt three different times by the English as we fought them for the freedom of Scotland. In one fire, my spinning wheel burned, taking with it one of our main sources of income. Sylvia told me I didn't have to worry about my home burning now, since I'd experienced it three times before and didn't need to experience it again. I followed this reading with a past life regression, and explored that life in Scotland. Sure enough, I remembered our home burning several times— a few of many difficult struggles in that life.

It was during the time of the Cedar Fire. I sensed something was very wrong about 2:30 in the morning, and I called the fire department. They told me there was a fire to the east, but not to worry—it was a long way away, and they already had men on it. I went back to bed but I couldn't sleep. I started to pack boxes with important files and pull together our family photo albums and videos. Just before sunrise, I sent my husband and daughter to where we boarded our horse, which was east of us. I felt our horse might need to be evacuated. At sunrise, you could start to see the magnitude of the unfolding disaster. A miles-long strip of fire headed our way, whipped by very strong Santa Ana winds.

As it turned out, I didn't even have time to go upstairs and grab the boxes I had so carefully packed. Patrol cars drove up and down our street, ordering us to evacuate immediately over loudspeakers. I barely had time to put the cats and dogs into the car with a few clothes. Before leaving, I projected a white bubble of protection around our home to protect it and our neighborhood. I asked God to send as many angels as possible to protect everyone and everything surrounding me. I knew what Sylvia had told me, but when I pulled out of my driveway, a wall of flame towered in front of me. I fully expected our home to be gone within the next few minutes. It would not have been logical to think otherwise.

Chaos reigned on the streets with people and cars everywhere. Some were slowly moving while others had stopped to gawk at the rapidly approaching wall of fire. I looked over my shoulder towards our home and the fire.

My ears popped. Instead of driving, I was walking next to a horse and we were quickly moving up a hill. The animal was breathing hard; heat radiated from it, even though the temperature around us was cold. A torch was thrown on the roof of my home, setting it on fire. My husband, who was again Richard, and my sons were resisting the English; as punishment, the English burned our home. After receiving a warning, the men had just enough time to ride back to our farm, and get me, several other women and our daughters out. We were heading into the surrounding hills for safety. I heard Richard's voice tell me not to look, so I turned my head away from my blazing home. In addition to feeling and hearing the horse, I listened to its steps and the sound of the saddle moving against it. I could feel constant cold dampness, the way it usually was in Scotland, wicking up my legs. (Even now, I can be cold or wet, but if I get cold *and* wet, I will wait for you in the car because I want to go home.) Our situation was grave; the English knew about us. Anyone who took us in ran the risk of losing their homes, too. We had lost everything.

I experienced and felt the "bleed through" for about 6 steps up the hill. Suddenly, I was back driving my car through the chaos of a mass fire emergency evacuation. While I was "gone" who or what had been driving my car? What triggered the bleed through? The strong emotion of feeling helpless to prevent my home from being burned, having to leave, and looking over my right shoulder toward the fire . . . all experiences I suffered in a distant past. The intensity of the emotion caused it to last longer than normal. Surprisingly, it had a calming effect on me. I knew we would be cared for by friends who did not have to worry about the English. We have insurance now; many of our things could be replaced. My family was not locked in a war with an overpowering enemy; once we were reunited later that day, we would be safe. Our neighborhoods would rebuild and we would be together again. So the memory/experience, while painful, calmed and consoled me now. Unlike then our house, and those immediately around us, was spared and this time we could offer help and comfort to those who lost their homes.

That evening in Tahoe the fire burned enough of the wood to make a sufficient bed of coals for us to create a good, long path to walk. One by one, we set an intention and then walked towards it over the burning coals. After we were finished, the coals were still glowing, so we were invited to walk again if we wanted to select another intention. Once again, I didn't feel any heat beneath my feet, so I went again. I decided to give someone else a chance to set an intention, someone who would never have the chance to walk in the fire themselves. I would do the actual walking for them. So I focused on my parents, that they find happiness and contentment during this stage of their lives. The third time I walked, slowly and with great intention. Again, I did not feel any discomfort on my feet. It was almost too easy; we all thought there was nothing to it. It is when one develops such an arrogant attitude that the universe reminds you that you are still human. The following year, when Edward again Dream Teamed the event, he walked the fire and he blistered the bottom of his foot. He said he didn't mind it, since it was a good reminder to stay humble and in gratitude. When we start to take something for granted, we get sloppy. If fortunate, we will only receive a gentle reminder from the universe, a tap on the shoulder, to be more mindful.

It is always interesting to work at the registration table. Some people arrive happy and full of energy; some do not. Two people stood out for me. First was Laurie, who arrived with her husband although they didn't act much like they were together. They asked to be on different teams and barely made eye contact. Laurie looked angry. It appeared more than a bad travel day; she looked like she was going to explode at any moment. I later learned this was "normal" for her. She was barely able to tolerate everything going on around her. She held her body so rigidly when it came time in the seminar to "give three hugs," most people dared not approach her. Another husband wife team registered, Don and Lisa. Lisa was bubbly and clearly happy to be there; Don was clearly not. Don refused to smile, no matter what you said to him. I remember thinking it would be interesting to watch these people as the week progressed.

There is one sure thing about working these events as a volunteer: you will work long and hard, every day. During a break, I realized how tired I was already. We were just starting a long week, and I was going to have to suck it up and get peppy. What always amazed me was invariably a couple of people would pay for the seminar, take time off work, pay for their transportation, arrive, decide they didn't like their hotel or other accommodations, turn around, and go back home. We had to change rooms when we first arrived at the hotel in 2007 because we were assigned a room with two double beds instead of a king or queen. We worked it out, but others just threw up their hands and left. I understand being tired from a trip and in a funk, but to give up so easily made me wonder if they gave up so easily on everything else in their lives as well.

I was amazed at the size of the group—it almost doubled the previous year's turnout. Instead of breaking up this longer event into multiple sessions with a smaller number of participants, James maxed out the amount of people the resort and the meeting room could hold. I know this might make good business sense, but the ability to interact with James continued to go down as the number of participants in each seminar went up. Furthermore, this was a spiritual event, which usually works best in a more intimate setting. He now had two bodyguards, always stationed on each side of the stage, who followed him off stage wherever he went. Their job? To keep people away from him.

During a break in the seminar the next day, I went over to see some of my WWS friends. I had been too busy to talk to them during registration, and wanted to say hello and meet some of the new members. While there I talked to Erica briefly since we hadn't seen much of her. We usually left the room before she was awake and we would return after she was asleep. James was still on stage. I saw him look at me. He called over a staffer, Susan, who was in charge of volunteers. The way they glanced at me, I knew I was about to get "spoken to." As I suspected, Susan talked to me right afterwards about the importance of letting Erica have her own experience, and that I should not talk to her much during the week. She asked me not to be with Erica when she participated in the challenges so Erica would rely on herself. I understood where Susan was going with this, but Erica and I are close, and I felt like I was abandoning her.

Erica was not happy when I told her about the conversation and the new "rules." I acted like I supported James' idea but had reservations. I don't think James really understands the parent/ child relationship since he is not a parent. He especially doesn't know the mother/child relationship at all. I raised Erica to be very independent, which she is, but we are still close. Children need to feel their mom is there for them, especially when overwhelmed or afraid. Someone needs to model the kinder, gentler side of the world for kids. It's our job and privilege to be there for them when they need us. So even though I agreed she should have her own experience, I would have liked to at least see her accomplish some of the challenges. I wanted to be there to root her on. But the king had spoken, and I needed to obey. For all I knew he may be right, even though it didn't feel right to me.

Later, we trained for coaching rebar bending. In all previous years of this challenge, only one pair of people would attempt the rebar at a time. James would coach one person, while a Dream Teamer would coach the other. This year, because of the large number of people, four pairs would attempt the challenge at the same time—and the Dream Teamers were going to be the ones coaching people at all four stations. After a short discussion, several people still had questions. James became annoyed and told us to stop making the activity harder than it was. I wasn't the one asking the questions, but I am glad someone was pushing James to be clearer as to which part of the throat we should place the end of the rebar. There was a lot more to this than holding a board in the air for someone to take a whack at.

At the fire I watched participants' faces as James picked up the rebar and held it like a spear to some of their throats. I sympathized with them. Fear, shock, disbelief, and acceptance must have raced through their heads simultaneously. I remembered it well. After James was done we manned our stations and couples started to arrive. The first few were always the adventurous ones, vying to be first to try everything. They were easy to coach. After that the couples grew more and more restrained. I just kept talking to them; their worst enemies were their own minds. One woman just barely started when she pulled up, looked at me and said, "That hurts!"

"Of course it hurts, it's rebar! What did you expect?"

She thought about it for a few seconds, and then determination crossed her face. The next time she dug in her feet and pushed forward until the bar finally bent. We often would put a foot behind the participant's feet so they had something from which to push. Otherwise, their feet slipped on the dry dirt and gravel and they couldn't get the traction they needed to move forward.

James made the rounds between the groups to see how everyone was doing. I thought I had seen a couple of people sneak out of the circle. I wanted to give them the benefit of the doubt that maybe seeing this scared the pee out of them—and they were running to the bathroom. It turned out they were running off; James called them on it the next day in class.

A WWS husband and wife team and their two children, who I would guess were about 9 and 12, came up to my station. JRI had ordered arrows for them to break, like the ones we use in Quantum Leap, instead of bending the rebar since it would be less intimidating for them. Unfortunately, the arrows were the wrong type. They were spiked hunting arrows and not the common archery target arrows we use. Believe me, the rebar looked less intimidating. James spoke with the parents, and the decision was not to exclude them from participating, but we were to watch them closely to see how they handled it.

I sent Carol to fetch James. I was not comfortable being the person to decide just how hard to push these kids. Coaching or coaxing along an adult is one thing, but when you talk to a child, you are a person of authority and I think you must be very careful not to push them too hard. They must attempt the challenge for their own accomplishment, not because I told them to. It was OK with me if they decided not to try. After a few attempts, the young boy was having trouble, so he stopped. We cheered him for his effort, and I told him, "That was brave of you for just trying, because many adults wouldn't have the nerve to even try to do it."

We needed someone to fill in for the boy because the girl wanted to continue. Her Dad stepped up, even though he had already bent rebar with his wife. I coached the Dad, while James instructed the girl. I asked the man how he was holding up with doing this twice in one night. "Don't you worry about me," he said. "You just take care of my little girl."

"I promise you I will; she is going to be just fine," I said.

The girl was wise beyond her years, an old soul, like Erica. She just kept hanging in there and trying again and again. When the bar bent and they finally succeeded, it was great to see him more excited than when he bent it for the first time with his wife. He held her up in the air, a moment she would never forget. I coached a couple more people, then started to lose my voice towards the end. You had to yell loudly to be heard over the supportive cheers of the people around us.

When I looked up to see if there was anyone else, Erica stood at the end of my line. She wore a huge smile on her face and held up her bent piece of rebar for me to see! I ran up to her and gave her a huge hug. Dream Teamers at her station said she did not hesitate at all and bent it quickly. I wish I could have seen her do it.

Before the start of Practical Mysticism and during the first few days of the event we frequently walked the trail which led to the top of the hill, which the group would follow at night carrying their life maps. We practiced the hike at least twice every day. Our first walk was around 5:30 a.m., and then we hiked it again at 1 or 2 a.m., after the day's events were over. JRI staffers wanted us to know the trail by heart, because we would need to know it in the dark and not get lost even if it was raining. Each night, I only had a couple of hours to myself after the night hike and before starting on the trail again for the morning hike. There were nights where I changed my clothes and sat up in bed, meditating for an hour with my eyes closed to give them a break.

Ironically, I didn't have to know the trail at all; I found out I would not be walking it with the group. Instead my assignment was to be the lookout, to signal the Dream Teamers at the top of the hill when the group arrived at the base of it. They still wanted everyone to know the trail "just in case." The fire would already be blazing when everyone arrived, so I signaled them to assume silence like the rest of the group, and start the drumming. During practices, we substituted a sound for the signal light from my flashlight. I made a silly bird sound—"CAW! CAW! CAW!"—Here they come! We were definitely well practiced for the ceremony.

Before the participants were to do the night hike, Laurie came up to me, fighting tears. She'd lost her life map. I could tell she was used to making everything perfect, exact. This was a disaster for her. She looked and seemed defeated. I asked her if she remembered what was on her board. "Yes, I know exactly what was on my board."

I got her a piece of blank paper and a pencil and I told her to sketch it out. She only had time for a rough sketch before the hike started. "If you run out of time, draw a letter to represent a photo; that'll be good enough to represent your board." The ensuing rushed and "sloppy" map was not what she wanted to represent her life, but time was very limited and she would have to "settle" for what she could get done. She sat in front of the stage while James talked and feverishly sketched until it was time to go.

That night, James took off hiking at the head of the line, with Carol and Richard accompanying him. We knew how long it would take and left an extra margin for error as the rest of us stayed behind and prepared the room for Holotropic Breathwork™. Our Dream Team drummer, Gary, moved slowly and needed more time to get to the top of the hill. We left Edward behind to help with moving the big speakers in the meeting room.

We headed to the hill, leaving in plenty of time to be among the first to arrive. I stopped where the path bisects the road, and waited to give the signal when the group arrived. The JRI event organizer joined me to test how effectively the light from my flashlight shone on the trees above. We were concerned that with the light from the fire, my flashlight might not be bright enough for them to see easily. She gave me her cell number to call when James and the participant group arrived. First, though, we needed to test to see if we could get a strong enough cell signal.

I was to wait until she reached the top and then call her. She was about halfway up the hill when Megan ran by and asked if Edward had started the fire. I told her he hadn't arrived yet. Though it was early, she decided to run up the hill to put lighter fluid on the fire, so it would be ready to light when Edward, the fire master for the week, arrived. I can still see Gary with his drum, rounding the corner atop the hill when Edward passed by.

Edward was about halfway up the hill when James showed up. As always, his lead group turned the walk into a race; he was way ahead of schedule. I tried shining my flashlight on the trees, but they weren't looking for a signal yet. I tried to call the JRI event organizer, but she thought I was rushing the test; she didn't pick up the call. I redialed over and over. James saw the light from my phone in the dark and glared at me. He whispered to Richard to tell me to turn off my phone. I respectfully declined and kept hitting redial while waving my flashlight around like a wild woman. I kept trying to stall James, a man who doesn't like to be stalled.

Finally, James walked over to me, extremely annoyed. "What's up, aren't they ready yet?" he asked.

I shook my head while continuing to redial, still no answer. I saw Edward at the top of the hill, but he had not yet rounded the corner. Without Edward, there was no fire. We were supposed to be silent, but I'd run out of options. James looked like he was going to storm up the hill any second. All I could do was to yell as loud as I could: "CAW! CAW! CAW!"

James looked at me like I had lost my mind! The rest of the Dream Team got the message loud and clear. At the top of the hill, Edward heard my call and ran around the top corner of the hill and poured additional lighter fluid on the fire. Megan stood by the fire pit and asked him if he thought I really meant it because it was still early, to which Edward yelled, "Hell yes!!"

They proceeded to dump two cans of lighter fluid on the wood and light it without setting themselves on fire in the process. Edward found another can and kept squirting. Gary started drumming. A few minutes later, I saw the fire's glow starting to rise in the darkness.

James continued to glare at me while pacing back and forth. I finally signaled to him they were ready for him to lead the group to the top. He was not happy about the delay. At the top, he started growling at me again to move the people around the fire so they were aligned to his satisfaction. The directions he gave were contradictory and resulted in more growling on his part.

A long delay ensued, more than 20 minutes before additional participants showed up from the trail. The first group went too fast and lost them. James stomped over to Edward and told him to make the fire bigger. It was already a huge teepee shaped fire, but following James' orders, Edward put on more wood. A few minutes later, James walked over to Edward. "I said, make the fire bigger!"

Edward and Carol started piling even more logs on the fire. It was huge and sparks were flying everywhere—while forests surrounding Tahoe were burning from wildfires. I stamped out embers as they hit the ground and the brush behind us. Other Dream Teamers did the same. A hotel employee who helped our fire ceremonies ran down the hill to stamp out sparks that were burning down there. James glared at me to hold still; after all, it was a solemn, sacred fire ceremony. More sparks blew past us and flew down the hill. The hotel employee scampered up and down the hill, stomping them out. Suddenly, James' big fire collapsed into a pile of coals, diminishing the flame to about a tenth of its original size! James was pissed. The rest of us looked at each other: *Where can we hide?* More group members ascended the hill, while James snarled at me to get them around the circle fast.

He started his talk about not wanting to carry your life's story around with you, while the fire collapsed more. I stifled a giggle. Edward and Carol threw every available log on the fire, but it continued to shrink. James held his hands up and starting to talk again when I saw the indicator light on his microphone's battery pack blip out, killing his mic. His brother, the sound guy, checked it out. Realizing the battery was dead, he sprinted to the meeting room to get another one. James must have left the mic on while hiking the trail.

After five minutes, James' brother cleared the hill and dropped to his knees behind James to swap out the batteries. The man could barely breathe from the run and altitude. Within a few moments, the new battery kicked in, and James resumed his talk. Finally, he invited group members to add their life maps to the fire. The flames grew again from the large amount of paper—twice as much as the previous year, because of the extra people. Sparks and pieces of burning paper flew everywhere.

When I looked down the hill, the sight of many small fires starting on the hill freaked me out! We were in the middle of a forest, in a terrible drought and extremely high fire danger, most of the fire-fighting resources were battling the forest fire at the other end of the lake, and at least five different small fires were starting from numerous pieces of burning paper that were still raining down. I ran down the hill to help the hotel employee stomp them out. The brush cut me up because I couldn't see it in the dark, and I twisted my ankle, but we managed to put out the numerous small fires. We looked at each other, sighed, and shook our heads. That was way too close to starting a forest fire at this end of the lake.

I returned to the top. The group prepared to head back down. When James passed me, he issued me another dark glare. *Yes, I* thought, *I broke the sacred circle when I ran down the hill . . . get over it.* Sometimes this man has no common sense of what is really important at the time. He gets so wrapped up in "his ceremony" while other more urgent issues, with possible disastrous effects on others or the environment, are going on around him. He is oblivious to what else is going on, and he gets mad at you if you don't ignore everything else as well. This made me think of his frequent admonition, that if we don't pay attention then we will pay with pain. I remember thinking *he needs to pay more attention!*

After James and the group left, Edward, Richard, Megan, Gary, a couple of other staffers and I circled up to close the ceremony and say a few words. Edward, Richard and I thought for sure we were going to get blasted for our "sloppiness." Instead, Megan smiled and said, "That was the best Fire Ceremony we ever had!" Edward and I looked up at each other, our eyes bugging out. The staffers returned to the meeting room for the start of the Holotropic Breathwork™ session, and the three of us stayed behind with the hotel employee to clean up. Edward bellowed, "The best Fire Ceremony ever? You've got to be freaking kidding me!"

We all laughed and shook our heads. "If that was the best, what the hell happened during the worst?" I asked. I gave the activity the title it is still known by today. "This was like 'The Three Stooges Do a Sacred Fire Ceremony!'"

The next evening, it was my group's turn for a Holotropic Breathwork™ session. I leaned down next to the participants' ears and demonstrated the breathing so they would remember to continue the rapid breathing pattern themselves. I had to be careful not to get smacked by them if they were startled or decided to roll onto their sides. The rest of the time, we watched to see if someone was moving around so much they posed a danger to someone lying near them. In that case, we would place pillows as buffers between people or grab the blanket under a person and drag them a safe distance from a "thrasher". Some never moved at all. They just lay there with the most angelic, peaceful smiles on their faces. A friend had been tucked into an isolated corner and was worried she was going to be pretty much alone, so she asked me to check on her often. She was among the "angelic" ones. Erica's session was on a different night, so I didn't find out about her experience until we were riding home. She was not impressed. As with every exercise, some will love it, and others will not.

All week I kept watchful eye on my two special participants. Laurie survived her lost life map episode, but stilled looked like a very angry person. Her Warrior Group continued to stay away from her. She would often sit by herself and look disgusted about everything. Over the course of the week, though, she seemed to mellow towards me. She was extremely intelligent, a very meticulous and capable person. I wanted to see her smile, just once. I really wished I could help her in some way, but I knew she wasn't ready yet.

My other special someone was Don, the man who did not share his wife's excitement at registration. He was a Vietnam Vet and a very angry man; I could not tell whether at himself, or someone else. During morning yoga, I saw him struggling. He would look around and try to emulate what others were doing, but was too inflexible, and he was getting very frustrated. When I tried to help him, he waved me off. His wife told me he had hurt his back and was in pain and that is why he couldn't move. James used to say an inflexible body is a sign of an inflexible mind. In my view, Don was trying very hard to stay rigid and not let something in. One day, the music was playing before the resumption of a session, and everyone was dancing except Don. He sat in his chair with his arms folded over his chest—his usual posture. James saw this and told him to get up and move. Don refused. When this happens, James will usually make the person dance on stage and he called Don to come up. Don refused. James verbally confronted him about not participating in the seminar or in life. I could tell Don was locking down more and more with every word. He was growing angrier by the second. Finally, James told him it was his life and choices, and he was way too young of a man to check out of life by using his back as an excuse. If he didn't move his back, he would lose the use of it. He needed to move, but it was his choice.

At the seminars, James had a rule: if your phone rang during a session, you had to sing on stage. The song was usually our national anthem or Canada's. He was particularly tough on staff members and Dream Teamers. This was harder for us, since staffers had their regular daily work responsibilities to keep up with, and the Dream Teamers often used their phones to interact with the hotel staff for things we needed in the meeting room. For example, two of my jobs were to keep the water container full and the room cool. Most hotels are not accustomed to supplying the amount of water needed at James' seminars, so I was always calling and asking them to fill up the water jugs. It was a constant struggle to keep enough water for the participants. I left a message with the manager to call me concerning getting more water containers for the room. I think you know where this is going.

The very last thing I want to do is to sing by myself in front of a group, so I was very careful to keep my phone on vibrate. When I was very young, I loved to sing. I even sang in the church choir. They weren't very picky about how you sounded; they just needed bodies. Anyone would do. One day, I tried out for a singing part in a school play. I didn't get the part. I was taunted mercilessly for years, kids being who they are. I was determined never to be embarrassed like that again, so I simply stopped singing around anyone. When my daughter was a baby, I sang to her when Richard was not around. One evening after I put her to bed, I came downstairs and Richard made the comment that he had never heard me sing before. He guessed it took having a baby to bring it out. I was mortified. I had forgotten all about the intercom system we used to hear her when she woke up. He never said I sounded bad, but in my mind I assumed the worst. I wouldn't sing to Erica unless Richard was out of the house. As she got older, I stopped completely.

There was a problem with my phone. I switched it to "Mute" by sliding a little switch on the outside of the phone. If it moved around in my bag or backpack, it could slide back to the "On" position. In an unusually quiet moment, my phone rang to the unmistakable sound of the Men at Work song "Who Can It Be Now." Everyone heard it loud and clear in the meeting room. I was so busted! James immediately stopped speaking and stood up, looking around the room to find the phone. When he saw me reaching into my backpack to turn it off, he started in with, "It couldn't be a Dream Team Member's phone, could it? They know better than that, don't they?"

As the phrase suggests, resistance is futile. I knew within a few moments, I would be singing on stage, so I might as well get it over with. However bad I sang, it would be OK. That is when I knew I had grown significantly over the past year. The old me would have tried to hide, argued with James that it was a call for his seminar, and/or it was my crappy phone's fault and I had set it to vibrate. James had taught us to take responsibility for our actions and our results. He would say nothing is your fault, but everything is your responsibility. I'm not sure I completely buy into the part about nothing being your fault, but I do accept I have to take responsibility for whatever happens, and that included my phone going off during the seminar. Sometimes you just have to get up and sing, no matter how much you don't want to, and then you can move on with your life.

As my feet made their way to the stage, my brain was trying to figure out why I was going up there. Eventually it caught up to the rest of me. James was going to wipe the stage up with me. He was already signaling for the microphone. You could hear cell phones shutting off all over the room. Susan ran the mic to him, and he asked who was responsible for the Dream Teamers and she said, "Me." He lightly bopped her on the head with the mic. *Great, now Susan was going to be mad at me as well.* James directed me to center stage and handed me the mic. He asked his brother, who was in charge of the music, to find a "good" song. His choice surprised me. Apparently, I would not be doing a rendition of the national anthem after all. They settled on a Beatles song: "All You Need Is Love." James was letting me off easy, which also surprised me. He said something to the effect of, "Well, you know the words to that, so let's go." I told him I didn't know the words, and he asked me if I was kidding, to which I said no, "James, I don't sing."

With that, he turned his head sharply at me and made eye contact. I think he realized this was more to me than just a little embarrassment, so when the music started, he actually sang along with me for a few of the words to get me started. When we started, the room followed. To my relief, I was likely not heard over everyone else. After a few lines of the song, he let me off the hook, and I walked back to my seat. Once there I removed the battery from my phone and waited until the break to check my message. To the utter amazement of those in the room, another phone went off within a few minutes. However they would not own up to it. James called them on it and moved on.

At the break I went outside to check messages. The hotel employee was telling me my water jugs were ready; just let them know when they could bring them into the room. The second came from a lady in real estate who I'd helped with a personal problem: "Hi Connie, this is Sandy, and I just wanted you to know you are my hero. See you when you get back from your meeting!"

It was time to take my group out to the Sierra Ropes Course. Erica was participating with the other group, and I was worried about how she was going to do. I didn't warn her about the wall. I was afraid she might decide not to do the course at all.

My group's first stop was more of a strategy game than anything scary. The next stop was the wall! There were several larger ladies in the group, but none as large as I was. There were also a couple of older ladies who were not looking too happy. At one point, two of them contemplated skipping the exercise, so I told them I had successfully done it. Most of the group stopped and turned to look at me. One of the ladies with cold feet pointed to the wall and asked me, "You got over that?"

"Yes, and you can too!"

The group did a great job helping each other over the wall, and I could see how it bolstered their confidence just as it had mine. They transformed into a caring team right before my eyes, except for one person, Laurie. We proceeded to a group balancing exercise, on which they worked very long and hard. Laurie was standing to one side, acting like she did not think they knew what they were doing, not wanting to participate. She eventually joined them, reluctantly. The group picked up on her attitude and started to exclude her from the decision-making process.

Our last stop was the Flying Squirrel. A cable stretched about two stories above the ground between two trees. Attached and over the cable was a rope, both ends of which hung to the ground. On one end of the rope was a clip for a harness, while the other end was used to pull a team member up—fast. The team lined up holding onto the rope and facing away from the cable. The "squirrel" was in a harness and helmet, clipped to the rope from the back, facing away from their team. When they got the order to start, they would all run as fast as they could in opposite directions. The faster they ran, the faster the squirrel got launched. At one point the squirrel could no longer stay on his or her feet because of being pulled upwards from behind. The person would fall forward, a scary feeling. At that point, the squirrel would be moving fast just above the ground. As the distance of the group from the high cable increased, the squirrel soared very high into the air and dangled a couple of stories above the ground. When they soar upwards, the person's hands instinctively swing out to their sides; hence, the "flying squirrel" name for the activity.

Some people will read this and go, "Cool!" while others will say, "You've got to be kidding me!" That is precisely what happens within the group. The "squirrel" places a lot of trust in their team, because it is completely up to the team to hoist them up and not let go of the rope and drop them to the ground. From two stories up, that would hurt!

One by one I worked through each person's issues if necessary as I strapped them into their harness. One very scared lady said to me, "Tell me again how you already did this." To which I had to respond, "I haven't done this one yet." She started to cry and say she just couldn't do it. I tried talking to her, but it was a no-go. "What will it take for you to give it a try?" I asked.

"For you to go first!"

I asked the rest of the group if they were OK pulling me up. They were, so I suited up in a harness and got hooked up. Have I mentioned I am not a big fan of heights? Before my experience with the wall the previous year, I never would have asked the group to put in the effort required to pull someone my size into the air, or have trusted them to do it. I would have assumed they either didn't want to do it or resented having to do it. As I asked them if they were willing, a few looked me up and down, likely thinking this is going to be challenging. I did not blink; neither did they. Together, we could do anything!

Still, I experienced some trepidation as I got ready. I quietly asked the ropes course facilitator if someone "my size" had ever done this before. She calmly told me far larger people than I were graduated "Flying Squirrels". When I was given the word to go, I started moving my 300 lb.-plus frame as fast as I could. I felt like I was falling forward, running too fast and losing my balance. A few seconds later, my feet were up and my body fell forward towards the ground. Just a few feet above the grass, my downward fall stopped and I was gliding above it. Suddenly, my body turned upwards and I was launched. My hands flew out to my sides and I did the "flying squirrel" as I soared upwards, squealing with delight. What a hoot! As I hung in the air doing my best Peter Pan imitation, I looked down at the woman who had been crying. Now she was laughing. The group lowered me back to the ground. If given the opportunity, I would have gone again!

Now I had to get the rest of the people up there. I adjusted her harness and off she went. I will always remember her smiling face as she hung at the top by the wire. I noticed Laurie was putting on her own harness, so I told her to be sure she had me check it for her before she went up. Her back was to me and I saw her nod in acknowledgement. She came to me, I checked her harness and tightened the back up, and told her she was good to go. She headed off to be hooked on by the ropes coordinator, and I moved my attention to the next person in line.

I heard a commotion from her direction. I looked up to see another woman trying to talk to Laurie because she was coming completely unglued. She yelled at her group member, "Don't talk to me!" and ran over to me and yelled, "I only want to talk to you!"

I lowered my voice and started asking her calmly what she was feeling. She was shaking and crying, and her words barely made sense. After talking with her for a few minutes, I figured out there were several issues. First, she was very afraid of heights. Worse, she did not trust her group to pull her up safely. Ah, trust issues. I understood a bit about that myself. I took her over to the waiting group and told them she was scared and she needed to know they would take good care of her.

"Yes," they said in unison.

I told her she may have some control issues; she admitted it. The idea that she would have no control over whether or not her group would drop her was frightening to no end. I talked with her about how hard and lonely it is going through life all alone, with no one who she felt she could count on, and that could stop right here, right now. The ultimate control would be hers; was she willing to make the choice to let them pull her up? "You have to make this decision sometime or die alone and scared, so what is it? Do you want to handle this once and for all right now—or not?" I reiterated. "Yes or no, it is your choice."

My voice grew stern. "Laurie, be brave and choose to trust."

Sobbing, she nodded and returned to the facilitator to be hooked up. I started adjusting the straps on the next person when I heard the coordinator yell, "Go!"

"Run, Laurie, run as fast as you can, leave the fear behind," I yelled.

Her feet left the ground and she soared into the air, doing a great flying squirrel. When she got to the top, she grabbed the harness around her chest. While she swung back and forth just below the wire, I couldn't tell if she was shouting from joy or terror. One of the ladies standing next to me said it didn't sound good, so I ran and stood beneath Laurie and told her to let go of the harness and fly. She refused. "It's your choice to let go of control and trust it will be OK," I said. "Control is an illusion anyway, so let go and have fun. Look at where you are, have fun, fly!"

Finally, she let go and put her hands out, but immediately pulled them back in and grabbed the harness again. We went back and forth several times until finally she put her arms out and left them there. I couldn't tell if she was laughing or crying, but she had released the illusion of control and trusted her harness and group not to drop her, at least for a few seconds. After she came back down, she took off the harness and I gave her a hug. She went over to a shady spot and sat there alone for a while. I remember looking at her, amazed that someone so capable was so unsure of herself and her surroundings. Did she become so self-reliant because she was always so afraid to trust anyone?

After we got back to the meeting room, I looked for Richard to see if he knew how Erica did. She did great, scaling the wall without any problems. Later, I asked her about it. She thought the wall was fun!

I learned a lesson. Unless I was really worried about someone's safety, I would keep my opinions about the activities to myself and let them have their own experience. That translated into our everyday life with my daughter. I can give her advice, but I need to give her the freedom to have her own experiences, both good and bad, untainted by my opinions.

We were heading to the later part of the week and James was increasing the sales pressure for people to buy boxes of his book, register for future events, and even to join the WWS. At events, he would bring the WWS members who were present up on stage to be introduced. At first, I didn't mind because I thought if people had questions about anything, they could seek us out during the events. But now it felt more like we were being used to sell more memberships, and we were now being told it was our responsibility to get others to sign up. Well, I had a problem with this, for two reasons. First, I didn't pay $75,000 to be his salesperson. If someone asked me about the group, I was happy to answer their questions, but I was not there to "sell them" on it. Second, we were promised at the very beginning the group would be no more than 60 people, and we were now larger than that. James was still claiming that he never said it was limited to just 60 members, and he held to the claim that what he said from the very beginning was the goal was to get 60 members the first year. That was a lie. Had it been true, we definitely would not have signed up as quickly as we did; after all, we were trying to get in before the 60 available slots were taken. As it turned out, we certainly could have waited longer to pull the money together for the membership. Also, the WWS was now clearly a business networking group, and James had started to promote it as such.

I didn't hear anything about the WWS project anymore, so I asked the responsible JRI staffer about it. She said they could not get a consensus from the membership on which project to pursue, so we were going to handle it at the WWS Congress in Cabo San Lucas in early 2009. Only WWS members would be at that meeting; it would be the perfect time to work it all out. It sounded like a reasonable plan.

We had been living on very little sleep for the entire week. We no longer had to walk the trail in the morning and evening, but we still endured very long days. After we officially ended for the day, we often helped participants with their homework until the wee hours. There were days when I would get back to the townhouse at 2 or 3 in the morning, take a shower and then join Edward in the kitchen for a couple of hours while we tried to maintain the shaky broadband connections on our laptops and answer emails. I had contracts and disclosures to finalize and return to my transaction coordinator as well. I would nap for about an hour, and then I would head back for breakfast and morning group yoga. God help you if you were late.

My one daily real estate commitment was to check in with the woman covering our clients for us during our absence. This five-minute call had to be made during each business day while she was in her office. One time during a break, I was on my check-in call when James walked past with his bodyguards in tow. He shot me the James Ray dirty look. He truly felt and acted as if he owned us every minute of the day and night, with no regard for the businesses or families we left behind to work for JRI for a week, for free. Not to mention paying for our own transportation, room and board. James always talks about coming from gratitude, but I couldn't help feeling he and his organization were in the habit of taking advantage of people.

The work schedule took its toll on Richard. Rarely is he sick, but he was down with a high fever and chills. He used a few meal breaks to return to the townhouse and lie down. I am sure James and company didn't like that either. Their attitude was they could always get someone else to replace you, but that was beginning to change. Fewer people were willing to bear the expense and long hours volunteering at these events required. In 2009, they were so short of Dream Team members for this same event they begged a participant who had attended it before to work the event. They were having a harder time recruiting volunteers for other events as well.

The last day finally arrived; time to get ready for the fire walk. My old Girl Scout leader experience came in handy when I built my bonfire. After the fire burned for a while, we collapsed the wood frames and pounded down the coals into smaller pieces on which people could walk. We then signaled to the meeting room for them to come back down to the fire ring.

During the fire walk, I manned my strip of fire and coals. If someone froze at the top of the fire path, and no one else was there to talk to them, then I had to coach them as well. Otherwise, it was just the fire and me that night. I kept turning and flattening down the coals. We had to use gloves and cover our faces with bandanas to protect us from the searing heat. Later, some of the participants asked if the fire was really that hot. We showed them how our plastic name badge holders had melted onto the paper inside them. The hair around my face was also singed.

The whole group finished quickly because we had four lines set up. Again, I did not see Erica walk the fire. I would have to wait until we were all back in the meeting room to find out how she did.

Some of the Dream Teamers stayed behind for a while putting out the fires, then we headed back up to the meeting room. They were still celebrating when we got there. I had a chance to look at the faces of the people who had experienced so much that week. You had to be brave to take a close, hard look at yourself, and this work was definitely not for wimps. Everyone came to improve him or herself, and the volunteers came to be of service to others. I looked through the room and saw Don, the angry Vietnam Vet, dancing in the corner . . . really shaking his booty! He lived in San Diego; over the next few years, he would be at a reception or Christmas party at my home and stand in the backyard, telling jokes and goofing around. I would look at him to see if I could recognize the angry man who'd arrived at this event. I also found Laurie, who I almost didn't recognize. She was actually smiling and giggling! The kids who worked together on bending the rebar were beaming. The girl came over and thanked me for my help, and said she would never forget that night when she bent the rebar. I finally found Erica in the crowd, and she, too, was happy.

James said a few words, then, "I love you guys," and disappeared with his bodyguards behind the stage. He just took off! People were stunned. They had already started lining up to get single and group photos with him, but he bolted the second the event was over. We took group shots of the warrior teams for them, thinking about James' rudeness. These people had paid a lot of money to see him, spent a week doing the hard work, and now he couldn't even be bothered to smile for a picture with them. This was not the James we knew when we started with him.

Something about him was changing, and not for the better.

The Dream Team decided to stay up late that night and pack up most of the stuff so we could awaken to an easier morning. The next day, Edward still had to clean up the mess left over from the fire walk. We planned to help, but first, we stopped at a WWS member's breakfast meeting. They wanted more representation of their own business products at James' events and were talking about ways to do that.

From this meeting, the future World Wealth Showcase was born. Unbeknownst to us, a storm was starting to brew. While there was harmony and mutual support on the surface, competition was developing between the members—and it would reach a head quickly.

After the meeting, a couple WWS members who were promoting the Kangen system, a special kind of water filter, approached us. We were interested in this great portable filtration system we had heard so much about. We were also looking for alternatives to plastic bottles, exploring the use of reusable stainless steel or glass containers to carry water instead. We went back to their room, took a look at the system, and signed up for one. We automatically became distributors by purchasing the product in this multi-level marketing system, but were not planning on quitting our day jobs anytime soon. We heard all week from people about how great the high pH water was, and we were happy to own a Kangen system.

We had no idea this seemingly innocent purchase set us up for a run-in with JRI and James.

CHAPTER 12

James' Sweat Lodge Gets Even Hotter

Spiritual Warrior • September 2008

If you can, help others; if you cannot do that,
at least do not harm them.

—Dalai Lama

We were encouraged by James to join one of his Journey Expansion Teams (JETS) that met monthly in cities and towns all over the world. He said the reason for these meetings was to "keep us plugged in with like minded people." We attended our first meeting just after we got back from Spiritual Warrior in '07, and found the group to be full of wonderful people. However, according to James' rules we were greatly limited in what we could discuss. We were not to talk about an event someone in the group had not attended yet. Often, there were people present who had attended very few events, so discussion of the seminar material and what we learned from it was very constrained. We were exploring some heavy subjects in the seminars, and it would be very beneficial to have a peer support group where everything was fair game.

So Richard and I invited a few people who were very serious about applying the material to their lives to come together as a group. We called ourselves the San Diego Warriors and met over dinner at our home once a month. We limited the group to only a few members so discussions would stay group-centered and not splinter off into sidebars, which I have seen happen when meetings became too big. We grew to know each other very well, and felt safe to give and accept advice freely. Edward, Dr. John, Stephen Ray, Richard and I were members. In this group, I continued to vent my concerns about the dangers of the sweat lodge. It was because of this that Stephen would eventually call us before attending Spiritual Warrior in 2009.

Even though Richard and I did not attend Spiritual Warrior in 2008 we made sure Faith and Edward knew some of our concerns about the sweat lodge before they arrived at the Angel Valley Resort in Sedona. We were still being somewhat vague about it because, again, we were not supposed to talk about an event they had not attended. That would change after Spiritual Warrior '08. At this time, though, we limited our cautions to the sweat lodge being too hot for too long, suggesting they enter early in order to sit on the outside ring, not to sit in the inner circle, and being careful about volunteering for anything during the event.

From what we were told the 2008 Spiritual Warrior was run similarly to 2007, with a couple of notable exceptions: they had a new cook with a larger choice of foods; and the dome on the sweat lodge was significantly lower than the previous year. The reason for the change? James complained the lodge did not get hot enough in 2007, and he felt lowering the top would concentrate the heat more. Edward remembers James saying the new lodge was built to his specifications. My mouth dropped open. The previous year, a woman was taken out shaking, unable to move on her own for several hours, another scraped the side of her face when she hit the ground hard while trying to make her way out, and many others were either throwing up or on the ground unable to move with fluids pouring out of their noses and mouths, and others were vomiting violently. *And it wasn't hot enough for him?* Remember James always took the seat in the cool spot right by the door, which also gave him a clear view of what was going on both inside and outside the lodge.

When Edward told me James had made the sweat lodge hotter I said the words that, tragically, proved true: "What is he trying to do, bake everyone to death?" Even as I spoke, I could not imagine he would push the temperature and conditions so far people would die, but I did feel certain someone would suffer brain damage if he kept up.

Other parts of the event remained the same, among them the writing assignments, which kept participants up all night. Sally talked about James using one of his favorite sayings, and I remember him saying the same words to us: "Sleep is over rated and you can sleep when you get home."

In the Samurai game, Edward, as I expected, ended up being a Daimyo, the group leader. He said his group chose him; what could he do? Today, I still ask him teasingly if he has heard the quote, "If nominated I will not run, if elected I will not serve!" One reason I warn people about not volunteering for the Samurai game is because if you get "killed" early, like most first-round Daimyos, you will have to endure without food and water for many more hours than everyone else because you have to lie there "dead" while they eat dinner. I thought the whole idea was mean-spirited. Lying "dead" on the hard floor without being able to move is excruciatingly painful.

Everyone to whom I spoke about Edward's "death" said it was unfairly ordered by "God"—James. Edward said aloud, intending to address either the JRI staff or Dream Team, "Can we go outside?" "God" James took it to mean he had talked to him, and no one but the priest can talk to "God." So "God" James pointed to him and ordered him in a loud and forceful voice to "Die!" Edward protested, "But I didn't ask you!" "God" ordered him to die immediately or multiple teammates would have to die as well.

Edward "dropped dead" to save his other teammates. What went through his mind while lying on the floor was, I believe, a result of the breach of trust he felt earlier that year in Kona. After we saw so many people injured during the concrete slab break, Edward and I discussed at our San Diego Warrior meetings that we would no longer blindly do what James told us to do anymore. We would set limits as to how far we were willing to go for "the lesson," because we could no longer trust James to look out for our safety. Edward slept for the first two hours on the ground, exhausted from staying up to do his writing assignments. After that he was too uncomfortable to sleep, no matter how tired he was.

He obediently laid there for several more hours to not "kill" a teammate, but then something happened. He set a boundary on how much more he was willing to endure. He decided he would hold still for only two more hours. If he were not allowed to move after that he would say, "The hell with James and his rules" and get up. Edward is a very honorable person. He paid a lot of money for this class and he wanted to "play full on," but he was going to decide for himself what was reasonable independent of what his mentor, James, was telling him to do. I believe this change in total faith and trust in

James is what saved Edward's life just a few days later in the sweat lodge.

The day of the sweat lodge arrived, and James gave his instructions. This is what he said, as taken from a 2008 attendee's notes:

"I have been in sweat lodges with shamans and I will tell you that you have never been in a lodge like mine. Most sweat lodges go 4 rounds—we will go 7 rounds or 12 rounds. That means that it will push your envelope of sanity, physical abilities and you can do it. You are more than that. . . . Please remember that once you enter, it is sacred as any temple, sanctuary or mosque. I am the priest. Hold it in as high a regard. Follow directions.

We know that levels of consciousness advancement are done in altered states. You will be in an altered state in the lodge. It will be hotter than hot. . . . No matter what you experience, remember that you are in a temple and you must act accordingly. . . . At some point, you will think, "Get me out of here now." You are more than that. . . . Once we are in, the ceremony will begin. We will bring in the Grandfathers (stone people). . . . The Fire Master is scorching the stones to a red-hot temperature right now. . . . I will start with 12 stones and buckets of water then close the entryway. As the stone Grandfathers come in on pitch fork, we all say, "A Ho Grandfathers." Give them you full attention, honor and respect. . . . Don't say a word unless you are asked to say a word. . . . On the physical level, sweat lodges are very healthy. . . .

There will come a time when you want to get the hell out of there. You will be straddling two worlds. Be honorable and see it through and there is power in doing that. Some of you may pass out. You won't die. . . . If you have to get out, do it ceremoniously and carefully. . . . A Dream Team member will assist you. Stay still until you are helped out. It's hot and you will not die. Opens your pores and toxins will come out. It is very healthy. When you exit the sweat lodge, you will be sprayed with cold water and you are birthed anew . . . .What has to happen for you to be in the moment and appreciate this moment even if it is uncomfortable?

What surprised me when I read the notes from this Spiritual Warrior was how close in content they were to mine. I had already written the chapter on my experience at Spiritual Warrior 2007. James must have used very similar words in 2008 as he had done in 2007. In addition to the expanded schedule (James called it a syntax) that the Dream Teamers and staff utilize at each event, on which every part of the seminar is broken up and put on a time line, I have also seen James refer to a binder he keeps on the table or on a stand near him during an event. When I saw that binder once close-up, it looked to me like it contained even more detailed information than what was on the syntax. Was James following a script? Is that why, when we saw an event multiple times, we noticed much of the material was delivered almost exactly the same way? We all marveled at James' memory, which is amazing . . . but was it also more than that? Was this former acting class student memorizing and delivering a script? If so, where is that black binder with the script he used for the 2009 Spiritual Warrior event?

Like 2007, there were no electrolytes or fruit. If there had been fruit in 2007, I would have dived in it after a week of "gourmet" vegan food! In 2008 the participants burned their journals and headed into the lodge like we had done. Edward and Faith ended up sitting on the side directly opposite the door—the worst place to be. Edward and Faith remembered it becoming ridiculously hot very quickly. As soon as the second round was over, approximately 20 people bolted for the door. James tried to persuade them to stay, but Faith said, "I'm out of here!" After that, it was pretty much the same unfortunate experience as 2007. Between rounds when the flap was open, people would rush out in various states of distress. Some were convinced of James' remark, "You are more than that, you are more than your body," and either stayed in the lodge or reentered it.

At one point, the concerned boyfriend of a JRI employee was outside the lodge and became very vocal about the safety of his girlfriend, who was still inside. People described it to me as "freaking out." Screaming her name, he kept calling to her to come out, and yelling she was going to die! She left in the middle of a round, likely to quiet him down, and is the only person I know of who left mid-round, with the exception of the guy who crawled out under the lodge in 2009. Inside James kept saying, "You know you're more than your body; you're more than that. You know you can do this," to encourage people to stay inside.

During Round 4 or 5, Edward managed to leave on his own, and then collapsed after being sprayed with the cold water. Our mutual friend, Lois, tended to him; twice, he stopped breathing. Others remember her yelling at him to breathe. Edward remembers having a "pleasant vision" of seeing his childhood and other long forgotten memories float by. After he returned home, he was pretty jazzed by his vision. I reminded him that he saw his life flash before his eyes. I can tell you from my own near-death experience that the sensation of being out of your body is indeed very wonderful. I believe Edward's vision was really a near-death experience.

Edward was not the only one experiencing serious physical distress. Sally came out at the end and said, "Somebody go get James right now because I'm gonna die." However, James had already left in his golf cart while people were still in serious physical trouble. He walked right past the people lying on the ground outside of the lodge to board his cart.

Our friend and fellow WWS member, Brenda, was unresponsive for hours, yet no one called 911. Why not? Was it because they knew James did not want them to? Somehow, this had become "normal" to the JRI staffers and volunteers. "Maybe that's normal to them 'cause that's what happens every year, but I don't think that's normal," Sally would later tell a detective.

"I don't either," the detective said in response to her statement.

Megan, his Chief of Operations, the person who always sat to his immediate right inside the lodge, later told detectives, "James was there after the lodge when people were passed out and there was . . . never a call for emergency help or call for a doctor or anything like that." She developed her attitude of accepting this situation as normal from her boss, James, the man for whom both she and her husband worked. This lack of concern was also demonstrated during her police interview after the 2009 sweat lodge incident:

Detective: "Were you aware that people could pass out in a sweat lodge?"

Megan: "Yes."

Detective: "Did you have any concerns ever about why people could pass out?"

Megan: "No."

It was because of Spiritual Warrior '08, Richard and I decided to completely ignore the directive of not discussing the specifics of the event with anyone planning to attend. If they were open to hearing about it, we would tell them. We chose to get specific about the sweat lodge and why we believed it to be dangerous. We also hoped our membership in the WWS would, at some point, give us a chance to speak privately with James about it. Our plan was to bring up our concerns with him when he might be in an open frame of mind. After all, we were supposed to be in his inner circle, we just needed to catch him at a time when our message might come across as friendly advice, rather than criticism. We already knew James was less and less open to hearing, never mind taking, other people's suggestions. Criticism would instantly launch him into attack mode and nothing would be accomplished. Catching him in the right mood and alone would be tricky, but we would look for the opportunity. In just a few weeks, we would be with him in Egypt, and we hoped it would offer us the chance to talk with him on a more casual level.

Back at our dining room table, the San Diego Warriors also speculated James and his staff certainly must have gotten the message after what just happened—tone it down and stop pushing people way too far. We again said, "James is a business man. He wouldn't let his clients get really hurt because it would be bad for business." We left out the part about not doing anything dangerous.

The distressing results from some of his "challenges" were so obvious we thought even "God" James would have to adjust his approach. At Modern Magick the universe gave him a *"tap on the shoulder"* to let him know he needed an attitude adjustment when all of those people broke bones and hurt themselves with the concrete slabs. Since he still had not gotten the message, he had just received *"a hard slap on the back of the head."* Really, would a man who professes to be a spiritual master let it go to the next step, to be *"pounded hard on the head by a 2x4,"* before making a course correction? Even with James' increasingly evident flaws, he was at least logical, right? We reassured each other he would get the message.

I thought of Spiritual Warrior 2007, and Spiritual Warrior 2008. The casualties were escalating. What would happen in 2009 if he didn't get the message?

We watched Edward walk to his car one night from our front door after our San Diego Warriors meeting. Richard said to me, "You know, we almost lost Edward in that damn Sweat Lodge."

"And Brenda too," I added.

While cleaning up the dishes, we talked about Dream Teaming future events and if we would ever work at Spiritual Warrior. Richard felt reasonably sure James must have learned his lesson, but I still had serious concerns. I told him I did not want to. "How can I tell a family member of someone who sustained severe brain damage I didn't call 911 as soon as I saw them in trouble? How could I defend that on a witness stand?" I asked.

Richard thought I was overreacting. Even though logic led me to believe James would back off now, my gut was still screaming "danger!" I bolted out of the lodge after the first round in 2007 because I wasn't feeling well. Could my upset stomach have really been my gut screaming "danger"; protecting me that day and forecasting what was to come two years later on the same spot?

I was willing to question if I was overreacting and if James knew better. He seemed to know a lot of things far better than I did. That is why we wanted to learn from him in the first place. But now, I was making it my choice to share my concerns with anyone who wanted my opinion.

I received a lot of valuable information and personal insights, and others did as well, so I didn't always feel comfortable saying, "Don't go to Spiritual Warrior at all." That was the rub with James. You could strongly disagree with some of his methods and behaviors, while at the same time benefit from much of what he taught. At what point do I have to let others make their own choices and walk their own path?

I decided if someone asked my advice about Spiritual Warrior I would suggest they take all the other events first. My hope was when the time came they would be better prepared to decide how far they wanted to go during the sweat lodge. I knew attending the other events first would prevent most people from ever going to Spiritual Warrior because of the exorbitant cost. If someone told me they already signed up for Spiritual Warrior, I told them they needed to call me before actually attending the event. For those who did call, I specifically warned them about volunteering and the sweat lodge.

Logically, I hoped the others were right predicting James had learned his lesson from the previous events and he would run the lodge at a reasonable intensity. He was a businessman, and continuing to have his clients engage in dangerous activities made no sense. My logic told me the sweat lodge should be much safer now, but my gut was still screaming "danger!" Sadly, I was still not at a point in my life where I fully trusted my intuition over logic.

CHAPTER 13

The Mother Ship

Egypt • September/October 2008

Perfection is a lie!
—Sekhmet

James often said Egypt is the "mother ship" of ancient spiritual places on our planet. It certainly sat on my short list of places to visit during my lifetime. Photos of the Sphinx and the Great Pyramid have appeared on Richard and my vision boards for as long as we have been using them. The energy I felt in Egypt was unlike anything I have ever experienced before or since. The other location on our board was Machu Picchu, in Peru

Just a few days before leaving, Richard's lower back felt tight. By the time we got to our hotel in Cairo, he could barely move. Luckily, we arrived several days before the rest of our group, to give ourselves a chance to adjust to the time change. Now we needed the extra time to get Richard up and walking again. We stayed in our room, waiting for him to get better. As each day passed, his back pain grew worse. Our friends began to arrive; they included a pharmacist and doctor. We headed out together to the local pharmacies to see what medication we could find. Unfortunately, nothing seemed to help. I became worried that we might need to head back home before our tour even began. Richard, however, would not hear of it. Nothing was going to prevent him from experiencing this trip of a lifetime.

During the tour, Richard was in so much pain from his back he could only walk for a few steps or stand for a minute or so before he would have to sit down. Why now? If I have learned anything, it is that nothing happens by accident or coincidence. If there is no logical explanation in this lifetime, then I look to a previous life for answers. Richard felt the same, and he already found clues from the images he saw in meditation during the first few days of the event.

One evening, we had a few minutes of down time and I led him in a past life regression, asking his unconscious mind to show him if his current pain resulted from an injury in a previous life. Not surprisingly, he went straight to a life in Egypt where he was working on a large construction site. He was the representative of a group of laborers who complained about the working conditions. Because of this, he was taken to a cave-like area, beaten severely, kicked in the back several times, and left to die. None of the other workers could come to his aid, because they would face the same fate. Returning to Egypt had tripped the unconscious memory of that past life event.

In my own experiences of leading past life regressions, I have often seen the power of "cell memory." There are books full of research on the subject. It is very common to experience physical symptoms now from something that happened in a previous life. Sometimes, they are physically obvious, such as a birthmark on the site of an injury sustained many lives ago. Other times, it is a chronic to acute pain that defies explanation or cure.

I had my own experience with this phenomenon years ago. I was rushing out the door of my home to pick up my daughter from school. Suddenly, I felt a sharp radiating pain in my chest and was unable to fully expand my lungs to breathe or stand. As I slid down the hallway wall, I was just a few feet from our kitchen phone, but I could not reach it to call for help. I thought I would die of a heart attack right there. My husband was out of the country on business; who was going to get and take care of Erica? The episode lasted for about five minutes, and then stopped as quickly as it had started. When I made my way back to my feet, I stood there for a minute, deciding if I should call for help. I was recovering very quickly and decided to get my daughter and call my doctor en route.

That afternoon, a battery of tests showed nothing was wrong with me. The doctor's diagnosis? Stress. He simply did not know what else to say.

Much later, when I was practicing a past life regression on myself, I asked my unconscious mind if my experience had its origin in a previous life. If so, could we go back to that time and recall it? I went straight into a previous life, where I was killed in battle by a spear that slid between my armor from below, entered my chest and pierced my heart. It was a traumatic death. I remember feeling that it was a stupid occurrence, because the battle was basically over and I had let my guard down. The frustration of the sudden forfeit of my life just as I was starting to celebrate winning the battle merged with the intense pain in my chest to form a strong cell memory. Richard was starting to generate physical symptoms even before our plane landed in Egypt.

James said joining the WWS was the only way to join him on this trip. Due to his connections in Egypt, we would have special access to areas that were off-limits to the general public; a once in a lifetime opportunity. In addition to our WWS membership fees, we still paid for the tour, food, hotel, and travel arrangements. He did provide a farewell dinner at the end and in exchange for his first class travel accommodations, paid for by our membership fees, we received the benefit of his instruction during the tour. I was surprised with the high cost of this membership that we were still paying so much for these activities. I remember thinking on one of the bus rides that JRI will have a nice amount of money left over at the end of this year to go towards the WWS charitable project.

In usual James Ray fashion, days were going to be long and packed with activity. At 2 a.m. in Cairo, our alarm clock went off. It didn't matter how excited I was to be on this trip—2 a.m. is really early to get up. Our group had a logistics meeting the night before at the hotel's hookah lounge. A hookah lounge is also known as a shisha bar, where people share flavored tobacco from a communal hookah pipe placed at each table. I didn't see anyone from our group smoking, but James told me more than once that he liked to smoke hookah and did so several times while in Egypt. It did seem a bit odd that someone so into health would be smoking tobacco, flavored or not, but this was not an everyday kind of thing for him. Several people spoke on the bus the next morning about smoking hookah with James.

During the orientation meeting we met our tour guide, who had worked with Egypt's Supreme Council of Antiquities for over 20 years. Over the course of the tour, he would describe the historical importance of each site, and then James would go into the more "spiritual" aspects of the location.

It was 2:30 a.m. We picked up our boxed breakfasts in the hotel and boarded a bus for the ride to the airport to catch our first flight of the day to Aswan. We would follow the path of the Initiate—initiating or starting the path of a spiritual aspirant. Traveling from south to north along the Nile, we first needed to engage our masculine/intellect and feminine/emotional energies. Our first stop was Philae Island with a temple complex dedicated to the Goddess Isis, and many depictions of the Goddess Hathor. While traveling in a small boat on Lake Nasser, which was formed behind the Aswan Dam, we turned to pass between some smaller islands. There it was, the majestic temple on Philae Island. Wow! It is still hard for me to wrap my head around how long ago these temples were built and how awe-inspiring they remain.

Once we arrived, James guided us in meditation, and then we toured the complex. In the center of the temple were two rooms, both completely covered from floor to ceiling with hieroglyphics and carved images. The room on our left presented scenes depicting the story of death and rebirth of Isis's husband Osiris, how Isis brought him back to life and then conceived their son Horus. In that room we did a group chant, during which Richard started to see himself walking over the sand towards a cave-like structure. The room on the right was the main sanctuary of the temple; inside stood a granite altar.

After our group left, I couldn't resist going back and putting my hands on the altar stone. I closed my eyes and envisioned with each deep inhalation that I was pulling the energy of the stone up through my arms and into my body. Almost instantly, I felt waves of energy moving from my hands and up through my arms. The harder I inhaled, the stronger the energy waves were. Every cell in my body vibrated and tingled. The strength of the energy was amazing, and it was the first time I was able to control the energy flow in and around me like that. My eyes were still closed and I was breathing in hard when I heard another tour group enter the room. Their guide told about the room in French; when he was finished, they all just stood there. I thought that they were busy looking at the carvings on the walls, but when I opened my eyes, I saw they were staring at *me*.

One young man stepped up to the altar and asked me what I was doing. I told him that I was absorbing energy from the temple. He asked if I could show him how, and I told him to just put his hands on the altar and "breathe in" the energy up his arms. We completed a few rounds of deep in breaths. When I opened my eyes to look at him, he still had his eyes closed and a huge smile on his face. He kept on breathing in hard, others from his group crowded around to do the same.

Not one for crowds, I took my leave and caught up with my group. I found James and told him about my experience. He told me to find Richard and have him sit with his back against the altar, because this temple was also known for its healing qualities. I did as he suggested. While Richard sat with his back against the altar and meditated, I repeated the process. I had the distinct feeling someone came up to the altar on my right and was doing the same thing I was. I could hear them breathing, so I matched my breath with theirs. When I opened my eyes, there was a flash of someone standing there—then they were gone. Richard and I were the only people in the room. I was too startled to resume breathing; besides, it was time to catch up with our group again.

We flew from Aswan to just a couple of miles north of the Sudan border to visit Abu Sibel, what some consider to be a masculine energy site. The colossal statues of Ramses II sat on both sides of the doorway of the larger structure, providing a hint at the spectacular rooms inside this UNESCO World Heritage Site. The temples were built into the side of the hill in 1244 B.C. by Ramses II, with the "smaller" one dedicated to his wife Nefertari. Pictures just can't do them justice. While we climbed the hill back towards the bus, the group stopped to watch a pair of hawks flying above us. James said it was a very good sign for our trip.

One of our assignments during this excursion was to journal our thoughts and impressions from each location we visited. When I got back to the bus and picked up my pen, I couldn't write anything. Finally I wrote just one word: *ineffable* which means indescribable beauty, beyond verbal expression. I looked over to see what profound statement Richard had made about Abu Simbel and he only had three words: WOW! WOW!! WOW!!! Yep, that summed it up, too!

Now the real work began. Our first step: Clearly state our intentions for our future. On day two we took an early morning boat ride to Elephantine Island, where the oldest ruins date back to 8,000 B.C.! We spent some time in the temple of the creator god Khnum, the Ram, which represents the first chakra, being grounded. Starting on the ground floor to intentionally build our future lives. We were instructed by James to find two volunteer stones or items on the island. We then found spots that felt "right" to be by ourselves. I held one stone in my right hand that I was to infuse with my negative emotions and leave behind on the temple grounds. I held another in my left hand to infuse with my positive emotions about the good things I was going to create for myself and those around me. My spot turned out to be the remaining

base of an ancient temple pillar. It was round in shape, with hieroglyphics inscribed around the bottom. Someone from our group
snapped a picture of me standing on it; it has become one of my
favorite photos. The negative thoughts I infused into the stone in my
right hand had to do mostly with just how disgusted and tired I was
with my constant weight battle. I begged to be released from it.

I thought we were going to keep our "positive" stone, but just
before we got back on the boat, James talked to us about setting our
intentions and then letting them go. He said you could not hold on
to them too tightly because the emotion of wanting something so
badly was not the same vibration as having something already. The
second vibration attracts what you want into your life. We need to surround ourselves with the vibration of abundance and gratitude.
Decide what you want, be very clear in stating what you want, feel the
good feelings of knowing it is already on its way since it already exists
in some form (everything is energy, and energy cannot be created or
destroyed; therefore, everything you want and will have is already
here), and do the actions (work) that will bring you into alignment
with what you want. Before we stepped back onto the boat, we had to
release our "good" stone into the Nile with gratitude for everything
we have, and everything already on its way to us.

Our second stop: the temple of Kom Ombo. Built for the god
Sobek, the negative or dark in the world, and the god Horus, the positive or light in the world, the temple was, in reality, conjoined twin
temples. We examined our anti-intentions, the less than desirable side
effects that would happen as we worked towards our intentions. Were
we ready to take them on as well? The law of polarity states that, to
carry the light, we must also carry the dark. The negative aspects of
our intentions will show up first. Say your intention is to double your
income over the next year. The negative side effects of more business
could be that you will be busier and therefore have less time to be
with your family, to travel, read, and exercise. You might feel rushed
more often or even most of the time. You will get busier *before* you see
your income grow, and that is why most people stop the process at
that point. They express their distaste with becoming busier by complaining, or by not working as hard. The universe acknowledges the
stopping of the process by saying, "your wish is my command" and
the goal slips away just before it was to arrive. Seeing the negative consequences of your request appear in your life means you are getting
close to your goal, but you have to persevere through the negative

first! Be happy to see the negative side effects, because it means the results you want are almost here. So in examining anti-intentions, we have to decide and commit to accepting the negative consequences that come with attaining our goals. Maybe you are not willing to take on the workload necessary to double your income. You could decide instead that you are willing to commit to doing what is necessary to increase your business by 50% over the next year.

While at this site, we moved down our list of intentions and adjusted them according to our willingness to accept the anti-intentions. It had really not occurred to me before to examine the negative consequences of working towards my goals, or to be conscious of the process and happy when these side effects showed up. We are conditioned to avoid the pain, or fix the discomforts and problems and make them stop. Pain to me meant I was doing something wrong. What if it really meant I was doing something right?

One interesting aspect of Kom Ombo is that on its back wall are carvings of what look like medical tools. The science of medicine was well known by the ancient Egyptians. There were also footprint carvings on the floor that marked the spots of healing vortexes. Richard and others stood on them for a while. After they were done, I stood on one to see if I would feel anything. To my amazement, the tension in my shoulders dissolved and my shoulders relaxed in a way I had not felt for over 30 years! They remain relaxed for the rest of the day. I would like to find some of those vortexes around San Diego!

The day's third and final stop was Edfu, which housed the temple of the falcon god Horus, the second largest complex after Karnak; it was built in 142 B.C. It was time for us to formulate our action plans to reach our intentions. The volume of knowledge depicted on the walls was almost indescribable. One wall showed the pharaoh dealing with one of his "black bags," or limiting beliefs, represented by an underwater hippopotamus. In the first scene, he tried to ignore it, but in the next scene, the hippo caused so much turbulence to the water around the pharaoh that he was forced to bring the issue to the surface, with the help of Isis, and deal with it. In the next scene, the large hippo now looked very small when on the surface, causing the pharoah to realize it was not as big a problem as he had originally thought. In the last scene, he killed the hippo, completing the cycle.

There are always more hippos/black bags lurking under the water (our unconscious mind) that will eventually cause so much trouble you can't ignore them anymore. So bring them up to the surface and deal with them. Once exposed, they don't seem to be such big deals after all, and you can finally be done with them. This is just one of several profound messages engraved on the walls of this ancient temple.

The start of day three took us to Dendera, the temple of Hathor, the goddess of music, singing & acting "childlike." This temple is related to the heart chakra. It reminded us to lighten up and enjoy life while we pursue our intentions. I was in awe of the massive solid stones that comprise the ceiling of the temple. On the walls, the Egyptians engraved the story of life in antiquity, how they grew and harvested their food, and how they built the temples. There was a detailed map of the zodiac on the ceiling of one of the higher rooms, and on a prominent wall, the Pharaoh and Horus used an "anti-gravity bubble" to raise the huge stone entry gate of the temple. Earlier in our trip, while pointing up to some huge stones that made up the high ceiling in a temple, I asked our guide, "Exactly how did the ancient Egyptians get them all the way up there?" He told us some speculated about the use of sand ramps. Along with many others in the group, I did not consider that a plausible way to move such massive stones into perfect position so high above the ground. The guide then added that later in the trip, we would see another possible explanation of how they did it. This carved image of the anti-gravity bubble was what he was referring to.

The next stop was the temples of Osiris and the Osireion at Abydos. Because much of the temple had been covered in sand, the amazing colors on the walls were better preserved. Ramses II finished this temple his father, Sety I, started. In addition to Osiris, there are rooms dedicated to his sister/wife, Isis, and their son, Horus. James instructed us to walk into one of three rooms to which we felt most drawn. James led us in a guided meditation, where we reviewed our list of intentions and asked for help in achieving them.

James became very emotional during this meditation. He said he was "on the skinny branches of the tree," meaning money was very tight, and he was asking for help from the universe to choose wisely and move beyond his present problems. I didn't think much of it at the time, but it seems odd he was having financial struggles during a time when his business appeared so successful—capacity turnouts at events that ranged in price from $1,000 to $10,000, over 65 members in a club that charged $60,000 to $75,000 for membership, plus all of his other products and business dealings thrown into the mix. Where was all the money going?

Finally, we stopped at Luxor after dark. It was illuminated and nearly empty, since it was close to closing. Seen from above, the temple of Luxor is thought to represent the human body. We moved up to the crown chakra area for a "silent" meditation, to connect with our higher conscious mind. James told us anyone can learn to meditate in a quiet room, but to become a master at it; we needed to discipline ourselves to meditate in a noisy area. This area of the head chakra was indeed noisy. Just a few feet away, on the other side of the wall, was a very busy intersection bustling with tourists, vendors and traffic. I think Egyptians use the horn just about as much as they use their car brakes. During our meditation, I felt the peace and silence "inside" the head/crown chakra area, yet at the same time knew that the "action" or life was to be experienced "out there" on the other side of the wall, outside of our heads.

The temple was closed and the lights off when we came out of the meditation. Now we could really "feel" the energy of the temple. We walked through and out of the Luxor Temple in the moonlight! We only heard the sound of our light footsteps. The silver moonlight reflected off the floor and walls around us . . . truly breathtaking! Many of us paused in the area that represented the solar plexus. There was a particularly good feeling in the main plaza, flanked by giant columns, which represented human ribs, on both sides. I would have been content to sit down and spend the rest of the night taking it all in, but the temple guards were busy trying to move us along as quickly as possible.

Day four started early. We arrived at the tombs in the Valley of the Kings at 7:30 a.m. It was already very hot and crowded. The Valley of the Kings receives an average of 10,000 visitors a day. We marveled at the intricate carvings of hieroglyphics and images on the insides of the tombs. Our guide explained that parts of the hieroglyphics were derived from the Egyptian Book of the Dead; a kind of "cheat sheet" for the pharaoh to follow after his death to ensure he takes the proper steps to receive eternal life. The rest of the people who did not merit such an elaborate resting place had to rely on their memory of the book to get the steps correct.

We marveled at the size of the sarcophagi that held the mummies, along with their multiple layers of boxes and wrappings. A heavy stone top covered each sarcophagus. We would use these for comparison later inside the Great Pyramid, which some say was also a tomb.

Our last stop on day four was the Karnak Temple Complex, the largest in Egypt. A sphinx-lined avenue once connected the Karnak and Luxor temples, two miles apart. Many Pharaohs added their temples and structures here over time.

We headed over to the statue of the scarab beetle, which represents rebirth and was dedicated by the pharaoh to the God Khepri, also known as the god of the morning. We walked clockwise seven times around the statue while meditating on our intentions. Then we stopped, stomped our left foot (side of spirit), sealed the requests and walked perpendicularly away. As we stomped our foot, we said to ourselves, "When the intention is clear and the commitment is strong . . . So be it . . . It *Must* Be So!"

James warned us to be very sure of what we were asking for, because it would happen, along with the anti-intentions. He told us he was nervous about doing the ritual again, and wasn't sure he was going to do it this time. The last time he said the "positive" and "negative" results were extremely powerful. About halfway through my seven circles, I saw James making his circles as well. Apparently, his desire to participate overcame his concerns. Looking at the "negative" results that showed up in his life just about a year later, it leaves you to wonder what "positive" things he requested as he made his way around the scarab beetle!

For the second part of the ritual, we walked to the Temple of Sekhmet, off limits to the general public and not often seen on many maps of Karnak. Sekhmet is the lioness-headed goddess of war and healing. She is the giver and taker of life, and guardian of the pharaoh. Our meditation centered on what continued to hold us back from being all we were capable of being. We had to go to war with our limiting beliefs, and expose them for what they are—lies—to truly heal. We experienced an extremely powerful meditation in a very pure vibration space that has been kept that way for thousands of years. James split us into two groups, with my group heading into the "waiting" room. We journaled and meditated while the other group did a guided meditation in Sekhmet's chamber. Even in the shade, we sweated profusely. The high-vibration energy manifested itself as high heat in that room.

After the first group was done, we were led into Sekhmet's chamber. The large black statue looked menacing; the lioness goddess with the solar disc on her head. The only light in the room came from a small slit in the ceiling, emitting a ray of light that struck her face. I was uncomfortable closing my eyes for the meditation in the statue's presence. When I first saw her, I could not help but notice how fierce her eyes looked. During the meditation, I peeked to make sure she was still standing only a couple of feet in front of me. Each time I looked back at her face during the meditation, it seemed to change from fierce, to concerned, and then at the end to compassionate. This was a solid stone statue . . . how could that be? Yet, several people from both groups made that same observation. Did the statue change—or did we?

During the meditation, we could ask her, if we dared, to reveal to us our most weakening limiting belief. Quieting my mind, I received the thought that I had stopped myself from doing or completing many things because I did not feel I could do them well enough. A second later, images of events flashed in my mind. Fun things I never did and chances I never took because I was afraid of not doing it perfectly. Satisfaction in a job well done I never allowed myself, because I did not do it perfectly. Then it hit me hard: there is NO manmade perfection on this earth. The attempt to strive for perfection was a complete waste of my time and a demoralizer of my spirit. Perfection is a lie!

More images flashed in my mind, events and accomplishments that should have brought me satisfaction, but instead felt like hollow achievements. My belief that everything had to be perfect to be good was my most weakening limiting belief. I understand where it came from. While growing up, I was always under pressure to do better or be better. When I got an A in a class, I remember my grandmother asking me why I didn't get an A+. I know she was trying to be encouraging, but it set me up for a lifetime of looking for the "+" for which, invariably, I would often fall short of attaining. Perfection is a lie, and good enough is good enough. I was a crying mess on the temple floor as I realized I had cheated myself out of considerable joy in my life while trying to attain something that did not exist in the first place.

At the end of the meditation, we could go up and thank Sekhmet for the lesson learned if we wanted. I looked at the statue. She appeared kind. Other people were patting or resting their hand on her. I cupped my hand around the jaw on her face. "Thank you," I said. Apparently, many other people had similar experiences, because as we slowly dragged ourselves out of her temple, we all looked like we had gone through hell—a hell of our own creation. As we slowly made our way to the parking lot, I heard one young boy ask his father while pointing to us, "What happened to them?"

To this day, a black stone statue of Sekhmet sits on my desk to remind me that perfection is a lie.

The next morning, after the sunrise meditation between the paws of the Sphinx (Chapter 1), we visited the Great Pyramid on the Giza Plateau to spend three hours alone inside. We visited all three levels, representing the Unconscious Mind (below ground level), the Conscious Mind (middle level, the Queens chamber) and the Higher Conscious Mind (upper level, the king's chamber). In the king's chamber was a small sarcophagus made out of red granite and without a top. Initiates would lay in the sarcophagus with their arms crossed over their chests after journeying up the Nile, then die to their old life and be reborn to their new one. We were told to leave behind "old life" elements in the sarcophagus. One problem: there was so many of us, we'd only have a few seconds apiece to experience this. We were going to be very rushed.

Before going into the pyramid, we had to decide if we were going to go to the lower chamber. James told me that it would be too hard for me because of my size and claustrophobia. Once we started down the very narrow passageway, we would not be able to stop for any reason because of the people behind us. James wanted those of us not going to the bottom chamber to wait for the rest of the group in the middle chamber. I asked our guide if we could start in the middle, proceed to the king's chamber and wait there for the group. That way we could have a longer time to lie in the sarcophagus. He readily agreed. When a couple of other people who were undecided about whether to go to the bottom chamber or not heard that, they jumped at the chance to have more time in the king's chamber and a less hurried experience of "death and rebirth" in the sarcophagus.

James and others tried to talk Richard out of going to the bottom because of his back. Richard said, "No way!" He was going. Our guide suggested he go last. If it was too hard on his back, he could back out of the passageway without blocking anyone else. He made it to the bottom, to an unfinished room a considerable distance below the surface of the ground. In the center was a "bottomless" pit. Richard kicked a small stone into the pit and said that he never heard it hit the bottom. It was too dark to see much of anything. Some books I've read say the pit connects an underground room below the Sphinx with the Great Pyramid. No explanation was given as to its purpose or depth. James led the group in a chant where they envisioned throwing down their "black bags" into the pit. Then he shimmied down a narrow passageway to what is believed to be the exact center of the pyramid. Other volunteers followed, holding onto the legs of the person in front of them, making a human chain up the small tunnel and out to the main group that had joined hands. They again chanted; I was told an incredible vibration permeated the space. While they were quiet, they could hear a noise that we later figured out was the sound of our small group chanting all the way up in the king's chamber! I have no idea how we were heard that far below and through all of that solid rock.

While the main group was heading down to the lower chamber, my group was making its way through the tunnel leading to the queen's chamber. This was a very small passageway as well. You had to crouch way down to get through. One of the pyramid attendants used a key to open a door made of steel bars that blocked the opening of the tunnel. The five members of my group started to make their way down the passageway. I held back. My claustrophobia was pitching a fit. The attendant shut the metal door and began to lock it. As uncomfortable as I was with tight places, I had already allowed my fears to stop me from experiencing the bottom chamber. I was not going to let it keep me from the middle chamber as well. I was shaking, but I would get to the middle chamber one way or another. I did not want the gate to close and block my way out, should I lose my resolve part way through that small tunnel. I asked the attendant if he had to close the metal door behind me. He said that he was going to lock us in until we were ready to come out to make sure that no unauthorized people entered. I signaled to him that I was going to follow my group. He understood, and reopened the gate. The thought of the metal gate locking me into a narrow passageway was downright disconcerting, so I asked if he could wait until I made it into the chamber before shutting it, in case I needed to turn around and come back out. English was probably his fifth language, and we were communicating with mostly hand gestures and a few words at best, but I thought he understood my meaning.

I tentatively started to make my way down the narrow tunnel. Not far in I heard the metal gate slam shut and lock behind me. Apparently, we did not communicate as well as I had hoped. When I looked back under my arm towards the entrance, the metal gate was closed and the lock hung on it, with no attendant in sight. I was determined that claustrophobia would no longer keep me from getting where I wanted to go. I dropped to my hands and knees and crawled as quickly as I could through the tunnel. I kept looking straight down to the area between my hands and moved one hand in front of the other as fast as I could go.

Finally, I made it to the chamber and stood up. The group was stating their intentions while walking in a circle, just like we had done around the scarab beetle. When finished, we headed back out the tunnel towards the gate. About halfway through, I heard the gate rattle and open. I was relieved to be out and climbing toward the king's chamber.

We had to climb the steep stairs in the Grand Gallery to reach the king's chamber. Often while inside the Great Pyramid, I reminded myself that the rooms and passageways were surrounded by countless tons of stone. The blocks used in the pyramid are believed to average 2.5 tons each, with some of the casing stones at the base weighting as much as 15 tons. The heaviest blocks, used to roof the king's chambers, weigh between 50 and 80 tons each!! At the top of the Grand Gallery, we ducked beneath several huge granite stones to enter the king's chamber. Once there, I noticed that there were no hieroglyphics or images carved anywhere inside the pyramid.

We were told that the pyramid was intended to be a place of initiation, not of burial. No book of the dead instruction "cheat sheet" on the walls for the pharaoh to follow after death. It was not needed here. The sarcophagus in the king's chamber was much smaller than those we saw in the Valley of the Kings tombs because it was not intended to hold the multiple wooden boxes that formed layers around the mummy. Here, it only needed to be large enough for a person to lie down. No top was needed on the sarcophagus, for the same reason. The top edges were rounded and not flat, showing that it was not intended to support a heavy stone cover. The room itself was amazing. The large stone blocks fit together perfectly.

Within a few minutes, we instinctively started to chant *Om* together. What we heard echoing around us was exceptional. All of our voices were in perfect harmony and we were able to hold the tone much longer than usual. It was as close as you can get to hearing angels sing on this plane. Later, when I researched the causes of this acoustic experience, I found an interview with Boris Said, the Emmy award-winning writer and producer of the feature documentary, *The Mystery of the Sphinx*, hosted by the late Charlton Heston. In the interview, Boris told writers Kenneth and Dee Burke that the king's chamber was built to enhance and amplify whatever sounds were made inside it. A special form of harmonic resonance existed there, and the pattern of notes described an F-sharp chord, which, according to ancient Egyptian texts, is the harmonic "tone" of the planet. F-sharp is also the frequency of the heart chakra, and the sound to which Native American shamans tune their sacred flutes. Nothing is by accident!

We took turns lying in the sarcophagus and meditating through "death" to rebirth. Since there were only six of us, we could take as much time as we needed. Soon after lying inside, I heard the distinct sound of someone breathing. I held my breath to see if it was me; it wasn't. I stuck my head up to see if anyone was near the sarcophagus . . . no one. Someone nearby was softly chanting *Om,* which would explain the in-breath, but not the exhaling breath. I continued with my attempt to release what did not serve me. The sound of someone else breathing, surrounded me like a cheesy horror movie, but it was not scary. I matched my breathing to it and felt in tune with a larger consciousness . . . the consciousness of the pyramid itself! I started to shake hard, but again I was not scared. I let the energy and my feelings flow. What did I want to leave behind? That was easy. I wanted to leave the struggle with my weight behind. Once again, I asked to be free of it.

After a few minutes, I stopped shaking and the breathing sounds stopped. I was exhausted, drained, but peaceful.

When I got out of the sarcophagus, I sat on the floor with my back against it. I continued chanting with the rest of the group and waited for the others to join us. After a while, I could hear approaching voices echoing from the passageway. I knew I had the best seat in the room, and that James would want to sit exactly where I was, so I got up and moved to the side of the room. About a minute later, James came bursting into the chamber. He clearly had raced up the stairs in the Grand Gallery and was out of breath. It was just like James to push himself to climb quickly. As I predicted, he went straight to where I had been seated and plopped down. I saved a place for Richard, and then James led the group in a chant while the second group took turns lying in the sarcophagus for about 20 seconds each. The group and James talked about feeling the floor vibrate, but I did not feel it. That may have been because I had been there longer and was already vibrating myself. Together, Richard and I jointly stated our intentions. James talked about research that showed chanting your intentions in the king's chamber would amplify the vibration that you were putting out. Men for some reason could get a higher amplification than women, but the highest amplification was achieved when a "committed" man and woman couple chanted their shared intentions together. So Richard and I chanted on. Another couple took the opportunity to exchange rings and renew their vows. Around us, we could hear people speaking in several different languages that blended together beautifully.

I asked Richard how his back was holding up. He returned the first smile I had seen on his face all week long. He told me the pain was completely gone. He was cured as soon as he entered the pyramid!

As we prepared to leave, James explained we were emerging to a different parallel universe where the world we knew would be changed (or was it *us* who changed?). Everything did look and feel "different" for many weeks afterward. Once outside, some of us noticed that our camera batteries had recharged and, unfortunately, Richard's back returned to its state of constant pain as soon as he stepped outside the pyramid.

We returned to Cairo for our farewell dinner. James came around briefly and asked each of us to name our personal highlight of the trip. Almost everyone else said the Great Pyramid, but Richard and I noted the Sphinx, which surprised him. Within a few hours, we were on planes heading home. During one of the long flights, I remember thinking that exactly 24 hours earlier I had been inside the Great Pyramid. This truly had been the trip of a lifetime!

CHAPTER 14

What Happened to Being Spiritual?

The End of 2008

It's no wonder that truth is stranger than fiction.
Fiction has to make sense.

—Mark Twain

James announced during one of our monthly calls there would be a WWS Showcase during the upcoming World Wealth Extravaganza (WWE). We would be given tables to present a product or service. There would also be one member or team selected—by James, of course—to do a presentation "spotlight" of their product/service during the event. To be considered, you needed to provide a video of your presentation to JRI. The only rule: he didn't want us to present more than one business at our table. James' sudden interest in our businesses resulted from the WWS breakfast meeting at the end of Practical Mysticism. Apparently, the members looking to leverage their considerable membership investment by promoting their businesses succeeded in getting James' attention.

Richard and I needed to decide between our real estate business or the portable Kangen water filtration system we purchased at Practical Mysticism. We were either going to be promote The Joys Of Real Estate or The Joys Of Healthy Water. We were also part of a team of WWS members who owned these water filters, and as a group, we wanted to see plastic bottled water replaced by great filtered tap water stored in reusable containers such as glass or stainless steel. We already noticed a dramatic increase in the amount of water we were drinking since we started using the Kangen system. It was great that we were no longer using plastic bottles. Working with this team provided a way of getting to know these fellow WWS members better.

We were leaning towards the Kangen filters, but before we made our decision, we needed to talk it over with the team. To our delight, they were thinking along the same lines: no one wanted to turn this into a competition between the different team members. We decided as a group to pool our resources, merge our tables, and inform people about the importance of great drinking water and using reusable containers. Any sales would be divided equally among the group. We would also have one person represent us as our nomination for the Spotlight presentation slot.

Excited about the synergy of this great group, we started working on the presentation materials and display. On August 19, we received the Showcase Agreement form from JRI, filled it out and returned it immediately. Our team member's video came out great and he was selected by JRI to do the Spotlight presentation.

Richard and I made our reservations to fly to Texas at the end of October, where some of our other team members lived, and put the finishing touches on everything. We were on schedule to have everything finished in plenty of time. It was wonderful to work with these positive and creative people!

Then, just 10 days before leaving for Texas and three weeks before Las Vegas, we received this email from an assistant to JRI staffer responsible for coordinating WWS activities:

> Hello!
> I am writing in regards to the WWE Showcase.
> You signed up to showcase Kangen Water, however, that business is already being showcased—and in an effort to really show everyone how diverse and great our WWS member's businesses are we would love for you all to showcase the business in which you entered the WWS as. If you have any questions or inquiries please don't hesitate to call or reply via e-mail. We look forward to seeing you both there, and attached is another showcase agreement as well.

Yes, we had a big question: *why didn't you say something about this before?* We never received the straight story from JRI, but our team learned that apparently, the person above all of us in the multi-level marketing chain for this water filter had feuded with someone on their downline—on our marketing upline. This individual insisted on being the only WWS member who could showcase the Kangen machines at the Extravaganza. The whole thing made absolutely no sense since she was above us, and anything that we sold would financially benefit her. She could have gone to the spa for the day and made money from our hard work. So much for not competing with other WWS members!

The WWS group had gone from spiritual to ugly in no time flat. They wanted to cut their own downline out of the event to spite someone one level below them and capture any sales directly and exclusively for themselves. I know this happens when money gets involved, but I thought we were working to rise above that type of behavior. Even stranger, JRI was enabling this by suddenly coming up with a new rule that there could be only one person showcasing a particular business. None of us had seen or heard the rule before and it only served to create deep divisions among the WWS members. So much for James teaching us to approach things from the viewpoint of abundance and not scarcity.

They tried to placate us by telling us not to worry; if another person joined the WWS and sold real estate, they couldn't showcase because we locked up that industry. This did not make us feel better at all. There was room for everyone, as far as we were concerned. Our teammate's presentation remained on the schedule, but if someone actually wanted to buy a Kangen machine, they could only make the purchase from this other woman. This was getting stranger by the day.

Many emails raced back and forth between our group and the JRI staffers, but we were getting nowhere. They didn't care about the work or money that had gone into our team's presentation. We were told to have nothing about the Kangen filters on our table. This also affected other WWS members who were not part of our team, but were also told that they could not present the Kangen machine. This whole thing was ridiculous! Richard and I thought certainly, if James knew this was happening, he would put a stop to it. Only one thing to do: see James. We insisted on speaking directly with him about it. After all, he had been promoting the WWS as his insider group with all of this exclusive access to him; it was time for some of that access.

The JRI staffers continued to do everything possible to prevent access to James. Other members wrote scathing letters about JRI and the way this was being handled, and decided not to participate in the showcase at all. Richard just kept insisting he wanted to speak to James directly. A couple staffers called me to "help me get through this." I'm going to give them the benefit of the doubt and hope that their hearts may have been in the right place, but we had a lot happening in our lives, and whatever patience remained towards the politics and feuding in the WWS was running thin. This was no longer about promoting water filters; it was about the entire team being treated unfairly and our concerns falling on deaf or uncaring ears. The JRI staff was blowing us off. We remained insistent on speaking with James.

To show the depth of frustration and anger among some WWS members, below is an email sent on October 24, 2008 from one member to James via the JRI staff person responsible for the WWS. Eleven other WWS members were cc'ed:

James & (JRI Staff Person),

(James, regrettably, I have not been entitled to your personal email, so I must send this email to (JRI Staff Person), in hopes you receive it.)

Allow me to personally express to both of you my absolute dismay at what is happening here with WWE. Why is JRI only allowing one Kangen booth at WWE? . . . . When someone enrolls with Kangen they are NOT just buying a water filter; they are becoming part of the vision and dream of passive income. Wouldn't you want to know who would be the best sponsor for you in achieving your financial goals? Wouldn't you want to be able to meet several people before you made such an important decision? Why play so small and in a model of scarcity? THERE IS MORE THAN ENOUGH FOR EVERYBODY! . . . .

Evidently, JRI has made it perfectly clear that (our team member) will present the Kangen water, and the person to buy from is (other woman). Did (this other woman) pay extra for her WWS membership? How do I sign up for that WWS membership? I would love to have someone give the sales pitch for me, and then sit at the back room and clean up, very sweet deal. Whoever made the decision of only one Kangen booth, should have consulted with a network marketing professional beforehand, they would have told you that this kind of decision would create an upheaval. Do you realize that (this other woman) is at the VERY top of the WWS Kangen pyramid, and that every time one of the 20+ people in HER organization sells a unit she gets paid? Months ago, when WWE was created, I announced to everyone in the MSI World Team, that I would not have a table at WWE and would rather support the entire team as a whole. Perhaps being a team player leads to success . . . something to think about.

In Egypt James, you personally told me that only (this woman) was to have a booth with Kangen at WWE. Obviously, I was surprised to get this news and made a few decisions based on this comment privately. One of those decisions was to NOT attend WWE, I will not participate in petty drama, I put a high value on my time and 2 days is priceless.

I really pondered whether or not to express myself in email and be considered politically incorrect by JRI. It is obviously easier to sit back and watch this drama play out, but as a leader of MSI World Team and by my very nature, I am choosing to let you know how I feel. Here you have it . . . I AM perplexed by the inconsideration of the JRI organization to its most "valued" clients! I'm not the smartest person on the planet, but I bet you both, that in April, when many WWS members go to renew their WWS membership, they might remember "their WWE event" in November 2008, I certainly will.

. . . I really invite JRI to consider allowing more than one table for Kangen, more than one table for financial planners, more than one table for numerologists, more than one table for (a vitamin brand), more than one table for chocolate confectioners, more than one table for everything and anything, allowing the entire room and event to be prosperous, abundant and drama free! Empower the people to decide who makes the best chocolate, or gives the best financial advice, or who they want to partner up with in a MLM company . . .

In Peace,
Rachel

PS— . . . I will not be in attendance at WWE. So at this point please understand, this is NOT about me, this about wanting to play full on with a team of people that allow the space for ALL to prosper.

The writer of this email, Rachel, came to the U.S. alone as a teenager. She didn't speak English. She has since built many successful businesses and is financially very well off. Rachel is a very ethical person who donates a lot of her time and money to causes in which she believes. As you can see from the email, she was majorly ticked off. Rachel was also right about the effect this decision would have on re-enrollment in the WWS the coming year.

True to JRI form, even though this email came from an "inner circle" member, there is no indication from the response later that day that James ever saw it. I now know that he did; he sees and controls everything. Imagine how you would feel if you took the time to write that email and received this as your only response:

> Hi Rachel,
> Thank you for sharing your thoughts. As a personal development company we are constantly growing, changing, and improving; we appreciate your feedback and will take this into consideration. If you or any of the other members of MSI World Team would like to discuss the decision of James Ray International further [JRI staffer] and I are more than happy to schedule a collective conference call.
> In joy,
> [JRI staffer responsible for the WWS]

Richard and I were disgusted with the politics and the heavy handedness. We considered skipping the event altogether, or as a team, defy the new rule and put water filters on the table. Our reservations for Texas had all ready been made, and we had arranged the trip to coincide with a real estate class we needed to attend, so we headed for Austin at the end of October.

It was wonderful to see our fellow WWS members, but our objective of pulling together our team display was a moot point unless we figured out what we were going to do. Those of us who elected not to ditch the showcase in protest did not want to cause more trouble by proceeding with a team table. We have found that confronting low-level behavior with more low-level behavior rarely results in a pleasant outcome.

On October 26, 2008, our team sadly acknowledged that we had resolved nothing. As we climbed into a truck to return to our hotel room, my phone rang. It was James. I asked him if he wanted to talk with the team, and he said no, he called to talk with just Richard and me. The other two people walked inside the house, eagerly awaiting the outcome of our talk. Everyone felt if one of us could talk to James, then being a logical businessman, he would see how this was unfair and the problem would be fixed.

Within the first few minutes, it was clear James was not going to change his stand on allowing only one member to present a specific product. He wanted to show the WWS as a diverse group and not have several of us promoting the same product or service no matter what it was. He did not want the showcase to look like a Kangen convention and that was that. As we all found out, it was only James' opinion that mattered.

Richard and I knew it was time to give it up. We received one thing we wanted: the chance to plead our case. Even though we did not like the outcome, we reached a point with James to agree to disagree. He asked us why we even got in the middle of this, because we did not join the WWS to promote these water systems. (True.) He told us to leave the Kangen business bickering to the members for whom Kangen was their main financial focus, and not waste any more of our time or energy on it. He said it was taking our attention away from our main business. (Also true.) Instead, he wanted us to concentrate on the profession at which we were expert—real estate—and not let ourselves get distracted by other things. (Good advice, even though the real distraction was this fuss over the showcase.)

He asked us to tell him one challenge we faced with our real estate business, and he would help step us through resolving it. We told him one of the reasons we were in Austin was to evaluate whether or not we should buy into our office and become its operating partners. Austin is our company's headquarters, and the class covered how the company and individual offices, called Market Centers, operated. We wanted to learn their unique business model. We talked about the challenges many other real estate offices in our area were experiencing due to the problems with the economy and the real estate market in general. Even though many of them were shrinking or failing completely, we believed we had a wonderful core group of agents to build a great office. If we could weather out the current economic storm, there was great potential. James asked us what differentiated this company from the others, and why we thought it could succeed as others failed. Our particular company was different because the management put the agent and clients before the company. When combined with true profit sharing, we could successfully grow the office while other offices shrank. This particular franchise's model was the future of a successful real estate office, while the others were based on a model that had long outlived its effectiveness.

The entire endeavor had its risks; James asked us to list them. We would be putting a substantial amount of our money into a real estate company during a time when all businesses were struggling—and one of the hardest hit sectors was real estate. After discussing the pros and cons, James helped us reach our decision to proceed with the investment because when we got to the bottom line, we believed this company had heart and felt it was the right thing to do. At the end of the call, he wanted our commitment to attend the event and showcase our real estate business. We agreed even though we would have to put a display together very quickly.

After we hung up the phone and were heading back into the house, I realized what James had done. He persuaded us to agree to give up the fight over promoting the Kangen filters by drawing our attention to a more serious business concern of ours. In providing us the value of his insight and time in working through our critical business decision, we ended the phone call "losing" on the Kangen systems, but "winning" by gaining his valuable help with an important decision. He also persuaded us to showcase our real estate business, which accomplished two things for him. He banked on it to stem the tide of ticked off WWS members planning not to attend the WWE, and also show diversification among the WWS membership. He hoped a wider range of businesses might make the WWS appear more appealing to a broader range of prospective new members.

Our intention was to be heard by Mr. Big, and we were. Unfortunately, we needed to pitch a major fit to accomplish it. He was right though. The dispute over showcasing the Kangen filters was a distraction we didn't need, and we were glad it was over.

We walked back into the house; our team was smiling. One of them asked if it was time to break out the champagne. "No," we said, and then we relayed our conversation with James. Their smiles quickly faded, and they drove us back to the hotel.

I learned something important about James in that interaction. Even when it appeared information was not piercing his JRI staff's armored barrier, it was. In all likelihood, he handled every decision made at JRI. He controlled everything very tightly, both inside and outside the events. I also learned he was just as good at manipulating words and reactions to his words off-stage as he was on.

Less than two weeks later, we were on our way to Las Vegas for Quantum Leap. We didn't have the time to pull too much together for our real estate presentation, but we were still carrying a lot in our bags—especially for two people used to traveling light. While walking through the casino on our way to the meeting room to register, I swear I saw the same older man camped out at the same video poker machine, and wearing the same cap, as last year. That couldn't be . . . could it?

Many of our friends were not Dream Teaming this time, so we decided to sit outside the WWS roped-off area so we could be with them for Quantum Leap. Because we were allowed into the room early, we grabbed great seats for all of us, up front and on the side, right next to the WWS section.

One of our MOTL friends, Ron, had become a coach for JRI. When we split up into pairs to do the exercises, he was my partner. One assignment was to work on a major limiting belief and expose it for the lie that it was; to be free of it. To my surprise, my major limiting belief remained my weight. With all of the work I had done over the last two years, I thought it should be completely gone by now. But it was like peeling the layers of an onion. You rip off the outer layer, just to find another layer still inside. I felt like this self-imposed belief that it was not safe to be pretty or look sexy would never go away. No matter how much I worked at it, it would still be there, just smaller.

Ron and I were working on this issue when I noticed James watching us intently from the stage. We were in the front row, just to the side of the WWS section. I knew him well enough to recognize that look; he did not approve of something. It was the same look he flashed when I Dream Teamed Practical Mysticism and he was watching me talk with Erica and other WWS members at a break. Why was I getting the look this time? Was this something left over from our phone call? Or because we had decided not to sit in the WWS section? Appearances were very important to James, and he may have been concerned with how it looked to see empty WWS prime seats. Time would tell what his issue was; he always let you know sooner or later, even if he did so in an inappropriate manner, like later "flaming" you from the stage when you ask a question on mic.

The rest of the event was nearly identical to 2007. The only change I noticed was the addition of safety goggles for the arrow break activity, undoubtedly due to the guy injuring his eye with a piece of the arrow shaft the year before. Dr. John held my arrow against my throat for me to break and Edward held Richard's. Between accomplishing this in 2007 and bending rebar, this no longer made even a blip on our concern meters. We used our time waiting in line to support people who were clearly stressed as they waited their turn.

There were many more Dream Teamers at this event than usual because James was working on an initiative to bring the Quantum Leap seminar to Dubai. To do so, he needed many people trained as Dream Teamers. Unless you participated as a Dream Team member during this event, we heard, you would not qualify to travel to Dubai. Speculation ran wild as to how much, if anything, James would pay for volunteer expenses—which were extensive, as he planned several back-to-back sessions. Many thought he couldn't possibly expect people to pay for something like that on their own, but I wasn't so sure. He planned some other stops around the world in conjunction with the trip. Plans were not firmed up yet, but James was becoming an international celebrity (at least in his own mind).

The announcement of the trip and dates was imminent. This was James' Dubai period. Dubai was enjoying a peak economic cycle. Astute businessmen figured out ways to conduct business there; that's where the money and action seemed to be.

At least that's what James thought. Over the next year, all talk about Dubai ceased. Apparently, James could not come up with a way to put a positive spin on why he did not do it. He said nothing and no one wanted to ask him about it.

At Quantum Leap, a suspicion of ours was confirmed. A couple of WWS members told us they never booked their hotel rooms under the "James Ray Discount Rate" because it was *more* than a regular reservation. When they told the JRI WWS staff person what they were doing, they said she looked "less than thrilled" at the news. We'd booked our rooms a time or two using the "James Ray Discount Rate," only to realize the rate didn't seem discounted at all.

Event coordinators have told me it is customary for an event's host to receive a small fee for every room a participant books. The group staging the event usually negotiates a reduced hotel rate so that, even with their cut added onto the "discounted rate," the total the visitor pays should be less than the regular hotel rate. One explanation for James elevated "discount rate" was he might have negotiated a higher kickback amount than usual.

I looked at our Participant Guides that stretched back to the first Harmonic Wealth Weekend in February 2007. Included were directions on making room reservations. The only part of the 12-page black and white guide they felt was important enough to be in color, bold red to be exact: To reserve a room at this special rate, please call the San Diego Marriott Hotel & Marina directly at 800.228.9290 prior to Tuesday, January 3, 2007 and identify yourself as a member of the James Ray International group.

After that, this additional bold-faced direction: We recommend that all participants, including local attendees, plan to stay at our host hotel, as the seminar will begin early and end late on both Friday and Saturday.

Why was it so important to JRI that they boldface the "recommendation"? JRI inserted this next section into the accommodations page, also in bold: So that we can ensure that you receive the group discount for your guest room, as soon as you make your reservation with the host hotel, please email your name, your roommate's name (if applicable), and your confirmation number to events@james-ray.com.

Dream Team volunteers received *the same participant guide and directions*. In addition to making hard-working volunteers pay for their own transportation, food, and hotel, was James also benefiting financially from them booking their hotel rooms under the JRI name and rate? Hotels also comp rooms (provide free of charge) to a group scheduling a large event, or at the very least, offer a number of rooms at a substantial discount. Couldn't James have offered comp rooms to the volunteers instead of making them pay for their rooms while working free at his events?

While we were setting up our table during the break between Quantum Leap and the Extravaganza, Carol, one of the other WWS members, eyed our display to make sure nothing related to the Kangen filters. She had also been told she could not promote them. This situation caused a general feeling of distrust among the members. Our teammate made his presentation, limiting his discussion to the importance of clean water in the world and using reusable containers without specifically mentioning the Kangen filters. During the showcase, a Kangen machine made its way onto his table. If anyone had questions about water filtration, we sent them to him.

Just like in the earlier WW Congress, we had four great speakers. One was the same gentleman who had talked about the current financial situation in the world; now, he is handling our money. There was also a speaker and writer who worked and conducted research in vibratory medicine, a well-known speaker and author on interpersonal communications, and a former performer on the TV show *American Gladiators,* a woman who talked about staying in shape even while traveling or not being able to get to the gym. So we covered the financial, physical and relational pillars this time.

We anticipated the announcement of the following year's WWS excursion. We all wondered how James could possibly top our recent trip to Egypt. He told us before that he wanted to take us to the Amazon to experience the psychotropic brew Ayahuasca. This drink, sacred to natives, became known to many Americans through William S. Burroughs' early sixties book *The Yage Letters,* consisting of letters he wrote to famed poet Allen Ginsberg about it. A specific brew made from the *B. caapi* vine and several other ingredients, Ayahuasca is said to help cure mental and physical illness and allow communication with the spirit world. Like its North American native religions counterpart, peyote, it also induces visions and magnifies one's psychological state. In other words, if you're happy, you could move into a truly exalted, euphoric space. If you're angry or brooding over something, well, it could be a long night. The brew is ingested in a very ceremonial way, often with a shaman chanting and drumming, communicating with the animal and spirit worlds, guiding participants, and serving as the bridge between the otherworldly realms.

Apparently James had ingested Ayahuasca before. As we listened to his stories of how it can make you very sick and vomit profusely, Richard leaned over to me and said, "I have absolutely no interest in going on this trip." I investigated and found out that, according to Wikipedia, Ayahuasca's religious use in Brazil was legalized in the mid-1980s after two official inquiries concluded it had valid spiritual uses. As we saw it, our next trip could be centered on something that would cause "intense vomiting and occasional diarrhea." Not so appealing. With all of the places in the world to visit, we hoped that James would select something different. Otherwise, our participation in next year's trip was definitely in question.

One place represented on our vision boards was Machu Picchu. Richard was definitely hoping for that. Even though I very much wanted to see it, I was deeply concerned about how I would do at such a high altitude. Machu Picchu saddles the end of the Inca trail, some 9,000 feet above sea level. Between my weight and lingering asthma,

I was worried I would not be able to take a trip like that. Many times, we had also heard the story of James' climb up Huayna Picchu, the steep cone shaped mountain that juts from the back of Machu Picchu. We heard how challenging it was —straight-up, switchback hiking along a pencil-thin trail that, in a few places, dropped two thousand feet to the river below. I knew in my present condition, I would not be able to even attempt it.

The time finally came for the big announcement, we were going to Peru. Richard was ecstatic. James even looked directly at Richard and me, checking our reaction, noting his approval. When he announced Egypt the year earlier, I jumped out of my seat. This time, I was having more of a panic attack while Richard bounced around with excitement. When James made eye contact with me and said, "Peru, isn't that great?" I had to say, "Oh yeah, great!" and applaud when I was really thinking *"Oh crap, I'm in deep dodo now!"*

Why does James always seem to look right at one of us when he announces these trips? In the front row, just a few feet from him, I had no place to hide; I had to fake enthusiasm. James told us later that his first choice was to go and experience Ayahuasca in the Amazon jungle, but his lawyers would not let him take us there. I had to wonder if his lawyers knew about the other things he already had us doing at his events.

He had another announcement as well. He told us by signing up for another year's membership in WWS, we would secure this fabulous trip to Peru—likely to include an amazing night-time ceremony on the death stone at Machu Picchu for which only James could provide the necessary special access. He offered the membership at a special discount of $45,000 for a single, or $56,250 for a team or couple. In addition to these great benefits, he was going to offer The Quickening seminar again, by invitation only, and the invitations would first go to WWS members who had already attended all of the other events. Since the class size was limited to a very small number, he said our only hope of getting in would be as WWS members. Dangling Machu Picchu was the carrot that caught Richard's attention; The Quickening seminar did it for me. I had heard from others who had attended The Quickening that it was a very powerful class that dived deeply into ancient spiritual teachings. It was only offered once every few years, and it was something I wanted to attend. But $56,250 was a bit out of our budget. On the other hand, we definitely were not going to "invest in" the regular membership price of $75,000, so if we were going to join, we needed to take advantage of the discount rate. Regardless, we were not sprinting to the back table like we did the first time to sign up.

James re-stated what he had said at the first Quantum Leap: his "goal" was to have 60 members join in the first year; he'd achieved that, with 65+ members. Unfortunately, we knew that wasn't true, and it just reinforced our decision to hold off rejoining. There were quite a few things that did not turn out the way we had thought they would. We were not happy with the large membership number, the way WWS had become a business networking group that left the spiritual goals behind, and the bickering and competition between the members. As for "special" access to James, we had only one private phone call with him, and that took a major hissy fit. Over the next few days, we learned he was also trying to take away some of the early members' privileges, such as allowing family members to attend events free. This did not sit well, especially for those of us with children. Apparently, he stopped offering many of those things to new members as the membership number swelled; now, he was trying to take these benefits away from us as well. He called it "making it fair and leveling the playing field." We saw it as more broken promises.

We waited to give it more thought.

After being around James for a couple of years, other aspects concerned us. He definitely had an obsession with money and his image. He spent money way too frivolously, in our opinion. James always told us the only way to travel was in the front of the plane (first class) and the back of the car (in a limo), and he was doing just that. However, in the next breath, he would complain about being short of funds— being "out on the skinny branches of the tree", as he put it. He told us that he spent over $1 million producing a TV infomercial that flopped. Then he said he was buying a $4 million home in Beverly Hills. His reason for moving to LA was he had been working on putting together a TV show; he hoped to become the "Dr. Phil" of spirituality. We didn't understand why he needed the Beverly Hills address for anything other than his ego. He could have lived across town, in Century City, Hollywood, Brentwood, Santa Monica or another nice LA-area neighborhood, for a small fraction of what he had paid. And he would've made it to the TV studio just fine.

James was also training speakers to handle his free two-hour intro events so he did not have to travel as much. We attended one of those events and didn't see anyone sign up for anything afterwards. James' two-hour event had devolved into a one-hour pitch session to get people to sign up for Harmonic Wealth Weekend with some question and answer time as content. Success had become more the result of a slick, well-delivered sales pitch rather than the quality of the material. The stand-in speakers could deliver the content, but no one was slicker at the sales pitch than James. We knew someone who applied for the speaking job, and he said the contract was heavily stacked in favor of James, with little money going to the speaker. "That contract was crazy!" The speaker was responsible for paying for the venue and other costs, and only received a small percentage from the people who signed up. In the end, James continued his road trips. Later, I heard this same contractual complaint from James' coaches. He was coming more and more from scarcity, trying to squeeze every penny out of everyone, instead of practicing what he taught, to come from a place of abundance and spread the wealth around. He seemed to forget about his direction to make everyone else successful, and then you will be, too.

In addition, James was filming the events, with the hope he would eventually stop doing them as well. He wanted to send a speaker onstage to introduce the film clips and lead attendees in the live exercises. Other well-known speakers have gone this route and succeeded for a while. It may be an acceptable format for some, but not everyone. Richard and I had planned to attend one of these well-know speakers' seminars, but then declined when we learned the speaker would not even be at his own seminar. James envisioned himself moving towards a TV show while facilitators ran his events for him—and commissioned speakers/salesmen signed people up. Obviously he was not successful in implementing this model. His popularity had just peaked. Over the next year, he would see a decline in attendance at his events. The buzz from his appearance in the documentary, *The Secret,* was wearing off.

During the showcase, James came by to see the displays. In a conciliatory tone, he offered to facilitate a free two-hour event at our office in celebration of us becoming the operating partners. I was starting to see the pattern: he pushes to "win" a discussion, and then appears to think it over and decide he may have been a bit too harsh, judgmental, and/or ungrateful. This offer was clearly a peace offering, his way of thanking us for letting him "win" the Kangen promotion argument. We will never know whether he decided we were right, that our team was treated unfairly, or was just happy he got his way.

His offer to do the seminar in our office was very generous, and we appreciated it. We told him we would wait until the transition was official first.

We gave the offer additional thought. In the end, we decided to pass on the private seminar. His hard-sell tactics had always embarrassed us, and we didn't want him to apply the same pressure to our agents, some of who were struggling financially due to the current real estate market. The last thing they needed was to go into debt purchasing a seminar they could not afford. There was still some of Mr. Buffini alive in us. We needed to support the agents in maintaining their budgets, so as much as we might love James to talk about goal setting, we could not risk exposing our agents to his hard sell tactics.

In early December 2008, we attended Creating Absolute Wealth in San Diego for the second time. I was curious how differently I would approach being "homeless" this time. They set the activity the same as before. We did not break for lunch, but instead selected our clothing from the two piles of men and women's garments in the meeting room. Again, I wore a Christmas top, but at least it was December so I would not look as daffy as I did during the earlier springtime event. Staffers smeared grease in our hair, put makeup "dirt" on our face and hands, and added extra holes and rips in our clothing. Same instructions as last time: we were not allowed to make eye contact with another member of our seminar. This time, a WWS friend from Canada brought along her two teen-aged kids. She had participated in this event before and planned to spend the entire time on the street shadowing her daughter while a group of us kept an eye on her son. Our bus dropped us off again next to an upscale shopping mall—a perfect place for a "homeless" teenager! Still, I understood why a Mom would want to have someone watching out for her kids during this exercise.

I wanted to handle the next few hours differently than the first time, just to see if it would leave me with a different impression. As soon as I got off the bus, I started walking around fairly quickly. It was a habit developed from always being in a hurry. Where was I rushing? I made myself stop and stand there for a few minutes. It almost killed me. I needed a mission, a purpose, and a task for every minute in the day. Right now, I didn't. I decided to slow down and see and hear more of what was going on around me. I looked at the flowers blooming so beautifully around the shopping center.

A flower stand flanked one of the main entrances to the mall. Much to the dismay of the woman working there, I smelled every flower at her stand. She smiled at me nervously, clearly wondering what I would do next. I commented that some of the giant long-stem roses had no smell, while smaller blossoms were wonderfully fragrant. I was trying to engage her in a conversation to find out more about her, but she would only answer my questions with as few words as possible. She wasn't unfriendly, she just seemed nervous about me being there.

After I finished smelling each flower, I sat on the bench directly across from her stand and continued to admire her flowers. She never took her eyes off me, except to help a customer. Several people came along; one at a time, and joined me on "my" bench. One very nicely dressed woman sat as far away from me as she could, leaning the other direction. I decided I had nothing better to do but to have a little fun with her. I asked if she knew what time it was; she told me without making eye contact. I made a comment about the beautiful roses at the flower stand. "Uh hum," she muttered.

Then I started to slide towards her, very slowly, so slowly that, after a few minutes, she must have wondered if I was getting closer or if she was imagining it. My goal was to see how close I could get before she felt compelled to get up. She started to lean farther and farther away, but did not stand. This was fun! I was also teaching myself patience. I had to move slowly and then wait for a minute or two before starting again. My experiment came to an end when her husband came along and they left together, but not before I had made my way to within a foot of her.

I glanced back at the flower stand. The woman who worked there smiled broadly as she looked at me.

A minute later another older woman, dressed in a janitor's uniform, sat right next to me. I scooted over to make more room for her. I asked her for the time. She smiled and held up her arm with her watch. She spoke very little English, but we spent the next few minutes pleasantly enjoying our time on the bench together. When she left, she smiled and nodded to me; I returned the gesture. About thirty seconds later, a very lovely 30-year-old woman sat down next to me. She looked up and down the road for her ride, then took out a square white Styrofoam container and popped it open. Inside the box was the biggest muffin I had ever seen. It approached the size of a small cake. "Wow, where did you get that?" I asked.

She gave me directions to the bakery stand. "This is my favorite muffin in the whole world. It's soooo good!" she said as she broke it in half and started to eat it. "You know," she continued, "right after I bought this huge thing, I got a call from my boyfriend and we are meeting people for an early dinner. He is on his way to get me right now. I need to eat something because I skipped lunch, but if I eat this whole thing I won't be able to eat dinner. Do you want part of this?"

She held out the other half for me. I suggested that she save it for later. She shook her head and smiled. "It will just go stale. Please do me a favor and take it before I eat it. You are doing me a favor, really."

I took it and thanked her. I took a bite. She was right; the muffin was amazing. I told her it tasted like lemon pound cake. We sat on the bench, eating the muffin until her boyfriend showed up. She bounced off of "my" bench, walked quickly to his car, and climbed inside.

I wiped my hands on my pants. When I looked up, the woman at the flower stand was still watching me. We smiled at each other. Now that three people had survived an encounter with me, she figured that I must be harmless.

I was having fun on the bench, but it was made of concrete, so it was time to get my butt up and move around. I saw my friend's son sitting on the steps of a large restaurant, so I positioned myself to watch both him and the fountain for a while. I knew him from the seminar. Like my own daughter, he was an old soul, wise beyond his years. He did not look the least bit concerned about where he was; rather, he looked bored. A very tall thin man came by and gave me a small envelope and said, "Jesus loves you," and kept on walking. I opened the flap; inside was a $5 gift card to a sub sandwich store. "To: A Very Special Person. From: Jesus," the tag said. What a great idea! Instead of handing out money to people living on the streets, give them food cards. I was really feeling the love now. Before I boarded the bus, I passed the gift card to someone who appeared to be really homeless. Jesus' love went a long way that afternoon.

Some people in our group asked for money and gave it away before they returned to the bus stop. Rachel, the very successful businesswoman on our Kangen team, raised enough money to buy over 30 sandwiches for a group of guys hanging out in a nearby park. This was the same woman who arrived in the U.S. with nothing, then survived and thrived by being resourceful. Apparently, she tapped into that resourcefulness very well as a "homeless" person.

While waiting for the bus, Martha approached me. I knew her from this and other seminars at which I Dream Teamed. She sat down beside me and started to cry. Knowing we were not supposed to talk yet, I did not say anything to her. We were not to make eye contact, but no one said anything about butt contact. I slid over until I was sitting against her. She responded by leaning over into my side, and there we stayed as we waited for the bus. She later told me an elderly lady who lived in subsidized housing downtown approached her and offered to pay her if she could come back to her place and do some cleaning and move a few things around her small one-bedroom apartment. Martha obliged, but in the end, refused the money. She was upset the elderly woman was so alone she had to rely on homeless strangers to help her. Martha looked around her little apartment and saw few possessions. A thought gripped her: what if she ended up helpless and alone when she was old?

James gave us a lecture about how our country's current economic mess was nothing more than the ebb and flow of a natural cycle, like the movement through the seasons. We'd heard this before. He said we were currently in the winter of our economic cycle and needed to get ready for spring and summer, because it would come. He added that there are never two winters in a row; summer would have to arrive. "Seasons come and seasons go" was his catch phrase. He followed with an idea of what we could do to "plant the seeds for a successful summer": sign up for more of his seminars. They would provide us the tools we needed to take full advantage of the approaching summer. And don't worry about the cost, because when summer comes, we'll make up the investment and then some. You will miss your big chance later if you don't act now.

Leaving my thoughts about the ice age aside, I still had some questions about his take on a natural financial cycle and there never being two winters in a row. I raised my hand and asked him if he was familiar with a documentary that suggested that our country's financial health was being manipulated by a group of people for their own gain. I named the film. "How do we change or align our thinking that the economy is just ebbing and flowing though a natural cycle if the cycle may not be natural at all but manmade?" I asked. "How can we best navigate through that and protect ourselves from it?"

Even though I did not agree with some of the documentary's conclusions, it did bring up some things to think about. Specifically, how our banking system had been manipulated in the past so a few larger banks could swallow up their competition. Or, how other groups could cause the stock market to plunge, allowing them to buy major interests in companies for pennies on the dollar. They could force a stock "fire sale" and smaller banks to fail, and then take full advantage of the situation. Heck, maybe they could also get the government to throw in some money to shore up their newly acquired assets at the same time! It happened in the past, and it appeared to be happening again. I wanted to know if he could suggest a way we, the "little guys," could ride out the storm.

Apparently, I hit a nerve. James did not want to enter into a discussion on how his "natural flow of the economic cycle" might have to be tweaked. He acknowledged he knew of the documentary and then started out his next sentence by saying, "I am usually tougher on my WWS members than I am on other attendees . . . " This meant trouble. Any time he started answering a question that way, the person who asked was about to be "flamed" by James. Most of us noticed the real mean streak growing in him lately. He likes to hide behind calling it "tough love", but he was quickly becoming just plain mean at times. When his meanness was present, he rarely answered the question. Was this becoming his way of dodging a question?

One of my friends in the row behind me said softly, "Oh oh." I was thinking the same thing. He launched into a nasty tirade that ended with calling me a "cosmic foo foo," and a conspiracy theorist. He said the movie was trash. We needed to stay focused. That I should know better by now than to pay attention to something like that. I did not fight back, knowing it would just set him off further. Also, the force of his attack shocked me. During the break, numerous people, including Faith, came up and said they thought he was way too hard on me, and others said I should have fought back.

Looking back, I realized several things from that exchange. First, he counted on the subject of his aggression not fighting back when he was on stage. If he had come up and said those things to me in person, we would have entered into a conversation—not what he really wanted. Secondly, he did not answer or address my question about coming out of our economic "winter" because he did not want to. Was his nasty fit a way for him to draw attention away from my question? Did I throw a wrench into his suggestion we should spend *more* on his seminars to prepare for the "summer" fast approaching? What if summer was really a long way away? I hit a nerve all right, but what did his calling me a "cosmic foo foo" have to do with economics? I had to think about that one for a while.

Later I watched him launch into another tirade that started out, "I am tougher on my coaches than on other attendees . . . " He went off on something that had nothing to do with the question his coach asked on mic. Now I understood why he called me a "cosmic foo foo." It had nothing to do with the economic question I asked. I believe he was sending me a public message to stay away from the MOTL members. Remember how James gave me "that look" when I sat with friends at Quantum Leap instead of remaining in the WWS section? I knew sooner or later, I would get "spoken to." James knew several MOTL members were friends of mine, and he wanted to distance himself and his WWS from them.

I was asking James questions off mic, such as if he was going to teach any of the ancient practices that used to be in the "old" Modern Magick events. James never gave me a straight answer, and appeared annoyed by the question. In Egypt, I asked him where he learned some of the ancient Egyptian ceremonies he was telling us about; he would not answer me. I was asking too many questions about things he did not want to discuss.

When I saw Faith after the break, she was laughing. She told me half the seminar attendees had returned to their rooms to Google the movie. James' over-reaction spiked everyone's curiosity—and probably sold some DVDs of the documentary.

Later, we repeated the trust exercise where we were blindfolded and led around the hotel grounds. This time Richard was not my partner, but someone I barely knew. The man leading me around was very attentive and careful, and I felt safe and OK. Then a hand grabbed mine quickly and started running with me, spinning me around. I knew from seeing him do this to others that it was James, and was fine with it. I had come a long way with trusting others in the last year. That whole thing would have bothered the heck out of me before.

James called a meeting of WWS members before the concluding black tie dinner dance on the third night of the event,. He was concerned that everyone had not jumped on the "opportunity" to rejoin the WWS when the discounted membership fee was announced back at the Extravaganza. The deadline for the membership discount was the end of the current month, and he needed to find out why people weren't rejoining. He pulled the chairs into a big circle. True to form, he sat with his brother on one side and his assistant on the other. Even after the trip to Egypt, he still acted like he might get cooties if he sat next to any of us. He directed us to join the meeting in the order we had joined the WWS. Since Richard and I signed up on the first possible day, we entered in the first wave, along with others who joined in the initial five-month period. The next wave would join the meeting in about half an hour, and the last to join the meeting would be the newest members who recently signed up. It was interesting that James broke us up according to our joining date because the primary interests of each wave had changed markedly, mostly due to changes in the way James pitched the WWS and its benefits. Our wave voiced concerns over the lack of a spiritual aspect in the WWS. We were no further along with the WWS humanitarian project than the day we started, and we did not like the commercialism and division that came with becoming a business networking group. We also did not like losing some of the promised privileges, like being able to attend events other than Spiritual Warrior for free and complimentary registrations for our children.

The second wave's primary concerns centered on not being able to promote their businesses as much as they wanted, and that James should be doing more to help develop their businesses and coach them. Both groups requested more personal interaction with him. The shift from primarily a spiritual group to a business group had taken place, and it was no wonder James was having trouble keeping both camps satisfied. After the last group joined us, Richard brought up the issue of having to pay the large WWS membership fee in a single payment, rather than making several installments. James agreed to look into it. The last concern the group discussed was the excursions: they were the most beneficial part of the membership. We wanted more—two smaller trips and one large excursion each year. When James asked for suggestions, Richard said he would like to take the hike in Sedona as they used to do at past Spiritual Warrior events. Shortly after the meeting, James announced anyone who rejoined WWS before the next WWS Congress (held at Cabo San Lucas in February) would be eligible to join him on a private hike in Sedona.

I noticed another change in James. His haughty arrogance was waning as the enthusiasm of the members in rejoining decreased. He was now willing to listen to our concerns and make some concessions. We thought he was finally listening and that things would improve when he came back to us and agreed to let our children continue to attend the seminars free, and produced a payment plan for the membership fee,. With the deadline approaching to join at the discounted price, and no hope of an extension (which is what we were told at the time), we made the difficult decision to rejoin for one more year. However, if we didn't see continued improvement over the next year, this would be our last.

The final event of the year was our WWS New Year's Eve party. James mingled with us almost like a "normal" person, more relaxed than usual, with no bodyguards. But not all was normal. We were not allowed to invite anyone to join us, other than one guest for each single member. James made his own separate rules for himself and invited his parents, in addition to a girl friend. True to form, he sat at a table with his parents, his brother and his brother's wife, and JRI staff members. James could only stand to mingle for so long. We stopped partying at around 11:30 p.m. and spent a few minutes setting our intentions for the coming year. James led us in a meditation and we welcomed the New Year.

I was thinking that night: the best thing about the WWS is the people. We made some close friends through WWS, and it was great to spend New Year's with them. At the same time, I missed commemorating the New Year with some of our other friends, and wished for a way to blend the two groups. Cabo and the WWS Congress were just a couple of months away. No one in that room had any idea what changes 2009 was going to bring.

Looking back, that night seems a million miles away.

CHAPTER 15

Desperate Times Call for Desperate Measures

Early 2009

A woman is like a tea bag. You can't tell how strong
she is until you put her in hot water.

—Eleanor Roosevelt

Richard and I headed to Cabo San Lucas, Mexico for the World Wealth Congress, the first WWS meeting for members only. This is not to be confused with the previous World Wealth Congress, which was free to everyone who attended Modern Magick in Kona. For some reason, James decided to re-use the name; the two events could not have been more different.

The night before the event, a few WWS members invited their image consultant from Beverly Hills to give us a demonstration of her work. Apparently, they must have thought some of us looked ratty and were in need of professional help. The consultant, Linda, was a lovely Persian lady with huge dark eyes. As soon as I walked through the large wooden double doors of her hotel suite, I saw that this demonstration would involve clothing. Clothing and I were not friends. In fact, we weren't on speaking terms most of the time. I picked up my champagne and made a hasty retreat to the large ocean view balcony, where I watched the beautiful sunset with several other members until her presentation began.

During her session, Linda discussed simple ways to look better in our clothing, and what to avoid when purchasing new clothes. I knew my wardrobe really needed help. I used to jokingly say that I purchased my fine couture at Costco, but really, I looked it. I am not the type of person to spend a lot of money on trendy or name brand clothing. However, I will spend money on a classic that's going to last awhile. My problem is there are not many classic styles in my size range.

Linda had an instinctual ability to determine, just from eyeing someone, which clothes would work great. Her racks were full of fun, classic clothing pieces that, for the most part, were reasonably priced. I wanted to know more. I needed help, and I knew she would not have anything on her racks to fit me. I imagined Linda was used to working with models, actors and actresses, so I made sure she was ready to take on a very plus-sized woman. We had a quick conversation, during which she assured me it would be her pleasure to work with me. I signed up for her weekend session, to take place two months later in April, just before Modern Magick in Dana Point.

When the congress started, James invited us to briefly describe our businesses by way of introducing ourselves to each other. This was very helpful, but I wondered if this entire weekend was going to pertain only to our businesses. Other than an afternoon session dedicated to the WWS project, and the intense sales pitch by James to sign up again, this weekend was clearly all about business. I thought the meeting would be a little more relaxed, but James carried a sharp edge. He was even more intense than usual. It probably had to do with the very small number of people who rejoined. The WWS was his major cash cow, and it was imploding. That left no time for a group meditation, which a few of us requested. There was plenty of time for the hard sell, though.

During introductions, a friend of ours, Lana, became the unfortunate target of one of James' "flame" sessions. As usual, the verbal tirade was mean and excessive. It made me wonder if there was something behind the scenes. What else could explain his angry attack? I knew from my own experience that he delivered a public message as a warning that may not relate to the subject being discussed. The reason he was "all over her," he said, was because he did not feel she was moving fast or decisively enough towards her goals. Lana didn't take the berating lightly; she stood up to him throughout the weekend. She told him his tough love approach had too much tough in it and not enough compassion. She later wrote that he needed to stop using force to get what he wanted. A theme was building: James' lack of compassion.

We finally discussed the WWS philanthropic project. There was still no consensus among the group regarding what we would undertake. With that, James declared we were going to have several projects; our choice on which project suited us. He devised a clever way of handling this in an orderly manner. If you actively and passionately supported a cause, he asked you to stand up and give a description, then stand at the edge of the room holding a sign with the project's name on it. After everyone was finished, he gave the sign-holders a chance to decide if they preferred to work on someone else's project. If that was the case, then they joined the other project. Next, each member was asked to select a project they wanted to support and go stand by the appropriate sign. With the different projects defined and groups formed, we talked within our groups about the project objectives, and then developed short- and long-term plans of action. For the final step, James told us to calculate how we were going to fund our group's objectives and report back to JRI with our results in a couple of weeks.

I was confused. Why did we have to put our money into these group projects? What about the tens of thousands of dollars we paid for our WWS memberships? I asked the JRI staffer how the WWS money was going to be divided up to support the different groups. She smiled, "It's up to you to financially support your own groups."

I was stunned! The dues money we paid was going only to James; none of it was going to be used for any charitable or socially conscious project. At the very least, this multimillionaire could throw some of his own money into the pot. How could he think what we were receiving as WWS members was worth that much money without at least part of it going to support a project? Richard and I noticed during the WWS sales pitch at the WW Extravaganza he did not mention anything about the special project. Like so many statements he made in the beginning, such as the 60-member maximum, he hoped the connection between projects and membership fees would fade. In the interest of complete disclosure, Richard remembers him talking about the project, but he does not remember him specifically saying what part of the membership money would be used to fund it. I checked with several others there, Edward as well, and they held the same impression; the reason for such a pricy membership was to fund the project.

It was clear we were receiving nowhere near our money's worth. The worst part: we had already taken the bait and signed up for the next year! We had given JRI a $15,000 deposit and an $8,250 payment. JRI had a no-refund policy, period. At what point do we cut our losses? Do we finish this next year? Whatever happened, this was definitely our last year in the WWS! Because we believed in our project—producing energy-saving devices—we still financially supported it, but I felt duped.

When we returned from lunch, James went into his hard sell mode. I was surprised to find out only four of the over 65+ members re-enrolled. Richard and I were two of them. As Lana put it, "His grand vision for the WWS was quickly crumbling." He needed to sell hard and fast, thus the hard edge he carried. James extended the offer for the private hike in Sedona for those who signed up during this meeting. So much for our special privilege for signing up before the Congress! Every sentence ticked me off more. We had to re-enroll no later than the end of December or the discounts on the membership fees would be gone. Now he was extending them as well. He emphatically added, "But for no longer than the end of today!"

Later, we learned some members were allowed to extend their payments further than previously permitted. Apparently, the "fixed" rules presented to Richard and me were very flexible for other members. Each member was being given different payment options, both in amount and term. We found out later at least four people were "honorary members;" they paid nothing at all for their memberships!

James' rules kept changing. His permanent rules were moving targets. We received an email from JRI saying that our children had to be younger than a specific age to attend the events free of charge. We fought the change and won. We heard new members could not attend the events free themselves. Later, as events struggled to fill and WWS membership numbers continued to decrease, James decided we needed to stay "plugged in." To help us, he was changing the rules yet again out of the goodness of his heart. All members could now attend the events for free, with the exception of Spiritual Warrior. He always put a spin on everything. The difference now was we recognized it immediately.

James talked again about his new Beverly Hills home and his upcoming TV show. He told us he was just getting started and we would be there with him, front row center for the whole thing! *Yippee,* I thought. *I paid all this money just to be in your fan club.*

On February 19, 2009, we received this email from JRI:

Hi everyone!! I am sooo excited to be the first to tell you . . . we just received word from Peru officials that we were granted after-hour permission for Machu Picchu!! Not only were we granted permission for this, but also after-hours for Ollantaytambo in the Sacred Valley . . . how awesome is that!?!

Everyone was truly excited about the permission to explore Machu Picchu after-hours. The death stone ceremony would happen; James discussed it often during the months leading up to the Peru trip. He was doing everything he could to fire up interest in the trip and the WWS. He hoped the exclusive time in Machu Picchu would encourage members to rejoin and new members to sign up. He promoted it heavily.

In a very tough decision, we decided that since we had already paid nearly half of the membership dues, we would stick it out. Many times, James had shared how the nighttime death stone ceremony at Machu Picchu had changed his life. We thought it a fitting death and rebirth ceremony for leaving James behind and progressing to the next phase of our spiritual education. I was also looking forward to taking The Quickening, which hadn't been offered in years. We started to tell people that if they wanted to attend Harmonic Wealth Weekend as our guests, do it right away. Next year, the option would be gone.

On April 4, we headed up to Dana Point, Calif. for Linda's two-day image workshop before Modern Magick. Before I arrived, she called me to find out what I wanted to get out of the two days. My intention was to put together a few good work outfits. She asked what my concerns were. "I see women who are getting older but still wearing clothing intended for someone 25 years younger," I said. "I want age and business appropriate clothing that is still fun and reasonably comfortable." Fun was completely missing in my wardrobe. Given my size, I had just presented her with a real challenge. I hoped for my sake she could rise to it.

We started by discussing our feelings about clothing in general. "I would rather walk on hot coals than go clothes shopping." The group knew I meant it literally. After Linda called on me, I headed to the changing room with the clothing I had selected from her racks, worried that there would be nothing that fit me. Sure enough, the first few things were too small. *How embarrassing is this going to be?* I didn't need to pay to feel this badly about my body. I could have obtained the same experience for free by wandering into a department store and trying on clothes. Finally, a pair of jeans fit; they looked great. I found some tops that fit well, too.

Linda did not want us to wear black. I could wear dark shades of plum, chocolate brown and navy blue, along with teal and a few other shades of blue that, she suggested, accented my blue eyes. Surprisingly, she kept putting me into oranges, which I thought were hideous—but everyone else in the group loved on me. I learned to like soft orange colors. She discouraged us from pointing to clothing and making gagging sounds when we saw something we didn't like. "It wasn't lady like." When she handed us things to try on, and we objected, she would always say, "Just try it on!" She was often right; we did look great in it. We had a higher failure rate when it came to our own selections from the racks!

I had a lot to learn. For many years, I went clothes shopping only when I desperately needed something. My only criteria: Does it fit? From now on, I would be more selective. I had to stop hiding behind the fat and the frumpy clothes. As I lost more weight, I would buy just a few good pieces of clothing so I always had at least one good outfit to wear.

Linda showed me it's not about the clothes, but how we feel about ourselves underneath them. We needed to stop beating ourselves up because most clothing straight off of the rack would not fit people well. Everyone's bodies are different. Each person had positive attributes, she said, so accentuate the strengths, forget the rest, and find a great tailor.

Next was the five-day Modern Magick event. Our friend Ron, a JRI coach and MOTL member, asked a fairly straightforward question. James began his answer with, "I am tougher on my coaches that I am on other people . . . ." *Oh crap, here he goes again.* Ron, who is one of the nicest, kindest people I know, was about to get flamed by James, whose meanness was growing right before our eyes. Ron's question was not controversial, and James' answer had nothing to do with the question. Instead, he pounced all over Ron for things that made no sense, then complained about how Ron's wife, Judy, was always taking notes, even during his stories. "You both should know better, and you need to stop and pay attention to what I am saying."

Judy was a meticulous note-taker, known for her detailed, accurate notes. Was he afraid she was going to "steal" his lecture material—which he had taken from someone else? Or did he want to avoid us having a record of exactly what he said?

Increasingly, I did not want to go on stage when the WWS was introduced at events. I was also being more direct in my advice about the different events. During a break, two women approached me. They were trying to decide which events to register for, and added they were leaning towards Spiritual Warrior. "What do you think?"

I asked them if they had attended Practical Mysticism. "No," they replied.

"Definitely do that first, and complete all of the other events before considering Spiritual Warrior."

They looked at me. "Why?"

"It is very hard on you both physically and mentally. And at least two of the activities in it were unnecessarily difficult."

They asked me if I had attended all the events, then wondered if I had learned the most from Spiritual Warrior.

"No," I replied. "I learned the most in Practical Mysticism; take that one first. It's also about half the price of Spiritual Warrior." I was not subtle about steering people away from Spiritual Warrior when asked.

They thanked me. As I turned to walk out the back door, I realized a JRI staffer had been standing just a few feet behind me and probably heard every word. It would be reported to James, for sure—especially the part where I talked them out of a more expensive event. Sooner or later, he would let me know his displeasure.

Apparently James heard our complaints about Holotropic Breathwork™ not being in the 2007 Modern Magick event, because this year it was the first night. Each time I did Holotropic Breathwork™, it grew easier to "lift off," as James called it. I had a real revelation. Thinking back to each time I was assaulted or sexually molested, I focused on my fear and powerlessness as it was happening. I did not realize in every case I was able to escape either by my own actions or by something else that helped me. In the case of the man trying to talk me into getting into his car when I was very young, my hesitation allowed enough time for Great Grandmother to arrive and drive him off. In the case of my swim coach, I found the nerve to defy him and physically twisted and kicked myself free. When he tried to give me a ride after practice, I refused to go, even though he was very insistent. When the guy was trying to pull me into the white van, I fought until another car came along. After the craft fair, when I was being stalked and chased by a group of guys on a side street, a police car miraculously showed up just in time. The last instance was at an open house. I was able to maneuver around the dining room table until Richard returned early because he had forgotten something.

Before Holotropic Breathwork™, I viewed these experiences as purely bad. I didn't see that each time I survived, it was due either to my own strength and wits, or because someone was looking out for me. I had survived, and if it happened again, I would survive again. The Holotropic Breathwork™ session caused the most amazing and empowering paradigm shift. I did not need to feel powerless anymore. I was powerful!

The next morning, I went to the hotel's fitness center and clocked my hour on the treadmill and then moved over to the elliptical machine. After another half hour, I felt the snap of a towel against my butt. Expecting to see Richard, I was surprised to see James standing behind me with a big smile on his face. He was all sweaty and clearly had been working out. I told him I had been working out about an hour and a half a day in preparation for Peru. He said he had been watching me and was happy to see I was exercising.

The next day, Richard and I were in the trance dance group. Again, I could have done without it. James would run around and pour water on the blindfolded dancer's heads, and sometimes grab one by the hand and spin them around. I could understand leading someone around to encourage movement, but dumping water on our heads seemed a bit juvenile. How did that contribute to a trance or meditative state? I could not see any profound spiritual experience from either the blindfolded dancing or being sprayed with water.

The next evening, it was our turn to form the ring around the trance dancers to keep them safe, but first we did an astral projection exercise. Remote viewing and astral projection are similar and often confused with each other. In remote viewing, the viewer "sees" something physically not visible to them or far away. The U.S. Army, Air Force, CIA and a variety of U.S. intelligence agencies, as well as the U.S.S.R, Germany and China, have researched and tried using remote viewing for obvious military and intelligence advantages. Things that were "seen" by this method included a big crane at a Soviet nuclear research facility, and a new class of Soviet strategic submarine.

In remote viewing, the viewer experience is usually limited to just "seeing" the remote object. During a meditation in Maui, I clearly saw a light left on in our home. If it was a candle, I would have called a neighbor immediately to blow it out. Since it was just a small light and we were just a day from returning, I was not very concerned. When we returned home the light was indeed on.

Astral projection or astral travel is different. In my experiences, I can see, hear and sometimes speak in remote locations. It is very similar to my near death experience and the only way I know the difference is that in a near death experience, you see yourself moving through the tunnel into the white light. In my common astral projections, I do not see the tunnel or the white light, but I will be the first to admit it is easy to confuse these two different but very similar experiences. Astral projection (AP) is also spontaneously experienced in association with sleep and dreams, illness, surgeries, and sleep paralysis. Sylvia Browne said all of us experience astral projection an average of three times a week during sleep. We may not remember or realize it, in the same way we often forget our dreams. I have frequently moved through my house during sleep, without my physical body, and found a candle still lit, my lost keys, or a window or door still open. I would wake up and do whatever needed correcting.

When Erica was a baby, I frequently checked on her in the crib to see if she had moved into an uncomfortable position, or thrown off her blanket. I would return to my body and go move her and rearrange the items in her crib. In each case of AP, I felt the sensation of moving, and heard noises, no matter where I was. Most of us who consciously astral project tend to have a favorite time. For me, it is between 3 and 5 a.m. A sign you may be projecting is when your body jerks suddenly because you feel like you are falling. Often you throw your hands to your sides to stop the "fall." In those instances, your ethereal self was either trying to leave your physical body, or return, and your body "woke up" early and startled at the transition. Sylvia told us to prevent that by asking God for a smooth exit and re-entry. The frequent experience ceased after I asked for it to stop.

Richard was on an international overnight flight and I was home in California. Before I fell asleep, I had been thinking about how much I missed him. Sleeping, I suddenly found myself on a plane. I could clearly see the cabin and hear the continuous drone of the engines. I moved through the back of the plane, looking up and down the aisles for him; most of the seats were empty. The cabin lights were turned down low. Finally, I found Richard leaning against a window, asleep. There was no one next to him, so his legs were propped up. I leaned over and called his name a couple of times. I saw him stir, but in a flash, I was back in my bed. One of our cats had jumped on me. After Richard landed, he called to let me know he had arrived safely. He told me he excitedly awoke on the plane because he clearly heard me call his name. He thought I purchased a ticket to surprise him! He was so sure he heard me that he searched every aisle, fully expecting to find me.

I did not know how to deliberately set where I wanted to go, or control when I left and came back. I was looking forward to doing this exercise since my chance of success was excellent. JRI staffers led small groups to different spots around the hotel, where specific features were pointed out to us. We were to seek the same features when we returned later, whether physically or through projection. Our group repeated the sequence a couple of times physically, always in the same order. Then we were told to repeat the process by ourselves, return to the main room, and lay down on our towels. While on the floor, in a meditative state, we were told to think and will our ethereal selves to leave our bodies and then repeat the circuit through the different locations.

In many of James' CD meditations, he guides us to move our ethereal selves outside our bodies; for many attendees, this was familiar. Not surprisingly, I projected out of my body after only a few rounds. When I returned from the circuit, I saw my body lying on my towel. At first, it is a bit spooky to see yourself from a distance, but curiosity takes over. As I approached my body, I felt a strong tug pulling me back into it. I wanted to take a good, up-close look at myself, but the closer I drew, the stronger the pull. Finally, it was too hard to resist; I was quickly sucked back into my body.

I stood up, physically completed the circuit, and then returned to the towel. This time, it was quick and easy for my ethereal body to lift from my physical body. When I got to the top of a large winding stairway, someone walked right through me. That was a strange feeling! I wondered if I could pass through parts of myself, so I tried to clasp my hands together. They just passed through each other. I tried to grab my forearm with the same result. I tried moving my hands into the trunk of my body. I was moving them through my chest when I bumped into something more "solid" I could not move through easily. Instinctively, I knew it did not belong there, so I grabbed it with one hand and pulled it out. It looked and felt like a sponge-shaped heart. After I threw the "heart" to the floor, I reached inside and found another, more solid object. Instead of being compact, this tentacled object intertwined throughout my body. I had to use both hands to loosen and remove it. I threw it to the ground as well. One more time, I reached inside myself, from top to bottom, but found nothing else "solid."

Looking back, it seems odd I did not mind pulling things out of myself. I somehow knew they didn't belong there. They were gone and everything was fine.

I turned and continued the circuit and visited the remaining locations. On my way back, I wondered about the objects I extracted. When I arrived at the top of the staircase, I stopped and looked around the floor to see if the "things" were still there. They were not. I proceeded to the room, where my physical body was lying on the towel. As soon as I felt the tug pulling me back, I moved back so I would not get sucked back in before I wanted to. Now I understood why we feel like we're falling at times while sleeping—the strong pull between the ethereal and physical bodies. If the physical body is not in the correct state to release or receive your ethereal body, then the ethereal body will either quickly "snap back in" or make a hard landing into the physical body, which creates the sensation of falling.

After examining my body from different angles, I moved slowly to see how close I could get before the pull became too strong to resist. When I passed the point, I was effortlessly pulled back into my physical body.

I opened my eyes and was preparing to lift myself off the towel when I felt something strange and unsettling inside my body . . . like my organs were moving around inside of me. Icky and yikes all at the same time! I laid there for a few moments, trying to steady and slow my breathing. I was freezing cold and shaking. I felt like there were hollow spots inside of me! I tried to pull energy down through my crown chakra. Each breath passed through me and exited through my feet rather than filling me. I was getting more concerned by the minute. I continued trying to breathe in the energy, but I was not feeling any better. I thought maybe getting up and repeating the cycles a couple of times might help center me, so I started heading for the door at the back of the room. With each step I felt stranger, as though a part of me was lagging just a little bit behind the rest.

I looked for James, but he was nowhere to be seen. When I got outside, a group of JRI staffers stood by the door. I asked one of them for help. She told me to go back to my towel and continue to breathe deeply until I felt better. I did so, but made no progress. I was really getting scared now. The feeling was unpleasant, I did not understand what it was or what it meant, and I could not get it to stop. Tears ran down my cheeks as I struggled to pull myself together.

Lights on! The activity was over. We picked up our towels and prepared for trance dancing. I told Richard and Ron what I was experiencing. Richard bolted in the direction of the stage when he saw James talking to a couple of people. Just as he arrived, James instructed his bodyguards not to let any more people ask him questions. They tried to hold Richard back. He persisted long enough to get James' attention, and told him I was having big problems from the last exercise and needed his help. James said that it was time to get the trance dancing going, and he moved to the center of the stage. So much for being a member of his "inside circle!"

Richard returned. I had a towel wrapped around me because I was still freezing. The super loud music blared. I could not stay in the room with the vibration of the music. It felt like the music waves were passing through me. I walked outside to find a seat in the atrium while continuing to pull down more energy through my crown chakra. Eventually, the energy stopped leaving me. It started to "stick" and fill my body, from my legs upward. Only a matter of time before I felt better; I was relieved. I stabilized the energy level as high as my chest. I turned to see a man watching me. He was dressed in a suit and clearly was not a participant. I thought he may be a concerned hotel manager. A few more breaths, I felt my energy increase, then stall. It would be all the way up to my crown chakra again soon. I just had to keep working at it.

Ron came out to check on me, followed by Richard and Edward. The man in the suit walked over and asked if there was something he could do to help. I assured him I was doing much better, and he said he could see that and wanted to be sure I was OK, and that I understood what was happening with me. Richard recognized him as someone who was just speaking with James. He told us he was our next speaker. He was here to talk about astral projecting and other altered states of consciousness. I don't remember much of what he said because my head was still swimming, but the guys became engrossed in conversation. What they learned, and I figured out on my own, was my consciousness and my body did not merge precisely when they drew back together. This was likely because I brought back a couple less things in my astral body than when I left my physical body. Somehow my body recognized the change and was trying to compensate. That's why things felt like they were moving around inside. My bodies were realigning.

As the trance dancing was ending, I went back into the room. The music still bothered me, but nothing like before. It would take several more hours of deep breathing and pulling in energy before I felt completely better. What amazed and bothered me was that neither James nor a staffer bothered to check on me.

Just after I went to sleep that night, I felt like I was falling. I slapped my arms hard on the mattress. This had not happened to me for years. I was surprised I was experiencing the exits or reentries again, and that I would astral project again so quickly. Apparently, my body was not ready for a repeat of the day; it refused to let me go again. Since then, I cannot recall astral projecting or the feeling of falling to the mattress. I believe I am still projecting, but not remembering.

On the last day, we did one of James' guided meditations. Towards the end, he took over from the CD. The meditation music kept playing and the lights stayed down low. He discussed how we were more than appearances, that we were capable of great things, and that we were more than our limiting beliefs. In other words, he gave us his usual "you are more than that" speech. Our eyes remained closed; the background music continued to play. He was getting emotional, repeating "you are more than that" in response to different challenges we might be facing. James mentioned we were more than our money and financial challenges. Then he launched into a sales pitch, including joining or rejoining the WWS. *During a meditation!* I was appalled! My training in hypnosis was sufficient for me to know he had just crossed the line of ethical acceptability.

There is not much difference between a guided meditation and a hypnosis session. In both, you are listening to someone's voice as an aid to focus on a task and guide you through it. In silent meditation, it takes incredible discipline to keep your mind from wandering, especially if you are dealing with something unpleasant. Having someone talk you through the process and keep you focused is very helpful. The moral responsibility lies in being careful what you inject into a person's open, unconscious mind. Your unconscious mind assimilates everything it hears as truth; it is as open and receptive as the mind of a child.

However, James induced a state of meditative hypnosis, where people knew and trusted his voice and were familiar and comfortable with the background music. Then he launched into a sales pitch. Wrong! Wrong! Wrong! There is no gray area here, it is just plain wrong—and he knew it. Conveniently, he ended the meditation/sales pitch with a break, so we would pass right by the registration tables on our way out the back door. I turned to Richard and expressed my disgust, then Edward. Neither of the men knew what to think.

While leaving the room, we saw one of our new real estate clients, Nancy, standing in line at the WWS table. She was excited she had decided to join the WWS! We had met Nancy a few months earlier at a JET meeting, when we presented a PowerPoint presentation on our trip to Egypt. She was getting ready to retire and needed to sell her home; she turned to us for guidance. We had told her about our townhome in Maui, and later she emailed me to ask if she and her son could stay there free for a few days while she attended a family reunion. She could not afford to go any other way. We told her our property managers keep the home scheduled out several months in advance, but that we would check.

Our townhome was booked solid and unavailable when she needed it. As the universe would have it, we received notice from our property managers a week later that the state was going to be doing some major road work right below our home, and that they couldn't book guests during that time. This was exactly the time frame Nancy needed a place to stay, so we let her have it instead of using the time ourselves.

Nancy's desire to join WWS was a big surprise to us. This lovely lady stood in line to spend $60,000 on a WWS membership . . . yet she was unable to pay for a place to stay during a family reunion? I always believed she told the truth about her tight finances, so this did not add up. When we met her a few weeks later to sign the contracts to place her home on the market, she said she decided not to join the WWS after thinking about it further. Richard and I were greatly relieved. I'm sure her sudden excitement at joining the WWS was ignited by James' sales pitch during the guided meditation. Luckily, she snapped out of it in time.

When we returned to our seats after the break, Edward told me another mutual friend and long time acquaintance of James was absolutely furious. His perception of what James did at the end of the meditation was the same as mine, except he used a specific term: black magick. This has many connotations, but in one sense, it means using your powers and knowledge to influence others to do something purely for your benefit and often detrimental to them. He can call it black magick. I call it just plain wrong.

The end of the seminar approached, which meant one thing at a James Ray event: the grand finale challenge to move us out of our comfort zone. After the previous year's broken bone fiasco during the concrete slab break, speculation ran wild. No one anticipated a repeat of the concrete slab activity. What would he put in its place?

After hinting at it all day, James announced that we would be working with the stars from the movie *Snakes on a Plane*. It was my guess he didn't mean Samuel L. Jackson and the other human stars. Always one for showmanship, James walked on stage with a giant snake over his shoulders. The snake raised his head eye level with James; it looked like they were having a stare-down. *Watch this: he is going to get his face bitten*, I thought. James quickly passed the snake to its handler, and explained in the back were open glass aquariums, each with a layer of wood shavings on the bottom. Under the wood shavings were skeleton keys —"the keys to your futures, the keys to the life you want to be living." As we watched, people walked up to the aquariums and dumped the contents of cloth sacks into the aquariums. Ten decent-sized snakes tumbled out of each bag. Yep, we'd have to dig through the snakes and wood shavings to reach the keys!

James ordered the first row, mostly WWS members, to the back of the room to retrieve the keys to our futures. Richard arrived first, reached into the aquarium quickly, and emerged with a key. I ended up going third. I had rolled up my sleeves as instructed so that a snake didn't scoot inside my shirt while I was digging. With the skin on my hand and arm exposed, I could feel snakes constantly sliding past my arms. As I rooted around for a key, they would bump into my hands with the tips of their noses. Even though I am not a big fan of snakes, I paused for a moment to look at how beautifully colored they were.

It didn't take me long to get my key. Richard and I went back to our seats. I slid my key onto the gold necklace around my neck. When I looked up, several people with major snake issues still waited in line. Two were WWS friends of ours, so I walked over, offered words of encouragement, and waited in line with them. This was one time it was a big benefit to go first. The longer you waited, the more you had to root around in the wood shavings to find a key. All the while, snakes slithered all over your arms.

The challenge ended soon enough. While walking back to our rooms to get ready for the celebration dinner, Richard, Edward, Faith and I discussed whether James had finally gotten the message about pushing people too hard and too far. This "snakes on a plane" challenge was a cinch compared to the concrete slab break. Even in the worst-case scenario, a bite from one of these non-poisonous snakes might hurt, even break your skin and bleed a little, but it certainly was not a broken bone or heat stroke. We felt hopeful James learned his lesson and would stop putting people in harm's way.

Richard started talking about Dream Teaming Spiritual Warrior again. If James was indeed backing off his dangerous activities, then the sweat lodge would be safer. In that case, it was possible we would volunteer. We were going to be there anyway for the private hike with James, scheduled before the start of Spiritual Warrior. I thought Richard might be right, but I still remained more cautious than optimistic.

Just before dinner, we had a WWS reception. I noticed James was actually mingling with the members without looking so pained to be with people. He talked with everyone like a "normal" person, which was unusual for him. After watching for a few minutes, I realized he was spending time with only a few people. When I passed him, I could tell he was working on holdouts in a last-ditch attempt to get them to rejoin. He was only partly successful.

There were about half the number of members as in 2008, and many of those were new. I saw four primary reasons why people were dissatisfied enough to not renew their membership. Interestingly, each reason involved a corresponding group with a distinct agenda. First, people had signed up because they were interested in being part of a society that really intended to make the world a better place. They knew we could and must treat each other and the earth better. This group was very attracted to the original idea of the WWS project. They were dissatisfied because the WWS had turned into primarily a business networking group. They also felt the cost of the WWS membership was too high, especially in light of finding out that they needed to provide additional financial support for a project.

The second group joined mostly to promote their businesses. They spent a majority of the time trying to sell their products to other WWS members. At one event, a woman told me, "If another person tries to sell me anything else today, I am going to scream!" Members of this group had sold everything possible to the other members; it was simply time for them to move on.

The third group included those disgusted with the way the WWS Showcase was handled, and the favoritism James and JRI showed towards a few members to the detriment of others.

The final group had joined for more access to James. They endured a year of very little extra contact with him, certainly not enough to warrant a $50,000+ investment.

When James spotted me in the hotel's fitness center, he probably thought working out was new for me because of my weight. It wasn't. After meditating between the paws of the Sphinx, I committed to making major changes in my health. I had high blood pressure and high cholesterol, and my fasting insulin levels showed I was within a couple of years of developing Type II diabetes. Our new doctor, whom we met in Kona at the original WW Summit, was working with me on improving my hormone levels. I started a thyroid medication after more extensive thyroid blood test. Now that I was being well monitored by a doctor, it was time to step up my exercise. I had worked years with a personal trainer for one-hour sessions, two to three times a week. Now, I was adding the aerobic machines to my routine to see if it would help me shed the extra pounds. All of my other hard work was barely making any difference. I kept cutting back more and more on my food and adding more exercise time, but the weight loss remained slow and frustrating.

With the trip to Peru only a few months away, I started to wonder if I would be going at all. I had to get into shape quickly to function at high altitude and make the steep climb up Huayna Picchu. We would be exploring the land of the Incas, at times over 12,000 feet above sea level. The capital city of the Incan Empire, Cusco, would be our home for the trip—at an altitude of 10,827 feet. I needed to pull off a miracle and fast. I committed to do whatever it took to lose as much weight as possible.

Then a break: Todd Durkin, the owner of Fitness Quest 10, the health and exercise center I belonged to, announced his first Biggest Winner weight loss contest. Exactly what I needed to speed up my progress! I felt the need to better educate myself on the reasons for my body's resistance to weight loss, so I purchased and read two books. The first was *Master Your Metabolism* by Jillian Michaels, one of the trainers on NBC's *The Biggest Loser* TV show. It is an excellent source of information on how the junk we eat affects our bodies and slows our metabolism. I was learning how to eat, what to avoid, and how processed foods helped me get fat in the first place. Food manufacturers insert additives in their processed foods to make us eat more and to sell more "food!" These products better resemble a science experiment than food—and most of us eat them every day. The other book, *The Power of 4* by Paula Owens, covers more areas of life we need to address in order to create and enjoy a healthy lifestyle.

Exercise is important, but as one of my trainers always says, "You can't exercise your way out of a bad diet." Exercise is primarily the accelerator to speed up the weight loss process. I started eating smaller meals more often. My goal was to eat every three hours and include a protein with every meal. I found if I drank more water, I desired less food. After we attended the first Harmonic Wealth Weekend, Richard and I both gave up soda and he gave up coffee.

Taking my clue from the TV series, *The Biggest Loser*, I knew even though I was working out three times a week, it was not enough. I had completely destroyed my metabolism with an unhealthy "diet" and processed foods, so I needed to do more than most to restart it again. From the show I learned there was a perfect blend of the amount of exercise and food that would yield the fastest amount of weight loss.

Every day during the contest, I worked out for three to four hours, until I burned at least 1,000 calories. One of my trainers wanted me to take one day off per week, but I was a woman on a mission and I was working against a deadline.

For the last week of the contest, I accelerated my workouts to see if my endurance had improved enough to handle the steep hour-long hike up Huayna Picchu. I completed a pair of five-hour elliptical sessions during the week, and then a six-hour session on Sunday. I only stopped because it was time for the center to close. I still refer to those as my "elliptathons." I was able to do them, thanks in large part to my portable MP3 player. I started each session listening to fast tempo music to get me going. In the middle of the long sessions, I enjoyed a "runner's high" where it suddenly felt easy for about an hour and then I tired and it grew difficult again. Pure determination kept me going. At the very end, I switched from music to chants. Gregorian, Hawaiian, Peruvian and Buddhist chants all worked well as I moved into a state more like a very fast walking meditation.

Another tool I used during these long sessions is something I learned from the guided meditations. I can imagine pulling down the "white light" energy through my crown chakra and into my body. It is the same thing I used to stabilize my life force energy after the astral projection exercise. With each long and hard inhalation, I visualize and feel the energy filling my body from my legs up to the top of my head. I do this for five or more breaths, until I feel so full of energy it radiates from me. This technique always brings a smile to my face and at least a few minutes of renewed energy. It works. What more proof do you need than a 250+ pound woman motoring for six straight hours on an elliptical machine?

Richard and I were prepping with weekly hikes up the side of a local mountain. At first, I was very slow and had to stop many times, but I did burn a lot of calories. Richard ran up the mountain ahead of me, and then we would meet at the top for an early lunch. As soon as I descended, I went to the chiropractor to have my knee adjusted. I was wearing a knee brace at the time, but the rocks were taking their toll, twisting my knee repeatedly as we climbed. Eventually, I walked faster and did not have to stop for breaks anymore.

I continued to use the sauna daily to purge the toxins my shrinking fat cells were releasing into my system. Fat is used to encircle toxins for the body's own protection. Now that my fat was diminishing, I needed to drink a lot of water to flush my system and rehydrate. I would preheat the sauna to 170 degrees and then set the timer to no more than 20 minutes as a safety precaution. My familiarity with saunas and steam rooms, and reasonable periods of exposure time and temperature, gave me the well-informed knowledge that James' sweat lodge was a disaster waiting to happen.

I won the Biggest Winner contest MVP award for being the only person to lose over 50 pounds during those six weeks! I did not have to get "skinny" to see incredible improvements in my health. I am still considered overweight, but what the scale projects is only a number; the improvements in my health have been profound and measurable.

I lost over 80 lbs. before we left for Peru, yet the question still remained: would that be enough for me to make the climb up Huayna Picchu?

In mid-June, we received an invitation to Dream Team Spiritual Warrior 2009. Richard accepted, and then came into my office to tell me. I was not very enthusiastic about his decision.

My major concern still centered on the sweat lodge. Richard had given me his word that he would never go in there again, but I was afraid he could be coaxed inside if they were short of men, which was usually the case. Every year, the men were needed to drag the barely conscious people out. Richard is a true gentleman. All a JRI staffer would have to say to get him inside would be, "You can't expect the women Dream Teamers to be doing that all by themselves, can you? That wouldn't be fair to them, would it?" You could count on the JRI people to do that. Plus, Richard would want to pull his own weight.

I had other concerns. What if the hike didn't happen? When we renewed our membership, we were promised it and The Quickening would be held. Six months passed without it being scheduled. It appeared The Quickening was another promise about to be broken. I think James did not schedule the event because people were having trouble paying for their memberships. If he was planning to charge a ridiculous fee for the event as everyone guessed, then it was unlikely many people could afford it. If James couldn't make a lot of money, he would likely bypass the event. Instead of saying he wasn't going to do it because of the financial challenges members were having, he said nothing. If confronted he would likely claim he only said there *might* a Quickening this year. We were only three months away from Spiritual Warrior, and talk about the hike had ceased. I questioned whether it would happen at all.

The price of travel, room and board for both of us to attend Spiritual Warrior in Sedona was the same cost as spending a week at our condo in Maui. Frankly, I was tired of being taken advantage of by James. When I brought up that argument, Richard walked straight back to his office and contacted JRI, asking them to provide us a lower lodging rate while we were volunteering. JRI knew what we meant, and we knew what they meant as when they replied we would have to pay the same rate as the attendees. Richard then declined to Dream Team Spiritual Warrior.

At the same time, we started to hear from other Dream Team members that James was increasingly pressuring them to sell his products and events. We had seen the start of it at the Harmonic Wealth Weekends we Dream Teamed. There was a contest in which the person who signed up the most people for events won extra "Manna money." How to cash in your Manna money, you ask? By spending it on more of James' stuff! Richard and I did not participate in the contest. We did not want someone to feel we persuaded them to attend an event for any other reason than it would be good for them. We found out from friends that Dream Teamed events right after us that James gave them direct sales training before the seminar started on how to "encourage" attendees to sign up for more events. James was already making a lot of money off of the volunteers' free labor. Now, even that wasn't good enough. He wanted to use them as unpaid salespeople as well. How desperate for money was this multimillionaire that he had to take such blatant advantage of his volunteers?

Richard held out hope the hike was still going to happen. Over the next few months, I grew concerned about even doing it. JRI was already having trouble getting enough volunteers, especially at the longer events. We knew they had to beg a WWS member who came to attend Practical Mysticism for a second time to be a Dream Team member because they were so short of volunteers. Would they be short of Dream Teamers for Spiritual Warrior as well? The scenario scared me: We would participate in the hike and, while there, be asked to help them out because they were short of volunteers. We usually drive to Sedona, so we would be the most likely candidates since we would not have to change our plane reservations. Worse, in my mind, would be if they only needed more men volunteers, disqualifying me. There was no way in hell I would leave Richard alone within 100 miles of that lodge!

For these reasons, I was fine when Richard accidentally scheduled our long overdue vacation in Maui at the same time as Spiritual Warrior and the hike in Sedona. We could move our Maui reservations, but it would be costly, so we decided to wait until we got back from Peru to deal with it.

Just before leaving for Peru I attended a three-day workshop in Palm Springs with Linda, the image consultant. Richard went along to hike nearby Mount San Jacinto, which juts more than 10,000 feet above sea level. Each day, he went for a hike; my plan was to join him on the final day. This would be my final high-altitude test before Peru. I was particularly anxious to see if the asthma would return.

This time, Linda's event wasn't about the clothes at all. We came to learn about empowering ourselves and other women by learning the different cultural customs and ceremonies in which women show love and support for each other. Many of us live away from our families and support systems; sometimes, we even live far away from our friends. Women take care of everyone else; here we learned how the women of other cultures care for each other.

We met an intuitive woman named Kimberly Joyce of Infinite Global Results, who came to give us a lecture on how to overcome emotional trauma and release limiting beliefs. She clearly connected with some of the women, but what caught my attention was her sales pitch at the end. She kept her voice low and soft, simply stating that flyers describing her services and fees were sitting at the back of the room. If we felt we could benefit, then take a look at the list. If the prices were beyond what we felt we could handle, she invited us to speak with her because she would offer the service at whatever price we could afford. "Money should not hold you back from getting the help you might need," she said.

Talk about the diametric opposite to a James Ray sales pitch! No high pressure, no neuro-linguistically programmed sales lines. She was operating from a heart-centered place of service; it was so clear to me that James was not. He could talk a good line, but really, it came down to how much money he could entice you to spend. The contrast between the two made me question how much further I would go with James. I knew I was quickly reaching the end of my journey with him.

During a break, a few of us tried to encourage Linda to attend the WW Summit later that year as our guests. She told us she wouldn't because a female JRI employee had called her a week before Modern Magick and asked her to move her workshop from before the event to afterward. Linda couldn't accommodate JRI; the request was too late. Her attendees already had purchased their plane tickets and made room reservations. Undeterred, the JRI staff person grew extremely persistent, demanding Linda move her seminar. Linda wanted to know why the switch was so important. Finally the JRI employee said that Modern Magick was James' event and he did not want his attendees to spend "all of their money with her," rather than on James' products and events. After Linda again refused to move her workshop, she was officially dropped from being considered as one of the presenters for the WW Summit!

Why was I saddened but not surprised? This is the man who had taught us to come from a place of abundance, yet it looked to me like James was coming from greed. We were little more than checkbooks and credit cards to him.

The day after Linda's event, Richard and I took the tram part way up Mt. San Jacinto to 8,515 feet above sea level. This was my final test before Peru to see how I could hike at altitude. We ran out of time due to a late start to go all the way to the summit, but I did get to climb above 10,000 ft., moving well, and showing no signs of asthma. I almost cried with relief. All the hard work had paid off; I was ready to take on Huayna Picchu!

In late July, our daughter Erica attended Creating Absolute Wealth in San Diego. James told us she played full-on during the activities and we should be proud of her. We could tell she really enjoyed the event. What she and other event participants didn't know was that one of the attendees, Colleen Conaway, committed suicide during the "homeless" activity in downtown San Diego by jumping from a balcony in the Horton Plaza shopping center. She was on Edward's bus. Edward, who was Dream Teaming the event, knew only that one of his riders was late in returning to the bus stop. Eventually, the bus had to leave, and a JRI Staff person stayed behind waiting for the "straggler" to show up. She never did.

The JRI people started to call, looking for her. When Edward checked with the staffers later that night, he was told not to worry about it: they were making calls, and they would find her. The next morning, Edward again asked a JRI staffer if they found Colleen. "We have found her," the staffer said. "She's fine. She's not returning to the event." He was relieved, but thought she must have done something really bad to not be allowed to return to the seminar. She was not fine; she was dead. Who told the JRI staffers to say she was fine? When did JRI know about her death? How much did James know about all of this?

Megan, JRI's Director of Operations, told investigators later in her immunity interview that JRI knew at 8:00 p.m. *the same night* Colleen committed suicide in the shopping mall. During breakfast the next morning, Melinda Martin, the JRI event coordinator, inquired about Colleen. According to Melinda, James said, "Well, I have talked to my attorneys. And, basically, it's really important that you're not involved in this. And we have found her, and she's fine, and she's decided not to return to the event. And if anybody else asks you that, we have found her. She's fine. She's decided not to return to the event."

Melinda said she thought it strange that James was angry with her for asking the question. She thought it was an innocent question. James *did* know all about it, and according to Melinda he personally issued the instructions to tell everyone that she was fine!

James' indifference continued after the event was over. According to an ABC News report, James Ray International never called the

Conaway family. The only thing they received from the company was a mailed sympathy card a month after Colleen's death. To date they've yet to receive any refund of the money that Colleen paid to JRI. Colleen's sister said that Colleen was $12,000 in debt to James Ray. "Ray's organization says they had no phone number for the family and claim they were not asked to repay the family," a JRI spokesman told ABC News.

Is that really their best excuse? James employed several high-end attorneys and PR people, yet this is what the great minds devised as the reason why a multimillion-dollar company run by a multimillionaire (according to him at the time) did not refund a dead woman's money back to her family. They simply could have credited the cost of that seminar and those for which she'd prepaid to the same credit card she used to charge the events. As Edward said later at my home over dinner, "Apparently death is not a good enough excuse to get a refund out of James Ray, either!"

I can see no acceptable excuse for this kind of behavior. What happened to being a spiritual master? I don't know what your spiritual beliefs are, but for me this type of behavior puts the wheels of karma in motion. If James values money more than people, then karma will separate him from money.

When Richard and I crashed the black tie dinner party at the end of Creating Absolute Wealth, I saw him for the first time since losing a lot of weight. I had emailed the WWS Staffer ahead of time asking for an estimate on when dinner would be finished, so we could come, pick up Erica, and say hello to a few friends. She gave us the estimate, yet, when we got there, they had not started dinner yet. That was true to form for James. While working my way across the room, I saw James sitting at the main table in front of the stage. James and his staff knew about me winning the MVP in the weight loss contest, but no one had seen me since Modern Magick, some 80 lbs. ago. When I approached the table to say hi to him, one of his bodyguards who I did not know came over to stop me. When James saw me, he told the guard that it was OK, I was WWS. Instead of reaching over the table to shake my hand, he walked around the long table and stepped down to the dance floor and gave me a long hug. Not his usual act; I appreciated the gesture.

Richard and I were planning to grab dinner at a local restaurant while we waited for Erica. However, our friend Brenda urged us to join them at the WWS table, which had several empty seats. We agreed to stay for wine, but ended up eating dinner. It was a fun evening, seeing so many of our friends and people we'd helped in previous events. Looking around the room, I could not tell that anything was wrong. There was no announcement of Colleen's death at the seminar, nor to the Dream Team during or after the event. Needless to say, Edward was shocked and saddened at finding out what really happened to Colleen. We figured it out after Spiritual Warrior 2009.

CHAPTER 16

But It's MY Goal!

Peru • August 2009

The World is a book, and those who do not travel read only a page.
—Saint Augustine

Even at 4:30 a.m., Lima Airport is a busy place. We started our second WWS Excursion with James in great health. Thank you, Lord! I was so grateful since Richard and I expected this trip to be physically challenging. I was both excited and apprehensive. Would all the hard training and weight loss allow me to handle the high elevations? Would it be enough to get me up the treacherous side of Huayna Picchu? I would find out in a couple of days.

We caught up with most of our WWS friends as they trickled into the hotel over the next two days. The women talked about the warm clothes they'd brought for the highly anticipated nighttime ceremony on the death stone in Machu Picchu. I was concerned so I asked our tour organizer, Vera Lopez, where I could purchase some heavier clothes. Vera told me it was warm during the day so not to worry about it. It wasn't the daytime that concerned me. I sat outside with James for hours in Tahoe and got really cold—even with a big fire burning. Vera seemed confused by our continued requests about how cold we should expect it to get during the nighttime ritual. Finally she said not to worry about it now. If we still wanted warmer clothes after we got to Cusco, she'd take us to one of the numerous sweater shops to buy some.

August 1 we flew from Lima to Cusco. It felt like we were climbing the Andes rather than soaring over them. Cusco's 10,827 ft above sea level altitude is felt as soon as you get off the plane.

Coca tea is constantly served to help the tourists acclimate. We could also chew coca leaves. Both are acquired tastes. There were also oxygen bottles in the lobby and bottles available for the room. We felt fine but could tell our resting heart rates were higher. We took it easy in our rooms for the afternoon before heading to the main square for dinner. Thanks to the suggestions from our amazing tour organizer, Vera, we found great food that was mostly organic and well washed in filtered water. The main square was a beautiful location to shop and dine, and especially lovely at night when it was illuminated.

Vera had arranged a tour of Cusco the next day with one of her great guides. Some of the WWS members had met a shaman and they wanted him to do an opening blessing for our group in the hotel garden. James made it clear he did not want the blessing to happen. He said there were a lot of shamans, but only a few were real and good. In truth, James did not like competition for our attention. His comments about bogus shamans proved to be ironic, considering what we later learned about his credentials.

At a member's suggestion we brought extra suitcases filled with clothing, especially children's clothing, toys and school supplies to take to an isolated village that does not receive help from outside organizations. Vera made the arrangements with a local aid group, That afternoon three vans of people and supplies headed to a remote area well outside of Cusco. We traveled down a long dirt road to the village. We unpacked and carried the supplies up the steep hill to where at least 50 children sat in a large circle outside a community building. We could feel their excitement. The children gave us wildflowers they'd picked in the fields, and we joined them in a welcome song and dance. After the "formalities," we started distributing small packages containing hot chicken meals, one for each child. I figured all of this was paid with WWS dues money, or perhaps, James, but later I learned the extra toys, chicken meals, and big bags of sugar and rice came from Vera and her foundation. She also brought big bags of dog food, which were opened and left on the ground. The village dogs ran over to join the feast. It was a smart move by Vera. Now that the dogs had their own food, they wouldn't hover around the children who out of the innate kindness in their hearts would be tempted to feed the dogs part of their chicken lunch. We were told the children usually only eat meat once or twice a year, so this was like Christmas for them.

With the kids finished eating, we gave out the toys and school supplies. It was great to see the older children made sure the younger ones were taken care of. The big hit was a soccer ball. Next we distributed the clothing. Everyone was thrilled with the clothing they received; truly grateful and joyful.

One of the elder men spoke to us through a translator. It broke my heart to hear him say he did not want us to think they were not good providers for their children. It had been very difficult lately on their farms; they deeply appreciated everything we did for them. I noticed in the background that a group of young boys were trying to estimate how tall we were and mark our heights on the side of a building. The Peruvian people and the Quechan tribe, who lived in this village, are small people. We must have looked like giants to the children! I walked over to the wall and stood with my back against it so that they could mark off my height. One of them to stood on another's shoulders to reach over my head. That drew big giggles.

On the long ride home, our van started planning to adopt the village. We talked about putting something together for Christmas, which we later did with Vera's help. Vera took the money she received from Richard and me, and other WWS members, and delivered hot chocolate and sweet bread for the entire village. Each child received a toy, and each elder received a blanket. Vera later sent us photos of the village's Christmas party. It felt like the best use of our Christmas money ever.

During dinner that night, James called me over to his table to ask how I managed to fit in four to five hours of exercise every day. I told him I got up early, answered emails and handled any paperwork that came in overnight, then went to the fitness center and worked out until I burned at least 1,000 calories, and then I worked on real estate until eleven or twelve o'clock at night. I couldn't tell if he thought I was nuts or if he was impressed.

Back at our table, there was more excited discussion about the upcoming nighttime ceremony on the death stone at Machu Picchu. We were just a few days away from the experience James had told us many times changed his life forever. I thought James must be excited to reconnect with his shaman mentor and teacher, don Javier Ruis (name changed to protect the man's privacy), who meant so much to him. When would we meet him?

Next morning, we sat for a group meeting in the hotel, where James lectured a bit and laid out the plans for our day. The reason we came to Peru, he said, was to reset and transform our lives. "You don't have to slow down, just calm down; but sometimes you do have to slow down to calm down and reset yourself," he said. "At the same time, there is no joy without productivity and expression. We are not here on this planet to kick back and relax. We are in this life to learn and produce." Our assignment was to define and examine what we were here on this planet to produce. James used the example of the seed, the symbol of the creative force. The pattern of an oak tree resides in an acorn but it must fall on fertile ground and have the proper environment to nurture it or else it will not come to fruition. The pattern of perfection is in us. We have to put ourselves in the proper environment to grow to our full potential.

The theme for today was death. "For something new to be born something old must first die," James said. It was one of his pet phrases these days. He often wore a dark t-shirt during the trip that read "Death to Death" and seemed to be preoccupied with talking about death. He talked about the angel of death being poised at our left shoulder with its finger out, ready to tap us, at any second. "You need to get moving now to accomplish what you want to do because none of us has a contract to live forever." He handed out Death tarot cards for us to study for a while and look at the symbolism.

I am not adept at interpreting the symbology in tarot cards. However, I do enjoy looking at different decks and comparing how they present the imagery, sometimes very differently. Some cards are beautiful works of art. As Dan Brown's books, *The Da Vinci Code* and *Angels and Demons* showed, ancient symbols are all around us, especially on churches and cathedrals, and often, we don't know what we're looking at. It's like learning to read another language.

I looked at my Death card. What does this image of a walking skeleton really mean? The Death card represents transformation, which is considered a good thing if you are OK with change. Drawing this card is especially good if things are not going so well. It signals something old or present is about to fall away, die, so that you can move on and bring in something new, a new birth, often for the better. Transformation can be a painful process while going through it, but often well worth it in the end. There was a discussion about the different symbols on the card, and a quiet meditation on its meaning in our lives now.

Afterwards, Richard asked James, "When are we going to meet don Javier Ruis?" Big smiles broke out on everyone's faces as we eagerly turned to James. Finally, we were going to meet this epic man.

However, James wasn't smiling. He looked a bit bewildered, an uncommon expression for a man who always appears to be in control. He said something to the effect that he didn't know, almost like he didn't care. How strange! *Maybe something has happened to don Javier Ruis and no one knows where he is,* I thought. Or, more likely, James did not want to tell us, because surely he must have tried to seek out don Javier Ruis as soon as he arrived in Cusco.

With that, James abruptly ended the meeting. We headed to our first stop, Kenko Cave outside of Cusco. Local tradition holds that Kenko houses the angel of death. We meditated and journaled on what must die in our lives so that we can achieve our goals. Afterward we headed to Saksayhuaman, one of the largest temples of the God Taita Inti (Father Sun). It overlooks Cusco, which is laid out in the shape of a Jaguar; Saksayhuaman represents its head. You have likely seen photos of the massive 130 to 200-ton stones that fit perfectly together without the use of mortar. The enormity of the construction is not dissimilar to the stone structure of the Egyptian pyramids.

The temple sits at 12,142 feet above sea level; I could really feel the altitude. We had only been at altitude for a couple of days, not long enough to acclimate. I kept my pace steady, my breathing deep. We climbed a long stone staircase—and it happened; my asthma returned. I climbed the stairs too quickly, and now I worked to keep my lungs well inflated. Within a minute, my breathing calmed down, but experience told me once my asthma recurred, it stayed around for a while. Damn! But then again I was grateful it had improved so much over the last year when I last suffered altitude-aggravated asthma at Lake Tahoe, a full 6,000 feet *lower.*

We walked past a natural rock formation shaped like a giant slide. It was speculated the Incas enjoyed sliding, judging from the visible wear marks. One of our wonderful guides, Gabino, demonstrated. Who ran up there next? Richard, of course! He might be 71, but I'm still waiting for him to grow up!

We proceeded to a round area where there was once a very large shallow pool. The Incans, great cosmologists, used it to study the reflection of the stars. We performed a release ritual, walking seven times counter-clockwise in a large circle, then seven times clockwise. We first released the things and actions which did not serve us well, then "resealed" ourselves so what we released didn't return; a bit like what we did in Egypt.

Our day's final stop was Tipon, the temple of the waters, where we would release some of our self-imposed limitations. Out of the three places we visited that day, both Richard and I loved Tipon the most. It felt deeply peaceful, perhaps because I am a water sign who loves to stand or sit near moving water. Tipon was fed year-round by multiple springs, even during the long dry season on this arid, high mountainside. The view of the valley was spectacular!

James frequently stopped to be filmed. Video was being uploaded via laptop to different social media websites, such as Facebook. Ever the promoter, James brought along Megan's husband, Josh, to handle the task. After we got home, JRI encouraged us to upload our personal photos to a public website, an additional forum being used by James to promote himself and membership in the WWS. Instead many of us chose to upload photos to our own Facebook pages so we could share them in a personal rather than promotional way.

We had been traveling all day with three Quero Indian shamans, one woman and two men. The Quero trace their lineage directly to the Inca and generally live in the Peruvian Andes, around 16,000 feet above sea level. The two male Quero shamans were conducting a Despacho ceremony for us, a tribute of gratitude to Pachamama (Mother Earth). As with most shamanic traditions, the Peruvians have great respect for Mother Earth and appreciation for the beauty of nature. As busy westerners, we have a growing disconnect with this reverence; a significant cause of the sorry state of our environment. Peruvians can't imagine being disrespectful of the land. Why would you trash your house? They deeply embrace the spiritual viewpoint that everything and everyone is connected, and the health of our planet affects all.

Shamans were the first tribal spiritual intermediaries in the human race. The tradition, shared by the vast majority of indigenous peoples worldwide to this day, stretches back at least 30,000 years. Quite simply, the shaman acts as an intermediary between the natural and spirit worlds. While in the spirit world, they ask spirits for help in healing, growing food or hunting, receiving favorable weather and other conditions. James told us many times that he was initiated as a shaman in two different groups, but there is no shaman university where you follow a published path of learning, take your shaman's test, and get your diploma to hang on a wall. The title bestows the highest levels of respect and is earned only after many years of study as an apprentice with a senior shaman, and the continued demonstration of a high level of skill.

For the Despacho ceremony, the shaman gave each of us three

coca leaves, considered sacred by the shamanic traditions of Peru. We held them in our hands and breathed our requests for Pachamama into them. Breath is the means by which we transfer our energy to something else, and also the means by which we absorb energy from our surroundings. One at a time, we presented our leaves to the senior shaman as we told him our name. The shaman went to great effort to make sure he correctly pronounced our names since each name vibration was different, and important, and he wanted to get each of them right. He sang a chant to each person that included their name, and then placed the leaves on a large piece of paper. By the time he'd collected all the leaves, he had fashioned an intricate woven pattern. He added items such as flowers, chocolate (Pachamama is a woman, after all!), and small items, such as seeds, symbolizing different objects from the earth. We all smiled when we saw the chocolate offering. It was a large round piece wrapped in a bright yellow wrapper with a "happy face" on it. Given the solemnity of the ceremony, and the natural beauty and colors of the other offerings, this item really stood out. One thing we were taught by James and other shamanic groups was the importance of being childlike, full of wonder and joy, and not taking everything so seriously. Have fun and enjoy the journey. This is not to be confused with being childish, which is all wrapped in ego and immaturity. Before the shaman started to put our leaves down, he sprinkled sugar over the paper to remind us that life is sweet. He topped the leaves with pieces of cotton to represent the clouds and air. He folded the leaves and objects into the paper, a gift to Mother Earth, to later be burned or buried.

The female shaman then led us in a chakra cleansing ritual using the sacred Tipon waters. Their tradition recognizes three chakra energy centers in the body, compared to other traditions with seven chakras. Their three are located at the crown or top of the head, the heart, and the middle of the trunk, at the solar plexus.

After the ceremony, James announced that one of the shamans was a relative of don Manuel, the teacher of don Javier Ruis. This piqued our group's curiosity: What's up with don Javier Ruis? When are we going to meet him? And now another question: Did the two men have a falling out? (It should be noted the three shamans conducting our ceremonies spoke no English, so James could have said anything and they would have still sat and smiled while he talked.) I noticed a quizzical look shot back and forth between Vera's guides, who did speak English. Something was up.

We boarded the bus for a steep, twisting ride down the mountain to Cusco. At one point the bus was moving precariously close to the edge of the dirt road with a steep drop below it. There were no guardrails. One of the women yelled to James from the back of the bus to ask if it was OK to end our study of death now and move on to the next subject. We all laughed, even James.

After dinner, we shopped for clothing that would keep us warm during the night ritual on the death stone. James had talked about how it was pouring rain when he laid on the long stone with a shaman standing over him. With circular motions, he loosened his three chakras and then lifted a part of his spiritual self, throwing it in the direction of the Jaguar to be devoured. The shaman and his apprentice then pulled in a new, "clean" version of James, and laid it on his body. He then retightened the chakra points. James could barely move off the stone and then collapsed to the ground . . . . a life changing experience. We'd have ours in just a couple of days!

Richard asked James again if he had heard anything about don Javier Ruis. James responded that he had found out don Javier Ruis was in Cusco. We fully expected the next words out of James' mouth to be "and we will be meeting him." Instead of looking excited about finding his master teacher, he looked down and away from us and changed the subject. After a few words, he just walked off.

A group of us looked at each other with our mouths hanging open. What the heck was *that* about? The only thing that we could imagine was that they might have suffered a falling-out. Otherwise why would he stay away from someone so dear to him when they were in the same city?

Our tarot card topic and subject matter the next day was Temperance, and according to James it represents the harmony of masculine and feminine energies in each of us. The discussion questions of the day: What enthusiastic action must I take to get where I want to go? How am I going to act if it takes longer than I think it should to get there? We discussed four truths of Buddha, which refer to *duka*, a state similar to a wagon wheel falling out of alignment and causing imbalance in the movement of the wagon. In short, the four truths are: 1) duka exists; 2) duka rises; 3) duka ceases; and 4) beyond duka lays a greater way, temperance. If you want a smoother ride through life, seek the middle path, where logic and emotion work well together and avoid extremes.

We took a long bus ride to Moray, home to huge concentric circular terraces apparently built for agriculture—but, in true Incan manner, also containing some spiritual significance. We walked down the very steep side of one of the smaller and older circular sets, which contained five levels. There, the female shaman greeted us. She gave us three seeds and three coca leaves apiece, and James instructed us to face east and set our three intentions during her chant. She blessed us, after which we were to pick a level, which signified the dimensional plane on which we would be working. There, we were to leave our seeds and leaves behind.

Throughout her chant, I held on tightly to my seeds and made sure I was facing and holding my leaves due east. I thought about what level I was going to climb. The 5th level (spirit—all elements coming together) seemed to be winning, when I opened my hand to check on my seeds. One was missing! I checked around carefully, but the grass was high; I wasn't going to find the seed. What to do now? Put my two remaining seeds on the 5th level? Which intention would I leave behind on the 1st level (earth—body and results)? Then I realized the universe was telling me to put my other two seeds with the first, along with my leaves. They belonged grounded at level one, Mother Earth. I needed to continue to work on my body to keep from backsliding and gaining the weight back, and I also needed to stay grounded and focus on my business. The great things I wanted in my future would come when the time was right.

James was sitting directly to my right, a few feet away. He looked down and opened his hand, just as I had. From his reaction, he also lost one or more of his seeds. He started to look around, but quickly came to the same conclusion, that he was not going to find it in the high grass around him. He still climbed a couple of levels to place his remaining seeds and leaves.

When we were done, we had to climb back out of the circles. It was so steep if we stopped moving we could slide backwards. The 11,611-foot altitude was messing with our lungs, but we had to keep moving. At one point, I was sliding backwards when one of Vera's guys jogged down the hill and offered to help me. I swear these people are all lungs and part mountain goat! He wanted to take my backpack and pull me up the hill, but I waved him off. I moved over just a few steps, stopped my feet from sliding, and worked my way up the hill. I did not know James was watching. When I got to the top, he said, "Connie, a year ago you could not have climbed up that hill."

I replied, "A year ago, I would not have been able to climb down it either!"

Our next stop was Ollantaytambo, in the Urubamba river valley—also known as the Sacred Valley. This was the temporary capital for the Inca during the Spanish invasion of Peru. At a mere 9,160 feet, we might be able to catch our breath here. Think again! James told us to practice a silent meditation as we climbed the estimated 230 to 275 steps to the Temple of the Sun. He said to think of it as climbing to higher levels of consciousness while also remembering the four important animals in the Inca tradition. During the lower third of the climb, we were to emulate the Serpent, reacting to the things around us. This meant taking one step after another, looking forward without much thought or consideration as to what we were doing. The next third represented the Jaguar, increased awareness of what is around you. We consciously felt steps under our feet, the wind and the sun, and listened to the sounds around us. For the final third of the climb, we were to picture the Condor, above it all, seeing everything and paying no attention to the aches and pains of the climb. The Condor sees the big picture. At the crest, we called upon the Hummingbird. Technically from an engineering point of view, this bird should not even be able to fly. Their wings are going so fast you can barely see them, but their bodies remain still in the apparent chaos around them. They are exact. Even though they fly and maneuver at great speeds, they hit the tiniest flower blossom target with complete precision. Even in a chaotic world, a person working at this level can be calm and still while a storm rages around them.

On the way up, I had to stop a couple of times to catch my breath. Once, I turned around to check on someone I had just passed, who was hanging onto the side of the wall a bit precariously. When I looked back, I saw how high I was and how steep the steps were! I snapped a photo of the stairs, during which I switched the camera to video by accident. It is still fun to watch that clip and hear myself sucking in air so hard while "resting" for a second. I wonder just how bad I sounded when I was really pushing it!

Onward and upward! Always upward, then steep downward, then upward again. The Andes have no flat spots.

At the top, we faced the sun with our feet together and arms straight out at our sides. The shadow we made behind us was a cross, the ancient symbol of Father God's light moving through man. The sky was a brilliantly intense blue with just a couple of small white puffy clouds drifting by. By some miracle, the tourist crowds had left the top of the temple and we had it all to ourselves, so James led us in a chant. When we were finished, we heard only the sound of the wind moving through this amazing structure. We then walked across the top and descended down a different set of stairs. At the bottom, the female shaman led another intention-setting ritual, using an egg, followed by a second chakra cleansing.

Most mornings and nights, we gathered in the hotel and talked about our day, then laid out the next day's schedule. Sometimes, James conducted mini-lectures. At one such meeting, just the day before we were to have the death stone ceremony, James announced that we would not be going into Machu Picchu at night.

What?

He said the Peruvian government was not going to honor their commitment to let us go. These types of things happen in other countries, which everyone who has traveled knows. There was nothing that could be done about it, James said. He mentioned that the group had already received special privileges for the boxed lunches, the Despacho ceremony, the water ritual in Tipon, and the ability to stay later at Ollantaytambo, none of which was usually allowed. In other words, he was saying be grateful. Then he just moved on to the next subject. He seemed to avoid eye contact. I just thought at the time that he was as disappointed as we were.

It took a while for it to register. We were stunned. The news was a major bummer! The death stone experience was one of the reasons we signed back up for the WWS. James seemed disappointed as well.

A full camera crew caught up with us. They were going to document the trip to Machu Picchu; maybe we'd receive a video of our experience to remember it by! Last time, even though a film crew followed us all over Egypt, we saw nothing except one short clip of James talking outside the Valley of the Kings. On the negative side, when the cameras were on, he tended to look and speak to them rather than us.

We spent the night in a lovely hotel close to Ollantaytambo, and then walked the next morning to the nearby train station for our ride to Machu Picchu. The next tarot card we studied was The World. The question of the day: what am I going to do with the knowledge that I have learned? Life really is not about slowing down, but about speeding up. Don't confuse being calm with going slow. Remember the hummingbird.

The train ride was great and the Urubamba River scenery breathtaking. The dry desert land was giving way to a more tropical environment as we entered the vicinity of the Amazon watershed. Gingers and other tropicals made it look more like Hawaii than the Andes! By the time we reached our final stop, Aguas Calientes, green, steep mountains surrounded us. We walked the short distance to our hotel, which sat on the banks of the rushing Urubamba River. This water sign gal was thrilled! I'm still not sure if I felt so invigorated because of my close proximity to fast-moving water, or because I was feeling some special vortex of energy.

We took a bus up the steep, winding road to Machu Picchu. Once there instead of following the main walkway ahead of us, we were directed to a smaller path to our left. After moving to the side of the trail closest to the mountain, we were each given a bandanna to roll up and use as a blindfold. We took the hand of the person to the front and behind us and walked further up the trail, slowly. I sensed Richard was much further up the trail. I really wished we were together. After a while, I could hear either Vera or one of her people warning us of a step, and helping us around a sharp turn near a steep drop off. (I found out later James did not like the fact we were receiving assistance. It was probably not scary enough that way, in his opinion). I appreciated the gestures of Vera's guides; that was reassuring. I did not completely trust James to look out for our safety anymore. I was trembling slightly, not because I was scared or cold, but because I could feel the energy around me! I was trying not to get too emotional . . . yet.

Finally we stopped. I could hear other people talking in different languages behind us. James walked in front of us, talking about living to the fullest. "To get where you want to go, you need to know where you are now."

At that moment, a man in a group walking in front of us said, "I'll tell you where you are now: you're standing blindfolded at the edge of a freaking cliff, that's where you are now!"

That cracked me up. I had no doubt we were indeed standing at the edge of a freaking cliff. James then asked, "Are you just taking up space or are you really living your lives?" He talked about the fact that we had *known about* Machu Picchu but because we had never experienced it we did not *know* Machu Picchu. He then told us to take off our blindfolds and *know* Machu Picchu. The man does have a flair for the dramatic!

I remember the exact moment I removed my blindfold. The beauty of the site defied description! It was surreal, to say the least. My eyes kept moving between a llama and the city. The llama stood to my left, only a few feet in front of me. He looked at me curiously while lazily chewing on a long strip of grass that hung from his mouth. Then I peered down at the city below. It looked just like the photo on my vision board for many years. *Now* it was time to get emotional! I was at the Sacred Crystal City of the Incas.

We headed even further up the hill, where we circled up and enjoyed a welcoming ceremony led by a different male shaman. He alternated between his native language and English as he performed the ceremony. We each selected a coca leaf, of course, and a few flower petals from either a red or white carnation. Each color meant something specific; I chose red. We were to find a place within Machu Picchu that felt personally special, and leave our offering there. We then headed to view the famous death stone. Like so many important stones, it was roped off. So close, yet so far.

Now a UNESCO World Heritage Site, Machu Picchu was built between 1438 and 1472 on a saddle of land about 8,000 feet above sea level. While not as ancient as the Egyptians, the Incans built an incredible volume of stone works during the relatively small amount of time they ruled. Again, like at Saksayhuaman, huge stones were perfectly fitted together without the use of mortar. I overheard another tour group member ask their guide how they were able to get these huge stones up this steep mountain. "According to legend, the 'others' spoke to the stones and they walked up into place on their own."

We entered the city through the Student's Gate, also known as the Front Portal. I stood in the doorway and put my hands up against the walls, asking permission of the city to enter. Then I awaited the reply. Everyone with whom I spoke afterwards had received a different message. After I got my invitation, I quickly slipped my offering between the stones on the right inside wall of the gate. We then walked over to a spot that would become one of my favorite locations in the entire city, the toning room. In groups of thirteen, we entered the room and put our heads into spaces in the wall located throughout the room. James led us in a specific chant to open the energy in a particular area in our bodies; we repeated each of two different sounds/tones three times each. There was wondrous acoustic resonance between these spaces, just like we'd experienced in the king's chamber in the Great Pyramid. Our voices were amplified and blended together beautifully. I could feel the effect the sound was having on a specific section of my body. The warm, tingling sensations lasted as long as we continued to chant. Richard came in with the next group and I was able to stand on a stairway above the room and hear the harmonious blending of their voices as well. In addition to the harmony, you could still pick out the specific voice of each individual. I could have played there all day!

We climbed up to one of the highest points in the city, the Intihuatana stone, also known as the "Hitching Post of the Sun." The stone looks like a giant sundial and is believed to be an astronomical clock or calendar. As I stepped over one of the steps to a high point on the trail, I held my hands over my head, looked up and allowed the fresh raindrops that had just started to fall hit my face. Still holding my hands up, I looked down to my right, across the small courtyard I'd just entered, and locked eyes with our shaman. He was doing the exact same thing. We smiled at each other, celebrating the rain together.

We reached the stone and encircled it. James led a ceremony he often did at seminars, invoking four different archangels. He started by calling on the archangel of the east, Rafael, represented by the element of air. When he finished, a strong wind whipped around us; it blew so hard we had to hold onto our hats and seek each other's help to stay standing. Next, he moved to the west and addressed the Archangel Gabriel, represented by the element of water. With that, the skies opened up and we were pounded by a torrent of rain. Several people claimed there was hail; I wouldn't doubt it. It was either raining or hailing so hard it stung when it hit my face. James proceeded to call upon the Archangel Michael, who is in the south, represented by fire. Lightning flashed all around us! Tourists scrambled to duck behind walls and in crawl spaces; a small group huddled in a corner just behind me. Now we felt like we were in a hurricane, the camera crew hung on to keep from blowing off the top of the hill; their camera soaked and trashed. I'd been around James long enough to know what came next. That would be Auriel (or Uriel), the Archangel in the north that represents the earth. James was preparing to call on this Archangel in the middle of one of the planet's most seismically active areas! We had just finished learning how the Incas had designed their walls to slope inward, to better absorb vibration during severe earthquakes. And now with wind, rain, and lightning all around us was he really going to call on the earth to respond as well? Several of us shot James a look of "don't do it."

He looked up at us and grinned. This was the first time I ever saw him not complete the full circle. Instead, he laughingly said we'd better stop. Several of us laughed and nodded in agreement. As soon as he stopped, so did the storm. As we walked down the stairs, a huge double rainbow arched across the sky directly in front of us. Was this storm just a coincidence? Vera and her guides said they had never seen it rain like that during the dry season, ever.

Just after the ceremony, we took one of my favorite photos of James, Richard and me together. You can see the last giant raindrops still falling, and it is obvious we were soaked, but big smiles beamed across our faces because we just had experienced the granddaddy of all Archangel Salutations!

We rode down to Aguas Calientes and circled up for our end of the day sharing session, with Vera arranging hot chocolate for everyone. James's personal assistant talked about what she had seen during the ceremony around the sundial—most of the other tourists in Machu Picchu, miserably huddled by the walls, trying to find some cover from the storm. We were blown around and soaked, and smiling about it. With wonderment in her voice and a smile on her face, she said something to the effect of, "What's with you people?" Yep, no one could accuse this group of being "normal."

James wrapped up the meeting by announcing a 10:30 a.m. starting time for the climb up Huayna Picchu. We needed to be all the way back to the train station by 1 p.m., any questions? Immediately, one of the women said several people who had done the climb told her to allow 1½ hours for just the climb up to the top because of the steepness and altitude—and allowing time to view the beauty of the trail. Also, I had been warned by climbers who were in good shape not to hurry, to allow plenty of time. James' timeline didn't seem to leave enough time. Several people agreed. The reason Peruvian authorities limited the number of people who could climb Huayna Picchu, and issued strict starting times, was because many people had fallen and died on that mountain. They were trying to space us out and keep tabs on climbers at all times. Rushing it did not sound like a good idea!

James acted like he did not care about the serious concern rising in the group. He brusquely said, "If you are still coming up the mountain and you see me coming down, you HAVE TO turn around and follow me down."

With that, the meeting was over. Carol moved over to sit down next to me and asked what we should do. I was surprised that she would be concerned, since she often worked and lived at altitude and was in great physical shape. I expected the climb would be no problem for her. However, Carol was very concerned; "We need to say something to James," she told me.

James walked behind us. We both stopped him. I looked at her. "Go ahead," I said.

"No, you do it," she stuttered, and looked down.

James looked at me. I told him that some of the people were really worried about their ability to make it up to the top in such a short amount of time. He brushed me off and said something to the effect that not everyone was meant to make it to the top, and off he went.

Well, didn't that just make us all feel better!

The hand wringing was building quickly. No one wanted the climactic moment of the trip, which was supposed to be once in a lifetime spiritual experience, turned into a race. With that, Richard and I swung into problem-solving mode. We needed to gather data: what were our fixed and movable constraints? We needed to maximize the time for the climb, so either we would start earlier or arrange later transportation back to Cusco. What were the ramifications of missing the train? Being delayed by an hour, or a day? How bad would it feel to be 90% of the way to the top, and then have to turn around for fear of missing the train, only to learn that the next train left just an hour later than our scheduled ride? So what if we got back to Cusco an hour or two later; no big deal! A day or week later would take more consideration.

One thing was clear; people were getting more concerned and upset by the minute. Some knew they would likely not have any problem with the climb. Others did have reason to worry, more so than me, and I felt their frustration at James' apparent lack of concern.

As we headed back to our room, I mentioned to Richard that James needed to show a little compassion for others. What was with him lately, anyway? Why did everything have to turn into an X-game?

At dinner, we asked the people around us if they would be willing to pay the cost if we missed the scheduled train. The answer was a resounding "Yes!" Diane and her husband, Mark, who sat at the table next to us, said simply: "Have credit cards, will travel." Next question: could we get a later train, or could we just start earlier? Richard checked to see if the other WWS members would be willing to miss part of the sunrise ceremony to start climbing earlier. "Yes!" again was their reply.

There was no one from James Ray International in the dining room. Our WWS contact at JRI was very sick, likely in bed, down for the count. However, our tour leader Vera sat at the next table, eating alone. Who would know better if we could get a later train or earlier start! She and Richard discussed the options. Starting earlier was not possible, since we were assigned that time slot to climb. Vera wanted to know why it was so important to us to climb the mountain. After Richard told her the extent of training many of us had done for the past year, Vera, loving soul that she is said that she would make it work. She would have Gabino stay behind with those who were slower, and, if needed, help them board a later train back to Cusco. It turned out a train left every 30 minutes. Problem solved!

After dinner, we stood in the back of the dining room, watching the band and a group of dancers, when I looked up and saw James on the second floor mezzanine talking to Helen. I smiled. I was happy to see him talking to her because she was having serious personal troubles. I asked him earlier in the week if he would talk to her and see if he could help her work through them.

James' return glance was anything but a smile. A glare was more like it. Odd, maybe he was engrossed in Helen's story, and a smile would have been inappropriate. Either way, I was happy to see them talking and didn't think any more about it.

Back in our room, we were trying to dry out our clothing and the inside of our hiking boots with the hair dryer before going to bed. Vera called us and said James was in the lobby talking to the people who were concerned about the time schedule for the climb; he wanted us to meet him there. As far as we were concerned, everything was set, but the king summoned us so off we went.

When we got to the lobby, James sat on a couch with a couple of women next to him, and a few others sitting on the floor at his feet. When he saw us, he went absolutely ballistic. He yelled that we were always the troublemakers, stirring everyone up, and he'd had enough. Richard and I were shocked by the ferocity of the attack. Why was he getting so bent out of shape? We merely arranged a later train back to Cusco, *if necessary*. What was so wrong with that?

James called us "the trouble makers in the WWS" and told us not everyone belonged in the WWS. He stopped talking while glaring right at us. Apparently it did not have the desired effect on Richard and me, because we did not instantly drop to our knees and beg forgiveness. *Well that's not a bad idea, really. Give us our money back prorated on the number of events that we attended and we will be gone,* I thought. We knew we would not be rejoining. His current attack was the last straw; never again would we make excuses for him.

He realized that threatening to eject us from the WWS was not going to beat us into submission, so he quickly changed his tactic. One thing above all else to remember: James is the best manipulator of words I have ever seen. Debating him is useless. I have seen people far more adept at debate than I am take him on and get shot down. It makes having a heart to heart talk with him very difficult when it is a *two-way* conversation. In other words, when he is counseling *you* to change, operating as the provider or leader, it can be a good talk. God help you if you try to suggest that *he* could do something better. Hope you're wearing your fireproof underwear, because you are about to get flamed big time! James is great at giving out criticism and what he calls "tough love." But he is probably the worst person I have ever met at listening to advice, never mind criticism. A true two-way conversation turns into a debate first, then into a contest he must win. I have seen him go into this mode, then come back later and act on the advice given him, even though he shot it down in the heat of the discussion. First "win" the debate, then consider. It's a trait possessed by insecure people.

The last thing I wanted to do was debate him in public. If I opened up and talked from my heart too much, he would use my words against me. I would have liked to help him understand that our plan was not that big of a deal, and find out why he was really so upset. I don't know what was said to him before we arrived, so I needed to understand his point of view, but that required an honest two-way conversation. In the best of circumstances, that was hard with him. Given his current state of rage, it would be impossible.

It took everything within me not to yell out, "What's your problem? I know you are probably pissed off we are not having the ceremony on the death stone right now. You need to calm down and let's talk this thing out!" Saying that would have just escalated his anger and he would *have* to win, no matter what I said. Besides, I'd already switched to de-escalation mode.

Not James. He took my lack of resistance as a sign of weakness, because he turned to me and started yelling about how I was not strong enough to make the climb so I was working . . . Richard cut him off. "Wait a minute, she didn't do anything. If you want to yell at someone for putting together a backup plan, then you need to talk to me, because I did it."

James proceeded to rip Richard apart. "You always have to be a hero. Always coming to someone's aid just to make you feel important," he yelled.

That made it official: *I have had it with James' flaming attacks on people.* Richard is the kindest, most decent person I have ever met. He does things anonymously for people all the time, while being quite happy to let others take the credit for it. It was clear James did not know Richard at all.

James was using another of his techniques based on the idea if you get bothered by someone else's activities, gestures, expressions or anything else, then you are projecting onto them something you don't like about yourself. It's your problem, not theirs. At an event, when someone said anything to the effect that they felt or did something because of what James said or did, he would deflect it by saying something like, "you're just projecting your anger/insecurity/whatever onto me. The problem is with you, not me." He often did this from the stage. He was using it on Richard and everyone else in the room, shifting responsibility for attitude problems to them—and blaming us for projecting our issues on him.

Well, it works both ways, James. Is Richard the one who always has to be the hero? Or is it you?

James kept ranting. He was mad we approached Vera for help instead of a JRI person. He didn't think either of us was strong enough to make the climb, no matter how much time he allotted. He added that Richard was a physical wreck. Again, I was surprised at how little he knew about us. Yes, Richard had the back problems in Egypt, but James was talking to "Mr. Fit," a man that ran a ridge trail in our local mountains every week for the past year. James started to yell at me again, "What's so important about climbing this mountain, anyway?"

"It's important to me because it has been my goal that I have been training for the last year," I replied.

To which he yelled back, "It's the wrong goal!"

I was really taken aback. For years, he taught the importance of setting clear goals and installing a plan of action to achieve them. I did that, but somehow it was now *his* call what my personal goals should be.

"You should have lost all that weight for your health, not to climb a mountain. Before, you were just a heart attack waiting to happen," he continued. "It's the wrong goal."

"But it is my goal."

Answering him only prolonged the attack. The floggings were definitely going to continue until the morale improved. At one point, he tried to stare down Richard again. It didn't work; Richard held his ground. I was surprised, for a couple of reasons. James can be a formidable presence, and I was actually impressed that Richard didn't blink, not even once. Also, Richard will bend over backwards to see someone else's point of view. He is not confrontational.

In that instant, I knew it wasn't just me who was finished listening to this temper tantrum. Richard would rather meet in the middle and work something out that benefits both sides, but if you try to take advantage and push him too far, his Aries kicks in and he won't take anymore. If you want to continue to be unreasonable, then do it by yourself.

Other people were trying to talk to James as well, but he kept repeating the same thing: "It's not about the mountain." It became his chant he repeated over and over. When another woman continued to argue he said, "You all can put just one foot on the trail and tell everyone that you have climbed it, you don't have to tell them that you didn't make it to the top."

I was floored. He looked at me, nodded his head, and said, "Yes; right?"

I shook my head and looked down. What could I say? It was a lie, like saying I ran a marathon when all I did was cross the starting line. The problem was some people in the group were not likely to make it to the top, and I didn't want to say something that would hurt their feelings, or take the option from them if it was going to give them some comfort. However, there was no way I could say I climbed the mountain unless I did. James could not understand that we were not climbing for bragging rights. Huayna Picchu had been calling to me. This was about meeting a challenge, and it was personal, very personal, between me and Huayna Picchu. I was going to reach the top, even if it was on my hands and knees.

Diane said in a disgusted voice to Mark, "I've heard enough, I'm out of here. Let's go buy some water." They turned to walk away. James called them back. Standing up to James takes some backbone, and both of them did. After Diane spoke her peace, James thanked her for her honesty.

He turned back to me, but this time the angry edge was out of his voice and he was speaking in a more normal tone. Was he calming down or switching to a new tactic? He said he heard everyone was mad at him, unhappy with the schedule and putting all the blame on him, and he didn't want to hear that kind of stuff.

Finally, I thought we were getting somewhere. He was talking about his feelings now instead of just blasting us. I really did want to know why he was so angry, because it did not make sense. He said Helen told him before dinner about the group's anger towards him. Now the sharp look he gave me in the dining room made sense. I thought he was talking to Helen about her problems, and he thought I was smiling because she was telling him how bad we thought he was. Truth is, neither Richard nor I spoke to Helen about the climb, so whatever she told him was coming from someone else. That may partly explain why we were attacked so harshly.

James then asked me, "Are you willing to miss the farewell dinner in Cusco with the other WWS members just to climb a mountain?"

That was easy one. I was hosting a WWS reception at our home in just a few weeks, the night before the WWS summit, and I would see everyone again then. I might never have another chance to climb this mountain. "Yes," I said.

He was clearly calming down now, or maybe we just wore him down. We had survived the attack, but I was aware of wounds on our side likely not to heal. Most of the women sitting near him or on the floor had tried to get their points across, too. Whitney frequently agreed with James, sometimes quoting us, but not too accurately, about Richard's dinnertime group discussion about making more time for the climb. Many ideas were being thrown around; according to her, they were all our ideas. It was interesting to watch how James' approval was so important to some they would agree and go along with whatever he said or did, just to maintain that approval.

James looked at the four of us. To Diane he said, "You're OK," then to Mark, "you're OK," and then to Richard, "you're OK."

When he got to me, he said, "Maybe you're not yet."

No, I wasn't. Some things he said were so untrue; perhaps now that he was calm and speaking normally, he might be willing to hear me. I knew he still had to win, but I was not going to let go of his wounds and insults without responding. "James, I am really having trouble with some of the things that you just said. I am not willing to throw anyone under the bus, so it is up to them to speak up if what I say applies to them. First, I was not the one who started the group off being concerned about the timing of the climb."

"I know, that was Carol," he said, looking at her.

Carol nodded. "We already talked about how I have to believe in myself more."

When I heard that I thought, OK, if he knew that I didn't start it, then why say that I did?

"You said that we were always trouble makers, and I know that we spoke up about what was going on with the WWS Extravaganza because we were not being treated fairly."

"I'm constantly hearing from my staff that you guys are complaining about something."

"We didn't think we were being treated fairly, and we just wanted to be heard," I said. "Once we spoke to you, we let it drop and went along with what you suggested, didn't we?"

He agreed. To Carol's credit, she spoke up and said, "You know James, I didn't feel like I was being treated fairly either, I just didn't say anything."

That surprised him.

"Others felt the same way too, but we were the ones who actually said something," I added. "Wouldn't you rather hear about something than have us just quit?"

"You threatened not to come to the event," James said.

"That was because we were getting the brush-off. After we spoke to you, we not only came, but with no prep time we put together a booth on real estate just like you asked us to, right?"

He nodded in agreement.

"We are still here and the person who caused all of that trouble is gone, right?"

He acknowledged that and added that there was an "element" in the WWS in 2008 that wasn't good, and it was better now that they were gone. I got the feeling he was referring to more than the one person I was talking about.

"So what other trouble are we constantly causing?" I asked. I was purposely keeping my voice low and calm. I was not trying to argue with him, and I didn't want him to get defensive again. I felt now we were at least communicating.

James couldn't think of anything else and he admitted it.

I did have an idea of what else we did that might have bugged him and his staff, and I knew he would not want to bring it up in front of the group. I would not promote Spiritual Warrior when we Dream Teamed, and instead encouraged people to take Practical Mysticism or Quantum Leap first. I know I was over heard by his staff at least once, and it likely went straight back to him.

"You know that you can always contact me directly if you need to talk to me," he said.

This surprised the women sitting around him; several told him they'd never known or felt that they could. I told James it was very difficult to reach him through his staff, "and that's why we had to pitch such a fit about the WWS Extravaganza, because they were not letting us talk to you. We just wanted to be heard by YOU."

There were other things I wanted to say, but I would not break confidences. Since a couple of those people were sitting there and not speaking up, I let it go. They had to fight their own battles. We were there a long time and everyone was exhausted, so James made a comment that sleep is overrated. Those who had been sitting rose to leave.

As he was getting up off the couch, James said, "Connie, don't leave yet, we need a hug." He exchanged quick hugs from the others as he made his way over to me. We hugged for a while. Did he intuitively know things had changed between us? Was he thinking maybe he had gone too far? Maybe he was thinking we really were a major pain in the ass. He can be hard to read.

We took the elevator with Whitney and one other woman. Whitney turned and, with a bright, happy smile said, "Wasn't that a great talk?"

I tried to say something back, but stuttered and stopped. What could I say? The other woman in the elevator raised her eyebrows and said, "I guess that depends on what side of the conversation you were on."

While returning to our room, I felt profound sadness. James really did not know either of us at all. Richard asked me if I had ever seen anything handled so badly in my life—from a life "master" no less. We had looked up to him, tried to emulate what he did, taken his advice and teachings to heart and incorporated them into our lives as much as we knew how. We would be the first to say that we were profoundly grateful for his positive impact on our lives, but he was heading in a direction we could not follow. We both knew it. His attack revealed a total lack of compassion for the group, and any understanding on his part that this was our trip, not just his.

Richard had managed more than 1,200 employees at one time. He was very good at listening to people and making them feel heard, even if he still decided to do exactly what he planned from the start. With that in mind, I asked him how he would have handled the situation if he were James. Without missing a beat, he said, "I would have called everyone together, told them I understand that they are concerned about having enough time to make the climb. That it is partly my fault for making such a big deal out of making it to the top in the first place, and that you will still have a successful trip and have learned a lot even if you don't make the climb at all. It's what is in your heart that counts. With that said, I understand it is important to some of you and my staff and I will do everything possible to give you as much time as we can. I can't promise you anything because we are working with Peruvian restrictions that we have no control over, but I can promise you we will do everything we can. Now go to bed and get a good night's sleep, we have a big day ahead of us tomorrow. Then we do hugs all around, ask Vera to do what she can to get us extra time, have the JRI employees look into what can be moved around in the schedule and then everybody go to bed."

Yep. It definitely could have been handled better.

Before sleeping, it is my habit to think of a lesson learned and something for which I am grateful. Today's lesson was easy to identify: Make other people fight their own battles. When Carol was so upset about the next day's schedule and she wanted me to do the talking for her with James, I should have responded, "No, you talk to him," and then shut up. I was grateful for James growing so angry and aggressive with us. It was much easier to see that we needed to move on. It was still a hard decision; we would miss our friends, and, believe it or not, we would miss James; but for some reason, the universe was pushing us quickly away from him.

The long anticipated hike up Huayna Picchu was just a few hours away as we headed to Machu Picchu for a sunrise ceremony. I'm not big on sunrise ceremonies. I am basically a night person who doesn't feel there is much you can do at 5 a.m. that can't happen just as well at 9 or 10.

People wanted to chitchat with me, but I wasn't in the mood. I still had not absorbed and processed everything that happened the previous day and night, and I'd slept precious little. My deep sadness was still there and I wanted to shake it off, but I couldn't just yet.

When we arrived at Machu Picchu, there was already a considerable crowd at the gate. Once inside, we went to one of the more isolated areas, where our shaman led a gratitude ceremony before James started talking. I had purposefully avoided eye contact with him, because in my mind, I was already separating from him. I also did not want to give him the opportunity to tell me again that I had to turn around and come down with him if I did not make it to the top during his time frame. That was the option of last resort. Richard and I decided he would climb with the main group, with me following as quickly as possible. If James started to come back down before I got to the top, then Richard would move to the end of the line. I would not turn around until I saw him. Richard could then give me an idea on how much further I had to go. If I was still a long way from the top, then I would likely turn around, but if I was 75% or more up the mountain, then I would continue and Richard would join me. James could be as ticked off at me as he wanted, but this might be my one and only chance to climb Huayna Picchu. I was going for it. It was my goal that I had worked so hard towards and I was going to do it!

During the ceremony, I noticed James trying to make eye contact with me, but I continued to avoid him. I was getting emotional during the ceremony and I could feel tears welling in my eyes. I was starting to feel the sadness of losing my role model. Hearing him talk during the ceremony reminded me of how much I was going to miss his talks and rituals. And I was going to miss this group. Crying is not advisable if you are at altitude with asthma, on the verge of a very challenging hike. I felt more like I was attending a funeral than a Sunrise Gratitude Ceremony. Something had just died.

James started talking about letting go of bad feelings, how they ate us up inside. I looked at him. He was peering directly at me. He kept saying to let it go. He was talking to me. At the end of the ceremony, James pointed to the roof directly behind me and told us to look at the eagle. The beautiful large blackish bird had landed on the rooftop and was sitting observing us from only a few feet away! First a pair of eagles circled over us in Spiritual Warrior, then the pair of hawks in Abu Simbel, and now this majestic bird in Machu Picchu. It sat there for quite a long time, as if posing for pictures as many in the group clicked away. Vera said she'd never seen an eagle come so close or sit so long here before.

Afterward, James gave Richard a big hug. They exchanged words and I tried to scoot away, but James caught my wrist, spun me around and looked me right in my eyes. No hiding now. We hugged. "You have to let it go," he said.

"I'm trying not to cry."

"Maybe you need a good cry."

I shook my head. "It's not a good idea for someone with asthma to cry before climbing."

With that, we hugged again. I really was going to miss him. "I love you," I said.

"I love you, too."

I meant it. I was so grateful for everything he taught us, and his positive effect on so many areas of our lives. The transformation in my life, particularly over the last year, was so huge even I could see it. I did the hard work, and he provided the tools and information. It came at a high cost financially, but the results were tangible and I wouldn't trade them for any amount of money. I felt like I was hugging a soon-to be-ex-boyfriend. He meant a lot to me, I loved him, and I wished him nothing but the best. However we were heading onto different paths because things were not as good as they needed to be between us anymore. Did he sense what I was feeling? Or just following his usual behavior, and now wishing he'd said things differently the previous night?

We headed over early to the start of the Huayna Picchu trail to see if we could start ahead of schedule. No such luck. At our scheduled time, we stepped up to the guard gate. Several women decided to stay in Machu Picchu and work with the shaman instead of climbing. One couple decided not to go, while one other person stayed in the hotel sick with food poisoning. The rest of the group was at the gate where we had to sign in and give quite a bit of information about ourselves. One of the guards told us that because people do fall and die on this trail, they want to know exactly who is on the mountain at all times. If someone does not sign out afterwards, then they search for that person. That is also why they don't let anyone start much later than the morning. If someone does not make it back, they want to conduct their search in daylight. This was not a mountain to take lightly.

James was one of the first people through the gate, followed by the camera crew. The line moved pretty smoothly until three of us remained, along with our rear guide, Gabino. Then, for some reason, they stopped letting us through. Meanwhile, James and the rest of the group took off up the trail. By the time the gate re-opened, 15 minutes had passed. Not good. Once the three of us started, the guards stopped Gabino and talked to him for a while. We walked a little way on our own, anxious about the amount of time we were losing.

We came to a sign and a fork in the road. Both had "Huayna Picchu" written on it, but not spelled like we were used to seeing it. It looked like we should go to the right, but that was just a guess. We could not afford to lose any more time by going the wrong way. We had to wait for Gabino. Finally, Gabino came bounding up the path and told us to go to the right. We were at least 20 minutes behind the main group. Richard took off to catch them. Yep, this is the man James called a physical wreck. He did in fact reach them just a short while later, while I stayed behind to hike with Rachel and Gabino. It wasn't long before I started to pull away from them. I was moving at a good speed, and my asthma was behaving. It was a steep trail, but not impossible. It was very similar to sections of a mountain trail on which we'd been training in San Diego, with altitude thrown in. And that wasn't so bad, now that we'd been in Peru for almost a week. If my knee and asthma behaved, nothing would stop me from reaching the top!

Soon, I couldn't hear Rachel and Gabino talk anymore. I was on my own. Now I had to follow the trail markers. It was well marked, but often people would stop and stand in front of one of the directional signs, which could easily lead to a wrong turn. That happened to me at one fork. It seemed like the trail wasn't climbing as much as it should. I asked a man coming the other way if I was on the right path. "No, this trail leads to a cave," he said. Luckily, I had not walked far, but time was precious and I could not afford too many mistakes. Sections of the trail were very steep, with sheer drop offs everywhere. There were spots with steel cables anchored into the rocks, to give you something to grab because it was almost straight up. At one of these spots, I first noticed the sound of a very big bug buzzing behind me. I was too busy hanging on to turn around and look, but we were in the Amazon watershed now and God only knows what kind of insects lurked out there, or in this case, just inches from the back of my head.

A nice thing about hiking alone was that I met people on the trail. If I had been with our group, I probably would have spent most of my time talking with them instead of the other hikers. At one point, I caught up to two men and one woman. They looked to be in their early twenties and their accents suggested they were from Australia. The man and woman I first passed were struggling. The man in front yelled back at his friends that this was embarrassing. "Don't you two realize that you were just passed by an older woman?"

When I drew closer, he asked me if I lived high up in mountains. "No, I live at sea level in California."

"This is really embarrassing," he repeated. "Oh no, now you're going to pass me!"

He told me they had just arrived, and I mentioned I had the advantage of being at altitude for almost a week. "No excuses," he said. He yelled back down to the other two, "We're going to have to cut back on the beer," to which his male friend replied, "let's not go and do anything that extreme without thinking about it first!"

Soon, I couldn't hear their voices anymore, but that big bug still filled my ears at times. Except it no longer sounded quite like a bug. The tone of its wings sounded a bit deeper. But I am certainly no expert on Amazonian insects. Every time I heard the sound, I was busy with both hands, climbing. I couldn't afford to get distracted, but I wanted to see what it looked like. It was always directly behind me. *Do beetles bite?*

I reached the middle of a particularly steep section of stones that twisted sharply up and to the left. At the bottom of the turn was a sheer drop off. Mud coated the stones, making them slippery. I used the cable in my right hand to pull myself up, and grabbed onto any surface I could reach with my left hand. When I found myself between rocks that didn't have a place I could grab, my right hand slipped and I skidded backwards a long way. My knees hit the stones hard and my right hand hurt from cable burn.

It was totally my fault. I had been thinking about James, the big blow up, what I could have done differently to prevent it, if I could have stopped the uproar after it started. I started to tear up. Now that my knees and hand hurt, I was exhorting myself, "Don't cry, don't cry, don't cry!" I was mad about having to rush, I was sad about the prospect of losing contact with my friends inside and outside WWS, the bug was back, I was frustrated that even if I tried to talk to James, he probably would not listen. I looked over my right shoulder, surprised to see how far I had slid. I could have slid all the way to the drop-off. I still could! If I slid off here, who would ever know what happened to me?

Suddenly, I felt very alone. "Don't cry, don't cry, don't cry!" I heard the bug again, took a deep breath, *don't cry,* then another slower deep breath.

The rock behind the cable came into sharp focus. It felt cold and rough on the back of my fingers, as my hand was again wrapped tightly around the steel cable. It was very quiet. I could hear no one either in front or behind me. Everything was still. I did not hear it approach; I just felt something land on the middle of my right shoulder blade. I looked as far as I could over my right shoulder without moving my head.

There, on my shoulder, was a very small hummingbird! When I turned my head slightly to the right to get a better look, it lifted off and hovered a few inches to the right of my head. It then hovered in front of me for what seemed like a minute before buzzing off. Wow!

My knees and hand still hurt, so I pulled myself up and pushed on. Two men came around the corner, heading down the mountain. They could tell I had fallen, and asked if I was OK. I assured them I was fine, and one man said, "This section is particularly nasty." They told me to be careful and they continued down the trail.

I washed off my hand with some drinking water. It was a bit scraped, but I was fine. What just happened? I truly don't believe in coincidences, so what did the hummingbird visitation mean? Often, I have been buzzed by the numerous hummingbirds around our home, but that usually happened when I wore bright colored shirts. Never had one landed on me—especially while wearing a pastel blue shirt. Why me, why now? Why a hummingbird? What had James told us about the hummingbirds when we scaled Ollantaytambo? *Be like the hummingbird, the calm in the chaos.*

I continued climbing, and every once in a while, "my" bird would show up. After getting my attention, it would fly off and hover over some beautiful plant or fly over the vista, enticing me to check out the view. Once, it buzzed by my face so closely I could feel the air move. It hovered over a beautiful purple pink wild orchid. I love orchids, and this one was magnificent. I would have missed it had the bird not shown it to me. I got it! It was telling me to stop and look around. *Don't be in such a hurry, human! Enjoy the view. Enjoy the journey.*

I sensed I was getting close to the top, but there was no way to gauge. There seemed to be more people hanging around at the level spots than before. Many stones now seemed to belong to walls and stairs. I marveled; *how did those stones get all the way up here?* I came to a large flat spot. A group of people stood to my right, looking like they were waiting for someone. Then I encountered stone slabs that would horrify someone with vertigo. The Incas have a fondness for "flying stairs." These stone slabs are anchored only on one side to a wall. Each slab was only supported at the point where it touched the wall; they did not touch each other. In front of me was such a tall, ridiculously steep staircase. Each step was barely deep enough to fit the ball of your foot, and there was absolutely nothing but air on the other side. OK, now this was scary!

No use in procrastinating. I started up the stairs. They were so steep I decided to climb with my hands and legs. I dug my fingers into any crevice I could find. It reminded me of crawling through the tunnel to the middle chamber in the Great Pyramid. I kept my eyes down and looked only at my hands. I heard the hummingbird again, just off my right shoulder. I was too busy hanging on to see him, but it was nice to know he was watching over me.

When I was halfway up, a man and woman atop the stairs were yelling something down to me in French. I could not understand what they were saying, but they kept waving their hands and yelling. I was three-quarters of the way up when I first heard a man calling to me from what sounded like far away. I could not look around much because of my precarious position on the stairs, so I kept climbing. Then I heard him again; this time, he was right behind me. It was Gabino! How the heck did he get up here so fast?

"This is too dangerous, you're going the wrong way," he said. "This is the way down; it's too hard to go up this way. I want you to turn around and go down with me, and then we'll go up the other way. It's much easier."

By then, I was nearly to the top of the stairs; no way was I going to turn around! I asked him if we could get to the top of Huayna Picchu if I kept going up this way. "Yes," he said.

"Then I'm going to keep going."

"Are you sure?"

"Yes."

"Then hold still." With that, Gabino *jumped* from behind me, landed his left foot between my left hand and my head, and jumped up to the stairs above me! How the heck did he do that? These people really are part mountain goat! He then reached his hand down and told me to grab on. I declined, since both of my hands were firmly clutching steps. He tried once again, but I insisted I was doing fine and would keep climbing.

When I reached the top, the French couple asked me if I spoke

English. "We were trying to tell you that you were going the wrong way. You can only go down these steps."

Well, apparently you can go up them, too. I just did, though it wasn't the recommended route. They told me of a directional sign pointing right at the bottom of the stairs. We looked down to the bottom of the stairs, and the large group was still standing there. "Trust me; behind all of those people there is a sign," the Frenchman said with a laugh. "I can't believe you came up that way. Weren't you scared?"

"I was just short of terrified," I said.

Gabino then told me he was going to take me back down another, much easier way. I asked about Rachel. "She made it about seventy percent of the way up and then decided she had to go back. She was worried about running out of time and wanted to be sure she had enough time to get all the way back to the train station."

I felt bad she didn't make it and hoped she was OK about it. Gabino went on to tell me about the structures around us, that we were looking at the high priestess' house, but what I really wanted to know was how close we were the top. "You're almost there, just a little bit further." I asked which way and he pointed to my right.

A few minutes later, Gabino announced our arrival. He pointed to the sign with the mountain's name and elevation. As he photographed me, I wondered where everyone was. I walked around the corner, and saw James and several from our group. I got a big hug from one of the ladies and a few of the others. James walked over and gave me a big hug. He said something either I didn't hear or don't remember because others were calling to me and I was searching for Richard. Gabino figured out who I was looking for, and pointed to the top of some huge rocks just above us. Richard was up there with a few others from our group and they all had their backs to me. I called to him and everyone spun around, surprised to see me. Richard signaled for me to climb up. Along with another woman, I tried to walk up the sheer-sloped edge of the huge stone which was very difficult and slippery. Gabino turned around and raced over. He just about pulled me off the rock. "No, no, too dangerous!" he exclaimed. "Come this way."

He led us around the side to a stone staircase. Up we went. It was great to see Richard again! He wanted to take pictures of me standing in all of the good photo spots. At one point, a friend took Richard's camera and told us to stand together. He held the camera over his head, pointed it down at us, and snapped away. Among those shots is my favorite photo of us together.

Richard said I arrived about 15 minutes behind them. Had I passed through the guard gate at the same time as everyone else, I would have made it to the top with them. The benefit from all those hours of hiking and gym time! I only stayed on top of Huayna Picchu for a few minutes, and then decided to head down before the group to allow extra descent time. I signaled to Gabino that I was going back and asked him how to return the other way.

We climbed down a wooden ladder into a cave. Gabino kept taking photos of me, then handed my camera to someone else on the trail to take a picture of both of us. I think he was more excited I summited the mountain than I was! When we reached the bottom of the flying stairs, he pointed out the sign. It had been behind the group of tourists, which is why I did not see it. "You'll be fine now," he said. With that, he turned around to go back to the top and check on the others. I enjoyed the walk down much more than the climb up.

We were walking out of Machu Picchu, I turned around to look back. I felt like I had not spent enough time there, that I would return one day. Richard said James looked for me at the summit after I had already started down the hill.

Returning to Cusco, we got cleaned up and ready for our last group meeting before heading to dinner. Before the meeting started, Carol informed me that while atop Huayna Picchu, James told the group he had lied: "It *was* about the mountain!"

CHAPTER 17

We're Done!

Spiritual Warrior • Fall 2009

When I've gathered enough information to make a decision
I don't take a poll; I just make a decision.
—Ronald Reagan

During the flight back from Peru, Richard and I talked about the confrontation with James in the hotel lobby. We were trying to make sense of the argument and getting nowhere. One evening, we have a heated argument; the next morning, James is almost conciliatory when he makes his way through the group to give us big hugs after the sunrise ceremony at Manchu Picchu. It is not like James to come to us; we usually have to try to approach him.

We'd reached the point of splitting from our teacher completely, so we wanted to make sure we were doing it for the right reasons. Did over-tiredness cause his blow-up? Was he disappointed because he couldn't conduct the night ceremony on the death stone in Machu Picchu? More to the point: was he being told something untrue about us that caused him to believe we were constantly causing trouble? If so, we needed to find out what it was.

The issue no longer concerned whether or not we were going to rejoin the World Wealth Society (WWS), because we were not. We had planned to Dream Team more events in addition to attending those for which we had pre-paid with our current membership; apparently, the Sedona hike was back on as well. We needed to decide which of these events to attend, if any, and we needed to make the decision soon. Going to Sedona for the hike would mean cancelling our flight and townhome reservations in Maui.

We needed an honest heart-to-heart talk with James—in private. Either we get *ponno* [right] with him about several things, or we would break with him completely, because we could no longer ignore or make excuses for his excessive behavior.

On August 14, we emailed the WWS staff person at JRI and requested a private meeting with James in his southern California office. In Peru, he'd said we and other WWS members could have one-on-one time with him whenever we asked. We were taking him up on it. We hoped we would not have a repeat of our last experience when his staff tried to block us from getting through to him.

No such luck. This was the response we received from the staff person in charge of the WWS:

> Hi Richard and Connie,
> It was great to connect with both of you in Peru . . . that was an experience like no other!! And I'm so excited that you both climbed Huayna Picchu . . . what an accomplishment!
> James is back on the road with an extensive traveling and work schedule. He isn't able to meet face to face at this time. The best way, as always, to connect with James is to submit your topic of conversation/question for the next Ask call and if applicable James can address it then. Also, special WWS- only meal times at events are another great way to talk with him.
> If there is something I can discuss with you both, or if there is something I can relay, I am more than happy to. Have a great weekend!

Nothing had changed: these were standard stall and blocking techniques of JRI. We reiterated this was a private matter, not intended for group discussion, and that James had told us in Peru we could talk with him. Can we arrange the meeting now, please? Several more rounds of emails followed with his staff; we got nowhere. We decided to wait until we saw him again, which would be soon, since we had volunteered to work at one of his intro events coming up in San Diego in late August.

August 25 just before the event, Richard spoke with James and told him we had been trying to schedule an appointment because we needed to talk. He acknowledged he knew we were trying to meet with him and asked Richard the specific matter we needed to discuss. Richard told him: we had some problems with what was said in Peru, and needed to discuss it further. James tried to brush it off by saying it was no big deal, that things were said on both sides that were not really meant and that we were "good." Richard insisted it was not yet good with us—we needed to talk. James said he would get back with us to schedule a time.

Within a few days we were contacted by his personal assistant and told he would only be available by phone. She scheduled a time about a week away.

Prior to the call, a former WWS member was at our home. She suggested we be very clear on what we wanted to resolve in this phone call and not let him lead the conversation in other directions. Great suggestion! We wanted to know why he considered us "the trouble makers in the WWS." We also wanted him to acknowledge that he overreacted in Peru and explain to us what was so bad about a backup plan for those people who needed more time to safely climb Huayna Picchu. If that went well and the discussion opened up, without his need to win the conversation, then I hoped to make some suggestions on how he could treat his volunteers better. Then, if he was still willing to listen, I wanted to bring up the upcoming sweat lodge at Spiritual Warrior and tell him my concerns about the health of people whose body temperatures elevate too high for too long.

It all turned out to be wishful thinking. Over the next couple of weeks, our phone conference was cancelled and moved several times. We reached the point where Richard and I decided if James cancelled again, we were not going to reschedule.

In the beginning of September, we attended the wedding of a neighbor's daughter. The father of the groom looked and acted like he'd suffered a massive stroke. He could barely talk or move. His wife spoke for him, including the reading the toast he wanted to give his son and the bride. Towards the end of the reception, we found out a couple of years earlier; a fever of 106 degrees caused the severe damage to his body. I shot Richard a look; he knew exactly what I was thinking. Richard saw the catastrophic effects of excessive heat on the body for himself instead of through my words and experience. I went into one of my rants about James' sweat lodge. Richard got it this time. He again gave me his word he would never go into James's lodge again, and we both decided we would never Dream Team Spiritual Warrior if the sweat lodge activity remained.

James finally kept his appointment with us on September 17. He started by thanking us for being so patient with all of the rescheduling. "Welcome to the world of my schedule." He added he only had about 10 minutes, "so let's get going." *Thanks for squeezing out a few minutes after we cleared our calendars numerous times for you!.*

My hopeful feeling of a productive call dissolved into the feeling of being brushed off again. We were barely going to have any time to discuss what had happened in Peru, never mind the volunteers or his sweat lodge. Looking back now, I wonder if that was his intention from the start.

James reiterated that he was fine with our relationship with him after Peru, but if there was something we wanted to discuss further, then go ahead. We wanted to know what was wrong about coming up with the alternate plan for those who might need more time to climb the mountain. Rushing people on that mountain could be dangerous. All we had done was to arrange for some of us to take a later train to Cusco, if necessary. And what was behind his statement that we were "the trouble makers in the WWS?"

He did not answer the first question at all. He moved to the second question and described a couple of complaints his staff voiced about us. One was that I did not give "100%" while Dream Teaming Practical Mysticism. I asked how they came to that conclusion. He responded I used my cell phone during the event. The only person who saw me on my phone the entire week was him, and that it was only once and during a break. James was hiding behind his staff, when it was really James complaining. I responded I spent 5 minutes max each day checking in with my office, and I was his for the other 23 hours and 55 minutes. The only calls I took during the event were from resort staff and had to do with something we requested for his event. How could that possibly be a problem for "his staff"? He didn't answer my question.

Next, "his staff" complained I had spent all my time with my daughter at Practical Mysticism and not with the other participants. My mind flashed back to the first morning break during Practical Mysticism 2008. I went over to greet several of the WWS members. Erica was sitting nearby; as I introduced her, I saw James watching us from the stage. He called over the staff person in charge of the volunteers, looking back over at us several times. She called me aside and told me to let Erica "have her own experience" and not talk or spend any time with her for the rest of the week. I felt really torn and sad about "ditching" my daughter, not being there to support and root her on. He got his way and he was still complaining.

That did it! I was furious. "James, I take real exception to that! You told your staff person to tell me to stay away from her during that event and because of that I didn't see my daughter bend rebar, do any of the ropes course challenges, and I never saw her walk fire. I didn't get back to our room until 2 or 3 in the morning after I was done helping the other attendees with their homework or cleaning up the meeting room. My daughter was asleep when I got in and when I left early the next morning. Saying that I spent all my time with her is just not true! In fact, it's outrageous to even say that!"

James' comments lit a fire under Richard. He had interrupted to agree with what I had said. Richard ran down the names of some of the attendees I helped that week. I'm sure James never expected us to come back at him so hard. He was used to people agreeing with whatever he said. I heard hesitation in his voice; very unusual for James.

Richard started talking about our concern that the volunteers were being pushed too hard. I was so mad I was shaking, and I don't remember everything they said, but James seemed to be back peddling.

James said I needed to be 100% behind all of the events when people asked my opinion of what to take next. I thought, *ah, he does know about me talking people out of Spiritual Warrior and/or warning them about the sweat lodge.* He had probably intended to give me a stern lecture about that as well, but this conversation was not going the way any of us had planned or hoped. We were moving into free-fall. Richard and I knew it; James was starting to get the message.

Richard said when someone asked our opinion, they were going to get our true opinion. Richard demanded to know exactly what else we had done to be considered troublemakers in the WWS. I wished we were meeting with him in person, so I could see his eyes and body language, because other than his tone and rate of speech, it was hard to tell what he was thinking. He said according to his staff, with which he agreed, "you have grown so much over the last couple of years that everything is just fine now." There were no more complaints.

Only one person in the conversation thought everything was fine. I was done with his profound lack of gratitude for us and the other volunteers. I told him Dream Teaming meant a significant loss of work time and money, especially when the events were held during our busiest times of the year. We would not be able to Dream Team for him any longer. It was time for us to focus on our family and business. That surprised him. After a pause, without raising his voice he said, "If you can't give 100%, then maybe that is for the best. It is your decision to make."

I knew I was making the decision without discussing it with Richard first, but he was not showing any objection. Richard was in agreement. I don't think James expected us to quit Dream Teaming entirely.

Suddenly James "remembered" he had to rush off to his next appointment, so in a chipper voice he said, "I've got to go now but I will see you two in Sedona in just a couple of weeks!" I told James we had to make a decision to attend either the WW Summit or Sedona. We were way overdue to spend some time at our home in Maui, and if we didn't go in the next couple of weeks, we would have to wait an entire year before our next opportunity. We could not take enough time off work for all three activities, so we decided to go to the Summit instead of Sedona. It was in San Diego and meant a minimum amount of time that we would be away from work. We would be in Maui during the hike and Spiritual Warrior.

"OK," he said. A few seconds of silence followed. I was again speaking for Richard without consulting him first, but I did not hear or see any disagreement from him. I knew Richard wanted to go on the hike, and James knew it as well. Richard had requested the hike in the first place. I had the feeling Richard's silence meant he didn't care to talk about it anymore. After the pause, James said we had made the right choice. The Summit was going to be amazing this year, with the great speakers he had lined up. I ended the call by saying we were looking forward to the Summit and we would see him there.

After I hung up the speakerphone, I looked up at Richard. We said at the exact same time, "We're done." There was no anger in our voices, just finality. His lack of gratitude and no acknowledgement that he overreacted in Peru left us with nothing more to say. After Richard left my office, I sat at my desk and peered out my office window. A hummingbird buzzed around the tropical flowers in bloom nearby.

We discussed our options. We were done with Dream Teaming. As much as we loved working with the people, we knew we were being taken advantage of. We felt used. We would finish off our pre-paid events, since they were non-refundable, and we would stay far away from Sedona. We would miss seeing our friends at the hike, but we needed to put some distance between us and James. It would be difficult to hide our dissatisfaction, and we didn't want another public confrontation since it wouldn't change anything anyway. I promised Richard we would do the hike on our own, or better yet, with our San Diego warrior group.

Others believed James would tone down the sweat lodge a bit after what had happened the previous year, but thinking about it gave me a bad feeling in the pit of my stomach. We didn't get the chance to discuss it with him during the call, but I don't think it would have made a difference. James was going to do what he wanted to do, and he was not open to suggestion.

Richard was now as willing as I was to break James' rules and talk openly about what happens at Spiritual Warrior and why we thought the sweat lodge was dangerous. The phone call marked the end of our journey with James. It also freed us emotionally. Later that week, when I returned to writing my book, I realized now I could write about what happened during the events without worrying about James' reaction. I had been concerned that if I wrote about the activities he would not let us attend any more of his events. Now, by the time my book was done, we would also be finished with him and his events.

Later that day we received this email from James:

> Hey guys . . .
> I just wanted to quickly reiterate how much it means to me that you cared enough to follow up and make sure we were "okay." You two have grown immensely since I first met you and I know that you have even greater things to come. You'll be missed in Sedona but I look forward to seeing you at The Summit.
> Lots of Love—I appreciate you

What to make of this? Especially "I appreciate you"? Did he really think about what we said and decide he should have shown some appreciation for our volunteer work? Or, more to the point, did he simply not want to lose two more members—and their precious membership fees—in the WWS?

On October 3, while shopping at a craft show in Maui, Richard came towards me while talking on his cell phone. It was our friend Stephen Ray (again, no relation to James). Stephen was en route to

Sedona to attend Spiritual Warrior, and we had told him numerous times to call us before going, so he did.

Richard told Stephen not to go into the sweat lodge at all, but Steve was an honorable man and a martial artist. With all of James' talk that week about being an honorable warrior, I knew Stephen would join the rest of the group, as would be expected. We told him if he was entering the lodge, to do so early so he could sit in the outside ring, close to the flap door. "Don't sit directly across from the door because it is hotter there and you won't be getting any fresh air when they open the flap. Lay down early with your head facing outward." Richard went on. "You can put your fingers under the tent and lift it a bit to let in cool air if it gets too hot. Leave often to cool down and drink water. You can go back in at any time, or better yet stay out and go back in for the final round if you really want to. Even if James does not tell you in the beginning, you can always go back in.

"And lastly, don't volunteer for anything! If you do, what will happen to you will be mean and unnecessary. You don't want to be the leader of anything while you are there!"

Stephen then discussed the possibility James had learned his lesson from the previous year's problems and would back off this year. He must have thought we were acting like overprotective parents, but he didn't argue and just listened.

Stephen sounded happy and excited. Several things had not gone well for him in the last few years in his relationships and his business, and he was ready to start anew. This was the best he had sounded in a long time. I hoped being around some of our mutual friends would be good for him. Also the release work at Spiritual Warrior was excellent, so it was my wish he would be able to leave behind the recent heartbreaks. I hoped he would get a fresh start while avoiding having to be "dead" too long in the Samurai game and minimize his exposure to the sweat lodge as well. Later he told us something we said during the call saved his life, and the lives of several others, but until the trials were over, he couldn't tell us what it was.

On October 8, the day of the now infamous sweat lodge, Richard and I went for a long walk and then headed down to use the fitness facility and the steam rooms. I had enjoyed using the new women's spa almost every day we were in Maui. After setting the timer to 20 minutes, I entered the steam room and climbed up the steps to my favorite spot, and then I laid down. The steam came on as usual and I closed my eyes.

Something unusual happened. It seemed like the steam machine was stuck. Steam kept filling up the room well after its usual stopping point. After a couple of minutes, I sat up and wrapped my towel around me and made my way to the bottom level. I positioned myself in a straight line to the door and estimated how many steps it would take to reach it. The steam was getting so thick, soon I would not be able to make out the door, and I wanted to be able to find it fast if needed. A second before I was about to head for it, the steam stopped. I could only stay for a couple more minutes because it was much warmer than usual. Once outside, I sat down at a bench nearby and cooled off. I tried turning off the timer and then turning it back on to see if the steam stuck on again, and this time it seemed to be working fine. I decided not to go back in.

Driving home Richard mentioned the men's steam room had acted strangely, that it seemed like the steam was never going to stop. I told him the same thing happened to me. We wondered if both steam rooms shared the same equipment, but it did not make sense since they were on opposite sides of the building. We chalked it up to a strange occurrence that defied explanation.

Later that night, after returning from dinner, there was a message on Richard's cell phone from Edward. He listened and raced downstairs to find me. I was working on a couple of sets of real estate files when he told me there was trouble again at the sweat lodge, and it looked like a war zone afterwards. Without looking up I said, "So what else is new? So much for James learning his lesson and taking it easier this year."

"No, it's even worse than usual. They took people away in helicopters and ambulances afterwards."

My fingers froze on my laptop keyboard. "Where's Stephen?"

"Edward didn't say."

"Call him back!" Richard was already dialing.

That night we received conflicting reports from people who were in communication with those who were there. We were getting inconsistent information about where everyone was and the seriousness of their conditions. It was already early morning in Arizona when we went to bed in Hawaii. We hoped by the time we got up, we would know more. Just before going to sleep, I thought about the steam rooms in the fitness center. They both appeared to overheat at the same time our friends were inside James' sweat lodge!

Early the next morning, I jumped back on my computer to find an Arizona TV news channel's internet site. I read the flashing headline at least four times before it would sink in: "Two die in sweat lodge."

I called for Richard. We stared at the computer screen in shock. Finally Richard said, "What the hell did he do?"

Again I asked, "Where's Stephen?"

Edward was in phone contact with our mutual friend, Lois, later identified as the Dream Teamer at Spiritual Warrior who also just happened to be a nurse. She was dating Stephen at the time and was with him at the Flagstaff hospital, where he was on a ventilator. He was the first person taken out by helicopter. My friend Liz Neuman was also in very serious condition in the same hospital. Liz was the second person taken out by helicopter. Information came to us from people who were spread out in hospitals from Cottonwood to Flagstaff. Many were hurt and many more shaken and shocked by what had happened.

Over the next few days, I got messages with updates from many people. Emotions flew all over the place. One came from our friend Carol, who had Dream Teamed the event. In her message, she guessed we probably knew what had happened, but in case we didn't, give her a call.

Her voice sounded flat, which worried me, so I called her right back. She was still in Angel Valley and went on to describe a ceremony they'd just finished—burning the sweat lodge "to try to find some type of closure" to what had happened there. I asked her how she was holding up. She was really tired and ready for a nap. I encouraged her to get some rest and call me back whenever she wanted to talk. She said after she hung up, she was going to lie down and get some sleep. It was the middle of the day. Her body and spirit were depleted.

CHAPTER 18

The Tragedy

Spiritual Warrior · October 2009

The ultimate measure of a man is not where he stands in moments of comfort, but where he stands at times of challenge and controversy.
—Martin Luther King, Jr.

When I first heard many of the following accounts from the 2009 Spiritual Warrior event, I was hesitant to write about them. They were so extreme and horrible, I wished they were untrue, or at least gross exaggerations. I had to sadly accept what I heard when some police interview transcripts were made public and I saw the same accounts given by multiple witnesses.

From all accounts that fateful week in 2009 started off the same as the Spiritual Warrior event we attended in 2007. From the first day, participants stayed up most of the night journaling. They played the Samurai game, where they were to demonstrate living with honor and integrity while doing everything to perfection. Again people were ordered to fall to the ground "dead" by "God"—James.

From what I have heard and read, it appears James' description of the sweat and instructions to the attendees were remarkably similar to what he said in previous years. I again wondered if he was working from a script.

James had talked about his qualifications, "I was trained in sweat lodges by Native Americans and even Native Americans agree that my sweats are hotter than theirs." Many people remember him bragging about it and how he was, " . . . quite proud of my sweat lodge; it is the very best and most intense. Even the Natives say I have the best sweat lodge ever."

We found out later that a local woman who stopped by to help out at the lodge told the police, "He completely disrespected the ceremony. I do not think elders would have taught that. I was told by (a man), who was told by elders, that they have gone to James Ray and told him to stop, that he wasn't doing it right and was hurting people. In normal sweat lodge, you walk out refreshed and ready to eat a nice dinner, you don't walk out sick."

James must have given himself another promotion, because one witness told investigators James said he was a member "of four shamanic orders" and that he was an " . . . employee of Tony Robbins." We had always heard he was a shaman with two different groups, as well as a kahuna.

Why didn't attendees bolt from the lodge when their bodies were telling them they were not OK? Like the previous year, the participants said James covered that concern beforehand when he said, "You think you are going to die, but you won't die." That, "it would get very hot but you would be okay." And, " . . . you need to surrender to death to survive it. It is going to be hotter than hell and you have to remove your mind from your body to survive this."

James had further promised them, "It's going to feel like you're going to die. I assure you will not . . . if you pass out don't worry, we will get you out" and, "if you pass out you will be taken care of." James also told them, "you may feel like you're nauseated and need to throw up." This established a mindset that kept many of them in the lodge past the point where they were mentally or physically capable of making the decision to leave on their own.

James' obsession with death continued. Originally a metaphor, it loomed constantly on his mind in Peru and Sedona. During the event, a JRI employee admitted James had said, "It was a good day to die." I had heard him say it many times, but now it was becoming almost a theme with him.

It was well known that James liked to use his Twitter account often, even during events and excursions. During this event, he sent out "tweets" he later deleted. But they didn't disappear. A couple of Twitter-savvy people claimed to find them, and this is what they reposted on the Internet:

JamesARay: is still in Spiritual Warrior . . . for anything new to live something first must die. What
needs to die in you so that new life can emerge?

JamesARay: Day 5 of SW. The Spiritual Warrior has
conquered death and therefore has no enemies,
and no fear, in this life or the next.

I have often heard him say these things in person.

Many of the participants either knew about sweat lodges or had
spoken to others who had been in traditional Native American sweats;
they knew or were told about pleasant experiences. For people familiar with a "real" sweat lodge, they have asked me, "How could someone die in one?"

This was not a "real" sweat lodge. According to Amarya Hamil-
ton, one of the owners of Angel Valley, "Sweat lodges traditionally
consist of four rounds with four to six hot stones brought into the
lodge in each round, yielding a total of around 20 stones." In my
opinion, what made James' lodge turn deadly comes down to time
and temperature, and only one person controlled those two variables.

After being told by James that he was trained and qualified to run
a lodge, and after promising they would be OK even if they passed
out, an estimated 56 people filed into the sweat lodge behind him
around 2:30 p.m. The lodge ran for a total of 8 rounds and an estimated time of 2 to 3 hours—twice the norm! James alone decided
how long the lodge would last. Later, a witness told police that when
the paramedics asked her what happened, she told them that they
were in the lodge for about two hours. "How f***ing ridiculous," the
paramedic responded. I couldn't agree more!

A JRI employee confirmed that no thermometer was used to keep
track of the temperature inside the lodge. James controlled the temperature intensity by the number of super-heated "grandfather"
stones added to the pit in the center. These rocks were heated in a
very hot fire and brought in one at a time before the start of each
round. According to participants, James called for _12_ stones for
rounds one and two. When they were in place, a 5-gallon bucket of
water was dumped over them to create steam, and the flap over the
door was dropped. In round three, he brought in eight stones, then
six more for the 4th round. He added 8 more stones for each of the
remaining four rounds. Do the math: If those witnesses are correct,

then *70* super-heated rocks were brought in to heat the lodge—3 1/2 *times* the number for a traditional sweat.

The combination of extended time and extreme temperature made this sweat dangerous—fatal for three people. I will not exceed 20 minutes in either a sauna or steam room. I don't know any reasonable person who would suggest that you spend 2 to 3 hours in one! James' lodges were much hotter than any sauna I'd been in. According to one witness, the heat in the sweat lodge was 10 times hotter than any sauna she had ever been in!

How did James keep people in the lodge? According to the witnesses, when people initially tried to leave, James told them, "you're more than that," and "you can do this." He also said, "If your bodies are feeling pain, you're stronger than that; you can overcome this." One woman crawled toward the door, intending to leave. When she passed James, he said, "Beverly, you are stronger than that, stay." According to two witnesses, he also verbally prevented two people from leaving the sweat lodge and told them they had to wait for the sweat lodge door to be opened. James was sitting just inside the doorway. You had to walk, crawl, or be dragged right by him to get out.

At about the fourth round, a man lifted up the back of the tent and rolled out. Later, he told people he didn't even know he had done it. James yelled, "Put that tent down; that is sacrilegious!" Another person heard him say, "We don't do that." He made it clear to the group that the only acceptable way in and out was through the door next to which he sat—and he controlled when it was opened and closed.

During one of the middle rounds, the first unconscious person was carried out. She remained unconscious for about 20 minutes. It required at least two people to carry her, which must have been difficult since they could not stand up straight with the low ceiling in the lodge.

Outside the lodge, people who previously left tried to speak with or help those in distress. Staff members and volunteers stopped them. They were also told to not interfere with those who were unconscious since, "they are okay, they will come back, they are having their out of body experience." Inside, someone said, "I can't take it, I am hurting." James Ray told them to quiet down. "I'm the one talking now."

During a police interview, one man, Dennis, told of crawling out at the end of the 5th round. According to the detective's narrative, "Dennis said he tried to crawl out but must have passed out, does not remember how he got out of the lodge. When Dennis came to he was outside and the Dream Team members were pouring water on him. He was really dizzy and could not get up. He thought he was down about 10 minutes and then started throwing up severely. Dennis thought he would then feel better, but he did not. Then he started having trouble breathing and thought he was having a heart attack. Dennis said he was trying to breathe but could not and thought his heart had stopped. Dennis said he was screaming, he did not want to die."

According to others, while this was happening, James was telling him from inside the lodge to "quiet down." Dennis kept yelling, "I'm dead, I'm dead," and James kept yelling out, "No, you're not dead." A JRI employee heard Dennis say he was having a heart attack. Another person described him as having "a seizure and flailing on the ground, screaming he was dying." James continued on with his lodge "experience" and no one called 911.

Other serious injuries developed in the lodge right in front of James. According to a witness, during round 5 or 6 a man, "became disorientated and started crawling out but crawled right into the fire pit." He "fell onto the heated stones in the sweat lodge and suffered severe burns to his hands and arms." Outside the lodge, another woman described seeing, "big chunks of flesh coming off his hands and arms." She said the man started to shake uncontrollably. After the lodge was over, another woman heard James say to the man, "Wow, you will have a good reminder of this."

Also during round 6, a man crawled back inside. According to the detectives, he told them, "there was a woman lying passed out where he needed to crawl so he squatted down where he was. James was telling someone to move the woman back, but the person said he couldn't because she was lying on his leg. He said he moved toward her to help move her and James told him not to. James Ray said, 'Well, we need to continue on.'"

James knew someone was passed out inside the lodge, yet he continued on with the next round without waiting for her to be carried out. So much for his promise! Apparently, the woman was not removed until the end of the sweat. According to this same man, once it finally ended, he knew he needed to get out of there or they all were going to die. Initially no one was really moving and he went over to the woman and was tugging on her to get her out.

James did not share these discomforts. As previously mentioned he always sat right by the door, receiving the full benefit of the cooler air when the flap was opened. As he had done in 2007, when I attended Spiritual Warrior, he would hang outside the open door and try to talk people back inside the lodge which cooled him off even more. In 2007, he also used towels soaked in cold water to wipe off his face, arms and chest. In 2009, Stephen, who was sitting close by him, said that he was splashing cold water on himself and staff members immediately to his right. The water bucket was not passed to the other people inside the lodge.

Even James' positioning himself by the door conflicts with many traditional sweats. I have been told that the person who runs a traditional sweat lodge often sits directly opposite the door, in the hottest position, the area with the least airflow. That way, they have more accurate knowledge of the temperature and can better manage the participants' safety. Unlike James, they don't have to sit by the door to prevent people from leaving. The police wrote one attendee's description as follows: "She said it was a lot hotter in the back than in the front. She knows because when she went around trying to get the people out who were in the back it was much hotter."

Signs that things were going horribly wrong were all around him, but James continued. One woman told police, "Kirby was breathing in a snoring fashion for four rounds. (This woman) kept telling them she was not breathing right and could see she was slumped over, but did not know if she was unconscious."

During the last few rounds, more people were carried out unconscious, while still others were left inside even though they were in very bad condition. One woman reported that James Shore pulled Sidney Spencer out of the sweat lodge at the end of round 6 and she believed that Sidney "was unconscious when [he] dragged her out."

And these witness statements: "Sidney had no voluntary movement. After Sidney was taken out, James [Shore] came back in and took that spot so now it is James [Shore] and Kirby to her left." And, "she heard his (James Shore's) cry for help before round 8 started . . . She said Shore came back to her position and shortly after he came back she heard him say, 'We need help over here to get her out.' She said there was no response . . . she could hear Brown gurgling and based on the direction of the gurgling and the direction of Shore's cry for help, she assumed that Shore was talking about Brown."

What was James Ray saying while all of this was transpiring in front of him? Two witnesses told investigators, "He (James Shore) asked that Kirby needed to come out. [The witness] said at that point James [Ray] said nobody else can leave at this time." And, "They closed the flap starting the 7th round. It was then someone said, 'she's not breathing; I can't get her to move.' James Ray said, 'Doors down; we will deal with it later.'"

That was at the start of the 7th round. During the break between rounds 7 and 8, Kirby Brown was still not removed from the lodge even though James Shore had asked for her to be taken out.

After the 8th round, James Ray walked out first and held up his arms in the air as he got hosed off. He was followed by his Operations Manager, then his personal assistant. Meanwhile, chaos reigned inside the lodge as people struggled to get out. Several never made it out on their own. Detectives noted one man's description of James' attitude after he exited the lodge: "When he left the lodge at the end of the eighth round, (another survivor), the two women, James [Shore] and Kirby were all inside. [The witness] said he crawled out on the tarp and he looked up at James Ray and his staff who were there standing up. He said he yelled at them, 'Hey somebody needs to get in there and help these f***ing people because they're in trouble.' (He) said in response to (his) request James Ray looked at one of his female staffers and said, 'They'll be okay.'"

All around James, people were lying on the ground, in serious trouble. When it was over and the people had made their way out of the lodge, Sydney was still unconscious. A witness said, "Sydney's eyes were rolled back in her head and she had drainage coming from her mouth and nose and was barely breathing."

Another witness described a woman who "had a blank stare on her face and began saying, 'Why did James Ray do this? Why did James Ray do this? Why did I look to James Ray? Why, why, why?' She was saying this over and over again. She said this woman did not appear to be fully conscious. She was shaking in fits . . . [She] started to convulse and had foam coming out of her mouth . . . [Her] body was contorting."

And another witness said, a "woman was rolled over and was foaming at the mouth and having an apparent seizure."

People were so disorientated that one woman came "out of the tent and she was staggering around and walking toward the fire." Luckily someone reached her in time or there would have been a second burn victim.

A witness describes that after she got outside, she "continued to look around and saw a woman lying on the ground and her arm was starting to turn blue and it did not look like she had circulation or was breathing."

Our friend Stephen Ray told someone later he got sick once he got outside and passed out. He may have been confused and disorientated because another person said he "was dragged out the front of the lodge at the conclusion of the ceremony; he was unconscious and his eyes were fluttering, as if he was having a seizure. He was the first flown out and Liz was the second one flown [out]." While Stephen was lying on the ground outside the lodge, another person described him as, "barely breathing and had drainage coming from his mouth and nose . . . she looked into his eyes and all the blood vessels were burst."

Later, Stephen told us he remembered feeling like he was experiencing a form of torture called water boarding. He felt suffocated and then things went black.

One person noted "many people continued to get worse even once they were outside." Why would that happen? Perhaps the reason was they would hose people off with very cold water right after they came out of the lodge. In 2007, I was handed a hose and asked to help rinse people off. I had to keep alternating the hand in which I was holding the hose, because the cold water numbed my hand. After a minute or two, I put down the hose and refused to continue. My basic first aid had taught me the importance of using room temperature water on heat stroke victims, because their blood vessels were extremely dilated due to the body trying to cool down. Hitting them with cold water could put someone into shock.

That could be what happened in 2009. Note some of the police interview descriptions of what happened after participants exited the lodge: " . . . After they hosed her down, and then she went into shock and started shaking." "[She] told me she felt fine until she came out of the sweat lodge, and she was in shock for a long time." "[She] hosed him off and he went into shock and was convulsing." And remember the man who thought that he was having a heart attack? "When Dennis came to he was outside and the dream team members were pouring water on him . . . Then he started having trouble breathing and thought he was having a heart attack." Rinsing severely overheated people off with very cold water might have exasperated the participant's conditions.

Why was 911 not called much sooner? One woman said, "That

around the 5th round so many people were being drug out unconscious with only two dream team members and two hoses they were
having trouble cooling everyone." A man added that, when he went
back into the lodge at the beginning of the 6th round, there were
"many indications that things were not going well." Dennis told investigators that he felt it took them too long to get emergency help on
the scene. Dennis said a lot of people were sick well before Kirby and
James [Shore] were found to be not breathing. Dennis described that
everywhere he looked people were crawling and throwing up. Dennis
wants to know why they did not call medical sooner when he went
out having trouble breathing in the 5th or 6th round.

Melinda Martin was the James Ray International Event Coordinator for Spiritual Warrior. She told a news reporter that her fellow
staffers forbade her to call 911 when things first started to spiral out
of control in Sedona. Why would they do that? Because their boss,
James Ray, had gotten angry in 2005 when 911 was called for an
attendee who suffered heat stroke. He knew that ambulances showing up at his event resulted in bad PR.

James Ray was standing outside the lodge, still seemingly unflus-
tered by what was happening, when according to an employee of
Angel Valley another Angel Valley staff person " . . . looked inside the
lodge and said there are three people still in here; can I open the
back of the lodge? James said, 'That would be sacrilegious . . . but if
you have to, go ahead.' [She] was already ripping open the back of
the lodge."

In witness interviews, person after person said they never saw
James Ray help anyone. In her TV interview, Melinda Martin noted
that he "made absolutely no effort to help any of the victims."
Another JRI employee said, "James Ray did not seem to respond at all
once it was realized there was a problem." She said she felt that he
should have gotten onto his knees and started talking with the people trying to help them back to consciousness." Another woman said
that, "at one point when this woman was yelling out James Ray's name
he just looked over and then looked away." Dennis told detectives,
"Even afterward James Ray just sat on a chair." All he told Dennis was,
"Oh, you were reborn, go take a shower and go to dinner."

This while CPR was being performed on two people!

Later I found two reports where someone said James did take
some action. "James Ray was just standing around and looking at people. He said it looked like James Ray was not concerned . . . He said

it seemed like they delayed calling 911 to avoid an incident . . . He
said he never saw James Ray help any of the people in distress except
he saw James talk to a specific woman who had been asking for him.
He said James got down on his knees because the woman was on her
back. Another woman said that he did ask, 'What can we do, what
else can we be doing?'"

There were marked differences in what some people experienced
and what others remembered. People who were close to the door and
kept their eyes closed or laid face down in the dirt for most of the
time would have a very different experience from those who were sitting up and watching what was going on, or who were in the hotter
part of the lodge, or who spent some time outside the lodge and saw
the distress that people were in as they came out. Even under the
same conditions people experience the same event differently, but
that does not make it any less true.

At some point, while the police were on-site, James and Megan,
his Director of Operations, disappeared. One of the owners took a
detective to find him and bring him back to the crime scene. This
was what the detective wrote in his report:

(Lieutenant) later arrived on scene. He asked me to locate
James Ray and bring him down to the sweat lodge area. (A
deputy) told me Mr. Ray was the one in charge of the group
and he needed to answer some questions. The owner of
the retreat grounds took me to where Mr. Ray was located.
He was in his room, which was located near the mess hall.
Mr. Ray was in the middle of eating and I told him he
needed to come to the site and answer some questions.

He asked me "right now?" I told him yes, now. He asked if
"Joshua" was down at the site and if he could answer any
questions we might have. He was referring to Joshua
Fredrickson.

I told him we needed him and asked him again to come
down to the site. He put on some pants and followed me
part way to the golf cart.

He asked if he was going to be answering questions for a
while and I told him he probably was. He then went back
to his room and got his jacket. He then went with me to

the site where he was contacted by (the lieutenant). During the rest of the call I either stood guard at the crime scene tape or detained Mr. Ray. We did not speak to each other during this time.

I don't know about you, but if helicopters had carried off the four most seriously injured while ambulances loaded up numerous others, the last thing on my mind would be dinner. What arrogance to ask the detective if he had to go "right now" and disrupt his meal! And to attempt to have an employee handle the police and their questions for him; utterly shocking!

It is shocking that James would leave the scene and force the police to look for him, especially since there were still people who needed counseling and support. But James is accustomed to walking off and leaving others to clean up his messes. He did it before at Spiritual Warrior 2005. His employee, Josh Frederickson, described the 2005 incident as follows:

> Josh: As soon as he got out of the lodge I believe . . . he just went back to his room and showered up . . . when the ambulance was called they went and got him from his room.
>
> DETECTIVE: so after this sweat happen and he just takes off and people need help then?
>
> Josh: Yeah.
>
> DETECTIVE . . . someone had to exit that sweat that day. They were having difficulties . . . did he check on that person to see how they were after the sweat?
>
> Josh: Not immediately after, no . . . So he's the first one to exit and so he got hosed off and then he just gathered his stuff and went.

After the 2009 sweat lodge, where did Megan, his chief of operations, disappear? What was she doing? James sent her to use the land-line phone in Angel Valley's gift shop to call his PR people and his attorneys! She stayed in the gift shop until 2 or 3 in the morning. Once Josh and James were released, they joined her there as well. A detective had personally told Josh before he was released that James Shore and Kirby Brown were dead.

After reaching the gift shop, James decided to send an email to JRI employees. Megan said in her immunity interview that James told them what to put in the email. According to the detectives, they were told that it read something like: some people took ill, but it was a great week and people had a great time.

Did he think he was going to sweep this under the rug like Colleen Conaway's suicide during the Creating Absolute Wealth seminar just a couple of months earlier? I was once again shocked. I realized the ease with which James could lie. He did not stay around to help with the investigation or to visit any of the people who were still in the hospital. He didn't even meet with the people who were still in Angel Valley and were up all night grieving deeply. Instead, he flew back to California. The news would read: "Police in Sedona, Arizona, say 51-year-old Ray refused to answer questions and flew back to California in the wake of last week's tragedy."

The spin was starting. James made his claim the sweat lodge tragedy was just an accident, and they had taken every precaution possible to prevent it. He claimed they hired a nurse to provide medical aid if necessary. I know Lois, the nurse who was at Spiritual Warrior '09, and she told me she was there as a member of the Dream Team to help out, and also as a James Ray coach. It just so happened that she was a nurse, just as one of the participants happened to be a doctor. According to former JRI employee Melinda Martin, "There was nobody contracted or assigned specifically to handle medical issues at the sweat lodge."

On October 15th, James arranged a "secret" conference call between him and the survivors. During this call, he encouraged the group not to talk to outsiders but instead to talk only to "harmonic minded individuals." One of the participants voiced her concern to police. According to the detective's report, "She is very frustrated because after the conference call all the other participants are not talking, or saying they do not remember. Beverly said during the conference call they were directed to only talk to people within the organization." One journalist who was able to get a hold of a transcript of the call said "it would appear that he is psychologically tampering with witnesses." During the call, the journalist said James and his staff repeatedly kept using the phrase "those who have fallen ill" in reference to the victims. The journalist added, "apparently he is choosing to portray this as some sort of disease or sickness, as opposed to the reality—they are suffering from overexposure to dangerous levels of heat that is a direct consequence of James Ray's actions in the sweat lodge."

Another survivor picked up on something I noticed as well. She told the police, "James Ray is saying how important it is to continue 'our mission' . . . prior to this, Ray made it very clear that this was *his* mission to spread his information." Suddenly, *his* mission became *our* mission, to try to promote the feeling that it was *us* against the world. I did not buy into it; apparently, neither did this survivor.

There was one other thing about this conference call. James instructed a Dream Team member to relay what someone else had channeled at Angel Valley shortly after the incident: " . . . of the two that had passed and they left their bodies during the ceremony and had so much fun they chose not to come back and that was their choice that they made." The volunteer has received a lot of criticism for saying this. In fairness to her, it is likely she had just experienced one of the most horrific days of her life and was dealing with her own shock and grief. The Dream Team members were victims of this tragedy, as well as the participants. I completely understand why people in general, and especially the family members of those who died, would be upset when they heard this, but consider who told her to relay the story in the first place, and his motives for doing so. After she finished on the call, James said, "Hopefully, all of you appreciate hearing that as well as I did reading it and hearing it again."

I think James Ray used her in his attempt to distance himself from his responsibility for the deaths. In his mind, how can it be his fault if the people who died "chose not to come back, and that was their choice that they made?" In my mind, he was using one of his victims to divert the group's attention away from what really happened.

CHAPTER 19

Did You Hear The Big Bang?

The End of 2009

Three things cannot be long hidden:
the sun, the moon, and the truth.

—Buddha

Richard and I tried to console and support our friends while working through our own feelings. Even though I was opposed to James' version of a sweat lodge, I never imagined he would act so callously, and that so many people would be hurt and killed as a result.

The first few days were filled with shock and profound sadness. As I started to receive phone messages and calls from the survivors, I heard the same emotions in their voices. Our community members, both the ones who had been there and those who had not, started to work their way through their stages of grief. Our first reaction of denial and shock was giving way to anger. This was happening at different speeds for different people and I could already see the seeds of future disagreement among the group start to take root. Some are still in denial even after many months have passed.

We received regular reports on Stephen's improvement from Edward. He was still in contact with our mutual friend Lois, the nurse, who was with him at the hospital. Stephen and Liz were in the same hospital so Lois was doing her best to check in on both of them. While Stephen was improving, Liz was not. She was in a coma. From my limited medical knowledge, I knew her condition was grave. I kept expecting to hear that James, or at the very least one of his top staff members, had arrived at the hospital to stay with Stephen and Liz until they were released, and that he was offering financial support for medical expenses incurred by those injured. That never happened, which only added to our community's state of shock.

The way James continued reacting to this disaster of his own creation, and the way he treated the victims and their families, sent many of us through repeated cycles of shock and anger. According to Kirby Brown's mother, Ginny Brown, in a *Larry King Live* broadcast, James called her five days after the tragedy to express his condolences. "He asked me, 'What can I do?' and I said, 'You can cooperate with the authorities.' He said, 'Oh I have'." Kirby's mother knew that wasn't true because she had been in close contact with the Yavapai County Sheriff's Department and according to them, Ray had still not given authorities a statement *two weeks* after the tragedy. In the *Larry King Live* interview, Mrs. Brown added, "Ray said he made a donation to the Surfrider Foundation in Kirby's memory, but to date, there's no record of any donation being made by James Ray for Kirby Brown.'" And, "We received a sympathy card, and in that sympathy card was a note that said 'please accept this financial assistance,' and on the check he wrote 'in honor of Kirby Brown' (along with) the amount on the check: $5,000."

"It's laughable," Mrs. Brown told King. "My daughter paid twice that to go to his event. We had to bring her body east, we had to bury her." For Kirby's mother, this may have been the point where James' dishonesty began, but James had been lying to all of us for a very long time.

Other family members reacted publicly about how poorly they and their loved one were being treated. In the reader's response section after a ABC *Good Morning America* report, "*Former Employee: Ray did not help people dying in sweat lodge—12/8/09*" was aired and posted on their website, this reader's response was posted below the story:

"Alex: My Mother, Liz Newman, was a 'friend' of James Ray for 7 years, yet she was admitted to the hospital as a Jane Doe and my family wasn't notified. We had to find out through the media 24 hours after it happened. James did not call or visit once while she was in critical condition for over a week before she died. He refused to cooperate with the authorities and immediately abandoned the state and all his people when they needed him most. James Ray said he was canceling his seminars to help with the investigation and the families, but multiple sources state that the convention centers were canceling on him. He has not helped my family at all! Is this really the kind of leader you want to follow? "

Things were not going much better for the seriously injured. Stephen told police investigators:

> "You know, I'm getting threatening letters from all the, you know from the hospital . . . one of the last things that I have left is my credit and now that's in jeopardy."
> "So James Ray didn't take care of those medical bills?" the detective asked.
> "No." was Stephen's response.

The last time I spoke with Stephen in July 2010, he still had not received any financial assistance from James or JRI.

Some of the people who continue to defend James' behavior use the excuse that he was in shock and that is why he subsequently reacted so poorly or not at all. Was he still in shock the next day, the next week, or the next month? Is he still in shock and unwilling to offer reasonable assistance over 6 months later to the victims and their families?

The survivors must continue to deal with ongoing health challenges. Some are more obvious than others. The issue of brain damage, or traumatic brain injury, is so difficult to quantify because not everyone shows the extreme symptoms we saw with the groom's father at the wedding, yet their bodies are still affected. One man told detectives in a police report, "[He] mentioned that since the sweat lodge he has had some speech and hearing problems. [He] said his speech and mental clarity is still not back to normal."

Then there is our friend, Stephen. He told detectives:

> "Yeah, I still don't have any taste or smell. I have trouble, I'm a college graduate and I used to pride myself on a very rich vocabulary and I find myself uhm like searching for words. I can't, you know when I'm trying to speak I, I get kind of you know try to search for words. I can't find words and just things that I normally would remember . . . Beyond that I still have ringing in my ears, traumatic headaches, trouble sleeping."
> "Okay, it sounds kind of similar to what, there was a guy in

2005 that had some problems and he still has those same problems," the detective said.

From this detective's response, we know the victim of James' 2005
lodge still has medical complications. In a June 2010 phone call,
Stephen told us he still had all of those health issues. Another victim
of James' lodge, Sidney Spencer, has according to a news report:
"multiple organ failures, neurological issues, and difficulty speaking."

At one point James and his legal team suggested that the reason
for this tragedy was due to the design and makeup of the lodge—not
his doing, he claimed. Over time, we learned that, according to one
of the owners of Angel Valley, they had contracted with a local Native
American man to build the most recent lodge in 2008. Two different
Native American men used this same lodge for multiple ceremonies—with no problems. The most recent lodge had been built in
2008 to Ray's specifications of holding up to 75 people, and it had
been used four times by other groups. A detective interviewed a JRI
contractor who was in the lodge. The detective noted, "I asked if
James Ray looks at it [the lodge] before people go in and if he
approves it to make sure it does what it is supposed to do."

"Yes, Ray met with them," the contractor said.

This information confirmed what many of us already knew: the
real issue was not the lodge itself, but how extremely long and hot
James made the "experience." Given his nature as a control freak,
we were not surprised to find out he was directly involved in the
design. A larger capacity would mean he could have more people at
the event, and that would mean more money for him. I am in no
way saying the lodge was ideal in its construction or materials. What
I am saying is that lodge construction is likely not the main cause of
the injuries and deaths. Plenty of people took sweats in that lodge
prior to Spiritual Warrior 2009, and there were no reports of problems.

Not everyone inside of JRI was excusing the organization's behavior or that of its leader. In addition to Melinda Martin, another
employee, Amy Hall, quit after getting an inside look at how JRI was
reacting to the tragedy. Amy resigned at about 5:00 p.m. on October
13th. She called the Yavapai County Sheriff an hour later, because she
was concerned that JRI employees may destroy evidence in the case.
Her resignation letter began:

It is with a heavy heart and mind that I must resign my job effective today . . . But for my values it is intolerable for me to work here any longer . . . As you, [another JRI employee] and I spoke when we met Monday I voiced my concerns over the lack of compassion that JRI has shown publicly for the victims. And thank you so much for sharing James' upset with me. But for us, as a transformational company, to take the stand that everything is business as usual is appalling and intolerable . . . For us to have Spiritual Warrior on the top of our list of events that we are selling at World Wealth Summit hurts me to the core. We are selling Spiritual Warrior just like nothing happened! . . . It seems to me like money is the driving force here and that is intolerable to me . . . And for a transformational company to hide behind the 'legal' way to handle a situation like this instead of being supportive and compassionate does not speak well about the company or their values . . . I can't fulfill my accountabilities of answering the phone and help desk tickets or managing the venues for the Introductory events for a company that has such a blatant disregard for their responsibilities to their clients and their staff.

The lack of compassion is the heart of the problem with James. She saw it from within his company and we saw it from the outside. We saw over several years the progressive disappearance of sincere compassion from James. His male energy went unchecked and allowed him to put the love of money over the love of people. The female, emotional energy of love and compassion was in short supply within him. I believe that is why he pushed people so hard and how, in his mind, his behavior was acceptable. I am not sure that even now he gets it. There is such a thing as tough love, but James had become tough, without the love.

Before Spiritual Warrior 2009, we were getting ready for the World Wealth Summit in San Diego, which we'd told James we would attend. Now we wondered if it would happen at all. This is the only JRI event that can run without James, since it consisted mainly of four great guest speakers, and anyone on the JRI staff could introduce them. Since most people had long since made their plane and hotel reservations, the consensus was that most of us would still attend since we needed to be with each other more than ever.

The night before the event we hosted our usual reception at our home for friends and their guests who were attending the Summit. Just a few days before our reception, I got another call from Carol. This time, she was concerned people were going to "talk bad" about James, and if I was going to let that happen, then she did not want to come. I told her everyone is entitled to work through his or her feelings, and some people will likely not have great things to say about him, but the reception was not intended to be a James bash. I told her I didn't plan on bringing him up because everyone needs space from him and Sedona to be together, grieve, and reconnect. She tentatively agreed to come. She would have to get used to hearing people criticize him, because James was certainly still providing enough material worthy of severe criticism.

The day of our reception, Mark, the man who joined us in standing up to James in Peru, came over early to spend the day. He and his wife had hiked with James in Sedona and attended Spiritual Warrior 2009. He wanted time to talk with us without any "sheeple" around. It was great to see him again even though I could tell he had been greatly affected by his recent experience. He was taking James' advice about being around "like minded people," and Mark thought Richard and I would be more "like minded" than many of the other members. We did not use much time to talk about James and Sedona. The three of us appreciated the time to be with people who were not trying to convince us we had to forgive and not judge, or tell us to forget what happened and focus on how great James' teaching were. We were able to spend time with someone else rationally working to come to grips with a terrible situation.

That night, the people who wanted to vent did so in smaller groups. Those who wanted to talk about the great things James' teaching had done for them or others did so as well. From what I could tell, the bulk of the people there were relieved just to see each other again. At one point, I checked in with Carol to see how she was doing. She kept insisting, as she had done in our phone call, that the people at Spiritual Warrior had amazing breakthroughs. All I said to her was that if the patient dies, you couldn't call the surgery a success. I saw a rift growing between us which saddened me. If she ever changed her mind, then I would be there for her, but if I had to agree with the premise that James was the real victim of a terrible accident, then we were going to part ways.

On October 16th the Summit began. WWS members were told to be there early to "set the space" in the room with James before the rest of the attendees were admitted. Personally, I had very little interest in setting space or anything else with James.

Our daughter Erica was with us, and I didn't want to drag her out of bed early just to leave her standing in the lobby while we huddled up with James to make him feel better. We arrived later than we were supposed to; they would have to get over it. We entered the meeting room and were surprised to see WWS members standing off to one side with a JRI staff person. No sign of James. The staffer said when the attendees arrived, we were to be their "hosts" since this was a WWS event. We needed to stand on each side of the door, clapping and greeting them as they came into the room. The "meeting" was concluded.

We went outside to pick up our registration packets and name badges. I asked the WWS staffer if James was here. "Yes," she said. Having no idea what to expect from the next two days, the three of us ate breakfast in the hotel restaurant. We still had a couple of hours before the event.

When we returned to the meeting room, I saw James standing in one of the main aisles. The WWS members who had gone in ahead of us queued up to speak with him and give him a hug. Without even saying anything to each other, Richard and I walked to the next aisle and made our way to our seats in the front of the room. We watched as one at a time the members approached him, said a few words and hugged. I thought about it, and decided I needed to show some compassion for James, even if for no other reason than he was a human being in a heap of trouble. Frankly, I hoped he would make an announcement during the event that he was sorry for what happened, for the way he acted since the tragedy, and that he was making financial restitution to all of the victims. I thought we needed to give him the space to do that.

Richard was not so inclined. After what happened in Peru, the private call afterwards, Sedona, and James' behavior since, my usually patient husband had given James every benefit of the doubt he was willing to give. He came to hear the great guest speakers, since he had already paid to do so. That was that. I grabbed Richard's arm and dragged him to the back of the line of people waiting to talk to James. When it was my turn, I gave James a hug and the advice I give to anyone in a really difficult position: "Just take one day at a time."

He had tears in his eyes, but I had seen him cry on cue before. He could be crying because he majorly screwed up his company and his money flow. When I hugged him, I felt no emotional energy coming from him. I usually have to work to keep myself from being overwhelmed by people's emotions, especially when they are under extreme duress, but this time, I felt absolutely nothing.

When we returned to our seats and James went backstage, I noticed more security guards inside the room than usual. They made a big deal about having our name badges showing at all times while we were in the meeting room. James' personal assistant sat to the left of the stage, as usual, but was joined this time by his executive assistant. A previous event planner had returned. It seemed there were more staffers present than usual for his events. I remember thinking "all hands were on deck" for this performance.

The volume of the music rose quickly, and we were given the signal to go to the back door to "welcome" the attendees. Even members who were in that sweat lodge, or outside it as volunteers, were encouraged to form a line on each side of the door to clap and cheer wildly as people came in. This struck me as so wrong. Just a week ago, some of them were doing CPR on dead people and others witnessed the lodge and its aftermath. A couple did jump around and clap enthusiastically, but many of them had a dazed and confused look on their faces.

When the signal was given, I rose and took a few steps towards the back of the room with the others, but then I pulled up. I was done being used by James. This may have been orchestrated to appear to participants or infiltrating press as a gesture of our support for him. I wanted no part of it. I walked back to my seat, where Richard was standing. Needless to say, he never budged.

To our great disappointment, James did not make an apology or promise financial support for the victims. He made a short comment about how he was in a very difficult time personally, and he chose to have the event out of consideration to everyone who already purchased their plane tickets. We had a private WWS reception with him and some of the guest speakers, but again he did not bring up the "elephant" in the middle of the room.

At the start of day two James pointed out the two long sheets of light-colored fabric hanging from the ceiling and reaching down to the floor at the far right of the stage. White lights shone on them, with green plants around their base. It was a memorial to Kirby Brown and James Shore. It was beautifully and tastefully done. He led us in a group meditation where we sent love and support to their families since, according to James; their funerals were going to be held that day.

The loud music returned with the Black Eyed Peas song, *I Got a Feeling*. In the song are the repeating lyrics, "that tonight's gonna be a good night." James stood up and started clapping and dancing on the stage, yelling at us to do the same. He was telling us to shake loose the sadness. I get that everyone handles grief differently, and I tried to go along with it in support of the other people around me, but this felt really wrong too.

I wished I was not in the front row, so I could be still with my thoughts for all of the families affected by James' actions. Reminders of the previous week were easy to see. I stood next to the first woman carried out unconscious. All around me were people who had just endured one of the most horrific experiences of their lives. We were all worried about our friends who were still seriously ill. This just did not feel right.

James was trying to raise the energy level in the room. I was not ready to move on so fast; neither were many of the other people in the room. The song was totally inappropriate, even though it was one of my favorites. It was the first song on my MP3 player, and the one I would use to get myself going when I started my aerobic workout. To this day, I cannot listen to it without feeling ill. When I can, I will know at least part of me has healed.

Not everyone was having trouble getting into the mood to jump around and dance. As soon as the music started, Carol, who was sitting front row center, jumped up and started to dance around the room while encouraging others to join her. I heard several people behind me exclaim phrases similar to, "Good God, Carol!"

During the two days of the event, James continued to promote the WWS and encouraged attendees who were not members to sign up for it. They replayed an old slide show of photos taken of us at WWS activities, set to the Queen song *We Believe*. When it came to the part where they sang about a hero who is "a man or woman who knows how to say they're sorry," they showed a photo of James. How ridiculously ironic!

James made the big announcement about the 2010 WWS excursion to India. There was a general lack of enthusiasm, just polite applause. I doubted he would be able to leave the country or that there would even be a WWS in 2010, never mind a trip to India. Was he that delusional to think that this trip was going to happen?

Apparently, many in the audience shared my concerns. As soon as he announced the destination, he looked right at Richard and me and said, "India! Isn't that great?" Richard nodded his head and said something about how India is great, but I seized the opportunity to root through my purse to look for another pen. At the break, people came up to us and asked about the WWS because they were thinking of joining. That amazed us, given events of the past week. We both told people to hold off and wait and see what happens first. Personally, I wouldn't even buy a CD from JRI and trust they would mail it to me, let alone give them $60,000!

During the final afternoon, Josh Frederickson hurriedly handed James a note while he was speaking on stage. Occasionally, a schedule-related message was given to him from the event coordinator, but this was not something Josh would normally do. I was sitting in the front row, just a few feet in front of James, and I carefully watched his face for any sign of emotion as he read the note. I saw none at all. Richard saw the same lack of expression, as did Edward, who was sitting directly behind us. James continued his talk. He took a break a few minutes later, and we all speculated that the police might have been waiting for him backstage. I doubt anyone would have placed a bet that James was going to return onstage after the break. But he did, and the event ended without any further interruption.

While we said our goodbyes to our friends, it occurred to me that this was likely the last time we would see many of them. Even with promises made to stay in touch, we knew it wasn't likely to happen. I heard one woman comment that a lot of the negative press coming from the Yavapai County Sheriff's department was because someone was running for reelection and was using James as a scapegoat to get more publicity.

I reminded the group that families had lost loved ones and they wanted and deserved answers. "If it had been your child that died in that lodge, then you would be on the phone every day to the district attorney wanting to know what they were doing about it, right?" The remark went over like a lead balloon. I didn't care. I was way out of the denial and shock phase. I was angry.

Just as we were getting ready to leave, Mark ran hurriedly down the hall. He had been looking for us; he'd just heard on TV in his hotel room that Liz had died. We stood there in sad silence. I knew she was not likely to get better, but still the news stung.

We looked for one of Liz's close friends who I had just said goodbye to a minute earlier. I wanted to tell her before she saw it on one of the big TV screens in the public areas in the hotel. I found her with a small group of people, some of who had been at Spiritual Warrior that year. When I tried to tell her, I stuttered and stopped. I was still having trouble absorbing the news. Aware of that moment in time just before something happens or is said, where there is no going back to the way you thought or felt before . . . I didn't want to be the one to tell her.

Richard understood my dilemma. He told me to tell her because she was going to find out anyway. I just couldn't get the words out. Richard finally told her. The shock was apparent even though she found out that morning they were going to remove Liz from life support. We speculated that the note Josh handed James may have contained the news of Liz's death. I flashed back to the absence of expression on his face when he read the note. Could he really have remained that devoid of emotion upon learning a loyal student who had been with him for over seven years was dead because of him?

News of Liz's death started another grief cycle before the previous two could take root. I felt like I could not get my emotional feet back under me before they were pulled out again. During the ride home from the event, we were mostly silent. Richard, Erica and I usually discuss what we learned from the speakers. I felt like I was going to throw up.

Two days later, I rushed to a local hotel for a real estate class that met every Monday. Since the events in Sedona I maintained my workload for our present clients and their current transactions, but had trouble reengaging with much of anything else. If I had not been part of a team in the class I would have skipped this week's session, because my head and heart were definitely not in it.

New rumors and speculation were running rampant that Colleen Conaway might have been the woman who committed suicide during the last Creating Absolute Wealth event. This was fueled by the rumors an email went out to all JRI employees from the JRI people in Sedona, saying something to the effect that Spiritual Warrior was great; that they had a good time and that some people fell ill. If an email like that went out, it was a monstrous lie. If they lied about that, would they lie about Colleen?

Then it hit me: I was standing in the same hotel where Creating Absolute Wealth is held!

Our regular meeting room for the class was part of the giant ball-room used for the seminar and the black tie dinner dance at the end of the event on day three. The room downstairs is where we sang the silly songs and had dinner after returning from the homeless exercise at the end of day two.

My mind started racing. Did I last see Liz alive here in this hotel? I couldn't remember. All the events and times we may have attended or Dream Teamed started running together. Then it also struck me: I was standing in the exact hall where Colleen stood before she boarded the bus to Horton Plaza for the homeless exercise! What if Colleen did die? If so, then this was one of the last places she had been.

When the hell was the last time I saw Liz? How can I not remember?

I hit a wall. I had been trying to support and comfort so many other people the last week and a half I had nothing left to give, even to myself. I felt lost. I felt confused; none of this made sense. The people who were dead were really gone, and so too was my extended family I was so happy to see when we crashed the black tie dinner party just a few months ago . . . in this very spot.

A passing hotel employee told me we were not meeting in our usual room, the class had been moved downstairs. When I entered the room, the round tables were set up just like at Creating Absolute Wealth for the dinner after the homeless exercise.

I was late; the class had started. As soon as I sat down an email pinged on my phone. The subject line said, "Confirmed, Colleen committed suicide at CAW!" I felt like someone just punched me in the stomach, hard.

Had Colleen survived the homeless exercise, she would have ended up in this very room laughing at the songs while having dinner. I didn't want to be in this room or hotel any longer! Of all of the hotels in San Diego, why was I in this one at exactly this moment? How could this be just a "coincidence?"

What I had been learning about James was draining me physically and mentally. We were fighting to reengage in our lives.

I wasn't the only one hitting a wall. Sedona survivors and others left messages, sounding like they were at the end of their own rope and needed someone to pull them back in. One heart-wrenching message was a minister who many people had turned to for advice on forgiveness and moving on. She couldn't do it anymore; she had nothing left to give. She was tired of trying to put a positive, forgiving face on this. She was angry with James. Her voice cracked in the message. I knew she was in the same emotional space that engulfed me in the hotel.

When I talked with her, I told her it was OK to be angry, that I was too. We needed to feel and experience our anger so we could move through it. Some of the survivors were feeling confused. They told me of feeling guilty because they were angry instead of being forgiving and non-judgmental, as James' supporters had advised. James had a saying: "Whatever you repress will be expressed in later days, in uglier ways." Independent of how I feel about him personally, I have to acknowledge that James taught us some really good stuff. Too bad he didn't pay attention to his own material.

I stopped writing the book that would eventually become this memoir. Who would care what I had learned from James now? What if anything he said, was true?

I was contacted by James' PR firm to do some pro-James news interviews. How terribly ironic that "the trouble makers in the WWS" were now so highly regarded by James and JRI. Some of the news media was referring to the victims as "cult members." James had hired a team of investigators to "find out what really happened in Sedona." Their actual mission, I believe, was to find something they could use to throw suspicion and fault on someone else other than James, and otherwise muddy the truth. They sought someone to blame, and didn't care who they threw under the bus. They interviewed survivors and had them sign statements likely without their lawyers present. They could have led the questions wherever they wanted. James later used quotes from these statements to publicly defend his actions. When a period of mourning and financial restitution would have been rational and responsible steps to take, James and his investigators were building a preemptive defense case outlined in a pair of "white papers" designed to make the prosecuting attorneys think they would not have a good case. It clearly did not work, but the statements contained within the white papers did succeed in pushing many of his students to no longer support him.

Right after the disaster in Sedona, I sent out an email stating one of two things was going to happen: Either I was going to learn by watching a master at work resolve a very bad situation; or the "master"

was going to show he was no master at all, and I would be very disappointed. James followed with an email to everyone, to which I replied
to my friends as follows:

> Is it just me, or does it seem that he is taking no responsibil-
> ity and is appearing to have no idea how this could have hap-
> pened? The only reason that he has a team investigating is to
> build a defense not to find out what happened. He baked them
> dead is what he did. Now that we know this vital piece of info
> that seems to be eluding him he can call off the investigators and
> save himself some money.
>
> He is continuing with "his work" to make more money.
>
> Remember when I said that in watching this, I am either
> going to get to watch & learn how a master handles a really big
> screw up, or be terribly disappointed?
>
> I think that I can make it official now . . . I'm disappointed!

Shortly after the Summit, the WWS members received an email
canceling the upcoming 2010 New Year's Eve party. It said we could
go to the one next year, whether or not we were still members of the
WWS. We saw the message as a stalling technique used to draw attention away from his next act, shutting down all WWS services while not
refunding any membership dues. We knew there was not going to be
a party next year—or a WWS, for that matter.

The last WWS email I received from James was on November 19,
2009:

> Dearest Friend,
>
> I just wanted to drop you a quick note and share that even
> in this most difficult time, you and all your fellow WWS mem-
> bers are in my daily thoughts. This is the most mentally and emo-
> tionally challenging time we've ever faced, and I'd love nothing
> more than to be with you and share our special times together
> as always. I miss our conversations.

Well apparently he didn't "miss our conversations" enough to use
a free conference call provider and make the hour-long call we had
with him each month. He was likely afraid of what some of our questions would be during our "ask James anything" call.

One big question still remained, one that fuels the "cult" flames in any of these situations: Why did intelligent people follow him into the lodge, and why did they stay? For one thing, he turned the heat up slowly during the week, instead of all at once. It reminds me of the adage: if you throw a frog into boiling water, it will jump right out. If you put the frog in lukewarm water and slowly turn up the heat, it will just relax until boiled to death. James slowly turned up the heat. He worked on our minds in all of his previous seminars, and all week in Spiritual Warrior, to get us to suspend our good judgment and to trust and obey him. Remember in Spiritual Warrior he had been "God" and you had to instantly obey him, even when he ordered you to die, or you were not an honorable person. It sounds ridiculous now, but he worked slowly, turning up the heat more and more over time. He built up to the lodge experience one day at a time.

We broke through many personal challenges and obstacles through James' events—with his once-sound guidance. Feats like bending rebar with your throat, breaking an arrow with your throat, and walking on fire were things we were not sure we could do, but he told us that we could, and we proved him right by doing them. Each time his credibility increased, while we learned to trust his judgment—sometimes more than ours. A quote directly from my Practical Mysticism notes: ***Have we not done things that by appearances would mean death and realize that death was just an illusion?***

One participant from Spiritual Warrior '08 said this in response to a detective's question of why she didn't think she would die: "Because I trusted him . . . It's a building of trust and it was obviously a false trust because I thought he had the certifications that he said that he had in order for me to feel safe doing what I was doing or what he asked me to do . . . I don't know what kind of a person he became but you know he became more about the money and not about the people."

A detective's notes on the man who thought he was having a heart attack during Spiritual Warrior '09 makes the point: "'At many of the events you do things that you don't think is possible and then you do.' Dennis had built a certain amount of trust because after doing those things you realize, 'wow I just did that.' Dennis said he came to believe that James would push your limits, but not do anything that would harm you. Dennis had doubts about the other things James Ray put them through and it all turned out okay. Dennis said he stayed longer because he had come to trust James Ray to know better than Dennis that he can do more than he ever thought . . . . Dennis said you combine everything they did through the week, and the trust he had in James Ray did not seem so strange."

James also presented us what seemed like very strong spiritual leadership credentials. We found out later many of them were not true. He also talked a lot about honor. If your teacher stresses the importance of honor, then you would consider him or her to be an honorable person . . . right? One survivor put it this way to detectives: "James Ray is a shaman and has done this sweat lodge for 8 years with no problem." Detectives also wrote she "also felt too much emphasis was placed on being the honorable warrior."

Many people stayed in the lodge too long because the heat, like alcohol, can impair judgment and increase lethargy. They were dizzy, made worse when they tried to sit or get up. They were so incoherent they could no longer tell up from down, and even if they wanted to leave, they were unable to move. They literally couldn't get out on their own. One participant who had a bad reaction to the lodge in Spiritual Warrior '08 was asked by detectives, "Would you be able to get up on your own and take care of yourself?"

"Absolutely not and had I'd been unconscious; how the heck would I get out of there?" she replied. "Even if I wanted to, how could an unconscious person make that decision? They can't. That's one of the problems that I have with this whole thing. They can't possibly make the decisions. "

Did James and JRI have any warning what they were doing was dangerous? Did they know about the serious problems suffered by past participants? We know in 2005 a man suffered heat stroke and was taken to the hospital in an ambulance. The Dream Team and staff also knew one woman was in serious physical duress for several hours after being carried out of the lodge in '07. The Dream Team member who took care of her believed that she was suffering from hyperthermia. We have confirmation from a JRI vendor's interview with the detectives that at Spiritual Warrior 2008 "there was two people who were incoherent, and it took awhile for them to come around (about two hours)." A woman who attended Spiritual Warrior '08 had this to say to detectives: "You don't think you're gonna go in there and die. My opinion and the reason I came forward, is because I was there and I know what happened and I feel that he had prior notice from people getting ill, that he was doing something wrong."

Why such division among the people who took his courses? I recognize perception of the truth differs for everyone involved. Each person had a different experience of James Arthur Ray. During a discussion with Dr. John over dinner at our house, he said he felt James was financially responsible to the victims for what happened but that he did not belong in jail. I did not argue with him because I respect his judgment and opinion. I did want to understand where he was coming from, though. After talking with Edward about it I realized Dr. John had not been to Spiritual Warrior. When I put myself in his shoes, I realized he had seen James push people to success at many activities. Other than the fiasco during the concrete block-breaking event, very few people had been hurt while attempting and succeeding at his challenges. The percentage of injuries and illnesses was very small compared to the number of people who attempted these things.

Then I drew it to a point: If I had trouble absorbing how extreme and crazy his lodge was, and I was there once, how could John imagine something so bizarre without any references to extrapolate from? It defied all logic to take clients to the point of projectile vomiting, disorientation, and unconsciousness. It would be very hard for someone to imagine people lying in pain on the ground around the lodge, and know James and his staff considered this "normal".

Like the many thousands of people who had attended some of James' events, Dr. John could not imagine or appreciate how hot it was in there because he had never experienced it. The James he knew pushed people hard. The James I knew didn't have compassion for his students, and he pushed people to the point of being reckless with their lives.

What our community experienced was another "Big Bang." Just like during the initial creation of the universe, we had all been forcibly propelled away from James. It was time to put to use what we had learned. We had studied enough, and taken more than enough of his seminars. Even though James would have kept us close for as long as possible so we continued to pay exorbitant prices for his training, we were ready to break free and do positive things for ourselves, our families, and our communities. Even with this massive explosion, some still stayed close to him, and others moved much farther away. Like the expanding universe in which we live, we are constantly expanding and moving farther away from him every day. Many of us have had a paradigm shift and nothing will ever be the same again. His hold on us is gone.

As a community, we were still struggling to come to terms with what happened. One woman put it well after Liz's death, "As I process the death of another James Ray participant, I ponder a very important lesson. How can I take the incredible teachings and transformation I have personally experienced over the past 5 years of studying with James and continue to apply them to my life without tainting them with the deep sadness, immense disappointment and outright anger I feel for the loss of lives involved? "

In February 2010, James Arthur Ray was indicted by a grand jury on three counts of manslaughter. He was arrested at the offices of his attorney and held for several weeks while his legal team worked to lower his $5 million bail. That's when his lawyers stated that this self-proclaimed multi-millionaire didn't have any money. All of the money that we paid him for our prepaid events and those $60,000 to $75,000 WWS membership fees, literally millions of dollars, disappeared into thin air. Does this make him a magician who works with magic, or someone who works with Magick, or both? His 7,234 sq. ft. Beverly Hills home he bought for about $4 million was now supposedly for sale seven months later for $5.4 million. You may have heard the term "priced to sell" for a home priced according to its current market value that should sell quickly. What we have here was a home "priced not to sell."

Questions started flying through my mind. Was the announcement of James' house going up for sale just another sympathy ploy, that he had no real plans on selling it? Was he planning on living there until it was foreclosed? What about his properties in Kona, and the two in Las Vegas? He may have very little equity in those properties, but I am still curious how he is paying for them, if he is still making payments. And the big question: where did all of OUR money go?

By now you know that I am angry with the man. What I haven't said is that in my opinion, for the sake of the victims, their families and all those hurt by his actions, he needs to have a serious time-out. It would also be beneficial to keep him from applying his considerable neuro-linguistic programming (NLP) and "stage" hypnosis skills on other people in the future, whether he is working live, recorded or in any form of broadcasted talks or classes. Even so, it was still hard for most of us to watch the news and see him being led into prison.

The bars closed on an era for our extended family, and us, and we saw wasted human potential in him and his victims. There's a saying, "A Warrior Dies Once, A Coward Dies A Thousand Deaths." Did he know this day would come, or was he really so arrogant he thought he was above it all?

We are still a house divided, and will likely stay that way. Recently

I received another call from Carol. She said she was feeling restless and wanted to put together an event where we could all come together again. But first she wanted to know how I felt about James. She only wanted people at this Spring 2010 gathering who supported him. After we talked, Richard and I were not invited to the get-together in Los Angeles. Apparently she did not like my attitude, which was all right with me, because the last place I wanted to be was at a James Ray pep rally.

For the first time in many years, the Joys of Real Estate decided not to hold our traditional end of the year Holiday Party for clients and friends. We were not in the party or holiday spirit at the end of 2009. We sent part of the money we would have spent to Vera's foundation to buy Christmas presents for the villagers we visited in Peru. We used the time to visit my parents in Prescott, Arizona just before Christmas; while there, we planned on visiting Vera in Sedona.

Something was calling us back to Sedona. We had unfinished business waiting for us there.

Epilogue

What Did We Learn From All Of This?

When there is no turning back, then we should concern ourselves only with the best way of going forward.
—Paulo Coehlo, *The Alchemist*

We sat in Vera's kitchen eating breakfast a couple of days before Christmas. A thick layer of snow had fallen on Sedona, an uncommon occurrence in this high desert town. The sight of the blanket of white lying over the red stone cliffs in the early morning light was stunning! Everything was still, yet you could feel the life force preparing to make its way back into full view as soon as the snow melted away. In a few hours, all traces of the snow would be gone, leaving just a beautiful memory. It seemed fitting we would find ourselves in Sedona just before the New Year of this particular year. As we drove into town from Cottonwood on 89A, we passed the road leading to Angel Valley. I thought about bringing flowers to place on the spot where the sweat lodge stood, but decided against it. The gate would likely be closed, and I didn't want to intrude on the owners.

James and his big ego were leaving behind equally huge wakes of grief and difficulty, swamping the owners of Angel Valley along with the rest of us. They are facing a lawsuit from the Black Hills Sioux Nation Treaty Council, which will likely take a considerable amount of their resources to defend. Their mistake was believing James when he said he knew what he was doing and would run a safe event on their property.

As we drove by the road, I could feel the heaviness. The last few months had been really sad for so many, including us. We could have been there that day. Richard could have been inside the lodge, and I could have been one of the people performing CPR. Would our presence have made any difference? Would one of us have had the nerve to disrupt the ceremony and/or call 911 in defiance of James? James was a formidable man, as we knew. Unlike our trip to Peru, this was his event. People had paid a large amount of money to learn from him, not to hear our opinions.

Could of, should of, would of . . . survivor guilt continued to spread, nearly three months later.

I don't know what we would have done if we had been there. I was concerned about people suffering brain damage from heat stroke; the thought that he would actually bake people to death was not something I could have even conceived of. However, I do not believe in coincidences. A higher force made sure we were not there. The universe, higher power, or our guardian angels went to great lengths to make sure we were not even on the mainland so that there was no way we would screw it up and still be there.

In Vera's kitchen, we drank our hot chocolate. Vera is an intuitive person and a healer. She started to gently ask me questions. We discussed the trip to Peru, and I was comparing it to Egypt. I told her about my experience between the paws of the Sphinx, the tasks I had to complete in this lifetime, and my spiritual assignment of sorts: to complete a book about my experiences over the last couple of years.

"How is the book going?" she asked.

"After what happened in the lodge, I stopped writing it. Who would want to read about what I learned from James now?"

At one time, a large group of people considered James to be their teacher. Within that group existed many different reactions over what happened. At one end of the spectrum, a small group of people are chronically co-dependent on him and living in denial. They will support him, no matter what he does. Several witnesses pointed out to the authorities that this co-dependent group appeared willing to lie, or at the very least have very selective memories of what happened. Then there are James' "supporters" who think that, like the Phoenix rising from the ashes, he will somehow dodge his responsibilities in this disaster and return quickly to his glory years. That group wants to be ready to hang on to his coat tails and rise up financially with him. These people and James are just using each other. He needs to keep some of them close to him, at least for now, so they don't suddenly regain their memories and testify against him.

At the other end of the spectrum are those who want to see him fry in hell, or at least experience significant jail time. Others, myself included, fall somewhere between the two. Let's not overlook the fact that not all JRI employees are raving fans of his either. So to try to dismiss such a diverse collection of people as a mindless group of cult followers is convenient, but inaccurate.

Vera and I discussed our mutual concern that the public perception of spirituality could be harmed by the tragedy and the trials to come. There are many great teachers and service providers who do not put money before people; now they, and virtually all spiritual practices not taught by a traditional religious institution, were falling into a negative light. I, for one, have learned and grown tremendously over the last few years. I would hate to see most of the opportunities for this kind of work evaporate just because of James. Vera and I talked about what could be done to help people understand what happened, and what needed to change so that it didn't happen again. I expressed my own need to understand all of this. The scientific side of me knew there must be an explanation; I just had to find it.

Vera convinced me that finishing the book was probably more important now than ever, for all of the reasons we'd discussed. She attempted to get my commitment to finish it. I evaded her question by saying I wasn't a good writer. She told me to just get over it. I really felt like running away from the whole thing, and she knew it.

The past few months had both drained and distracted me. Now I had to make a decision on whether or not to focus on it further—and from different angles and perspectives. She persisted. I made the commitment knowing it would likely pull me into a firestorm. In truth, one of the reasons I chose to complete this book was for my own sanity. I had to understand what the hell happened to help me not repeat my own lapses in judgment again. Peace is easier when you can see more clearly, and I wanted peace.

Vera put me in touch with a publisher that, she said, I could trust to include the spiritual aspects of my journey. A while later I sent them my chapters I had written before Spiritual Warrior 2009.

Vera also said completing the book would help me clear the anger from my system. I thought about that for a while. Was I still angry? I thought I was making progress through the grief cycle. True, the anger rose when I spoke to someone who had been injured, or when I heard more details of what happened or how James was behaving, but I thought I was getting over each reoccurrence well.

A couple of months later, I attended a Transformational Breathing Seminar with Edward and Faith. During the breathing exercise, the facilitators come around and identify what issues your body may be having, based on how you are breathing. One bent down and told me I had issues with righteous anger that was justified, but taking a toll on my jaw and body. For my own health, I needed to do what was necessary to release it and move on.

Well, all righty then. Maybe I was not doing as well as I hoped. Edward and Faith teased me later about who deserved such righteous anger from me: James, of course. His actions caused the death of three great people and nearly several more, and broke up our extended family. Up to this point in time he has left everyone high and dry with huge medical bills and funeral expenses, and ripped off those who pre-paid events and membership fees. He continued to act like he had no idea how the tragedy happened, that somehow he was the real victim.

Vera was right: I was harboring anger, and it was time to get it out of my system.

Eventually, our conversation turned to how strange James acted at times. I still thought James' blow-up in Peru may have resulted from his disappointment at learning the permission for our night ceremony in Machu Picchu had been revoked. I asked Vera exactly when she found out that our permission had been rescinded. That hit a hot button! She told me we never had permission in the first place—and JRI and James knew it. He knew there would be no death stone ritual long before we left the U.S. James stood by for months before the trip, listening to our excited chatter about the ceremony—and never said anything!

Why would he and his staff do that? Maybe he promoted the night ceremony at Machu Picchu to entice more people to join the WWS. He certainly had no problems breaking promises he had made to get people to join, so what would stop him from creating a benefit that didn't exist? At Spiritual Warrior, he stated Colleen Conaway was "*fine*" when he knew she was dead, and that people "*had taken ill*," when two of them were dead as well. Remember the email that the WWS members received on February 19, 2009 from JRI? Let me refresh your memory:

Hi everyone!! I am sooo excited to be the first to tell you . . . we just received word from Peru officials that we were granted

after hour permission for Machu Picchu!! Not only were we
granted permission for this, but also after hours for Ollantaytambo in the Sacred Valley . . . how awesome is that!?!

There was much more deception. James' staff sent photos of him
in Peru to Vera wanting to know the identities of the locations. The
photos were taken at Sacsayhuaman and Ollantaytambo, two very
famous Incan sites. Even I know their names and locations. How
could James not know if he had spent so much time there? Vera was
led to believe he had only been to Peru one time.

But wait: If he hadn't spent a lot of time studying in Peru, how
could he have experienced the adventures he told us about? How
could he have become a shaman? Looking back, I realize it takes
many years of training to become a shaman in one group, never mind
two. I have since found out, that for the most part, according to South
American native spirituality a group's next shaman is considered to
be preordained. In one Amazonian tribe near the Peruvian city of
Iquitos, the shaman is selected as a child, usually after some sort of
spiritual sign. The child is taken from his parents, placed in the care
of spiritual elders, and taught the ways of plants, animals, human
spirit and the "other side"—then how to operate in both the seen and
unseen realms. This training, most of which takes place in the raw
jungle, continues for eight years or more before the selectee is considered old and wise enough to be the spiritual intermediary for the
tribe.

That just addresses James' claim to be a shaman in South America. Add the number of years of intensive study to become a Kahuna,
and it was clear James likely could not have attained all those levels of
mastery, if any.

We also found out that while we were in Machu Picchu James did
not want the other shaman to talk to us after the first ceremony. One
of the great things for us about this shaman was he also spoke English, which is very rare, and we could have understood what he said
during the ceremonies. What a spiritual gift for us, to hear a traditional ceremony, likely delivered very similar to how an Incan high
priest might have done six centuries before? Why would James not
want him to lead any more? Did James want to stay the main shaman,
or just preserve the illusion that he was a shaman at all?

The revealing news kept rolling in. Before visiting Vera, we had just
learned that James was likely not a kahuna either. I saw a TV interview

with Dr. Matthew James, an instructor in the ancient Hawaiian spiritual system of Huna and James Ray's former spiritual teacher. He said, "I remember when he [James] was attending the trainings . . . after only taking a handful of trainings, he began to teach some of the things we had specifically said people aren't allowed to teach. A person picks up a book, they read it, they think they know something and they begin to teach it." Dr. Matthew James said they asked James to stop and he refused, so he was no longer welcome at their events or trainings. Furthermore, we later learned James was not trained by Dr. Grof in Holotropic Breathwork™. According to the management of Dr. Grof's company, James Ray is not certified in the use of their techniques, and Dr. Grof said he never heard of James Ray before the disaster at Angel Valley. James often told us that Holotropic Breathwork™ was dangerous to practice on our own, because you needed to have someone alongside with the training to "bring you back" if there was any trouble. Want to guess how many hundreds of us did this activity thinking James was properly trained, when in fact he wasn't trained by Grof at all?

James had no trouble using other people's material and claiming it as his own. In addition to teaching Dr. Matthew James' Huna practices even after he was told not to, he also ignored Dr. Grof's trademark on Holotropic Breathwork™. Some of James' staff later tried to claim that they only referred to the exercise as Breathwork, but I and others have heard James refer to it numerous times as Holotropic Breathwork™. Here is one exchange between a detective from Sedona and Josh, a James Ray International high level employee, where he acknowledges that they know about the trademark but still tries to claim that what they do and call it is different:

> Det.: Okay. So your training of holotropic breathing came from James Ray.
> Josh: My understanding of it. I also read Stanislov Grof's book Holotropic Mind. And to be clear I know that holotropic breathing is Stan's trademark and I don't know how that specifically differs if anything from what we do that we call Breathwork.

But if we look at the 2009 Spiritual Warrior waiver that was part of the Participant Guide for the event it says, "These activities may include . . . Holotropic Breathwork (a psychotherapeutic approach believed to allow access to non-ordinary states of consciousness) . . ."

James used the name and process of Holotropic Breathwork™ without the permission or the knowledge of the trade mark's owner, and also claimed to have been trained in it by Dr. Grof himself.

I also flipped back to the *Fortune* magazine article about James: "Ray's bio also says he spent four years working with Stephen Covey, the author of *The 7 Habits of Highly Effective People* . . . But Debra Lund, the spokeswoman for Covey, said no one at the company has any recollection of Ray."

All those stories James told us about his teacher, don Javier Ruis (name changed to protect the man's privacy), had to be true, right? After I was told that James' shaman mentor could be a Cusco tour guide and not a shaman, I was in shock; another big fib. Of course, it is not as bad as saying that people are "*fine*" or have "*taken ill*" when they're dead, but it was a biggie. Amazingly I was still having trouble believing it. Could there be more than one don Javier Ruis in Cusco? I had to be sure we were taking about the same man, and I remembered how to confirm it. After our trip to Egypt, James challenged us to give a presentation to our local JET groups and share what we learned during our trip. I made a PowerPoint presentation from the photos. It was on the laptop with me at the WW Extravaganza. I was surprised James did not have any of the video he took and only a few photos of Egypt displayed on the big screens, so I offered to let them auto run my Egyptian presentation. When I talked to Josh about it, I asked him if I should bring him my laptop. "No, just load it onto this," he said. He unplugged a small thumb drive from his computer and gave it to me.

During a short break, I hurried to my room and tried to bring up my computer and copy over my file. Let's just say that I had a certain operating system on my brand new laptop that ran ridiculously slow and hung up often. When it finally booted up, my computer had trouble recognizing the thumb drive. I tried to copy and paste the file over to the small portable drive. When that would not work; I tried to drag it over. It was a tablet PC and the stylus was not picking up the files accurately due to the constantly stalling system. I had copied too many of my files onto the thumb drive by mistake, and now the little drive was full. I struggled to drag all of my files back, popped open the tablet PC to make it into a "regular" notebook, and tried again using a mouse I attached. Finally, I transferred the right file and raced back to the meeting room and gave the thumb drive back to Josh.

Several months later, I needed to use the laptop again. That's when I noticed strange files on it. While looking for my Egyptian PowerPoint presentation, I found something called "social proof." I opened it: it was the PowerPoint presentation James used to show during breaks, featuring all of the places he'd been and people he knew. If I remembered right, there were photos of James with don Javier Ruis. I found them. I stripped off the titles, sent them to Vera, and asked if anyone she knew could identify the man in the photo with James. She told me there was someone who interfaced with most of the tour guides in Cusco. If anyone would know, they would. She emailed the photos.

What a learning experience! The first photo, originally captioned, "James with don Javier Ruis—Peru" was a photo of James standing by a short man wearing a red flannel shirt and blue jeans. The other photo carried the caption, "Qu'ero Shaman—Peru." It showed "don" Javier Ruis in the same red shirt and blue jeans, sitting next to a person dressed in traditional Peruvian shaman clothing. Vera's contact wrote back, "The man is Javier Ruis and the *shaman* is don Geriano; I don't work too much with them." Note the distinction—Javier Ruis was not called a shaman or given the title of *don.*

Now I knew we were talking about the same Javier Ruis. Looking at the photos, it is now obvious that Javier Ruis was wearing regular western clothing. While we were in Peru, as far as we could tell, the shaman wore traditional clothing. Is it possible that Javier Ruis was a wild and crazy guy who did not follow the norms of traditional clothing for shaman? Sure, but unlikely. Vera's contact would not address a person without the "don" title unless he was not a shaman. It would be like introducing a Priest by saying, "the man's name is Joseph Kennedy" instead of "the Priest's name is Father Joseph Kennedy." Even in casual conversation, you would still call him Father Joe. He also would have identified Javier Ruis as a shaman, and not just as a man. I wasn't sure if I was happy or sad over confirming this deception.

However, it did lead me to ask: What did James actually tell us that *was* true?

I wasn't alone. In light of learning James was not trained by Grof and was probably not a Kahuna, a group of committed JRI event attendees started asking the inevitable question: does anyone have any proof that James was indeed a shaman? Below is what I posted to them on Facebook:

James, the night ceremony at Machu Picchu and his shaman teacher . . .

Reading this will be one of those moments where some things may never look the same to you again. It is my hope and prayer that in telling you this that it will help some people learn, let go and heal. When I heard it I finally "got it." My heart ached, but I finally "got it." I am grateful to James for giving me the tools that I decided to take and use to transform my life over the past few years. Now I need separate James the man from the lessons I learned.

Some of you may know that we went back to Sedona just before Christmas to visit family and spend some time with Vera, the incredible lady who was the tour organizer for the WWS trip to Peru. While we were there we learned some things that shocked me down to my bones. Why I could still be shocked goes to the fact that I had still apparently not let everything sink in. We now know that James was not trained by Grof in Holotropic Breathwork™. We now know that he is most likely not a Kahuna according to the man whom he took Huna courses from. So why would it shock me to find out that James' shaman experiences might be "off" from what we were told by him as well? Still I was stunned and this is what I found out.

We all remember the lead up to the Peru trip. James on stage telling us that he had most of the signatures necessary to get into Manchu Picchu at night and do the death stone ritual. Each progressive seminar we were told that due to his extensive connections in Peru we were getting closer and closer to having the final permission. Then, finally, the big announcement. James was able to get the final approval! The WWS was going to have that incredible experience, and the only way for you in the audience to have it as well was to sign up for WWS. Yeah . . . how great . . . a once in a lifetime opportunity! I was jazzed.

When we got to Peru, Vera was confused by all the questions from us about having enough warm clothing for the night ceremony at MP. You see, Vera was James' connection in Peru, and it was her employees standing in line at the government offices working on getting us permissions to do special things. She NEVER EVER told anyone at JRI that we had permission to be in Manchu Picchu after dark never mind get on the death stone. UNESCO and the Peruvian government do not allow it anymore. Her employees were able to get permission for the meditation/ceremonies in Mapi and Ollantaytambo, and they tried while they were at it for the nighttime ceremony at MP but it was always a no go. JRI always knew that and they certainly knew that before we got there. Vera has emails from the JRI employee where they acknowledged that they were disappointed but fully aware that we did not have permission for entering any temple at night.

Vera only spoke to James once via phone before the trip and it was after most of the plans had been firmed up. He asked what could be done to get the extra permission and she told him NOTHING, UNESCO had restricted entrance and that was that. It might be possible, a big MAYBE to try to hang around a little later in the day but no go for at night and no ceremony on the death stone.

As far as James' extensive travels and studies in Peru . . . Vera was always under the impression that he was there only once. On that single phone call when she asked him how he came by information on where to visit in Peru he said that he had taken good notes. The JRI people had sent her a photo of James at Ollantaytambo and at Sacksayhuman and asked her if she knew where these places where since James did not remember the names or where there were but that they were "quite nice." Now I have only been to these places one time and even my menopausal brain remembers their names and where they are. So I will let you draw your own conclusions about James' extensive travels throughout Peru.

Last but not least James' shaman teacher. One of the things that the WWS members were excited about was to meet this guy. He was our teacher's teacher . . . how cool! This was the man responsible for setting James out on his path to change the world. We have heard about him for as long as we had known James and now we were likely going to meet him. How excited James MUST BE to get to see his teacher again . . . right? At one point during the trip a group of us asked him if he had found his teacher and he said that he had found out that he was in Cusco (that's where we were at the time). He had a strange look on his face then immediately changed the subject. Well, that was downright strange. His great teacher was close by and he was neither excited nor even wanted to talk about it. We later were told by Vera that her two incredible guides were confused by our excitement about James' teacher. Vera did not know the man personally but they knew him and he was a tour guide in town. They were both surprised that James was so impressed with the guy. So it was no wonder that we were not treated to the opportunity to meet and talk with him.

So to all those people like me who charged money they didn't have to join WWS and get that once in a life time opportunity to die on the death stone . . . well we will have to settle for having a piece of our hearts die a little bit now. What does not kill us makes us stronger . . . right? Yes, it does.

So for those who are interested in having a once in a lifetime trip through Peru I strongly suggest you contact Vera Lopez from Spirits of *the Earth. You don't have to pay $65,000+ for an incredible spiritual experience. And THAT is my lesson from all of this. That and to be my own Guru. There were numerous red flags all over the place and I wanted so much to believe in James that I suspended my own good judgment. . . . This experience exposed me to a magical group of people and showed me that I could hold myself, my environment, and my companionships to a higher standard. It hurt to grow over the past years. It would have hurt more to stay the same. It hurts NOW to grow through this. It would hurt more not to face it. We ARE warriors, and we will take our learning's and be all the better for them.*

    Love you all,
    Connie

Nancy Ogilvie responded, "Reading Carlos Castaneda doesn't make him a shaman any more than reading about the Royal Family makes me a Queen." She goes on to say that she had been studying the work of a Zen Master to help her move on from the Sedona tragedy. "No, that does not mean that (I'm) now a Zen Master either," she wrote. "Every one of us spent thousands of dollars to a teacher that we believed was something he wasn't. It doesn't really matter if he was good at synthesizing the material, because while he sounds good, in practice he is only living the cliff notes version. We all have a better grasp of the 'message' than he does. Is the message valid? Of course it is—but it is about time that we stop attributing the message to James and maybe go back to the source."

Breaking up is hard to do

It was especially hard for everyone who had reached the painful point of no longer supporting James. We began working together to validate the value of the lessons we learned and the changes we made in our lives, while seeing our teacher's shortcomings. Another issue we are having concerns James Ray's body of work: what do we do with it? Many of us still have boxes of his books he "encouraged" us to buy. Some people threw out, shredded or burned his material. As much as I hate to see something useful being trashed, I understand where they are coming from. Right now, I can't listen to his voice on the numerous CDs I have, or read anything he has written.

I am still getting bombarded with emails from him, enticing me to pay to listen to his new radio show, or to watch his next free video. Remember, he still owes us $56,000+ we paid for our membership/

event fees in the now defunct WWS. He has never sent us a letter, email or made a phone call telling us how or when he would reimburse us. BUT, because he is such a good guy, and out of the generosity of his heart, he sent us an email on June 16, 2010. It links to his newly branded website and this spectacular offer: "Now You Can Get James as your Virtual Coach in his *Success Certain Coaching Training System* For 40% OFF! The course sells like hotcakes every day for $497.00 . . . but you can save 40% and get the entire copy for just $297!"

This "system" has been around for a long time; we bought two of these binders with CDs in November 2007. I remember selling them for a lot less than $297 at the 2008 Harmonic Wealth Weekends at which we worked. The man has taken $56,000+ from us and has the nerve to try to sell us more of his old stuff. If *ineffable* is a word that refers to indescribable beauty, what word to use for inexplicable audacity?

Maybe it's just me, but I see something else amiss here. How can a man in James' current state of affairs send me video emails promoting ways he can teach me how to live a better life? Or watch a video in which he discusses the importance of coming from gratitude? A friend who has also been receiving his video emails asked me, "Is he for real, trying to tell me how to live my life? That dude needs to get a real job!" Another person said on Facebook that it would be fitting if he did life management videos while wearing an orange jumpsuit.

Some people have found a way to have fun with their James Ray paraphernalia. For Christmas, Edward and Faith gave us each a beautifully wrapped present. We peeled off the paper and found a copy of James' book and his DVD. "No backies!" they yelled.

There is always the danger of believing your own press. At one time, James arranged to be introduced as:

> A self-made millionaire, James is transforming the way the world thinks. Called "The Rock Star of Personal Transformation" by the press, James is a "World Thought Leader" Our co-host for this interview is James Arthur Ray. James is the President and CEO of James Ray International, a multi-million dollar corporation dedicated to teaching individuals to create wealth in all

areas of their lives: financially, relationally, intellectually, physically and spiritually.

What's with this guy? The quick answer: James has a Messiah complex. He's a person who thinks that he is the next coming, and that you need to work through him to find spiritual enlightenment. James would save the world, and he would save your world . . . for a high price. I suggest you keep these two things in mind when evaluating anyone who promises to show you the path to enlightenment. Are their fees exorbitant, and is there continual pressure to sign up for more events and services? At this point, I reached an understanding of some of the questions that once baffled me. I share them with you now, accepting that from your unique perspective, your answers may be different than mine:

Why are many American Indians angry about the Sedona tragedy?

First, their spiritual tradition of a sweat lodge ceremony has very little in common with what James Ray called a sweat lodge ceremony during his Spiritual Warrior event. This was not a real sweat lodge; it was an endurance test James created. Now, the reputation of one of their most sacred rites, part and parcel of their spiritual paths for countless centuries, has been damaged. I understand their anger.

Why are we so surprised that James behaved this way before, during and after Spiritual Warrior 2009?

From the very first Harmonic Wealth Weekend, James taught us to take responsibility for our results—good or bad. My notes of his comments from Practical Mysticism state: "Anytime you think you are 'the bomb,' the universe will drop a bomb on you. When you are tapping into higher levels of consciousness, it generally will tell you to stretch and keep growing. If it is telling you that you are the second coming that is your Ego, not the Divine."

Because James kept teaching this, we assumed he would not fall into the trap because he would know better. Obviously, we were wrong. He hinted at his own karma in his book, a title in which reads, "We teach what we most need to learn." James was also fond of quoting a comment made by the Morpheus character in *The Matrix*: "There is a major difference between knowing of the path and walking the path." Ultimately, James violated the most basic rule of all: first, do no harm.

Why did we all spend so much money?

Nancy Ogilvie answered this question well: "Tell me that IF YOU HAD KNOWN THE TRUTH about James that you would have spent half the money he charged . . . It cost me over $20,000 to do 7 events with him in 13 months. Why did I do it all so fast? James told me it was best . . . . I am a single parent with one income. Why did I take the chance and pay that kind of ridiculous money for this experience? Because James was a mystic that could give me experiences I would get nowhere else and I would have practical results . . . we were making huge decisions based on lies . . . We ARE the lucky ones—we escaped with our lives. Credit scores and financial portfolios can be rebuilt."

We believed his credentials and training. I would not have imagined that someone would stand on a stage and make those huge claims in front of hundreds of people if they weren't true. We thought that we were paying for his years of training and experience as a shaman, kahuna, Holotropic Breathwork™ and sweat lodge facilitator. I thought that it was worth paying him that much money; after all, where else can you find someone with such broad training? In truth, the answer to that question is nowhere.

Given the extensive training, and lifelong adherence to a singular path that mark the sacred, centuries-old traditions of true tribal or spiritual shaman, or kahuna, that multi-faceted person likely does not exist. To state that you're studying these paths of ancient spiritual knowledge is another matter. Many people are well-versed in a variety of spiritual paths, the best of them able to follow these teachings to their originating points, their roots. What they do with that knowledge separates researchers from teachers, and humble great souls from megalomaniacs. I'll leave it to you to decide where James falls.

James also used stage hypnosis techniques and NLP to get people to sign up for events and services they could not afford. I heard him claim once on stage that he was a master at NLP and could teach it . . . Red flag, red flag, red flag!

Why was it these three wonderful people were the ones to die?

If Richard and I had died in that lodge, the headlines would have read:

"Overweight fifty year old woman and man over seventy die in a sweat lodge accident."

Maybe they would have dug deeper; maybe they wouldn't. The possibility that our deaths resulted from my weight and Richard's age would have made it easier to dismiss it as an accident. Instead, two healthy middle-aged people with no pre-existing medical conditions died inside the lodge (Liz died in the hospital). This cannot be dismissed so easily.

While Kirby Brown and James Shore were relatively newcomers, Liz was a member of the "old guard' and had been affiliated with James for seven years. He knew her well, yet she was in the hospital for nine days before she died and her family never received a call or visit from James during that time. This sent a message to the rest of his students that if he could treat Liz this way, he certainly would not treat anyone else any better. Look to his actions for his real intentions and feelings, not his words.

In all, three people died as a result of an activity James was leading. First off if only one person had died, again it would have been easier to dismiss. There might not have been the instant uproar from the public or volume of attention from the press, and James might have been able to continue on with his seminars, at least for a while.

If you believe nothing happens by accident, consider the significance of the number three. In many of the older spiritual traditions, a person would hold a pointed object during a prayer or ceremony, symbolizing their intention or prayer must come to a focused point for it to manifest. That fine focus can be represented by a wand, a crystal or achieved very simply by using your pointed finger. As a demonstration, lift your arm straight in front of you and point your index finger outward. Your intention or prayer goes out into the world through your pointed finger. If you look at your hand, you will see three fingers pointing back at you. The symbolism: for every intention or action you put out into the world, it will return three times over. Current practitioners of these ancient belief disciplines would never willingly push negativity into the world, because it will come back at them three times over.

Earlier, I talked about how the wheels of karma started to turn when James lied about Colleen's suicide in San Diego and then he did not return the money to her family for the seminar or the other events she prepaid. His actions put out a clear message to the universe: he was disrespectful of Colleen and her death, and his love of money exceeded the love of people. What did the universe send back to him? Exactly three deaths. He tried to spin it by saying some of the people had "taken ill," but the universe made him acknowledge the deaths in the three counts of manslaughter and by separating him from money.

While I am not a big supporter of regulation, if something doesn't change, a tragedy like what happened at Sedona will happen again, and abuses within this industry will continue.

Here are my suggestions for change:

Provider's credentials must be easily available and give verifiable references to training and education claims. A third-party peer review panel would be helpful. If someone claims to be trained in Native American sweat lodge ceremonies, great! Now prove it. Give facts: dates, places, length of training, the instructor, and the instructor's contact information. You can't apply for a job without giving your resume and verifiable references; this should be no different. Even in real estate, every one of our home sales informational packages contains a copy of our broker's licenses, my Accredited Staging Professional and Advanced Feng Shui certificates, and other certifications as well. A true teacher will have no trouble with this requirement. People who have done the work are proud of it and happy to show the proof of what they have accomplished.

Full disclosure during the time period that a person can cancel their purchase and get a full refund. The period does not start until the consumer has received all of the necessary disclosures. This must include the provider's credentials, copies of any waivers, and specifics of event activities. If there are unusual food or water restrictions, disclose that as well. Disclose the approximate length of time per day of all sessions—including any homework assignments. If you don't want to attend an event where you will be getting one hour of sleep a night for five consecutive days, then you need to know if that's part of the event for which you are signing up. If you don't want to walk on fire, then Practical Mysticism may not be the event for you. The consumer needs to have the basic right to make a fully informed decision what they are paying for and getting themselves into.

If the current system had not been so terribly abused, all of these disclosures requirements would not have been necessary.

James, for example, routinely sent copies of the consent forms shortly before the event, long after the time period had elapsed to get your money back if you saw something disagreeable. Essentially, attendees were being placed in a position where they had to sign the consent and release forms. JRI had a "no refund" policy, with the exception of Harmonic Wealth Weekend—and that came with a list of conditions designed to greatly limit eligibility for refunds. It was pretty safe to say that other than within the first three days after signing up for an event, you were not likely to receive a refund, no matter what you found out. If you refused to sign, then you could not attend the event. The best that JRI would consider doing is to offer you another of James' events or services in exchange—and they weren't going to disclose anything about that other event in advance, either. If you decided that you did not want to pick another mystery event, your only other option was to receive a credit for his products. Most of James' events ran thousands of dollars—a ridiculous number of CDs!

Provider's ratings maintained online by an independent group. I can buy a $2 soap dish from eBay or a book at Amazon.com, and be able to rate the provider on their service, and the product purchased. Why is it, then, that I can spend $10,000 on an event or $75,000 on a membership and not have the opportunity to warn other consumers about poor service or bad products? Or recommend a great seminar to them through my review or rating?

Are they a good presenter(s)? Was the event or service what you expected? How was their refund policy? How do you rate this service/product? Any comments? Such a system would have allowed previous JRI seminar attendees to warn those after them about the dangers of the sweat lodge.

Insurance/bond coverage requirements in line with activity risk levels and number of attendees. Clearly, you need more coverage for activities outside the usual lecture experience.

Escrow or trust accounts must be established where prepaid seminar fees that are over a thousand dollars are held, minus a small deposit around 5%, until the event or services are delivered. James had taken over $56,000 from Richard and me in WWS '09 membership fees alone. That was supposed to provide us with services and events from April '09 to April '10. Obviously, that didn't happen. We are far from alone.

Besides other WWS members, hundreds of other people prepaid for events and services, a total outlay that enters seven digits.

Where is all of that money? Supposedly, this multi-millionaire owner of a multi-million dollar company did not have enough money to post his original bail. He claims to be unable to pay all the victims and victims' families for their expenses other than his one insurance policy. The man who always bragged about sitting in the front of the plane or the back of the car when he traveled was peddling his lifestyle on OUR money. Money that he had not yet earned, prepaid money. If we had given this amount of money to an investment firm, and they had spent it on themselves or other pet projects instead of providing the agreed-upon service, they could go to jail. If we had taken the $56,000 to buy a car, and the car was stolen, the thief would go to jail—even if he or she eventually returned it. Why should practitioners in the self-help industry not be required to offer some form of assurance that the money will either be there to finance the service or event, or be automatically refunded back to the consumer?

The immediate solution is simple: know your teacher. If they appear unapproachable, unwilling to let you get to know them well, then move on until you find one who will. At the same time, keep in mind the only teacher you really need now or ever is within you. "The kingdom of heaven is within you," Jesus admonished his disciples. **Be your own guru**; that may be the most powerful lesson you or I will ever learn from any teacher. Ironically, James is still our teacher, whether we like it or not. The difference now is that he can't charge us anymore for the life lessons he is giving us. Sometimes, having a demonstration of what not to do is more powerful than being told what to do.

I hope you understand the people who died and were injured in the sweat lodge were not mindless cult followers. They were smart, positive, brave, and hard working people who only wanted to better themselves, and the world around them. They wanted to be better moms, dads, sisters, brothers, friends, sons, daughters, and co-workers. They are exactly the type of people you would want on your team or in your life. You would have counted yourself lucky to know them. I do. Here's how I remember Liz: Sitting in Kona, a huge smile on her face, beaming; a joy to be around. She was also an angel, always willing to lend a helping hand or a shoulder to cry on. I would expect those who knew James Shore and Kirby Brown would have similar things to say about them. This is why many of us stayed around, even as it was getting harder and harder to overlook some of the behaviors we were seeing in James. We lingered to be around this extended family of participants and volunteers. That is why we grieve not just for the loss of these wonderful people, but also for the loss of our "like-minded group."

To the families who lost loved ones, it is my fervent wish that you will be able to find closure through the trials, and eventually peace. Many people pray for you every day.

We also hold those who were injured in our prayers, to heal as quickly as possible and find closure. Nearly a year later, Stephen still deals with many health issues and high medical bills. At the writing of this book he has not received any help from James or JRI. He is attempting to get some financial relief from James' and Angel Valley's insurance carriers. One day, we talked about gratitude. Stephen cherishes every day; he knows he was among the lucky ones. He still feels guilty he lived while others died. He is aware he was airlifted out first, before Liz; if she had gone first, he said, maybe she would have survived. He is a kind soul still struggling in James' wake.

James taught us in Practical Mysticism, "Juries make their decisions within the first five to seven minutes of the trial and spend the rest of the trial convincing themselves they are right." I wonder how he feels about that truth right now! Expect him to be very deliberate in everything he does and wears, especially in those first few minutes of his trial. He is a master of stage presence, and we have seen him cry on cue at Harmonic Wealth Weekends. Nothing he says or does will be insignificant.

In 2005, when one man was sent to the hospital with heat stroke, the universe gave James a "*tap on the shoulder*" that he was pushing people too far. In 2007, the universe ramped up to a "*slap on the back of his head*" when a woman experienced a severe heat-induced reaction for several hours after the lodge ceremony. He decided to increase the heat. In 2008, the universe "*hit James over the head with a 2x4*" to get him to stop when Edward stopped breathing twice and another woman was unresponsive for a least a couple of hours. Then, in 2009, the universe "*delivered a bomb*" to finally stop him.

As James often said, when you don't pay attention, you will end up paying with pain.

When I started to write this book, I was willing to overlook much of what I saw in James that worried me because I was getting so much from his seminars and events. Now that I come to the end, I am able to separate James the man from the material he taught. I no longer feel torn about him. Nancy temporarily changed her Facebook picture to Dorothy from the *Wizard of Oz*. Dorothy wears a look of shock when she discovers that the great and powerful Oz is not what he appeared to be. We saw the illusion James wanted us to see. Now, especially in the aftermath of Sedona, we know he is not the illusion, but the little man behind the curtain. James can continue to bellow all he wants, and try to pull our chains and push our buttons to manipulate us, but most of us have had a paradigm shift and there is no going back to the way it was.

Will I ever be completely over my weight issues? Ask any alcoholic or addict if they are ever free of concern about maintaining their sobriety. It took me 50 years to build up my conscious and unconscious habits. Now, at least, I have a better opportunity to intercept some of the negative behaviors before they get too far out of hand.

Believe it or not, I would like to try a REAL sweat lodge someday. That would be a rebirth for me, a true release, letting something old die so that something new can be born. While I was typing this last line, I noticed a hummingbird just returned outside my window; he'd been hovering all day, a couple of feet away from me. This buzzing blue and green wonder must be seeing its reflection in the glass because it stops and looks in the window almost as if it is posing for a picture. Every time I viewed the bird, my mind returned to that time when one of these magnificent creatures was my companion as I climbed the steep trail up Huayna Picchu alone. Suddenly, I remembered to pay attention! The hummingbird had paid me an unusually long visit. I had forgotten exactly what it meant to have a hummingbird visit you, so I Googled "animal speak hummingbird." This is what I found: "In the high Andes of South America, the hummingbird is taken to be a symbol of resurrection. This is because each hummer becomes lifeless and seems to die on cold nights, but it comes back to life again when the miraculous sunrise brings warmth."

I am ready now for the sunrise to bring the warmth back into my life.

About the Author

Raised in a very religious Roman Catholic family, Connie had a paradigm shift as an adult that put her on a lifelong path as a student of spirituality. She has belonged to several spiritual groups, including leading a Sylvia Browne study group, and was trained as a Practitioner of Hypnosis with emphasis in past life regression. After watching the movie *The Secret*, Connie attended one of James Arthur Ray's seminars in 2007 with her husband Richard and signed up for his Harmonic Wealth Weekend (HWW) event held in February, 2007. Over the next three years, Connie and Richard participated in or volunteered for 27 James Arthur Ray seminars and events.

In 2007, Connie and Richard attended the following James Ray seminars and events:

01/07   Learning Annex: Secret of Attracting True Wealth with James Ray, San Diego, CA

02/07   Harmonic Wealth Weekend (HWW), San Diego, CA

05/07   Creating Absolute Wealth (CAW), San Diego, CA

07/07   Practical Mysticism (PM), Tahoe, CA

09/07   James Ray International's Grand Opening Reception, Carlsbad, CA

09/07   Spiritual Warrior (SW), Sedona, AZ

11/07   Quantum Leap (QL), Las Vegas, NV

11/07 While attending Quantum Leap (QL) we became one of the 5 founding members of the World Wealth Society (WWS) when it was first announced

11/07 Volunteered at The Secret of Attracting True Wealth, Del Mar, CA

In 2008, Connie and Richard attended the following James Ray seminars and events:

01/08 Volunteered at Harmonic Wealth Weekend (HWW), San Diego, CA

04/08 Modern Magick (MM), Kona, HI

04/08 WWS members worked for Habitat for Humanity, Kona, HI

04/08 World Wealth Congress, Kona, HI

07/08 Volunteered at Practical Mysticism (PM), Tahoe, CA

08/08 Volunteered at Harmonic Wealth Weekend (HWW), San Diego, CA

10/08 WWS excursion to Egypt (WWS members only)

11/08 Quantum Leap (QL), Las Vegas, NV

11/08 World Wealth Extravaganza, Las Vegas, NV

12/08 Creating Absolute Wealth (CAW), San Diego, CA

12/08 We reenrolled for the 2009 membership in WWS

12/31/08 WWS New Year's Eve Celebration, San Diego, CA (WWS members only)

In 2009, Connie and Richard attended the following James Ray seminars and events:

02/09 World Wealth Congress, Cabo San Lucas, Mexico (WWS members only)

04/09 Modern Magick (MM), Dana Point, CA

04/09 Secret of Attracting the Life You Want, Carlsbad, CA

06/09 Invited to Dream Team 2009 Spiritual Warrior (SW), but declined

07/09 Their daughter attended Creating Absolute Wealth (CAW), San Diego, CA. (Colleen Conaway commits suicide.) We attended the final night black tie dinner dance.

08/09   WWS excursion to Peru (WWS members only)

08/09   Volunteered at Secret of Attracting the Life You Want, Carlsbad, CA

10/09   World Wealth Summit, San Diego, CA

In preparation for a trip to Peru with a group led by Ray, Connie lost 80 lbs which she credits in part to what she learned from James and her goal of being in better physical shape before going to Peru.

Connie and her husband Richard are among the few people who were members of the World Wealth Society (WWS), Ray's inner circle, from its inception. They attended every event that he offered as either participants or volunteers. Connie has a unique insight into how his organization was run and has developed friendships with Ray's employees, other members of the WWS and participants in his events. She was trained in activities such as fire walking, breaking a board with your hand, and rebar bending using your throat, and coached participants through those activities at his events.

Connie has a B.S. in Computer Science from the University of Santa Clara, and an A.A.S in Medical Laboratory Technology & Electron Microscopy. She has worked as a medical laboratory technician, chemical engineer, and a large computer systems sales person. Currently she and her husband are real estate brokers and own The Joys of Real Estate which operates under Keller Williams Realty. Connie resides in San Diego, CA, with her husband Richard and daughter, Erica.

Contact Connie Joy at:
Connie@TragedyInSedona.com

For more information, references and photos:
www.TragedyInSedona.com

Transformation Media Books

Transformation Media Books is dedicated to publishing innovative works that nourish the body, mind and spirit, written by authors whose ideas and messages make a difference in the world.

Please visit our website:

www.TransformationMediaBooks.com
For more information, the latest titles or to purchase direct

Sereni-Tea: Sipping Self Success
Dharlene Marie Fahl

ISBN: 978-0-9844600-3-8
Retail List Prices: $15.95 USD,
$17.00 CAD, £ 12.95 GBP

Certified tea specialist, Dharlene Marie Fahl, guides you on an inner journey of self-discovery through the simple practice of sipping tea. Quiet your mind, open your heart and nurture your being as you drink in the peace of self success. Anywhere, anytime, your cup of *Sereni-Tea* awaits you.

"*Sereni-Tea* is not a typical book about tea. Yes, it contains all the necessary information to help both novices and experts alike to better appreciate this near-miraculous beverage, but then it uses tea as a means for discovering who we are and what we could become . . ."

—Joe Simrany, President, Tea Association of the USA

Dying for a Change
William L. Murtha

ISBN: 978-0-9823850-8-1
Retail List: $19.95 USD

Dying for a Change is the gripping, true account of William L. Murtha's fight to survive hypothermia in the freezing waters off the coast of Britain. At a crucial time when his life was rapidly spiraling out of control, William was swept out to sea by a twenty-foot freak wave. Drowning, losing consciousness and convinced that this was the end, he relived many pivotal moments from his past and experienced a life-changing conversation with a Higher Presence.

William's compelling message inspires readers to come face-to-face with their own deepest fears and challenges perceptions about God, life, death and miracles.

"An amazing story! . . . takes away any doubt that there is an energy force out there ready to help us find our way . . . we need only listen."

—Susan Jeffers, Ph.D, Author, *Feel the Fear and Do It Anyway*®

The Key of Life: A Metaphysical Investigation
Randolph J. Rogers

ISBN: 978-0-9823850-9-8

Retail List: $18.95 USD

Newsman Randy Rogers takes you along on his riveting journey investigating past lives, present events and reincarnation. Randy proves that "ordinary" people can experience the extraordinary when they open themselves to the possibilities.

The Key of Life is a true story about who we are, why we are here and how we are all connected.

". . . a consciousness-raising self-help detective story . . ."

—Peter Michalos, Author of *Psyche, a Novel of the Young Freud*

"... a very personal and life changing experience . . . We emerge from it . . . enlightened, inspired."

—Maria Shriver, First Lady of California, Author

EAT IT UP!
The Complete Mind/Body/Spirit Guide to a Full Life After Weight Loss Survey
Connie Stapleton, Ph. D.

ISBN: 978-0-9823850-7-4

Retail List: $15.95 USD

Eat It Up! is the first book incorporating a whole person, mind/body/spirit approach to prevent weight regain in the months and years following weight loss surgery. Written with humor, compassion and a "firm and fair" approach, *Eat It Up!* is a must-have for the millions who are obese or overweight.

"*Eat It Up!* is a must-have book for surgical weight loss patients. Dr. Stapleton goes beyond the "how to" of maintaining weight loss following surgery to providing skills, wisdom and the support necessary to create a fully healthy and balanced life."

—John C. Friel, Ph.D., Licensed Psychologist,
New York Times best-selling author

MONEYLICIOUS

A Financial Clue for Generation Y

Ornella Grosz

ISBN: 978-0-9845751-1-4

Retail List: $12:95 USD

Spend and invest your hard earned dollars in an effective way! *Moneylicious* is an easy-to-understand guide for Gen Y and everyone needing to understand how money and personal finance work. Twenty-something Ornella Grosz will help you recover, or better yet avoid, the slippery slope of debt!

Moneylicious: A Financial Clue for Generation Y explains the basics of: investing, banking, purchasing a first home, the importance of spending with a touch of humor (yes, you can buy $100 pair of jeans). And much more!

"For Gen Y . . . written by Gen Y . . . *Moneylicious* provides a great financial roadmap. Ornella's willingness to share her own stories not only engages the reader but creates a learning environment where the basics of money and investing are not only explained...but shared in a way that is entertaining as well as experiential. This book should be required reading for all young people in high school and college. Armed with the knowledge that Ornella shares, the readers will be prepared to not only survive . . . but to thrive in the financial world they face."

—Sharon Lechter, Founder and CEO of Pay Your Family First, member of the first President's Advisory Council on Financial Literacy, the AICPA Financial Literacy Commission and co-author of the National Bestseller *Think and Grow Rich – Three Feet From Gold.*

Sooner or Later
Restoring Sanity to Your End-of-Life Care

Damiano deSano Iocovozzi MSN FNP CNS

ISBN: 978-0-9842258-6-6
Retail List: $12.95 USD

Sooner or Later offers patient, family and caregivers a safe place to help process turbulent emotions during the diagnosis phase of a serious or terminal illness and remain sane, rational and in control.

Sooner or Later provides the information and tools to empower patients and their families to seek the appropriate level of care, take control and make good decisions to maintain the best quality of life.

"*Sooner or Later* is a rare treasure. This book shines with compassion, wisdom, humor, and truth. I believe it should be must reading for everyone. Really!"

—Christiane Northrup, M.D. ob/gyn physician
and author of the *New York Times* bestsellers:
Women's Bodies, Women's Wisdom and *The Wisdom of Menopause*

LaVergne, TN USA
11 August 2010
192946LV00003B/2/P